T0403269

Public Uses of Human Remains and Relics in History

The principal theme of this volume is the importance of the public use of human remains in a historical perspective. The book presents a series of case studies aimed at offering historiographical and methodological reflections and providing interpretative approaches highlighting how, through the ages and with a succession of complex practices and uses, human remains have been imbued with a plurality of meanings. Covering a period running from late antiquity to the present day, the contributions are the combined results of multidisciplinary research pertaining to the realities of the Italian peninsula, hitherto not investigated with a long-term and multidisciplinary historical perspective.

From the relics of great men to the remains of patriots, and from anatomical specimens to the skeletons of the saints: through these case studies the scholars involved have investigated a wide range of human remains (real or reputed) and of meanings attributed to them, in order to decipher their function over the centuries. In doing so, they have traversed the interpretative boundaries of political history, religious history and the history of science, as required by questions aimed at integrating the anthropological, social and cultural aspects of a complex subject.

Silvia Cavicchioli is Researcher of Contemporary History at the University of Turin.

Luigi Provero is Full Professor of Medieval History at the University of Turin.

Routledge Approaches to History

For more information about this series, please visit: www.routledge.com/
Routledge-Approaches-to-History/book-series/RSHISTHRY

Public Uses of Human Remains and Relics in History

Edited by Silvia Cavicchioli
and Luigi Provero

Routledge
Taylor & Francis Group

NEW YORK AND LONDON

First published 2020
by Routledge
52 Vanderbilt Avenue, New York, NY 10017

and by Routledge
2 Park Square, Milton Park, Abingdon, Oxon, OX14 4RN

Routledge is an imprint of the Taylor & Francis Group, an informa business

© 2020 Taylor & Francis

The right of Silvia Cavicchioli and Luigi Provero to be identified as the authors of the editorial material, and of the authors for their individual chapters, has been asserted in accordance with sections 77 and 78 of the Copyright, Designs and Patents Act 1988.

Trademark notice: Product or corporate names may be trademarks or registered trademarks, and are used only for identification and explanation without intent to infringe.

Library of Congress Cataloging-in-Publication Data
Names: Cavicchioli, Silvia, 1971– editor. | Provero, Luigi, editor.
Title: Public uses of human remains and relics in history / edited
   by Silvia Cavicchioli and Luigi Provero.
Description: New York : Routledge, [2020] | Series: Routledge
   approaches to history ; vol 32 | Includes bibliographical
   references and index.
Identifiers: LCCN 2019035527 (print) | LCCN 2019035528
   (ebook) | ISBN 9780367272722 (hardback) | ISBN
   9780429295904 (ebook) | ISBN 9781000751864 (adobe pdf) |
   ISBN 9781000751994 (mobi) | ISBN 9781000752120 (epub)
Subjects: LCSH: Human remains (Archaeology)—Italy. | Relics—
   Italy. | Burial—Italy—History. | Tombs—Italy—History.
Classification: LCC CC79.5.H85 P84 2020 (print) | LCC
   CC79.5.H85 (ebook) | DDC 930.10937—dc23
LC record available at https://lccn.loc.gov/2019035527
LC ebook record available at https://lccn.loc.gov/2019035528

ISBN: 978-0-367-27272-2 (hbk)
ISBN: 978-0-429-29590-4 (ebk)

Typeset in Sabon
by Apex CoVantage, LLC

Contents

Figures

Tables

Introduction

Silvia Cavicchioli and Luigi Provero

Human Remains From Antiquity to the Contemporary Age

The relationship between the living and the dead is central in any historical context: human remains weigh on and affect the world of the living,
who as a result work and fight for control over bodies and burial places.
Venerated, collected and studied, or else repudiated, forgotten and redis-
covered, human remains and relics ensure a continuity with the past, and
in some contexts receive new force and efficacy.[1] As has recently been
noted, "in their physicality relics are only contingent material objectifica-
tions of ideas and gestures endowed with their own specific and histori-
cised genealogies."[2] There is therefore a basic tension which arises from
the desire to manage and manipulate the meanings of these remains, the
past and the history which they convey.

In the West, over the centuries the preservation of human remains and
the veneration of relics have been most widespread in the religious sphere,
in the awareness of a continuation of life after death.[3] In similar ways
political authority has resorted to using human remains of the past to root
and legitimise its strength, and to propagate its prestige.[4] Secular power
then created its own relics, enabling the processes of transferring sacredness from the religious to the political level. These re-semantifications
appear very evident from the French Revolution onwards and then
throughout the contemporary era, in the Italian case giving rise to
extremely interesting case studies during Fascism.[5]

In this volume we consider a broad notion of "human remains," not
necessarily celebrated or venerated. The object of our investigation in
fact encompasses a diversity of human remains (real or imagined), such
as those of saints (not least the crucified body of Jesus), of kings and of
famous people, as well as unidentified corpses. And that diversity has a
vast range of components, different in substance and in nature: whole
bodies and parts of them, and even so-called contact relics. The research
collected here intends to reconstruct—thanks to its significant number of
case studies—the complexity of the cults of veneration, the symbols they

generated, and also the religious, political, commemorative and scientific uses assigned to them in different historical periods.

This theme is developed by means of a comparative and long-term approach—from antiquity to the contemporary era—without any pretence to exhaustivity but nevertheless with the aim of bringing a new scientific and historiographical perspective to the investigation of the theme. Whereas the subject is of recognised importance and topicality, the studies thus far conducted on human remains appear extremely dispersed.

In recent years the treatment of dead bodies and its many ramifications have attracted the attention of the scientific community. This is demonstrated, on a more general level, by the ongoing theoretical debate on the "repatriation" of remains of indigenous populations of America and Oceania and on the musealisation of human remains. It can also be seen in the contrasting viewpoints of communities in our society: the meaning given to human remains by the religious community changes when another community—scientific, anthropological, archaeological, museological, legal or historical—talks about them.

The latter, the historians, have been relatively slow to grasp the extraordinary richness offered by the study of human remains and to decipher the political and social constituents of the rituals, mnemonic processes and identity relationships expressed and mediated by them. However, the growing interest in "body politics," in other words corporeity and thanatopolitics (the politics of death), as well as the expansion of the sub-discipline of memory studies, have undoubtedly helped to draw the attention of historiography to these subjects. Furthermore, the way that these objects of study have been assimilated into the *lieux de mémoire* codified by Pierre Nora has stressed the importance of the study of human remains in defining the processes of conflict and stability, propaganda and consensus seeking, invention of tradition and nation building.

The important studies carried out in a purely historical perspective have gradually identified various historiographical models and cultural reference points: the subject of human remains is important, but research has resulted in very different threads and lines of enquiry, demonstrating its richness and noteworthiness. It is probably not a coincidence that the bibliographies of the 14 chapters gathered here are so profoundly different from each other: this is probably not only due to the different contexts of analysis, but also to the absence of a real historiography on human remains, and the absence of a scholarly debate that has brought into full contact those who have studied the relationship between the living and the dead from a historical point of view.

Intended therefore to fill a historiographical void, the main purpose of this collection is to investigate the multiplicity of meanings that has been applied to the use of human remains over a long span of time. We have sought to produce an organic reflection on the subject and to develop fresh angles for historical investigation enriched with anthropological and cultural implications, adhering to the research lines already followed mainly in the English-speaking world.[6]

At the same time, the authors of these chapters have had to cope with a specific weakness inherent in studies relating to Italy, on which they have chosen to concentrate their attention. Despite the recognised poly-semic richness of the many areas involved and of the potential research developments, the subject has long been partly neglected and subject to historiographical prejudices, at least if one excludes contributions linked to religious traditions, the cult of saints and hagiography, and the history of art.

This collection therefore restores the historical interpretation of human remains to a time-span that crosses profoundly dissimilar historical and cultural eras in order to highlight the layers of traditions and customs that have formed over the centuries (in addition to the increasing conflict around their conservation). At various junctures human remains have been given different roles to play: from an object of worship charac-teristic of Christianity, to an element of sacralisation and legitimisation of dynastic and political authorities; from weapons used in struggles between religious and civil power, to anti-relic forms either oppositional or expiatory; from identity symbols of religious and political minorities, to a building tool of a "religion of the homeland" founded on the venera-tion of civil remains and on the sacralisation of secular relics; from de-humanised exhibits in present-day scientific collections, to a driving force of the recognition politics of native communities worldwide.

The authors have given careful thought to the areas of production, discovery, preservation and exhibition of human remains by examining their many uses in terms of memory, cultural identity, political claims and scientific heritage. The research projects presented here investigate the different religious, political, memorial and scientific meanings attributed to human remains in order to decipher their function over the centuries through the interpretative high points of political history, religious his-tory and the history of science, in accordance with questions aimed at combining the anthropological, social and cultural dimensions of such a complex subject. While Prosperi had underlined the complexity of the theme of the material and immaterial relationship between those who die and those who survive, works by Ariès and Kantorowicz, centred on the thanatopolitical practices and symbolic uses of the dead body, had already understood the need for a multi-century and multidisciplinary approach to the subject.[7]

The adoption of a long chronological perspective also makes possible the emergence of the different territorial declinations within which indi-viduals, groups and authorities worked in order to recover, safeguard, study and catalogue, enhance or destroy human remains: on the one hand, the national contexts wherein we investigate the relics of saints, popes, kings and emperors of Catholicism or the symbols of identity, dynasty and politics activated during the unification processes; and on the other hand, the regional contexts wherein we reconstruct analytically the mechanisms of relationships between the cult of dead bodies and local power and the practices of political legitimisation.

A Unifying Complexity

The long-term reading of human remains has been approached from different angles, but is governed by a shared methodological framework and an interdisciplinary viewpoint that also addresses anthropological and cultural elements capable of enriching the historical and socio-political interpretations of the various contexts considered. It has favoured the emergence, construction and restoration of a comprehensive unified framework in which continuities, ruptures and transformations are highlighted.

The unifying key of interpretation is therefore that of the interaction between the living and the dead, but this allows us to underscore how, through different eras, customs and gestures, human remains have taken on a variety of meanings, which often refer to a variety of disciplinary statutes. Thus, the reading of the contributions gathered in this volume—thanks to the broad chronological and thematic articulation of the chapters—suggests many positive threads of continuity and discontinuity and brings to the fore conceptual oppositions of great interest, such as those between celebrated and repudiated bodies, between inclusion and exclusion, and between individuality and anonymous collectivity.

Some of the human remains examined belonged to a prevalently static group, that is, one where the interest is in the scientific practices of verification, measurement, study, preservation, musealisation and standardisation: hence the contribution by Simone Baral which focuses on the skulls of famous Italians, from Leonardo to Raphael, that underwent anthropometric and phrenological measuring aimed at uncovering the characteristics of genius or nationality; or, similarly, the research by Silvano Montaldo in which the corpses made available for research and teaching in the anatomical institute of Turin at the end of the nineteenth century comprise the centrepiece. In these examples the static and scientific dimension of observation, cataloguing, preservation, collecting and, finally, regulation dominates: the same is true of the chapter by Maria G. Castello, which seeks to demonstrate by dint of a study of late-classical important normative instruments (the imperial legislation and the newborn ecclesiastical law) how the empire and the church attempted, in different ways and yet not systematically, to regulate the traffic and commerce in relics, their uses and misuses, their proliferation and attempted misappropriation, and also to find means of certifying their authenticity.

In contrast, some of the human remains that feature in other contributions belonged to a prevalently dynamic group, that is, one where the spotlight is on the ceremonial and ritual sphere, well-publicised moments of restoration, celebrative choreography, media-relayed ostensions and collective rituals involving body-monuments, where the spectacularity of the event (with all its political, identity and symbolic implications) is an integral part of the intervention on human remains. This is the substance of the study conducted by Silvia Cavicchioli into the repeated exhumations and relocations of the bodies of the martyrs of the Roman Republic of 1849, carried out from the Risorgimento period to that of the Fascist dictatorship, to serve as instruments of political legitimisation and transmitters of patriotic sentiment. It is also central to Paolo Cozzo's study of the postponed funeral processions of the many bodies extracted from Roman catacombs which, despite not belonging to local hagiographic traditions, still became the focal point of cults, often overlaid with meaning for the identities of the Piedmontese communities to which they were moved between the sixteenth and eighteenth centuries.

It is therefore first and foremost individual relics that were charged with enormous community and identity significance, such as the phenomenon of the prodigious liquefaction of the blood of Saint Januarius, the long story of which has been recounted by Francesco Paolo de Ceglia; or such as the remains of Simon of Trent, which were used to support an anti-Semitic agenda, as detailed by Emanuele D'Antonio; or such as, finally, the ostension and exhibition of the body of Padre Pio of Pietrelcina in the sanctuary of San Giovanni Rotondo, an event of 2008 which Maria Teresa Milicia uses to reflect on illustrative practices of the social treatment of human remains in the contemporary world.

The importance of the individual becomes a prerequisite for the development of memorial practices and collective celebrations. Thus, Mauro Forno describes the solemn celebration accorded to the mortal remains of another "popular saint," Giovanni Bosco, in particular during the canonical recognition of his body (on 16 May 1929 just before his beatification) and its subsequent translation, events that were transformed into gigantic collective rites in which hundreds of people participated; contrarily, in stark contrast, there is the example of condemnation provided by the ignominious burial of Jesus Christ, which Andrea Nicolotti reconstructs through an evocative rereading of the texts of the Gospels which, in the light of Jewish law and noting the apologetic objective of the evangelists, reveals a knowing attempt to ennoble the consignment of the body to a rock tomb. The notion of condemnation, degenerated into annihilation and destruction, sank to its nadir in the form of the contemptible cannibalism described by Luca Addante in his chapter on the fall of the Neapolitan Republic, in which he considers the two-way use of tortured bodies in an attempt to detect signs of an important change in the discourses on power and in its representations: with the Bourbon restoration, and through the daily passing of public death sentences, royal power reaffirmed its sovereignty over those that it considered traitors to the Neapolitan fatherland.

In that case study, while individuals are clearly of importance, the focus is shifted decisively onto a collective dimension and the creation of political identity. This dimension, in profoundly different ways, can be found in the contributions that place the emphasis on the importance of cemeteries as places for the development of collective funeral practices, cults and community identities: these are issues considered in Luigi Provero's chapter on the community function of medieval village cemeteries, and in Natale Spineto's work on the collective exhibition of "mummies" in the Capuchin Catacombs of Palermo from the end of the sixteenth to the twentieth century, and also in Diego Carnevale's work on the stratification of hundreds of human remains in the Neapolitan Fontanelle cemetery.

The first part of the volume tackles the subject of the relationship between norm and praxis in late antiquity. The second, which takes a particularly broad chronological and geographical view, is dedicated specifically to relics, to their cult and their circulation, and to the battles to control them. The third part offers reflections on the collective dimension of death, on the symbolisms of funeral rites linked to the display and manipulation of human remains, on the collective uses of places for the preservation and exhibition or else the burial of corpses. Finally, the fourth part investigates the public uses of human bodies as instruments of celebration and scientific study but also of annihilation in the contemporary era.

This volume—a significant stage of a research path rather than a point of arrival—concludes a two-year project funded by the University of Turin (Linea B—2016) entitled *Religious relics, secular relics, human remains: symbols of collective identity, instruments of power, cultural legacy, and scientific memory*, and coordinated by Silvia Cavicchioli. We wish to offer our sincere thanks to a number of scholars who accepted our invitation to participate as discussants in a series of seminars organised as part of the project in order to confer about the cornerstones of the research, namely Andrea Augenti, Pierre Antoine Fabre, Dino Mengozzi and Angelo Torre. Our thanks also go to Nicolas Laubry, the coordinator, together with Guillaume Cuchet and Michel Lauwers, of the *Transitions funèraires* project, which gave us valuable food for thought.

Finally, we extend our thanks to Ester de Fort for her generous support and Matthew Armistead, who translated this volume with great care and with special attention to English readers.

Notes

1. Michel Bouvier, "De l'incorruptibilité des corps saints," in *Les Miracles, miroirs des corps*, ed. Jacques Gélis and Odile Redon (Paris: Presses et Publications de l'Universite de Paris-VIII, 1983), 193–221. The ideas in this

introduction are shared by both authors. The first section was edited by Silvia Cavicchioli, the second by Luigi Provero.

2. Luigi Canetti, *Frammenti di eternità. Corpi e reliquie tra Antichità e Medioevo* (Rome: Viella, 2002).

3. Edina Bozoki, *La politique des reliques de Constantin à Saint Louis. Protection collective et légitimation du pouvoir* (Paris: Beauchesne, 2006).

4. Philippe Boutry, Pierre-Antoine Fabre and Dominique Julia, eds., *Reliques modernes: cultes et usages chretiens des corps saints des reformes aux revolutions* (Paris: Éditions de l'EHESS, 2009); Dominique Julia, "Reliques: le pouvoir du saint," in *L'Europe. Encyclopédie historique*, ed. Christophe Charle and Daniel Roche (Arles: Actes Sud, 2018), 296–300.

5. Mona Ozouf, *La fête révolutionnaire. 1789–1799* (Paris: Gallimard, 1976); Emilio Gentile, *Il culto del littorio. La sacralizzazione della politica nell'Italia fascista* (Rome-Bari: Laterza, 2001).

6. Alexandra Walsham, ed., "Relics and Remains," *Past and Present*, Supplement 5 (2010); Thomas W. Laqueur, *The Work of the Dead: A Cultural History of Mortal Remains* (Princeton: Princeton University Press, 2015).

7. Ernst H. Kantorowicz, *The King's Two Bodies: A Study in Medieval Political Theology* (Princeton: Princeton University Press, 1957); Philippe Ariès, *L'Homme devant la mort* (Paris: Seuil, 1977); Adriano Prosperi, ed., *I vivi e i morti* (Bologna: Il Mulino, 1982).

Part I

Norm and Praxis
in Late Antiquity

1   An Ignominious Burial

The Treatment of the Body of Jesus of Nazareth

Andrea Nicolotti

The story of what happened to the mortal remains of Jesus of Nazareth—put to death on the cross in Jerusalem on an Easter Friday between the years 27 and 34 CE—is told in the Gospels. Of these, the oldest and most useful to any historical reconstruction, which is at least probable, are those attributed to Matthew, Mark, Luke, John and Peter.

Their accounts are compatible as a whole, are partly interdependent, and are most likely drawn from sources now lost to us. Sometimes, however, their narratives are contradictory, each being influenced by the personal perspective of the compiler, who based his account on information available to him and which he believed was well-founded. Many of their differences could be due to the fact that there were a number of coexisting streams of information about Jesus, probably arising from several places. It is therefore possible, with due caution, to treat the Gospels as broadly reliable recollections, though we should not forget that they were written, in the form in which they have reached us, several years after the facts and using not always exact memories and stories as their foundation. Furthermore, they are not dry historical accounts, but rather testimonies of a faith lived in the light of belief in the resurrection of Jesus, in constant dialogue with the ancient Hebrew scriptures and with an explicit parenetic and apologetic intent. Thus the events that will be discussed from here on should not be automatically considered facts corresponding to reality because the truth of every detail of the Gospels cannot actually be proved and is the subject of debate among scholars. What I will reconstruct in the following pages is above all what Jesus' followers could and/or wanted to remember about him.

An Ignominious Burial

The funeral of a first-century Jew[1] began with a procession that accompanied the deceased to the sound of flutes and the keening of weeping women, and then there followed laments, ceremonies, blessings and eulogies, ending with the inhumation in the family tomb.[2] Jesus, however, had none of this. His burial recalls, at least in part, the punishment that

Josephus demanded for blasphemers: "Let him that blasphemes God be stoned, then hung for a day, and buried ignominiously and in obscurity."[3] The *Mishnah* described this custom as follows:

> They did not bury [the felon] in the burial grounds of his ancestors. But there were two graveyards made ready for the use of the court, one for those who were beheaded or strangled, and one for those who were stoned or burned. [. . .] And they did not go into mourning, but they observed a private grief, for grief is only in the heart.[4]

These were the two essential characteristics of what is known as "ignominious burial": the prohibition of burying the criminal next to his "fathers"—in other words in a family tomb that housed the bodies of innocent people—and the ban on carrying out all the public ceremonies of mourning. Dishonourable burials were an ancient practice and can in fact be found in texts predating the time of Jesus.[5]

The burial of Jesus described by the Gospels has certain characteristics that identify it as dishonourable.[6] The joint condemnation by the Roman and Jewish authorities (this is what the Gospels say) excluded the possibility of a solemn funeral for those guilty of blasphemy, and so the ignominious suffering of the cross had to be matched by an equally ignominious burial. The Gospel of Peter confirms this when it mentions that the women were not able to perform the usual lamentations on the day of the burial, and adds that they meant to do so later:

> Now at the dawn of the Lord's day Mary Magdalene, a female disciple of the Lord—who, afraid because of the Jews since they were inflamed with anger, had not done at the tomb of the Lord what women were accustomed to do for the dead beloved by them—having taken with her women friends, came to the tomb where he had been placed. And they were afraid lest the Jews should see them and were saying: "If indeed on that day on which he was crucified we could not weep and beat ourselves, yet now at his tomb we may do these things."[7]

But isn't all of this in contradiction with the Gospel passages where it is said that Jesus was buried in a new and dignified tomb, and not in the criminal cemetery mentioned in the Mishnah? Some have replied that their account is false, and sometimes go as far as to claim that Jesus was thrown into a mass grave. Yet there are good reasons for believing that things did not turn out like that.

The Handing Over of the Body

The Jews did not deprive anyone of a burial. Leaving a corpse unburied was considered an unworthy act; it could only happen in moments of great tension, such as war, when relatives feared that burying their dead might put their own lives at risk or when they were prevented from doing so.[8] In the case of Roman executions governors reserved the right of deciding whether to return the body, and generally preferred to comply with Jewish custom. It is therefore likely that Jesus' body was handed over to be buried. Even Yehohanan, a man crucified in the first century whose bones have been found in Jerusalem, did not end up in a mass grave, but rather in a tomb, and the same is true of other executed people whose remains have come to light. The Mishnaic norm prescribing burial in a separate cemetery concerns criminals judged by the Sanhedrin, not those executed by the Roman civil authority.

Furthermore, Jewish law did not allow a body to remain exposed overnight, something that according to John even Jesus' opponents brought to the notice of Pilate.[9] Jesus' closest followers and friends were not present either at the Deposition or at his burial. It might be assumed that they had escaped, fearful and confused at the death of their master. Yet somebody had to take care of the necessary, and the Gospels name Joseph of Arimathea, who obtained permission from the Roman governor to remove the body from the cross and arrange for it to be buried.[10] According to Matthew and John, Joseph was a disciple of Jesus, but Mark and Luke say that he was a member of the Sanhedrin, while Peter says that he was a friend of both Jesus and Pilate.

Assuming that the evangelists had credible information about him (something that cannot be taken for granted),[11] some think, as suggested in the Gospel of Peter, that Joseph did not act out of any sympathy for the deceased, but had instead been formally assigned to do so by the Sanhedrin,[12] which would not have allowed night to fall on an unburied victim of crucifixion.[13] This would also explain the apparent anomaly regarding why Joseph was never mentioned in the Gospels as a follower of Jesus either before or after the burial, when we might otherwise have expected that he would have assumed a prominent position among the disciples. Joseph was not a witness either to Jesus' death or to his subsequent resurrection: it is as if his task lasted only a few hours, in other words, the time needed to take care of the burial in accordance with Jewish rules. This hypothesis may be indirectly corroborated by the passage in John where it is stated that it was the Jews themselves who asked Pilate to bring down the corpses of Jesus and the two criminals from their crosses, while the Acts of the Apostles, which quotes the words of Paul, states that it was they who also took measures to ensure the burial.[14]

Removing the body from the cross, transporting it and burying it, and sealing the tomb with a large stone were not tasks that could be carried by one person. Joseph may have used his own servants or else staff of the Jewish authorities.[15] It is also possible that he tried to avoid the contamination deriving from any operation that involved contact with a corpse, something which rendered a person impure for seven days. In such an eventuality Joseph would have been unable to take part in the Passover festivities.

The Cleaning of the Body

The practice of cleaning a corpse, known as *taharah*, is also mentioned in the Acts of the Apostles.[16] One would think that the ablution of a crucified and bloodied body was an obvious course of action, and the Gospel of Peter specifically states that Jesus was washed.[17] The four older Gospels, however, do not mention any washing, perhaps because it went without saying.

Some, however, have maintained that it could not have taken place, making reference to the modern Jewish custom: those who die a violent death or through bleeding must not be washed, but must be buried together with the clothes impregnated with their blood. The oldest known formulation of this precept is the work of Yaakov ben Moshe Moelin, known as Maharil (d. 1427):

> About one woman who fell from a roof and died due to her fall—may it not happen to us—the Maharash taught that if blood came out of her, she should not be purified, because if she was, the blood would be washed off. But she would be buried as she is clothed. And he also said that if a quarter-log[18] of blood came out of her a priest should not rend himself unclean to her. [. . .] And it is customary to bury all those slain by transgressors and oppressors simply as they were found, with all their clothes, to raise anger and get revenge.[19]

Maharil had probably been taught this rule either by his master, Maharash, or by Shalom ben Yizhak, the rabbi of Neustadt in Austria (died c. 1413). In the nineteenth century the Hungarian rabbi Shlomo Ganzfried elucidated it by talking of lifeblood:

> If a person collapses and dies instantly, if his body was injured, and blood flowed from the wound, and there is reason to fear that perhaps his lifeblood was absorbed in his clothes and his shoes, he should not be ritually cleansed, but he should be buried in his clothing and his shoes. Over his clothing, he should be wrapped in a cloth. The sheet is called *sovev* ("wrapping"). It is customary to scoop up the earth from the spot where he fell, if any blood is there. The earth nearby that spot should also be dug up, and he should be buried with all the earth that contains blood.[20]

The current justification for this is that the last drops of blood, shed in the instant when a person passes from life to death, is lifeblood. If those drops had been absorbed by clothing or the ground, these too must be buried together with the body. But since with bleeding wounds lifeblood cannot be distinguished from blood lost before or after the moment of death, everything must be preserved.

If these provisions were applied in the case of Jesus, the situation would be clear: the corpse and shed blood would have to be buried together, without washing. Jesus did not have clothes, since he had died naked and his clothing had been shared among the soldiers.[21]

The difficulty raised by this interpretation has to do with the risk of blithely integrating the silence of the sources by making use of later texts. It is not historically correct to found the exegesis of first-century Hebrew writings by relying on other works written much later.[22] The only thing to have been found in texts closer to the period in question is evidence of concern for the management of the blood of those who died of wounds. A passage from the Mishnah (second century) presents an interesting example of a hanged man (who could be compared to a crucified man, although it should be noted that Jewish law allowed the bodies of the condemned to be hanged only after death and not before). According to the passage, the blood that escaped from the man's wounds could be deemed impure owing to having been mixed, since some would have been shed when the man was still alive, and the rest after his death. This meant that anyone who had been exposed to it would have to be purified—exactly as in the case of touching a corpse—because he had been rendered impure.[23] From this passage we learn that at least until the second century there was some sensitivity regarding the purity of those who came into contact with lifeblood, although this is a different problem to that of what should be done with it, meaning that even this source does not allow us to deduce that there had been a rule regulating such a circumstance either in that century or the one before.

We should also bear in mind that the essential and original function of washing the body was simply hygienic. The ritualisation of the process transpired slowly, surfacing appreciably in the period of the Medieval Ashkenazic Hasidism in Europe. The Hasidim of Ashkenaz attributed great importance to the physical preparation of the body in view of the day of judgment for all souls (especially those of martyrs, marked with blood), which they considered imminent and not, as their predecessors did, an event that would arrive in a more distant eschatological time. The killing of many Jews during the twelfth and thirteenth century must have given rise to new discussions on the best way to bury murder victims. Indeed, the rare occasions when corpses were buried in their blood-soaked clothes concerned men murdered in Europe during the late Middle Ages: according to the beliefs of the Ashkenazi Jews, the blood would serve as proof of their martyrdom and was a substance that would unleash God's vengeance on the killers.[24] It seems highly significant that the rules written on the burial of blood with the corpse and on not washing do not go back beyond the Middle Ages,[25] and it is possible that the current rule mandating burials with the blood began with this motivation linked to blood-revenge.[26]

Ultimately, there is not enough evidence to exclude the possibility that Jesus' body was washed.

Covering the Body

According to the Gospels of Matthew, Mark, Luke, John and Peter, the corpse was immediately wrapped in a cloth after being brought down from the cross, even before it reached the tomb. It must therefore have already been covered when being transported, which is understandable because the Jews did not permit displays of nudity.

The five authors state that, after laying the body down Joseph covered it in cloth known as *sindón* (σινδών).[27] At the time, this word had two meanings. First, it referred to a type of fine fabric, especially linen but which could also be cotton. Second, and by extension, it identified any item made from that fabric: we find instances of it being used to refer to a variety of objects, such as cloths, tunics, sheets, flags, burial cloths, ribbons, cloaks and curtains. This double meaning has an immediate consequence as far as the text of the Gospels is concerned: if the writers used the word *sindón* in the first sense, in other words as the name of a type of material—surely linen since in the first century cotton did not exist in Palestine—the translation would be: "Joseph wrapped it in linen,"[28] in other words in one or more pieces of this specific material (from which strips, bandages, clothes and sheets could be made). If, on the other hand *sindón* referred to a single piece of cloth, the translation would be: "he wrapped it up in a (single piece of fabric made of) linen."

There is no reason to choose arbitrarily between one solution or the other, as for example those who translate it as "in a sheet of linen" do. The term *sindón* does not in fact tell us anything about the shape of the fabric or fabrics to which the Gospels refer, but the associated verbs do at least inform us about the way that Jesus was wrapped. Luke and Matthew use the word *entulísso*, which means to "wrap" or "roll up," while Mark, the oldest source, instead uses the more restrictive *eneiléo*, or to "wrap tightly," "envelop," "wind" or "entangle." Thus, for these evangelists, the body of Jesus was not simply covered or dressed, but, rather, bound up fairly tightly. There is no way of knowing whether it was wrapped in strips of linen, in one or more sheets, in a tunic or other form of clothing, or whether it was wrapped in bandages, ropes, cord or something else. We cannot know if Joseph's *sindón* was used in the form in which it had been purchased, or if it was cut to make pieces or strips with which to wrap the corpse. The only thing that is certain is that this linen had to fulfil the function of wrapping and tightly binding the body.

It may be that the Gospel writers chose to utilise the term *sindón* because they wanted to underline the value of the type of material used, their concern being not so much to describe the way the corpse was dressed, which could have easily been imagined by their contemporaries, as to remove any suspicion that Jesus had been buried naked or was covered in cheap material. Matthew even specified that the *sindón* was *kathará* (καθαρά), that is "pure" or "clean." This might signify that the material was new and unsoiled, in other words unused (Mark states that Joseph purchased it for the occasion); or else that it was made of pure linen, that is, not mixed with other textiles (which, among other things, would have meant that it broke Jewish laws which in certain cases—but not in burials—forbade the mixing of different fibres); or even that it was "white," that is, that it had been subjected to bleaching processes. White was a colour typically attributed to priests, philosophers, angels and gods, even pagan ones:[29] the evangelist, then, might been implying that the cloth had a sacred quality.[30]

The Gospel of John, conversely, does not speak of Jesus' *sindón*, but rather of *othónia* (ὀθόνια) which served to bind (δέω) the body of Jesus.[31] *Othónia* is a diminutive plural of *othóne* (ὀθόνη), which means, generically, "linen cloth," "garment," "veil" or "band." In our case, the diminutive might have been utilised to indicate a very fine and delicate textile (like linen), or one made out of the material *othóne*, in small quantities, or else a textile different in quality to *othóne*, that is small, or long and narrow, perhaps made of something bigger (like bandages obtained by cutting down a larger piece of cloth). Among Greek writers *othónion* is used to denote a "cloth," "little curtain," "placemat," "hand towel," "handkerchief" or a "bandage" for wrapping, and more rarely as "cloth" or "linen" generally, regardless of size. Papyrological evidence reveals a constant use of *othónion* in the generic sense of "cloth" and also of "clothing." Clearly John was thinking of more than one item, but he did not say what these were like. Thus the phrase "they bound it in *othónia*" should prudently be translated as "they bound it in linen cloths." The translation "they bound it in strips of linen" that is sometimes used is not incorrect, but interpretative and influenced by the fact that John himself used the same verb *déo* (to "bind") when he said that in the tomb Lazarus's hands and feet were bound in "swathing-bands," "bandages," "strips" or "girths" known as *keiríai* (κειρίαι).[32]

Moreover, John added to the linens a *soudárion* (σουδάριον), that is, a cloth that was placed on the head of the deceased. He then recounted that on Sunday morning the apostle Peter went to the tomb that had been found empty and, looking inside, saw that there remained only "the linen cloths lying there, and the *soudárion* that was upon his head, not lying with the linen cloths," but wrapped up in a different place (or in a particular way).[33]

Unfortunately, we have no clear idea about how the Jews normally wrapped the dead in Jesus' time. Some findings made in the Cave of Letters show that most sepulchral materials were made from recycled cloths, particularly of tunics made into rags or sacks.[34] Even the fabrics in 'En Gedi had probably been reclaimed. In two coffins a piece of knotted cloth was found in the position of the right shoulder: could this be the "knot in the undergarment at the shoulder" to which the Mishnah refers?[35] The presence in a tomb of two types of material, one coarse and the other fine, confirms that a variety of fabrics were used on the same person. A momentous discovery was made in the region of Akeldamà: although, because of the fragmentary state of the original form, the number and size of the materials cannot be determined, the surviving fabrics were made up of overlapping layers.[36]

Ointments and Aromas

In general the corpses of Jews were cleansed and covered in perfumed oil. It is normally believed that the washing of a body was an operation that preceded its anointing, and indeed if the aim of the anointing was to perfume the body, it makes sense that this came after the washing.[37] However, a passage of the Mishnah has this order in reverse, affirming that a corpse can be "anointed and washed" even on the Sabbath.[38]

Following an extensive investigation of the Jewish sources, Adolf Büchler has compared this funeral practice with that of rubbing one's hands with oil after meals to remove the dirt sticking to the fingers before washing them, as well as to the custom of covering the body with oil in the bath to remove dirt and impurities before scraping it off the skin or rinsing with water. The purpose of washing the corpse would therefore be to remove the oil previously used to give the skin a pleasant smell.[39]

The fact that anointing the deceased was a widespread practice in this period was confirmed by Jesus himself in the episode of the sinful woman of Bethany who one day approached him with a jar filled with perfumed oil and began to anoint his body. Jesus interpreted this as a symbolic precursory sepulchral anointing.[40] The question has been asked, without agreement ever having been reached, whether this story allows us to deduce that Jesus was not anointed after his death.

Let us therefore return to the Gospel accounts of the burial.[41] Matthew, Mark and Luke say that after Jesus' body had been removed from the cross Joseph of Arimathea wrapped it in linen, placed it in the tomb, and nothing more. Matthew does not speak of any perfume, while Mark states that "when the Sabbath was over, Mary Magdalene, Mary the mother of James, and Salome bought aromatic spices so that they might go and anoint him," while according to Luke, on the Friday evening the women "returned and prepared aromatic spices and perfumes, and on the Sabbath they rested according to the commandment." All three agree on the fact that the women returned to the tomb on the Sunday morning, but only Mark and Luke specify that they took perfumes with them.

John provides a very different account, introducing a new protagonist, namely the Pharisee Nicodemus. At the Deposition he came "carrying a mixture of myrrh and aloes weighing about a hundred pounds." He and Joseph of Arimathea "took Jesus's body and bound it by *othónia* with the aromatic spices, as is the custom of the Jews to prepare for burial." John makes no mention of the women's morning visit, making reference only to the arrival of Mary Magdalene but saying nothing of aromas. The accounts are therefore contradictory: Matthew does not talk about perfumes, Mark and Luke say that these were brought to the tomb by the women on Sunday, Mark asserts that they were purchased late on Saturday, while Luke says that they had already been prepared on Friday night. John excludes the women from anything involving aromas and he alone reveals that on Friday evening Nicodemus had brought a mixture of myrrh and aloe and that Jesus was buried with it.

Myrrh is an odoriferous gum resin that can be extracted from the trunk and branches of various plants of the genus Commiphora.[42] It was a precious resin that the Magi gave to the baby Jesus along with gold and frankincense. On the other hand, there are two types of aloe: a juice that is extracted from the leaves of the homonymous plants of the liliaceae family, and the fragrant wood known as agarwood or aloeswood. The juice, which has anti-inflammatory and healing properties, is very odorous, while the wood is taken from trees affected by a particular fungal infection which causes them to spontaneously secrete the resinous compound that makes the wood fragrant. The plant that provided the most highly sought-after fragrant wood was the *Aquilaria*, and the most widely used variety was the *Aquilaria agallocha*.[43] In order to release the smell, the wood would be burned, and it appears that John was in fact thinking about the wood rather than the juice. In any case, it is necessary to take into account the fact that the myrrh and aloe referenced by John were probably solid and would therefore be different from the aromas mentioned by Mark, which were liquid. One should therefore avoid conflating the two things. In an attempt to reconcile the difference between them, some have speculated that the solid aromas were pressed into a liquid oil.

As for the mixture of aloe and myrrh provided by Nicodemus, the quantity mentioned is large, both from the point of view of purchase and of transportation: 100 Roman pounds equates to around 32 kilograms. Some commentators have therefore suggested that John may have used a different unit of measure or that he was simply exaggerating with the intent of symbolising a messianic abundance or a regal burial. This brings to mind the funeral procession of Herod the Great, when the corpse was transported on a litter while 500 slaves and freemen carried aromas.[44]

And the thought of Herod's funeral recalls a traditional custom referred to in the scriptures: that of transporting and offering aromas for the deceased, which would have been laid down on his bedding and burned in his honour.[45] The Mishnah also mentions some specific "spices of the dead," which the Palestinian Talmud explains were placed on or in front of the coffin and which the Babylonian Talmud says were used "to remove the bad smell."[46] The Tosefta also refers to the ancient use of carrying incense ahead of the coffins of those who died from intestinal problems, a custom that was then extended to everyone "because of the honour owing to the dead." This gesture evidently became widespread over time so that eventually the Babylonian Talmud no longer considered it a sign of honour, but merely a "deference to the living that suffer from intestinal disorders."[47] Thus, in addition to the anointment occurring during the preparation of the corpse, the Rabbinical texts also spoke of the custom of burning aromas with the deceased or of transporting them during a funeral procession, as well as of using liquid perfumes either on the body or in front of the coffin.[48]

Should we therefore consider the possibility that Nicodemus brought his fragrances in order for them to be burned or sprinkled on the bench of the tomb or around the body, perhaps having them transported during the brief funeral procession and even sprinkled on that occasion? In that case we should take into account the tendency to ennoble Jesus' burial that emerges in the Gospel of John. Or were these fragrances perhaps intended to be part of the funeral goods? There is in fact evidence of a contemporary Jewish practice of leaving objects in the tombs, including jars, bowls, unguents,[49] whose function is unclear. Were these votive offerings? Materials used during the burial? Aromas to perfume the stale air in the sepulchre?

After telling us about Nicodemus, John affirms that Jesus' body was bound in linens "with the aromatic spices." Were these the mixture of aloe and myrrh just mentioned? They might have been, but we cannot completely exclude the possibility that the evangelist intended to distinguish between Nicodemus's mixture, brought for one of the aforementioned reasons, and other aromas (solid or liquid) used to perfume the sepulchral cloths: an informed reader would of course have been able to identify them without need for further explanation. It may be that the aromas were placed between the body and the fabric, or between the different layers of cloth, or else that the fabrics had been perfumed beforehand by them.

In the end, we have no precise idea about what John was attributing to Nicodemus with his mixture of aloe and myrrh, and neither do we know whether the aromas used when wrapping the body of Jesus inside the linens were the same or not, or whether they had been put in contact with the fabrics during the inhumation or before.

Were the aromatic spices brought by the women that Mark and Luke talk about poured on the body at the moment of burial? If this were so, we must conclude that they had no means or time to perform the operation at the right moment on the Friday evening, that is, before the burial, and thus had to leave Jesus, having in mind to return later to complete the task.

But the Gospels do not tell us this, nor do they speak about a provisional or incomplete burial. It may be that the anointing took place without the evangelists feeling a need to recall it explicitly, since it was a customary act. Or else maybe the perfumes that the women prepared to take to the tomb on Sunday morning were not meant to be the anointment of the deceased called for by the ritual preparation for burial. The women's visit on the third day may simply have been an act of piety performed by spreading aromatic oil on the already buried body of Jesus. In fact, "it would not be unnatural for the women to wish to make their own offering of devotion, even if they knew that someone else had already done what was required."[50] The verb *aléipho* ("anoint") could very well indicate the act of pouring oil on something, perhaps even on a body already wrapped in its burial cloths, without it needing to be poured directly onto the skin:[51] a little like what the angels did for three days, according to the Testament of Abraham (first century), to the already wrapped body of the patriarch, and like the archangels did with the body of Adam that had already been dressed in three linens, according to the Apocalypse of Moses (first to third century).[52]

Mark writes about spices (ἀρώματα), Luke about spices and perfumes (ἀρώματα καὶ μύρα) and immediately afterwards only about spices.[53] But when we distinguish between ἀρώματα and μύρα it is possible that we are differentiating between solid spices and oily liquid perfumes. This reading, however, seems to be invalidated by Mark, who uses the verb "to anoint" when referring to the ἀρώματα: but not invalidated if the oil had been mixed with spices to create a substance suitable for being poured or sprinkled on the corpse.

The visit made on the third day can also be understood in the light of the Rabbinical texts, which mention the custom of visiting the tomb in the days after the death, especially during the first three, following which the most intense phase of a family's mourning comes to an end. The Babylonian Talmud formulated a series of precise instructions for these first three days, establishing rules that had two prime purposes, namely those of regulating the behaviour of grieving parties in the post-burial period and declaring the irreversibility of the death.[54] For the first three days the absence of signs of putrefaction could in fact lead the grieving to think that the departed was not dead but only appeared so. According to the Palestinian Talmud,

> for the first three days after death the soul floats above the body, thinking that it will return to the body. When the soul sees the body, that the appearance of the face has changed, it leaves the body and goes on its way.[55]

Thus the third day marked the moment when the family of the deceased could be certain of the demise of their loved one. The visit of the women to Jesus' tomb on the third day, that is the Sunday, can therefore be interpreted as an act of obedience towards a Jewish tradition, which has perhaps also been confirmed by the later Semaḥot treatise.[56]

The Coffin, the Litter and the Problem of Time

Was Jesus taken from the cross to the tomb on a litter? Did he have a wooden coffin? We do have contemporary testimonies of these objects, and the Gospel of Luke mentions the coffin of another deceased but not of Jesus.[57] The Rabbinical texts lead us to believe that coffins were necessary for burial but archaeological findings relating to first-century Jerusalem are ambiguous: some coffins have been found, although they do not appear to have been used consistently.[58] The specific conditions in which Jesus was buried suggest that his body was moved when wrapped simply in burial cloth, and in any event there must have been some men acting as carriers.

It has sometimes been argued that Jesus' burial took place in a hurry due to the late hour and the supervening of the Sabbath, a festive day on which many activities were forbidden. In the remaining hours before nightfall those involved had to go to Pilate, await his response, arrange for the burial cloths, remove the body from the cross, cover and transport it, open the tomb and bury it. Luke informs us that at the end of all of this "the Sabbath was beginning."

It is certainly true that the fast-approaching Sabbath created some urgency and perhaps the need to find a nearby tomb to avoid a long funeral journey,[59] but it would not necessarily have created the same problem for the other practices involved in the burial, which were another matter. These two passages from the Mishnah are informative in this regard:

> Whoever allows his deceased to stay unburied overnight transgresses a negative commandment. But if one kept a corpse overnight for its own honor, to bring a bier for it and shrouds, he does not transgress on its account.
>
> [On Shabbat they can] prepare all that is needed for a corpse. They anoint and rinse it, on condition that they not move any limb of the corpse. They remove the mattress from under it. And they put it on sand so that it will keep. They tie the chin, not so that it will go up, but so that it will not droop.[60]

If this practice was already in force at the time of Jesus—that is, at a time when such rules were the subject of debate, even if they had not been written down in a definitive form—then we have no reason to consider why at least this part of the funeral operations had to have been hasty and incomplete. It is true that the prohibition on moving the limbs prevented the manipulations of a body typical of burial, but since in Jesus' case there had not been a funeral with the transportation of the body and subsequent inhumation, once his body had been laid in the tomb the completion of the burial could have taken place in the evening. Nor would all this have taken an inordinate amount of time: according to the Acts of the Apostles, when Ananias died he was buried in the space of three hours.[61] If Jesus died around three in the afternoon, sunset would come just four hours later: there was not much time, but neither was there too little.

The preparations—which were usually carried out at home but on this occasion had to be done near the tomb, or at least not far from the cross—meant that the body had to be anointed, perhaps washed, and wrapped in linen before burial. The more recent rabbinic custom also calls for the face to be shaved and the hair to be cut.[62]

The New Tomb

The new tomb in which Jesus was placed is an indirect confirmation of the ignominious nature of his burial: a tomb in which nobody had ever been buried (thus an empty one)[63] was the only acceptable compromise to make. In this way burial in a cemetery for criminals was avoided and, in addition, a breach of the rule against burying a condemned man in a family tomb along with innocents was averted. According to Josef Blinzer rather than a compromise, this was an out-and-out necessity:

> If there had been enough time Jesus would have been buried in the official cemetery for criminals. Since after the removal of the body from the cross and its preparation for burial, the day had begun to decline—and with the sunset the Sabbath would begin, during which no work could be done—transporting it to an official cemetery some distance away was no longer possible, and thus a nearby rock tomb was chosen instead. This was not against any legal scruple, since the tomb had not yet been used so there was no need to fear bringing any dishonour to the pious deceased.[64]

The choice of a new tomb would also serve, later on, to counter the claim that the story of the discovery of the empty tomb was due to an error by the women and the apostles in identifying the corpse, which could only have happened in an already populated tomb. Thus despite the dishonourable torture of the cross, Jesus was able to receive a burial, and there are no grounds in any of the texts to believe that he did not.[65] But this was a dishonourable burial, without a procession, flutes, prayers, lamentations and public demonstrations of mourning.

In conclusion, the evangelists demonstrated good knowledge of Jewish customs and their stories are broadly consistent. One notes, however, an increasing tendency to stress the fact that the body of Jesus was not thrown among the criminals, but received a burial, if not quite sumptuous then at least dignified. A process of progressive ennoblement of details concerning the burial is clearly evident: Mark and Luke's burial cloth becomes, in Matthew, "pure"; for Matthew the tomb belonged personally to Joseph, while for John and the Gospel of Peter it was located in a garden, like that of the kings of Israel.[66] John adds the presence of Nicodemus and the aromas, and the Gospel of Peter speaks of the washing of the body and of the women who intended to carry out the ritual lamentations. John, it is clear, describes a burial that is more than dignified, and in him is realised what Raymond Brown has defined as a "triumphal orientation . . . as the culmination of the enthroning crucifixion."[67]

Notes

1. On Jewish funeral customs, see Siegfried Klein, *Tod und Begräbnis in Palästina zur Zeit der Tannaiten* (Berlin: Itzkowske, 1908); Samuel Krauss, *Talmudische Archäologie*, vol. 2 (Leipzig: Fock, 1911), 54–82; Shmuel Safrai and Menahem Stern, eds., *The Jewish People in the First Century*, vol. 2 (Assen: Van Gorcum, 1976), 773–87; Harold Liebowitz, "Jewish Burial Practices in the Roman Period," *The Mankind Quarterly* 22 (1981): 107–17; Joseph Patrich, קבורה ראשונה על-פי מקורות חז"ל—לביאורם של מונחים, in Itamar Singer, ed., קברים וצוהגי קבורה בארץ-ישראל בעת העתיקה, (Jerusalem: Yad Izhak Ben-Zvi, 1994), 190–211; Nissan Rubin, קץ החיים: טקסי קבורה ואבל במקורות חז"ל (Tel Aviv: Hakibbutz Hameuchad, 1997); David Kraemer, *The Meanings of Death in Rabbinic Judaism* (London: Routledge, 2000); Byron McCane, *Roll Back the Stone. Death and Burial in the World of Jesus* (Harrisburg: Trinity Press, 2003).
2. There are allusions to these customs in the Rabbinical texts: *Mishnah, Baba Batra* 6:7 (procession); *Ketubot* 2:10 (procession and funeral speech); *Ketubot* 4:4 (flutes and women); *Megillah* 4:3 (ceremonies and benedictions); *Mo'ed Qatan* 3:9 (singing women); *Talmud babilonese, Baba Qamma* 17a (very long procession). According to Josephus "the funeral ceremony is to be undertaken by the nearest relatives, and all who pass while a burial is proceeding must join the procession and share the mourning of the family" (*Contra Apionem* 2:205). Jesus himself crossed a funeral procession (Luke 7:12) in which the people "were all weeping, and beating themselves" (Luke 8:52), and according to Mark 5:38 were "weeping and wailing," while according to Matthew 9:23 there were "the minstrels and the multitude making tumult." Funeral lamentations dated back to the ancient world: see Roland De Vaux, *Ancient Israel: Its Life and Institutions* (Grand Rapids: Eerdmans, 1997), 60–61.
3. Iosephus Flavius, *Antiquitates Iudaicae* 4:202; translation of Henry Thackeray, *The Jewish Antiquities, Books I–IV* (London: Heinemann, 1930).
4. *Mishnah, Sanhedrin* 6:5–6; translation by Jacob Neusner, *The Mishnah: A New Translation* (New Haven: Yale University Press, 1988). See Adolf Büchler, "L'enterrement des criminels d'après le Talmud et le Midrasch," *Revue des études juives* 46 (1903): 74–88. See also Beth Berkowitz,

Execution and Invention: Death Penalty Discourse in Early Rabbinic and Christian Cultures (Oxford: Oxford University Press, 2006).

5. 1 Kings 13:22 says of an unfaithful prophet: "Your corpse will not be buried in your ancestral tomb"; Jeremiah 22:18–19, says this about Jehoiakim: "They will not mourn for him [. . .] He will be left unburied just like a dead donkey. His body will be dragged off and thrown outside the gates of Jerusalem"; Isaiah 53:9, on the suffering servant: "They intended to bury him with criminals, but he ended up in a rich man's tomb"; Flavius, *Antiquitates Iudaicae* 5:44: "He was straightway put to death and at nightfall was given the ignominious burial proper to the condemned"; *Tosefta, Sanhedrin* 9:8.

6. See, for example, Byron McCane, "Where No One Had Yet Been Laid: The Shame of Jesus' Burial," in *Authenticating the Activities of Jesus*, ed. Bruce Chilton and Craig Evans (Leiden: Brill, 1999), 431–52; Jerome Murphy-O'Connor, "The Descent from the Cross and the Burial of Jesus," *Revue biblique* 118 (2011): 554–57.

7. *Evangelium Petri*, 50–52; trans. Raymond Brown, *The Death of the Messiah*, vol. 2 (New York: Doubleday, 1994), 1320.

8. See Iosephus Flavius, *Bellum Iudaicum* 4:317 (burial of the crucified); 4:331–32 and 381–83 (fear of burial).

9. Deuteronomy 21:23: "His corpse must not remain all night on the tree"; see Flavius, *Bellum Iudaicum* 4:317; John 19:31: "The bodies should not stay on the crosses on the Sabbath."

10. Matthew 27:57–61; Mark 15:42–47; Luke 23:50–56; John 19:38–42; *Evangelium Petri* 23–24. A legal discussion of the question of the Deposition and burial of the condemned is in Barbara Fabbrini, "La deposizione di Gesù nel sepolcro e il problema del divieto di sepoltura per i condannati," *Studia et documenta historiae et iuris* 61 (1995): 97–178, although I do not share all of Fabbrini's conclusions.

11. According to Jerome Murphy O'Connor "none of the evangelists had any reliable historical information about Joseph of Arimathea"; his inclusion in the story may simply be owed to the fact that he was the owner of the tomb ("The Descent from the Cross," 553).

12. *Evangelium Petri* 23: "And the Jews rejoiced and gave his body to Joseph that he might bury it, since he was one who had seen the many good things he did."

13. Adriana Destro and Mauro Pesce, *La morte di Gesù* (Milan: Rizzoli, 2014), 133–59.

14. John 19:31: "The Jewish leaders asked Pilate to have the victims' legs broken and the bodies taken down"; Acts 13:27–29: "The people who live in Jerusalem and their rulers . . . asked Pilate to have him executed and . . . they took him down from the cross and placed him in a tomb."

15. According, for example, to Paul Gaechter, "Zum Begräbnis Jesu," *Zeitschrift für katholische Theologie* 75 (1953): 222; Josef Blinzler, *Der Prozeß Jesu* (Regensburg: Friedrich Pustet, 1969), 394; Destro and Pesce, *La morte di Gesù*, 148–49.

16. Acts 9:37.

17. *Evangelium Petri* 24.

18. A log is a measurement of between 345 and 597 cubic centimetres, so a quarter log would have been at least 85 cc (8.5 cl).

19. ספר שאלות ותשובות מהרי"ל - *Schalot utschuwot Maril* (Krakau: Fischer und Deutscher, 1881), 25v, translation by Daniel Klutstein, with slight revisions.

20. Shlomo Ganzfried, *Kitzur Shulḥan Aruk* 197:9; trans. Avrohom Davis, *Kitzur Shulchan Aruch* (New York: Metsudah Publications, 1996). The current law is described by Maurice Lamm, *The Jewish Way in Death and Mourning*

(New York: Jonathan David, 2000), 284. See also the explanation provided in Chaim Denburg, *Code of Hebrew Law* (Montreal: The Jurisprudence Press, 1954), 161, n. 39.

21. This is according to Alfred O'Rahilly, *The Burial of Christ* (Cork: Cork University Press, 1942), 3–4.

22. An excellent approach to this topic can be found in Kraemer, *The Meanings of Death*, 4–11.

23. *Mishnah, Ohalot* 3:5; see also 2:2 (impurity due to mixed blood), the comment on the subject made by the *Babylonan Talmud, Niddah* 71a, and the treatment of Jacob Neusner, *A History of the Mishnaic Law of Purities. Part 4: Ohalot* (Leiden: Brill, 1974), 95–102.

24. For this interpretation of the blood, see Israel J. Yuval, *Two Nations in Your Womb: Perceptions of Jews and Christians in Late Antiquity and the Middle Ages* (Berkeley: University of California Press, 2006), 92–143.

25. In fact there is a passage in the *Eichah Rabbah* (4,1) that may date back to the fifth century after Christ, in which it is stated that the quarter-logs of blood of the king Josiah "that flowed from him while there were three hundred arrows shooted at him" were buried by Jeremiah "each in its place" (ed. S. Buber, מדרש איכה רבה [Wilna: Wittwe & Gebrüder Romm, 1899], 140–41). This also explains why in Lamentations it is stated that Josiah "was buried in the sepulchres of his fathers," plural. But this account is isolated and has nothing to do with the cleaning of the body but only with the burial of the blood escaped from an injured man. The blood, in any event, was not buried with the body, but elsewhere. Each quarter-log deserved a burial, as an impure substance that might be touched unknowingly, and perhaps also because it was considered part of the life force. The action of Jeremiah can probably also be explained as an act of extreme veneration towards his sovereign. There is no evidence that there was a rule about this and if there was, that it was also followed by ordinary people.

26. These considerations were suggested to me by Paul Mandel (Schechter Institute of Jewish Studies, Jerusalem) who also consulted some of his colleagues on the subject. I would like to dedicate an in-depth study to this topic in the future.

27. Matthew 27:59–60: "And having taken the body, Joseph wrapped it in pure *sindón* and laid it in his new sepulcher"; Mark 15:46: "And he, having brought *sindón*, and having taken him down, wound him with the *sindón*, and laid him in a sepulcher"; Luke 23:53: "And he, having taken down, wrapped it in *sindón*, and laid him in a tomb"; *Evangelium Petri* 24: "And he, having taken the Lord, washed and tied him with *sindón* and brought him into his own grave."

28. As happens, for example, in Luke 16:19: "A certain man was rich, and was clothed in purple and fine linen."

29. See the sources collected by Craig Keener, *The Gospel of Matthew* (Grand Rapids: Eerdmans, 2009), 700–1.

30. See Pier Angelo Gramaglia, "La Sindone di Torino: alcuni problemi storici," *Rivista di storia e letteratura religiosa* 24 (1988): 550–59, which contains many examples.

31. John 19:40: "They took, therefore, the body of Jesus, and bound it by *othónia* with the spices."

32. John 11:44: "And the dead man came out, being bound feet and hands with *keiríai*, his face wrapped in a *soudárion*."

33. John 20:7.

34. See Yigael Yadin, *The Finds from the Bar Kokhba Period in the Cave of Letters* (Jerusalem: Israel Exploration Society, 1963), 171 and 205; Orit Shamir,

"Shrouds and Other Textiles from Ein Gedi," in *Ein Gedi*, ed. Yizhar Hirschfeld (Haifa: Hecht Museum, 2006), 58.

35. See Gideon Hadas, תישעה קברים מימי הבית השני בעין-גדי, *'Atiqot* 24 (1994): 56; Shamir, "Shrouds and Other Textiles," 71–74 and 57–59; *Mishnah, Miqvaot* 10:4.

36. See James Tabor, *The Jesus Dynasty* (New York: Simon & Schuster, 2007), 6–15; Orit Shamir, "Textiles from the 1st Century CE in Jerusalem," in *Ancient Textiles: Production, Crafts and Society*, ed. Carole Gillis and Marie-Louise Nosch (London: Oxbow Books, 2008), 77–80; Shimon Gibson, *Final Days of Jesus* (New York: HarperOne, 2009), 143–47; Orit Shamir, "A Burial Textile from the First Century CE in Jerusalem Compared to Roman Textiles in the Land of Israel and the Turin Shroud," *SHS Web of Conferences* 15, no. 10 (2015): 3.

37. As can be seen in 2 Samuel 12:20; Ezekiel 16:9.

38. *Mishnah, Shabbat* 23:5: סכין ומדיחין.

39. Adolf Büchler, פירוש המשנה שבת פרק כ"ג, ה, עושין כל צורכי המת סכין ומדיחין אותו in ספר היובל לפרופיסור שמואל קרויס (Jerusalem: Rubin Mass, 1937), 36–49.

40. Matthew 26:6–12; Mark 14:3–8; Luke 7:36–47; John 12:1–7.

41. Matthew 27:57–28:1; Mark 15:42–16:2; Luke 23:50–24:1; John 19:38–20:1.

42. See Jean Langenheim, *Plant Resins* (Portland: Timber Press, 2003), 368–70.

43. Ibid., 448–50.

44. Flavius, *Bellum Iudaicum* 1:671–73; *Antiquitates Iudaicae* 17:197–200.

45. See 2 Chronicles 16:14; 21:19; Jeremiah 34:5; Flavius, *Antiquitates Iudaicae* 15:61; *Babylonian Talmud, Abodah Zarah* 11a.

46. *Mishnah, Berakhot* 8:6; *Palestinian Talmud, Berakhot* 8:6 (61a); *Babylonian Talmud, Berakhot* 53a. On the Rabbinical sources, see Deborah Green, "Sweet Spices in the Tomb," in *Commemorating the Dead*, ed. Deborah Green and Laurie Brink (Berlin: De Gruyter, 2008), 145–73.

47. *Tosefta, Niddah* 9:16; *Babylonian Talmud, Mo'ed Qatan* 27b.

48. *Tosefta, Sheqalim* 1:12; *Palestinian Talmud, Yoma* 8:1 (39a).

49. See Rachel Hachlili, *Jewish Funerary Customs* (Leiden: Brill, 2004), 378–86.

50. Charles Cranfield, *The Gospel According to St Mark* (Cambridge: Cambridge University Press, 1977), 464.

51. So thought François-Marie Braun, "Le Linceul de Turin et l'Évangile de Saint Jean," *Nouvelle revue théologique* 66 (1939): 1038–39; Josef Blinzler, "Die Grablegung Jesu in historischer Sicht," in *Resurrexit*, ed. Édouard Dhanis (Vatican City: Libreria EditriceVaticana, 1974), 81.

52. *Testamentum Abrahae* (long version) 20:10–11; *Apocalypsis Mosis* 40.

53. Mark 16:1; Luke 23:56 and 24:1.

54. See Kraemer, *The Meanings of Death*, 123–26.

55. *Palestinian Talmud, Yebamot* 16:3 (83a), a saying attributed to the third quarter of the third century. Parallel passage in *Mo'ed Qatan* 3:5 (14a). In the *Paralipomena Ieremiae* (BHG 777) 9:10–13 it is said that Jeremiah came back to life three days after his death.

56. Thus Braun, "Le Linceul de Turin," 1037. *Semaḥot* (8:1) also prescribed that "one may go out to the cemetery for thirty days to inspect the dead for a sign of life." There are proposals to amend "thirty" to "three" (for example Safrai and Stern, *The Jewish People*, 784–85) since after 30 days such an inspection would make very little sense.

57. Luke 7:14.

58. *Mishnah, Berakhot* 3:1; *Mo'ed Qatan* 1:6; *Babylonian Talmud, Mo'ed Qatan* 27a–b. Images of some Judaic coffins from the first century can be seen in Hadas, תישעה קברים מימי הבית השני, 6–54. See Amos Kloner and Boaz Zissu, *The Necropolis of Jerusalem* (Leuven: Peeters, 2007), 103–4.

59. This is also said in John 19:42: "And so, because it was the Jewish day of preparation and the tomb was nearby, they placed Jesus's body there."
60. *Mishnah, Sanhedrin* 6:5 and *Shabbat* 23:5.
61. Acts 5:6–10.
62. *Babylonian Talmud, Moʻed Qatan* 8b.
63. Some Biblical manuscripts in fact substitute καινόν (new) with κενόν (empty). The pronunciation is the same.
64. Blinzler, "Die Grablegung Jesu," 101–2.
65. In response to those who believe that a person condemned to death was necessarily destined to remain unburied or to be placed in a mass grave, see Craig Evans, "Jewish Burial Traditions and the Resurrection of Jesus," *Journal for the Study of the Historical Jesus* 3 (2005): 233–48; Craig Evans, "The Family Buried Together Stays Together," in *The World of Jesus and the Early Church*, ed. Craig Evans (Peabody: Hendrickson, 2011), 87–96; John Granger Cook, "Crucifixion and Burial," *New Testament Studies* 57 (2011): 193–213, in particular against the opinions expressed by John Dominic Crossan, who in fact repeated what had been written a century earlier by Alfred Loisy, *Les Évangiles synoptiques* (Ceffonds: chez l'auteur, 1907), 223. Crossan believes that Jesus ended up in a mass grave at the mercy of wild animals and that the whole history of his burial is merely the result of the pious wishful thinking of his disciples.
66. See 2 King 21:18–26.
67. Brown, *The Death of the Messiah*, 1278.

2 The Cult of Relics in the Late Roman Empire
Legal Aspects

Maria G. Castello

The cult of relics has been of great academic interest for a long time, but *The Cult of the Saints*, the fundamental work by Peter Brown,[1] has manifestly given a major impetus to the research. Through the years the study of this cult has never been the hunting ground only of historians—be they specialists of the Roman era, of religion or of Christianity—but has been resolutely open to the perspectives of sociology, anthropology and even economics, thereby broadening the spectrum of investigations into the phenomenon. This contribution takes a strictly historical-juridical approach, aiming to analyse the cult of relics from the point of view of its formalisation by the imperial and canonical-episcopal authorities. It will therefore focus on "official" sources, such as the late imperial juridical collations—although the status of the *Codex Theodosianus* is still debated[2]—and on the acts of the ecclesiastical councils, ecumenical and otherwise, albeit reference will also be made to less formal sources, such as episcopal letters and homilies which, due to the prestige of their authors, were soon equated to canonised sources. In particular I will concentrate on the forms of control of the cult of relics, hoping to demonstrate how these involved not only religious, but also political and social issues.

From a methodological point of view, it is important to make one initial point. While many contributions to this volume have embraced a localised perspective, in this case that cannot be done because of the nature of the sources examined. As we know, late antiquity legislation handed down by the codes would have been intended as general:[3] it referred to events that were clearly of a local nature but whose practicability the legislators thought worthy of general application, or even valid for the entire empire. This means that it is not always possible to go back to the specific episode that gave rise to a law that was later made *generalis*. Indeed, we should remember that the Justinian Code was intended to be "living" and suited to the legislative practice of the sixth century, for which it included existing rules adapted to that period, and the link to the original circumstances that generated them is often impossible to trace. This point also applies to the norms that were borrowed from the Code of Theodosius, then dissected and redistributed in different parts of the Code of Justinian.

The cult of relics followed and developed in lockstep with the rise and legitimisation of Christianity. We have evidence of it from the second half of the second century CE, but it really proliferated from the second half of the fourth century, having started to be codified from the end of the third and beginning of the fourth.[4] As early as 324 Constantine cited it in an epistle published in Eusebius's *Life of Constantine*, granting the church ownership of the tombs of martyrs:

> Eus. V. Const. II 40: Καὶ μὴν καὶ τοὺς τόπους αὐτούς, οἳ τοῖς σώμασι τῶν μαρτύρων τετίμηνται καὶ τῆς ἀναχωρήσεως τῆς ἐνδόξου ὑπομνήματα καθεστᾶσιν, τίς ἂν ἀμφιβάλοι μὴ οὐχὶ ταῖς ἐκκλησίαις προσήκειν, ἢ οὐχὶ καὶ προστάξειεν ἄν.[5]

This early evidence makes clear how the question involved not only the religious sphere, but also the politic and economic ones. We should not forget that this was the eve of the Council of Nicea. As can be deduced, in late antiquity, as in the modern and contemporary ages, relics were also a political fact and represented, as we shall see, one of the areas of confrontation between the empire and the church.

The First Imperial Legislation

Although the cult of relics had become widespread, probably first in the East, well before the Edict of Milan, it became systematised only when the empire created the conditions for it, in other words with the great Diocletianic Persecution. Although the likely number of victims has been reduced over the years, the impact of the persecution on the collective imagination has not, thanks in part to the work of Eusebius of Caesarea.

The first law included in the codes, specifically the Code of Justinian, concerning the translation of bodies, is not, however, attributable to a Christian emperor, but, paradoxically, to Diocletian, the "great persecutor." This is *C. I.* 3, 44, 10, promulgated in 287, before the persecution began.

> Imperatores Diocletianus, Maximianus. Si necdum perpetuae sepulturae corpus traditum est, translationem eius facere non prohiberis. Diocl. et Maxim. AA. Aquilinae. A 287 pp. VIII Id. Dec. Diocletiano III et Maximiano AA. Conss.[6]

The code incorporated other, earlier laws, but these concerned material objects and not the body as such.[7] This first law, then, was probably a rescript—unfortunately the original *suggestio* has been lost—that allowed the translation of a body only if it had not already been interred. It is likely that it reflected the traditional Roman religious notion according to which a body that had been exhumed and removed from its place of burial, a *locus religiosus*, was impure and in need of ceremonial purification. Thus the translation of bodies was permitted—when authorised by the emperor, perhaps in his role of *Pontifex Maximus*—only if they had not yet been definitively laid to rest.[8] What interests us here is not so much the historical and religious context in which this law was issued, as the reason why it was included in a code whose Christian influence is very clear. It is possible to assume that in the age of Justinian the law was used to regulate, and even facilitate, the transport and transfer of bodies and relics, and hence it was included in the *Codex*.[9] Support for this interpretation comes from the fact that, as F. Millar has underlined,[10] the rule appears to have been less restrictive than the one laid out by Ulpian, which is also found in the *Digesta*.[11]

There are therefore several ways of interpreting this. The first, formalistic one, recalls a view from Paul, according to whom for a *locus* to be religious—and as such a place of perpetual burial—the inhumed body had to be complete, or at least had to have a head:[12] the practice of relic hunting, which did not require that the relic must be whole,[13] was already quite widespread at the time of Justinian, and had clearly been made easier by this rule. Moreover, considering that the *perpetuus* status of a burial was decided by the tomb's owner and was often not hereditary,[14] it would have been easy for the empire or the church to claim ownership and thereby eliminate the restraint of *locus religiosus* and, accordingly, the penal sanctions linked to the *translationes*. Nevertheless, more pragmatically but also more in keeping with the sixth-century reality of a now-Christian empire in which the dominant force was the *Heilsgeschichte*, the Diocletianic law could justify the custom in which the *sepultura perpetua* of the body or remains of a saint or martyr might be identified with a sanctuary under ecclesiastic control or—basically the same thing—with an imperial reliquary, legitimising a *translatio* from a burial site that was clearly not definitive.

And since history often has unpredictable outcomes, it is possible that it was precisely on the basis of this law that Julian, in 362, felt that he had the authority to move the remains of Saint Babylas—a well-known case of public translation recorded in the sources—which lay in the Temple of Daphne.[15] It is also interesting to note that the law was one of the 14 in the *titulus De religiosis et sumptis funerum*, only one of which was post-Constantinian; this was *C. I.* 3, 44, 14, ascribed to Diocletian but which should in fact be post-dated to 386. It is actually part of *C. Th.* 9, 17, 7, to which we shall return, promulgated by Theodosius in 386 and, divided into sections, placed in the Justinian Code. Julian, in keeping with what we glean from his writings, attempted to curtail the spread of the cult of relics, which he regarded as obsessive: not by chance in 363 with *C. Th.* 9. 17.5 he condemned the violation of tombs and, in the second part, daytime funeral services.

It should be a cause for reflection that a law by the "apostate" emperor was not only accepted in the Theodosian, but even in the Justinian Code (*C. I.* 9.19.5), although it was in part defective. We should never underestimate changes of position, amendments and reorganisation in the texts.

Table 2.1 Julian's law on burials

C. Th. 9.17.5	C. I. 9.19.5
Imp. Iulianus a. ad populum. *pr. Pergit audacia ad busta diem* *functorum et aggeres consecratos,* *cum et lapidem hinc movere et terram* *sollicitare et cespitem vellere proximum* *sacrilegio maiores semper habuerint.* *Sed et ornamenta quidam tricliniis aut* *porticibus auferunt de sepulchris.* *Quibus primis consulentes, ne in* *piaculum incidant contaminata religione* *bustorum, hoc fieri prohibemus poena* *manium vindice cohibentes.* *1. Secundum illud est, quod efferri* *cognovimus cadavera mortuorum per* *confertam populi frequentiam et per* *maximam insistentium densitatem;* *quod quidem oculos hominum infaustis* *incestat aspectibus. Qui enim dies est* *bene auspicatus a funere aut quomodo* *ad deos et templa venietur? Ideoque* *quoniam et dolor in exsequiis secretum* *amat et diem functis nihil interest,* *utrum per noctes an per dies efferantur,* *liberari convenit populi totius aspectus,* *ut dolor esse in funeribus, non pompa* *exsequiarum nec ostentatio videatur.* *Dat. prid. id. feb. Antiochiae Iuliano a.* *IIII et Sallustio conss. (363 febr. 12).*	*Imperator Iulianus. Pergit* *audacia ad busta diem* *functorum et aggeres* *consecratos, cum et lapidem* *hinc movere et terram* *sollicitare et cespitem vellere* *proximum sacrilegio maiores* *semper habuerunt: sed et* *ornamenta quaedam tricliniis* *aut porticibus auferri de* *sepulchris.* *1. Quibus primis consulentes,* *ne in piaculum incidant* *contaminata religione* *bustorum, hoc fieri prohibemus* *poena sacrilegii cohibentes.* **Iul. A. ad Pop. <A 363 D. Prid.* *Id. Febr. Antiochiae Iuliano* *A.III et Sallustio Conss.[1]>*

1 C.Th. 9.17.5: Emperor Julian Augustus to the People. Criminal audacity extends to the ashes of the dead and their consecrated mounds, although our ancestors always considered it the next thing to sacrilege even to move a stone from such places or to disturb the earth or to tear up the sod. But some men even take away from the tombs ornaments for their dining rooms and porticoes. We consider the interests of such criminals first, that they may not fall into sin by defiling the sanctity of tombs, and We prohibit such deeds, restraining them by the penalty which avenges the spirits of the dead. 1. The second matter is the fact that We have learned that the corpses of the dead are being carried to burial through dense crowds of people and through the greatest throngs of bystanders. This practice, indeed, pollutes the eyes of men by its ill-omened aspect. For what day is well-omened by a funeral? Or how can one come to the gods and temples from a funeral? Therefore, since grief loves privacy in its obsequies and since it makes no difference to those who have finished their days whether they are carried to their tombs by night or by day, the sight of all the people must be freed from this spectacle. Thus grief may appear to be associated with funerals, but not pompous obsequies and ostentation. Given on the day before the ides of February at Antioch in the year of the fourth consulship of Julian Augustus and the consulship of Sallustius. February 12, 363 (trans. Clyde Pharr, *The Theodosian Code* (London: 1952), 240). C. I. 9.19.5: Emperor Julian to the people. Audacity extends to the tombs of the dead and to consecrated mounds, whom our forefathers considered it almost a sacrilege to even move a stone therefrom, or disturb the earth or tear up the sod. And some of the things are removed for ornaments for dining rooms and porticoes. 1. Consulting their interest, we prohibit this to be done, lest they (the transgressors) fall into the sin of disturbing the sanctity of the dead (bustorum) under the penalty fixed for sacrilege. Given at Antioch February 12 (363) (trans. Blume, *Justinian*).

This law shows the life of the imperial constitutions in the course of the centuries. Enacted by Julian in 363, it is nothing other than a sort of abstract of a much wider text drawn up by the chancery, an epistle by the emperor Julian (136b) that unfortunately has only survived in mutilated form and in which are argued, in accordance with Julian's philosophic and religious credo, the provisions of a legislative text (136a) that appears to be much more neutral, of a general nature, and in line with the content of other provisions on the subject in the *titulus*. These are the reasons why the compilers the Thedosian *Codex* chose to place it in their work.[16] It was then also included in the Justinian Code, although its second paragraph—dealing with funerals—was cut out because it was deemed overly pagan despite its generality.[17] Finally, further testimony of the adaptations made to eliminate any type of pagan heritage in the laws of the *Codex* is the fact that the expression *manium vindice*, which was still present in the Theodosian text, was substituted by Justinian's compilers for the more Christian *sacrilegii*.

The Voices of the Church

One should not, however, believe that the legislators were the only ones to speak about a phenomenon that from the fourth century had stimulated reflections also among the church fathers who expressed their views in writings, councils and synods. And neither were the secular intellectual elites excluded from the debate: they looked upon the cult of relics with suspicion and undisguised contempt: for Eunapius of Sardis, relics were nothing but bones and skulls of outlaws,[18] while what Julian wrote about them in his *Misopogon* and *Against the Galileans* was no less harsh.[19]

There were several issues that triggered a reflection about this matter: issues about public order, theology (for example, the debate about the integrity of relics) and economics, while increased demand, as summarised by F. Carlà, created a flourishing market.[20] The demand was for bodies (level I relics), the possessions of holy men (level II) and, finally, relics made up of items that had come into with the corpse of a saint (level III).[21] Thus the words of Gaudentius of Brescia are hardly surprising:

> Gaud. Brix., *Sermo*, 17, 34 [MPL 20, 970B]: *Cum cineres exustorum corporum, mandato persecutoris, in fluvium jacerentur, non defuerunt religiosae manus, quae partem cineris vel furto eriperent, vel pretio compararent.*[22]

While Zeno, bishop of Verona in the second half of the fourth century lamented the excessive proliferation of cults of improper deaths and the tenfold increase in *inventiones* of martyrs, giving voice to a phenomenon clearly perceived as widespread:

> Zeno, *Tract.*, I, 25, 11 [MPL 11, 366A]: *Non hi solum, qui tales sunt, displicent Deo, sed et illi, qui per sepulcra discurrunt; qui foeterosis prandia cadaveribus sacrificant mortuorum; qui amore luxuriandi atque bibendi, in infamibus locis lagenis et calicibus subito sibi martyres pepererunt.*

Athanasius and Theodoret explained the theological issues of the private conservation and dismemberment of the bodies of saints, reporting some curious cases:

> *Athan.* V. Ant. 90–91 (MPG 26, 689C–690A; 691A):

> When the brethren urged him to stay with them and die there, he refused to do so for many reasons, as he indicated, thought without saying anything, and especially because of this. The Egyptians have the custom of honoring with funeral rites and wrapping in linen shrouds the bodies of good men, and especially of the holy martyrs; but they do not bury them in the earth, but place them on couches and keep them with them at home, thinking in this way to honor the departed. Antony had often asked even the bishops to give instructions to the people on the matter. [. . .] [Antony said to them] If you have any care of me and think of me as a father, do not allow anyone to take my body into Egypt, lest they should keep it in their house. This was my reason for going to the mountain and coming here. You know how I always put to shame those who do this and charged them to stop the custom. Therefore, carry out my obsequies yourselves and bury my body in the earth and let what I have said be so respected by you, that no one will know the place but you alone.[23]

> *Theodor.* Hist. Mon., 3, 18 (V. Marciani):

> Many everywhere built him burial shrines—in Cyrrhus his nephew Alypius, in Chacis a certain Zenobiana, glorious in birth, preeminent in virtue and flourishing in abundance of wealth, and not a few others did the same thing, in competition to carry off this victorious athlete. Knowing this, the man of God adjured that wonderful Eusebius, imposing on him oaths fraught with very terror, to bury his body in that spot and inform no one of his grave, save two of his more intimate companions, until a great number of years had passed. That wonderful man carried out this oath: when the end of the victor had

come and the choir of the angels transferred that sacred and godly soul into the abodes of heaven, he did not announce his death until, with the two companions most close to him, he had dug the grave, buried the body, and leveled the surface of the ground. Fifty years or more passed by, a countless number hastened along and searched for the body; yet the grave remained undetected.

Theodor. Hist. Mon.*, 21, 5 and 9 (V.* Iacobi*):*

Fourteen years ago, a grave illness came upon him which caused him a condition to be expected in one with a mortal body. [. . .] It was then that I witnessed the great endurance of this man. For while many men of the country had assembled with the intention of seizing the victorious body. [. . .] Noticing this, I addressed many exhortations to those who had come, and many threats, ordering them to go away. Finally I applied to them my Episcopal authority, and in the evening, with great effort, sent them away. [. . .] A later time he fell ill of a more serious disease. As many come together from all side to seize his body, all the men of the town, when they heard of it, hastened together, soldiers and civilian, some taking up military equipment, others using whatever weapons lay to hand. Forming up in close order, they fought by shooting arrows and slinging stones—not to wound but simply to instill fear. [. . .] He was not even conscious of his hair being plucked off by the peasants.[24]

In addition, this is what the *Testamentum* wrote about the Forty Martyrs of Sebaste:

Testamentum LX martyrum 3–4 (ed. Musurillo):

Ἔτι δὲ ἀξιοῦμεν πάντας μηδένα τῶν ἐκ τῆς καμίνου ἀνελομένων λειψάνων ἡμῶν ἐν ἑαυτῷ περιποιήσασθαι, ἀλλὰ καὶ τῆς ἐν ταὐτῷ συναθροίσεως φροντίσαντα ἀποδοῦναι τοῖς προειρημένοις.[25]

In these passages we see, apart from the issues already mentioned, the emergence of others, among which was the problem of certifying the authenticity of a martyr. This is mentioned by Optatus of Milevis, who recounted the perplexity of Cecilianus of Carthage on seeing a woman who carried with her the bones of martyrs that had not been identified.[26]

These matters resurfaced in different ways in the councils of the fourth century or were appropriately enhanced with political-ecclesiastical meaning in the works of charismatic exponents of the clergy. Thus in 343 the Council of Gangra condemned those who did not venerate the relics and the memory of the martyrs:

Gangra 343, Can. 20:

Εἴ τις [αἰτιᾶται] ὑπερηφάνῳ διαθέσει κεχρημένος, καὶ βδελθσσόμενος τὰς συνάξεις τῶν μαρτύρων, ἢ τὰς ἐν αὐτοῖς γινομένας λειτουργίας, καὶ τὰς μνήμας αὐτῶν, ἀνάθεμα ἔστω.[27]

Later, at Laodicea in 364 and Carthage in 401, when contending with an uncontrolled explosion of the phenomenon, the cities tried, if not to limit it, at least to regulate it. At Laodicea attempts were made to sanction the clergymen committed to fuelling the relics market—in this case not human ones—by inviting them not to become mathematicians or astrologers.

Laodicea 364, Can. 36:

Ὅτι οὐ δεῖ ἱερατικοὺς ἢ κληρικοὺς μάγους ἢ ἐπαοιδοὺς εἶναι, ἢ μαθηματικούς, ἢ ἀστρολόγους, ἢποιεῖν τὰ λεγόμενα φυλακτήρια ἅτινα ἐστι δεσμωτήρια τῶν ψυχῶν αὐτῶν. τοὺς δὲ φοροῦντας ῥιπτάζεσθαι ἐκ τῆς ἐκκλησίας ἐκελεύσαμεν.[28]

The choice of words is interesting because it follows exactly that of the contemporary imperial legislation which outlawed the *superstitiones* of mathematicians, soothsayers and astrologers.[29] While there may be no direct correlation, the comparability to the episode of the illness of the newly elected emperors Valentinian and Valens, which unleashed an out-and-out witch-hunt against mathematicians, astrologers and fortune-tellers is certainly suggestive.[30]

In 401 in the council of Carthage, on the other hand, an attempt was made to regulate the cult of martyrs and their remains by endorsing cer-tification criteria on a topographical basis.

Carthago 401, c. 14 (Mansi, Conc. III, col. 971):

Item placuit, ut altaria quae passim per agros aut vias, tanquam memoriae martyrum constituuntur, in quibus nullum corpus aut reli-quiae martyrum conditae probantur, ab episcopis, qui eisdem locis praesunt, si fieri potest, evertantur. Si autem propter tumultus popu-lares non sinitur, plebes tamen admoneantur, ne illa loca frequen-tent, ut qui recte sapiunt, nulla ibi superstitione devincti teneantur. Et omnino nulla memoria martyrum probabiliter acceptetur, nisi aut ibi corpus, aut aliquae certae reliquiae sint, aut ubi origo alicuius habi-tationis, vel possessionis, vel passionis fedelissima origine traditur. Nam quae per somniae et per inanes quasi revelationes quorumlibet ubique constituuntur altaria, omnimode reprobentur.[31]

Human remains lent themselves very well to validating claims of a politi-cal nature. This was fully understood by Eusebius of Caesarea when,

according to a far-fetched hypothesis, he avoided talking about the rediscovery by Helena, mother of Constantine, of the holy relics linked to
the passion and death of Christ, during her journey to the Holy Land:
this would have reinforced the position of the diocese of Jerusalem to the
detriment of that of Caesarea over which he presided.[32] The political use
of human remains became systematic later on, in around the second half
of the fourth century with key personages of the then ecclesiastical scene,
Damasus and Ambrose. Paradigmatic is the case of the *inventio* by the
bishop of Milan of the relics of Gervasius and Protasius and the use that
he made of them to enhance the primate of Milan as an episcopal see as
well as—as we shall see—to counter the Arian drift of the imperial court
promoted by Justina, mother of Emperor Valentinian II. Much the same
was done in Rome by Damasus with Saints Peter and Paul and in Bologna,
again by Ambrose, with Saint Vitalis.[33] These were "functional" saints
whose political and not only economic standing in the hierarchy of relics
was immeasurable, given the authoritativeness of their "promoters."

Finally, returning to the sources concerning the severing of bodies in
order to increase the number of relics, Gregory the Great's opposition
to the *crurifragium* when he was asked for parts of the remains of Peter
and Paul is noteworthy. His objection could easily have been motivated
by theological considerations or by a desire not to disrespect the remains
of two princes of the church. But, in fact, it was no more than a form of
opposition to the dispersion of prestigious relics of which the church of
Rome had claimed total ownership.[34]

Thus, the church oscillated between the need for relics, in terms of
how they were used by Ambrose, Gaudentius of Brescia and Damasus of
Rome, later successfully replicated by Gregory the Great, and the need to
regulate their use.

Empire and Church

Relics also become instruments of contestation (not always peaceful)
between the empire and the church. And so while Gervasio and Protasio's
386 *inventio* can only be read from an anti-Arian point of view,[35] specifically as an act against Justina and in open controversy with a law of the
same year that allowed the Arians freedom of worship,[36] so a law by Constance II in 346 (*C.Th.* 9, 17, 4) against the violation of tombs, of buried
bodies and relics can easily be read as a peace-keeping measure, but also
as a position taken by the Arian emperor against the uncontrolled trade of
human remains.[37] This was the first law that equated offences against fune-
real monuments to those against the remains (*reliquiae*) of the deceased:

> C. Th. 9.17.4: *Idem a. ad populum.*
> *Qui aedificia manium violant, domus ut ita dixerim defuncto-*
> *rum, geminum videntur facinus perpetrare, nam et sepultos spoliant*

destruendo et vivos polluunt fabricando. Si quis igitur de sepulchro abstulerit saxa vel marmora vel columnas aliamve quamcumque materiam fabricae gratia sive id fecerit venditurus, decem pondo auri cogatur inferre fisco: sive quis propria sepulchra defendens hanc in iudicium querellam detulerit sive quicumque alius accusaverit vel officium nuntiaverit. Quae poena priscae severitati accedit, nihil enim derogatum est illi supplicio, quod sepulchra violantibus videtur impositum. Huic autem poenae subiacebunt et qui corpora sepulta aut reliquias contrectaverint.

Dat. id. iun. Mediolano Constantio a. VIIII et Iuliano caes. II conss.[38]

Until then the legislation regarding this matter—contained in the *titulus* 17, 9, *De sepulchris violatis*—had been focused on buildings and structures: now, not unintentionally, attention turned to bodies.[39] The law is also preserved in C. I. 9, 19, 4 with one significant change: the pagan locution *aedificia manium* was substituted by the compilers with the Christian *sepulchra*.[40]

Finally, in 386, a key year in the history of relics, came C. Th. 9, 17, 7, a law by Emperor Theodosius and addressed to the Christian prefect Maternus Cynegius:

C. Th. 9.17.7
Idem aaa. Cynegio praefecto praetorio.

Humatum corpus nemo ad alterum locum transferat; nemo martyrem distrahat, nemo mercetur. Habeant vero in potestate, si quolibet in loco sanctorum est aliquis conditus, pro eius veneratione quod martyrium vocandum sit addant quod voluerint fabricarum. Dat. IIII kal. mart. Constantinopoli, Honorio n. p. et Evodio conss.

(386 febr. 26).[41]

This law, which would appear to be lapidary, exemplifying a total rejection of reliquary and martyrological practices, not only arises in the context of the struggle against heresies that was then tearing apart the city of Constantinople, despite the severe measures taken by Theodosius—for example, the so-called "Edict of Thessalonica" and the councils held in Constantinople in 381 and 382[42]—but does not seem to have been recognised as such by Justinian's compilers.

D. Hunt places the Theodosian constitution in direct opposition to the actions of Ambrose:[43] while in the same year the bishop of Milan promoted the practice of *intra moenia* burials, giving them the character of a public worship, Theodosius sought to confine martyrs within their *extra moenia* burial spaces, at least in the East. These were therefore different measures, promoted in different geographical contexts by different authorities, namely a "local" bishop—albeit one of an imperial residence—and an emperor with jurisdiction over the entire eastern area, whose normative acts had, at least in theory,[44] authority over the whole empire. Even so, considering the controversial relations between the two, one cannot fail to think that there was some contiguity between the two situations, as had already been the case with the almost homologous councils of 381 in Constantinople and Aquileia.

Nevertheless, the subsequent history of the law, when it was incorporated into the Justinian Code, is interesting. Most of the Theodosian constitutions in the *titulus* of 9, 17 were included in the *titulus* of the Justinian Code, 9, 19, with the exception of *C. Th.* 9, 17, 6, a law that forbade burials *apud sanctos*, which was carried over into *C. I.* 1, 2, 2, and *C. Th.* 9, 17, 7, which was broken up and divided between *C. I.* 1, 2, 3 and *C. I.* 3, 44, 14.

Justinian's compilers worked in the sure knowledge that a Code would become part of everyday legal practice, and therefore the splitting of the Theodosius's *lex* in their *Codex* deserves attention.

Table 2.2 Theodosius's law on relics

C. Th. 9.17.7	C. I. 9.19	C. I. 3.44.14	C. I. 1.2.3
De sepuchri violati	*De sepulchro violato*	*De religiosis ed sumptibus funerum*	*De sacrosanctis ecclesiis et de rebus et privilegiis earum*
Idem aaa. Cynegio praefecto praetorio. Humatum corpus nemo ad alterum locum transferat; nemo martyrem distrahat, nemo mercetur. Habeant vero in potestate, si quolibet in loco sanctorum est aliquis conditus, pro eius veneratione quod martyrium vocandum sit addant quod voluerint fabricarum. Dat. IIII kal. mart. Constantinopoli Honorio n. p. et Evodio conss. (386 febr. 26).		*Imperatores Diocletianus, Maximianus. Nemo humanum corpus ad alterum locum sine augusti adfatibus transferat. Diocl. et Maxim. AAA. Cynegio pp. <A 386 D. IIII K. Mart. Constantinopoli Honorio Nob. Puero et Euodio Conss.>*	*Imperatores Gratianus, Valentinianus, Theodosius. Nemo martyres distrahat, nemo mercetur. Grat. Valentin. et Theodos. AAA. Cynegio pp.*

If the dispositions of Constantine and Julian recalled above (*C. Th.* 9.17.4–5 = 9. 19. 4–5) were included in the Justinian Code under the same *titulus*, the same could not be said of the Theodosian law, whose two chapters constituted, from the juridical perspective of the fourth century and the start of the fifth, a synthesis between traditional legislation— which explains its inclusion in the aforementioned *titulus de sepulchris violatis*—and a newer one that recognised ecclesiastical canons, homiletical prescriptions and the cult of relics as "bodies." Twenty-three years had elapsed between the law by Justinian and that of 386, during which time the church fathers, but also lay and pagan voices, had in effect explicitly recognised the cult of the relics of martyrs. The legislation took account of this, hence the clause in the second paragraph of the law, which was plainly designed for them. This was a law perfectly modulated for the historical context in which it was conceived, a setting in which the translation of bodies and trade in corpses were treated in the same way, in accordance with a point of view that I dare to define most pragmatically as "Theodosian": a perspective within which past issues and contingent ones merge in the wake of a consolidated legislative tradition. We return to the theme of *realpolitik* of which the same Theodosian Code remains an expression. Things changed in the next century with the publication of the Justinian Code that underlay a more rationally managed codification project. The outcome of this is clear even in the case of the legislation on human remains.

C. *Th*. 9, 17, 7, which up to that period represented, from the imperial standpoint, the norm of reference on bodies/relics, was divided into two *tituli*: *De religiosis et sumptibus funerum* and *De sacrosanctis ecclesiis et de rebus et privilegiis earum*, significantly avoiding the original *titulus* relating to the violation of sepulchres. The first part, so similar in content to the Diocletianic disposition of 287, was relegated to a prescriptive section, perhaps a sign of the state's attention to the protection of burial spaces. The second, of an apparently sanctioning nature—no penalties were foreseen—freed the Theodosian law from the religious ambiguity to which Theodosius had relegated it: included in book I of the Justinian Code, it exemplified its Christian nature, conceived for a Christian empire. It should not be forgotten that book I of the Justinian Code, save for the pragmatic constitutions, was dedicated to the *Catholica Fides*. The law sanctioned the trade in relics and, at the same time, now recognising their cult[45] and its political potential, ascribed—in the other *titulus*—its management to the emperors alone.

There is a final, but fundamental aspect of this constitution that must be underlined: the one in the Justinian Code indicates that bodies were not to be moved to another place *sine augusti adfatibus*, a clarification that is absent from the Theodosian law.[46] Can it perhaps be theorised that, at the time of the drafting of the Justinian Code, this clause was aimed at bringing under the aegis of political authority the intense traffic in human remains recorded by the sources between the fourth and fifth centuries, removing it from ecclesiastical control in a challenge that, while certainly political and economic, also aimed to emphasise status?[47]

The inclusion of the two dispositions in the same *titulus* does not appear casual. If it had been so, the law would be further confirmation of how the Justinian Code had reworked the legislation to adapt it to its times. This, as has been suggested, might explain the failure to mention religious authorities, which traditionally were in charge of such practices,[48] in *C. I.* 3, 44, 1,[49] and which once again regulated the translation of bodies,[50] making clear the imperial will to assume the responsibility at a time when it was very active in this area.[51] But at the same time, it must be admitted that Christianity in the age of Justinian, much more than in the Theodosian one, despite the religious orientation evidenced in the programmatic constitutions,[52] exerted a certain influence over the compilers' work. This is made clear by the change of language in *C. Th.* 19, 7, 4 and 5, and also in *C. I.* 3, 44, 10, which, having been added to the sixth century *Codex*, also shows how the concept of *perpetuus* and *locus religious*, so carefully codified by the jurists of the classical age, was transformed, with real consequences, by the *nova religio*.[53]

Legislation is the final act of processes that have been codified. This is how we should interpret all the laws, imperial and canonical, as well as the dictates of the church fathers I recalled above. Legislation reacted quickly and over the long term. As an expression of political power, if interpreted in the right way, it perhaps illustrated certain historical, political and religious processes. The re-exegesis of legislative sources has made it possible to re-evaluate the religious policy of champions of Christianity like Constantine and Theodosius, but such investigations have not involved laws specifically related to worship. In this analysis we have been able to verify that this interpretative model is valid also for more sensitive cases such as the cult of relics, for the standardisation of which, still in Justinian's age, in spite of solid historiographic constructions, the attention to the safety of the state remained the main focus.

Notes

1. Peter Brown, *The Cult of the Saints* (Chicago: Chicago University Press, 1981).
2. See Adriaan Johan Boudewijn Sirks, *The Theodosian Code: A Study* (Friedrichsdorf: Tortuga, 2007), 208–14; Benet Salway, "The Publication and Application of the Theodosian Code: NTh 1, the *Gesta senatus*, and the *constitutionarii*," *Mélanges de l'École française de Rome—Antiquité* 125, no. 2 (2013): 1–40, in part. 11–14.
3. *C. Th.* 1, 1, 6.
4. John Wortley, "The Origins of Christian Veneration of Body-Parts," *Revue de l'histoire des religions* 223 (2006): 12–13; Filippo Carlà, "Exchange and the Saints: Gift-Giving and the Commerce of Relics," in *Gift Giving and the 'Embedded' Economy in the Ancient World*, ed. Filippo Carlà and Maia Gori (Heidelberg: Universitätsverlag Winter, 2014), 404; Margherita Bolla,

"Sepoltura non perpetua: la riapertura delle tombe e il caso concordiese," in *Le necropoli della media e tarda età imperiale (III–IV secolo d.C.) a* Iulia Concordia *e nell'arco Altoadriatico. Organizzazione spaziale, aspetti monumentali e strutture sociali. Atti del convegno di studio (Concordia Sagittaria, 5–6 giugno 2014)*, ed. Federica Rinaldi and Alberto Vigoni (Rubano: Grafiche Turato Edizioni, 2015), 357–77.

5. "Furthermore the places themselves which are honoured by the bodies of the martyrs and stand as monuments to their glorious decease, who could doubt that they belong to the churches, or would not so decree?" (Averil Cameron and Stuart G. Hall, trans., *Eusebius: Life of Constantine* [Oxford: Clarendon, 1999], 109). See Filippo Carlà, *"Res tamquam proprias retinebat:* Personal and Collective Property in the Late Antique Church Between Normative Regulation and Social Practice," in *Himmelwärts und erdverbunden? Religiöse und wirtschaftliche Aspekte spätantiker Lebensrealität (4.-7. Jh.)*, ed. Rudolf Haensch and Philipp Freiherr von Rummel (Rahden: forthcoming).

6. "Emperors Diocletian and Maximian to Acquilina. If the dead body has not yet been buried in a permanent sepulcher, you are not forbidden to transfer it. Promulgated December 6 (287)" (Fred H. Blume, trans., "Annotated Justinian Code, ad locum," www.uwyo.edu/lawlib/blume-justinian/ajc-edition-2/books/).

7. Apart from *C. I.* 3.44.1 (213), which allows bodies to be moved in the event of their being threatened by a flooding river. On this law, see Arnaud Paturet, "Le transfert des morts dans l'antiquite romaine: aspects juridiques et religieux," *Revue Internationale des Droits de l'Antiquité* 54 (2007): 352–63. The law was taken up again in *Paul. Sent.* 1, 21, 1: *Ob incursum fluminis vel metum ruinae corpus iam perpetuae sepulturae traditum sollemnibus redditis sacrificiis per noctem in alium locum transferri potest.*

8. Fergus Millar, *The Emperor in the Roman World* (London: Duckworth, 1977), 361; Yan Thomas, *"Res Religiosae:* On the Categories of Religion and Commerce in Roman Law," in *Law, Anthropology, and the Constitution of the Social: Making Persons and Things*, ed. Alain Pottage and Martha Mundy (Cambridge: Cambridge University Press, 2004), 60–62; Nicolas Laubry, "Le transfert des corps dans l'empire romain. Problèmes d'épigraphie, de religion et de droit romain," *Mélanges de l'École française de Rome—Antiquité* 119 (2007): 171–75; Éric Rebillard, *Religion et sèpulture. L'Église, les vivants et les morts dansl'Antiquité tardive* (Paris: Éditions de l'École des hautes études en sciences sociales, 2003), 77–79; Bolla, "Sepoltura," 357–77. The locution *perpetua sepultura*, already present in the sentence by Paul cited above, also recurs in the acceptation—even if this is more restrictive—of the Diocletian law, in Ulpian D. 47, 12, 3, 4 and in *Paul. Sent.* 1, 21, 4; see Laubry, "Le transfert," 157–60 which argues, on the basis of D. 11, 7, 44, that the perpetual nature of burial—and thus its transformation into a *locus religiosus*—depends on the wishes of the owner of the tomb at the moment of its inauguration. See also Paturet, "Le transfert des morts," 360 n. 45.

9. Millar, *Emperor*, 361; Liz James, "Bearing Gifts from the East: Imperial Relic Hunters Abroad," in *Eastern Approaches to Byzantium: Papers from the Thirty-Third Spring Symposium of Byzantine Studies, University of Warwick, Coventry, March 1999*, ed. Anthony Eastmond (Aldershot: Ashgate, 2001), 126.

10. Ibid.

11. See *n. supra.*

12. D. 11, 7, 44 (Paul, *Quaest.* III).

13. Sean Lafferty, "*Ad sanctitatem mortuorum*: Tomb Raiders, Body Snatchers and Relic Hunters in Late Antiquity," *Early Medieval Europe* 22 (2014): 261–62.

14. Laubry, "Le transfert," 159; Bolla, "Sepultura," 358–59.

15. Andrea Pellizzari, "*Libanios et la* Monodie sur le temple de Daphné *(Or. LX)*," forthcoming; Gilvan Ventura da Silva, "Un imperatore in cerca della città perfetta: Giuliano e l'immagine di Antiochia nel *Misopogon*," *Chaos e Kosmos* 14 (2013): 13–15; Christine Shepardson, *Controlling Contested Places: Late Antique Antioch and the Spatial Politics* (Berkeley: University of California Press 2014), 59–74; Marco Falcon, "Il corpo di San Babila nelle concezioni ellenica e Cristiana," in *Il corpo in Roma antica. Ricerche giuridiche II*, ed. Luigi Garofalo (Pisa: Pacini, 2017), 389–409.

16. Joseph Bidez and Franz Cumont, eds., *Julien. Oeuvres Completes*, I–2 (Paris: 1924), 129–32 and 197–200; Matilde Caltabiano, *L'epistolario di Giuliano imperatore* (Naples: D'Auria, 1991), 212–15 and 275–76. See also Rowland B.E. Smith, *Julian's Gods: Religion and Philosophy in the Thought and Action of Julian the Apostate* (London: Routledge, 1995), 111–13 and Rebillard, *Religion*, 80–81.

17. The aversion to bodies is well-documented in pagan Rome, where this had even prompted the banning of funerals and translations of bodies during daylight hours. In this sense this one of Julian's laws' has a strong "paganising" or religiously traditional flavour. See Paturet, "Le transfert des morts," 369–73; Bolla, "Sepoltura," 360–61.

18. Eun. *V. Soph.* VI 11: δήσαντες τὸ ἀνθρώπινον. ὀστέα γὰρ καὶ κεφαλὰς τῶν ἐπὶ πολλοῖς ἁμαρτήμασιν ἑαλωκότων συναλίζοντες, οὓς τὸ πολιτικὸν ἐκόλαζε δικαστήριον, θεούς τε ἀπεδείκνυσαν, καὶ προσεκαλινδοῦντο τοῖς ὀστοῖς καὶ κρείττους ὑπελάμβανον εἶναι μολυνόμενοι πρὸς τοῖς τάφοις. μάρτυρες γοῦν ἐκαλοῦντο καὶ διάκονοί τινες [. . .]. "For they collected the bones and skulls of criminals who had been put to death for numerous crimes, men whom the law courts of the city had condemned to punishment, made them out to be gods, haunted their sepulchers" (W.C. Wright, trans., *Philostratus: Lives of Sophists. Eunapius Lives of Philosophers* [Cambridge, MA: Harvard University Press, 1921], 425).

19. Iul. *Misopogon* 344A; *Contr. Galil.* 335C; see Wortley, "The Origins of Christian," 9–10.

20. See David Hunt, "The Traffic in Relics: Some Late Roman Evidence," in *The Byzantine Saint: University of Birmingham, Fourteenth Spring Symposium of Byzantine Studies*, ed. Sergeï Hackel (London: Fellowship of St. Alban and St. Sergius, 1981), 171–80; Carlà, "Exchange," 403–6; 414–20; Andrea Nicolotti, "Doni e controdoni nel culto delle reliquie," in *Dono, controdono e corruzione. Ricerche storiche e dialogo interdisciplinare*, ed. Gianluca Cuniberti (Turin: Edizioni dell'Orso, 2017), 401–2.

21. See Carlà, "Exchange," 411.

22. "When the ashes of the burned bodies were thrown in a river by order of the persecutor, religious hands were not lacking which either obtained by theft or bought with money a part of the relic"; Stephen L. Boehrer, trans., *Gaudentius of Brescia: Sermons and Letters* (Washington, DC: The Catholic University of America 1965), 200.

23. Robert T. Meyer, trans., *St. Athanasius: The Life of Saint Antony* (Westminster, MD: The Newman Bookshop, 1950), 94–96; see Wortley, "The Origins of Christian," 16–18.

24. Both passages Richard M. Price, trans., *Theoderetus: A History of the Monks of Syria* (Kalamazoo, MI: Cistercian Publications 1985), 45 and 135–36.

25. "Furthermore we beg you all that no one should take for himself one particle of our remains from the furnace; they should hand them over to the afore-mentioned, bearing in mind that they are to be collected in one place" (Herbert Anthony Musurillo, trans., *The Acts of Christian Martyrs: Introduction, Texts and Translations* (Oxford: Clarendon, 1972), 355–56). Musurillo (L) underlines how the main focal point of the text, or rather of its first part, is in fact the treatment of the bodies of martyrs: nobody was to keep any relics for themselves. See Hunt, "The Traffic in Relics," 174–75.

26. Optatus, *Adv. Don.* 1.16–17 [MPL 11, 916B-917A]; for the discussion on the passage see Robert Wiśniewski, "Lucilla and the Bone: Remarks on an Early Testimony to the Cult of Relics," *Journal of Late Antiquity* 4 (2011): 157–61; Carlà, "Exchange," 411–12.

27. "If any one out of pride and scorn censures the συνάξεις of the martyrs or the services there held, and the commemoration of the martyrs, let him be anathem" (Karl Joseph Hefele, trans., *A History of the Councils of the Church from the Original Documents*, vol. II (Edinburgh: T. & T. Clark, 1896), 334). The date of the council of Gangra is still under discussion; see Timothy D. Barnes, "The Date of the Council of Gangra," *The Journal of Theological Studies* 40 (1989): 121–24; Avshalom Laniado, "Note sur la datation conservée en syriaque du Concile de Gangres," *Orientalia Christiana Periodica* 61 (1995): 195–99.

28. "They who are of the priesthood, or of the clergy, shall not be magicians, enchanters, mathematicians, or astrologers; nor shall they make what are called amulets, which are chains for their own souls. And those who wear such, we command to be cast out of the Church" (Hefele, *A History of the Councils*, 318).

29. *C. Th.* 9, 16: *titulus De maleficis et mathematicis et ceteris similibus.* It is interesting to note that the same register is used in Eus. *V. C.* II, 4 to refer to the individuals that Constantine surrounded himself with: Egyptian soothsayers, sorcerers and magicians.

30. Rita Lizzi Testa, *Senatori, popolo e papi. Il governo di Roma al tempo dei Valentiniani* (Bari: Edipuglia, 2004), 209–48.

31. Charles Munier, *Concilia Africae* (Turnhout: Brepols, 1974), c. 82 and 204–5; Marianne Sághy, "Martyr Cult and Collective Identity in Fourth-Century Rome," in *Identity and Alterity in Agiography and the Cult of Saints*, ed. Ana Marinković and Trpimir Vedriš (Zagreb: Hagiotheca, 2010), 25; Bolla, "Sepoltura," 360–61.

32. Jan Willem Drijvers, *Helena Augusta: The Mother of Constantine the Great and the Legend of Her Finding of the True Cross* (Leiden: Brill, 1992), 84–88 and bibliography; Filippo Carlà and Maria G. Castello, *Questioni tardoantiche. storia e mito della "svolta costantiniana"* (Rome: Aracne, 2010), 185–86.

33. V. Filippo Carlà, "Milan, Ravenna, Rome: Some Reflections on the Cult of the Saints and on Civic Politics in Late Antiquity," *Rivista di Storia e Letteratura Religiosa* 2 (2010): 197–270 and bibliography.

34. See Robin M. Jensen, "Saints' Relics and the Consecration of Church Buildings in Rome," *Studia Patristica* 71 (2014): 162–65.

35. On the political significance of Ambrose's "disovery," Neil McLynn, *Ambrose of Milan: Church and Court in a Christian Capital* (Berkeley: University of California Press, 1994), 209–15; Carlà, "Milan, Ravenna, Rome," 199–203.

36. *C. Th.* 16.1.4. The inclusion of this law in the *Codex* can probably be ascribed to a mistake made by the compilers on the Council of Constantinople, which was mixed up with the "orthodox" one promoted by Theodosius in 381; McLynn, *Ambrose of Milan*, 181.

37. On the Arian aversion to the cult of the relics of martyrs and to martyrs in general, see Charles Pietri, "L'évolution du culte des saints aux premiers siècles chrétiens: du témoin à l'intercesseur," in *Les fonctions des saints dans le monde occidental (IIIe–XIIIe siècle). Actes du colloque Rome, 27–29 octobre 1988* (Rome: École francaise de Rome, 1991), 25.

38. "Those persons who violate the habitations of the shades, the homes, so to speak, of the dead, appear to perpetrate a twofold crime. For they both despoil the buried dead by the destruction of the tombs, and they contaminate the living by the use of this material in building. If any person, therefore, should take away from a tomb, stones or marbles or columns or any other material for the purpose of building or if he should do this for the purpose of selling such material, he shall be compelled to pay ten pounds of gold to the fisc, whether someone defending his own tombs should bring this complaint into court or someone else should accuse him or apparitors should report his crime. This penalty is added to the severity of the ancient laws, for nothing has been derogated from that punishment which is known to have been imposed on violators of tombs. Moreover, those persons also who disturb buried bodies or the remains of the dead shall be subject to the same penalty. Given on the ides of June at Milan in the year of the ninth consulship of Constantius Augustus and the second consulship of Julian Caesar" (Clyde Pharr, *The Theodosian Code* (London: Princeton University Press, 1952), 239).

39. Rebillard, *Religion*, 80.

40. Paola Ombretta Cuneo, *La legislazione di Costantino II, Costanzo II e Costante, 337–361* (Milan: Giuffrè editore, 1997), 299–300.

41. "The same Augustuses to Cynegius, Praetorian Prefect. No person shall transfer a buried body to another place. No person shall sell the relics of a martyr; no person shall traffic in them. But if anyone of the saints has been buried many place whatever, persons shall have it in their power to add whatever building they may wish in veneration of such a place and such building must be called a martyr" (Pharr, trans., *Theodosian*, 240).

42. On Theodosius's conduct in religious matters see Rita Lizzi Testa, "La politica religiosa di Teodosio I. Miti storiografici e realtà storica," *Rendiconti dell'Accademia Lombarda* 9, no. 7 (1996): 323–61.

43. David Hunt, "The Church as a Public Institution," in *The Cambridge Ancient History XIII, the Late Empire*, ed. Alan Cameron and Peter Garsney (Cambridge: Cambridge University Press, 1998), 254. The same theory has also been put forward by Jill Harries, "Death and the Dead in the Late Roman West," in *Death in Towns: Urban Responses to the Dying and the Dead, 100–1600*, ed. Steven Basset (Leicester: Leicester University Press, 1992), 63; see also Laubry, "Le transfert," 169–70; Rebillard, *Religion*, 81–82.

44. Paolo Lepore, "Un problema ancora aperto: i rapporti legislativi tra Oriente e Occidente nel tardo impero Romano," *Studia ed Documenta Historiae et Iuris* 66 (2000): 343–98.

45. See above, n. 42, for the translation of the first law. C. I. 3, 44, 14: Emperors Gratian, Valentinian and Theodosius to Cynegius, Praetorian Prefect. No one shall transfer a dead body to another place without a rescript of the emperor. Given at Constantinople February 26 (386). C. I. 1, 2, 3: The same to Cynegius, Praetorian Prefect. No one shall sell, or barter in, the relics of the martyrs. Given at Constantinople, February 26 (386) (Blume, "Annotated Justinian Code.").

46. On the clause *sine augusti adfatibus* see Salvatore Sciortino, "Sull'adozione da parte delle donne," *Annali del Seminario Giuridico dell'Università di Palermo* 51 (2006): 23–24.

47. James, "Bearing Gifts from the East," 124–28; Holger A. Klein, "Sacred Relics and Imperial Ceremonies at the Great Palace of Constantinople," in

Visualisierungen von Herrschaft. Frühmittelalterliche Residenzen, Gestalt und Zeremoniell, ed. Franz Alto (Istanbul: Ege Yayınları, 2006), 81–88; Lafferty, "*Ad sanctitatem mortuorum*," 265–66; Carlà, "Exchange," 407 and n. 23; Carlà, "*Res tamquam proprias retinebat*."

48. Millar, *Emperor*, 359–60.
49. On which, see above.
50. Paturet, "Le transfert des morts," 353.
51. James, "Bearing Gifts from the East," 126.
52. C. *Th*. 1, 1, 6. See Emilio Germino, "Il *Codex Theodosianus*: un codice cristiano?" in *Società e diritto nella Tarda Antichità*, ed. Lucio De Giovanni (Naples: D'Auria, 2012), 11–43.
53. See above.

Part II
Cults, Circulations and Battles for Relics

3 A Liquid Miracle

The Origins of the Liquefaction Ritual of the Blood of Saint Januarius

Francesco Paolo de Ceglia

Rising Again After a Thousand Years

From that summer on Naples would never be the same again. The situation in a community devastated by infighting between the supporters of the House of Anjou-Durazzo and the House of Valois-Anjou, those of the pope and the antipope, was dramatic. The city was ravaged by famine, hunger, fires and fighting.[1] But on 16 August 1389 two ambassadors arrived by sea bearing a letter signed by the king of France with news that was considered to be of enormous importance for the uncertain future of the Kingdom of Naples. And, most importantly, they brought with them food which was just then needed as never before. To celebrate the ambassadors' arrival and to let them know who of the city's self-styled elite was on their side, lights were set up. At that point something unheard of happened, which the anonymous author of the so-called *Chronicon Siculum*, whose attention was concentrated on the evolving political scene, reported almost in passing:

> and the morning of the following day 17 there was a great procession for the miracle that Our Lord Jesus Christ showed with the blood of Saint Januarius that was in a certain ampule and that was then liquefied as if it had come out of the body of Saint Januarius on that very day.[2]

More than a thousand years after the presumed date of the death of a man traditionally remembered as a martyr, this is the first testimony to have reached us of the so-called miracle of the liquefaction of his blood. The source in question is also the very first to mention the precious relic: as far as we know, the blood entered history through the news of its prodigious behaviour.

After examining the few sources on the historic Januarius and briefly reconstructing the story of his relics, my aim is to cast light on how, in between the late Middle Ages and the early modern era, the conceptualisation of the miracle (or prodigy, as it is formally defined by the Catholic

Church) connected to the saint and his relics evolved. In other words, can it be argued that the *quid* of the miracle has changed in relation to the manner in which the relics were exhibited?

In Search of a Meaning

One might imagine that in the aftermath of that astounding event the Christian world talked about little else. But no, this was not the case. Indeed, what occurred to the blood of Saint Januarius was a sort of "unnoticed revolution," at least in the immediate term. One must not forget that throughout the late Middle Ages there had been blood miracles of every kind,[3] so it would be a long time before news of this particular blood's singular behaviour resounded outside the city. Episodes of melting continued to reveal the blood's intimate vitality, so it may well be that after the first one the ampoule was in some way monitored. Nevertheless, for around a century the few surviving sources, generally very vague, do not mention specific dates in the liturgical calendar when the dark substance liquefied, instead they merely summarised the features of a blood "now [*modo*] solidified, now [*modo*] melted,"[4] that "carries out and has carried out several miracles."[5] It was as if the martyr now enjoyed a burst of renewed energy with which to express himself in ways and times of his own choosing. In essence, the Saint Januarius of the early years of the miracle was free of patterns and rhythms: "alive" through his blood, as at the time the learned legal expert Matteo d'Afflitto described him.[6]

Much has been said about that distant 1389, but to try to understand what happened it is necessary to read the facts as they were known at the time. Hence we must leave aside the subsequent institutionalisation of the miracle's periodicity, which, belonging to the future, obviously could not in any way have been taken into account by people living in the medieval period. Likewise, the possibility that blood, a vital fluid profoundly endowed with meaning—especially when of a martyr—could be found in a liquid state due to unknown natural causes was never contemplated by the mindset of the period. The blood's revivification therefore had to signify something. And it is true that during wars, epidemics and famines the prodigious events attributed to a city's patrons were generally understood as the message with which they communicated their decision to regather the community under their protection. But the case in question was not the reassuring apparition of a saint giving blessings from among the clouds: it is difficult to see how dissolving blood, in particular when one is not prepared for the possibility, could herald some positive change to a situation that was already painful in itself.[7] Was the liquefaction perhaps predicting that the Neapolitans had to shed yet more blood? Rather than generating enthusiasm and jubilation, at the beginning the phenomenon might in fact have given rise to anxieties and fears: it would have been understandable to discern the epiphany of a numen, irate or sorrowful, that stigmatised past events or gave warning about those of the future.

Furthermore, the blood, as the Neapolitans would soon have learned, was not consistently liquid. Its liquefaction could not easily be classed as a "continuous miracle": something which, with its immutable fulfilment, ensured a perennial and therefore psychologically reassuring confirmation of the numen's active presence and benevolence. In other words, the miracle's instability meant that it was not in itself enough to serve as a visible expression of the peaceful renewal of the alliance between saint and city. Some element of consistency therefore had to be identified in those mysterious changes of phase, as only this would give the impression of controlling them symbolically. To stabilise the meaning. But where to begin?

A switch in perspective: the blood, it was true, was not always liquid, but, paradoxically, in order ensure the fundamental continuity or "perenniality," as it would have been defined in sixteenth- and seventeenth-century literature, it was possible to make use of this very incessant transformation and change of phase. The bodily fluid was "changeable by mystery, not by default,"[8] and the fact that it was "alive" was the very thing that constituted a great miracle, as d'Afflitto would observe, albeit with a few years of delay. The instability thus lost the negative or at least uncertain connotation that characterised it at the start, and instead acquired an antithetical significance: the essence of the miracle was not in the liquidity itself, but in its mutability; the inclination to change was in its own way constant, and therefore able to be normalised even while remaining abnormal. The transition from one phase to the other thus became the epiphany of a tenacious, autocratic and inscrutable will, as only that of a bishop martyred when in full physical vigour could have been.

But Who Was Coming Back to Life?

We might think it likely that the people had long known for sure that the blood belonged to Saint Januarius. Perhaps. But for a thousand years the Neapolitans had spoken only about his bones, without ever referring to blood relics, which, if nothing else, ought to have attracted attention for their peculiarity. Nor, ultimately, was Januarius a particularly key figure in the "Neapolitan paradise": he was one of the city's seven protectors, but relatively little was known about him. Tradition, rather than documentary evidence, had it that he died young, and even his name did not seem right, being more like a surname than a forename.[9]

So who was he? In general, it is believed that he lived between the third and fourth centuries and, as bishop of Benevento, went to visit the deacon Sossius in jail. Recognised as a Christian, he himself was imprisoned and condemned to be fed to wild beasts. The sentence was commuted to decapitation, carried out near the Solfatara in Pozzuoli, apparently on 19 September in (perhaps) 305.

Are these the first solid grounds from which to start? To be frank, no. Even this rudimentary information—the best we have given the lack of more authoritative sources—has over the years been repeatedly called into question by specialists.[10] It is generally based on a *Passio*, of which there are two versions. As we know, however, the texts belonging to this literary genre, which recount the last days in the lives of martyrs and the torments which they endured before the end, have more to do with the ideals of Christian death held by their authors than the real experiences of their heroic protagonists.[11]

What is more, the so-called *Acta Bononiensia*, the oldest of the two passions of Januarius, dates back only to the sixth and seventh centuries: in other words, the two texts were written at least 200–300 years after the saint's presumed death. This of course does not mean that they do not translate, reproduce or incorporate older narratives or that they were not based on a faithful oral tradition. It only means that it is difficult to determine their historical reliability; this is not only because there are few other sources with which to compare the two passions, but also because of the structure of the manuscript handed down, which in the opinion of hagiologists results from the juxtaposition and reworking of two earlier passions, one concerning the martyr Sossius and the other Januarius.[12]

Moreover, it would be naive of us not to take into proper consideration how much any story, particularly one with such strong symbolic value, might have been—even in good faith—altered over only a handful of generations. Indeed, the most recent version of this passion, namely the *Acta Vaticana*, which the experts estimate was written between the seventh and eighth centuries, while supplementing the earlier account and aggrandising the figure of the martyr Januarius, provides clear evidence of the constant process of rewriting to which this type of narration was subjected.[13] This is why, as has been said, "looking for historical information here is like drawing water from sand."[14]

Since it is not possible to learn more about the saint's life, let us turn instead to his body, that is, to his relics. It appears that shortly after his execution Januarius's remains were buried near Pozzuoli, in a locality known as *Ager Marcianus*, whose whereabouts have been much discussed to no avail, making it seem like a sort of "non place." This is where they languished for a long time:[15] for more than a century, it is said. Afterwards John I—who according to the chronotaxis of Neapolitan bishops occupied the episcopal chair for a little less than 30 years before departing this life on Holy Saturday 432—had them exhumed in a period when Christians were free to live their faith openly, and then had them translated, ostensibly on 13 April, into the lower catacomb of the extra-urban cemetery complex at the foot of the Capodimonte hill, which then took the name of Saint Januarius, its most illustrious guest.[16]

A *translatio* always gives rise to new sources, and the arrival of the body to Naples duly signalled the year zero of the documentation of the cult, about which it is possible to say a few things,[17] whereas one can only hypothesise about what happened before. One cannot even exclude the possibility, as Domenico Mallardo—the scholar who carried out the most accurate survey of the ancient sources on the saint—was willing to do, that the *translatio* ensued from an *inventio*, that is, the rediscovery (we do not know how) of his remains.[18] Saint Januarius might therefore have been a *martyr inventus*: a designation often used to classify abuses and fanciful identifications.

Mallardo's thinking matured by degrees within the context of a controversy of the 1930s and 1940s regarding the veracity of the image of the saint, which in the judgment of the Lutheran evangelical Christianist Hans Achelis—and basically in that of the Jesuit Hippolyte Delehaye—was the fruit of a reworking of the legend of the historical figure of a certain Januarius, bishop of Benevento, who took part in the Council of Serdica, modern-day Sofia, in 343. Had this bishop been martyred? It would appear not: at the very most he had been exiled or had suffered a violent death, but the hagiographic legend subsequently reworked in the form described above was yet to be proved. After all, as Mallardo himself admitted, "in antiquity the title of 'martyr' was given not only to those who died for the faith, in the midst of torture, but also to those who died in exile, and sometimes even to the exiles who returned home."[19] Januarius, whose later medieval cult was almost entirely revamped on the strength of his "living" relic, would in this case have been, paradoxically, a martyr *sine cruore*, without shed blood.[20]

Many years have passed since that scholarly debate, and the question still remains open. The only sure thing is that Naples already venerated with particular devotion the remains of Agrippinus, a bishop of the city who had not experienced the glory of martyrdom. The *translatio* of Januarius therefore gave the local church the martyr that perhaps it needed. The *inventio*, if there was one, might have conferred the palm of martyrdom, in other words the accreditation of a grisly death borne in the name of God, to someone whose life had ended in a less exemplary way. But it was also true that the bishop John I had brought to Naples the body of a man who could seemingly have been rightly claimed by the citizens of Benevento: it is conceivable that he would not have knowingly embarked on such a potentially problematic undertaking if the *translatus* had not had a *fama sanctitatis* such as to override that of Agrippinus and to give the local cult a boost in quality that repaid, in ideal and material terms, any diplomatic repercussions triggered by the unjustified appropriation. What can be affirmed with certainty about Januarius is that, as was said of others, "with his blood," that is, with his martyrdom, real or purported, "he changed country" or at least diocese.[21] He ended up not in Pozzuoli but in Naples, where John had wanted him and had taken a real risk to acquire him, perhaps because he knew he was worth it.

Gennaro Luongo has explained that with the passing of time "the mediating function of the saints between the fourth and sixth centuries" was "felt to be more efficaciously active where they had made their supreme testimony and where their bodies were laid to rest."[22] The new bones therefore exerted a beneficial, almost euphoric effect, so as to justify the claim, stated just before the translation, that "Januarius, bishop and martyr, brings prestige to the Church of Naples."[23] Everyone wanted to be buried *ad sanctos*. For this reason, the martyr's remains constituted the building propellant of the cemetery complex of Capodimonte, giving impetus to the cult and attracting pilgrims.[24] In short, serving as the Archimedean point for Saint Januarius's patronage of Naples. And this is why it is so hard, after the fact, to understand whether the martyr generated the cult or the cult generated the martyr. Yet there can be no doubt that the veneration gave shape to the hagiographic features of the saint, which could not have been anything other than heroically extraordinary. On this question we may conclude with the words of André Vauchez:

> The precise context of this "abduction"—translation or *furtum sacrum?*—of the relics remains shrouded in mystery. But it should probably be placed in the more general setting of the process, studied by Peter Brown, which, between the end of the fourth and the start of the fifth century, made the bishops the "impresarios" of the cult of the martyrs.[25]

Bones on the Road

Saint Januarius's bones knew no peace during the Middle Ages. It is said that while besieging Naples, in circa 831 the Lombard Prince Siconulf broke into the basilica of the extra-urban cemetery where Januarius's remains were at rest and took them away to Benevento. We do not know if things really went that way, seeing as the sources are rather late and for all we know untrustworthy.[26] Nevertheless, the Neapolitans always described the act as a sacrilege, even though the Lombards probably only wanted to recover what they thought was theirs given that the body was that of a bishop of Benevento and ergo Januarius was Beneventan himself. What is sure is that at a certain point the citizens of Benevento began to glory in having possession of the saint's relics. But whether they were really his, the same that once were in Naples and were looted by Siconulf, has for some yet to be ascertained.[27]

It also appears that also in the ninth century part of the supposed Neapolitan remains somehow ended up in the famous Abbey of Reichenau, located on a picturesque islet on Lake Constance, where they can still be found today.[28] In any event, most of the bones remained in Benevento, where, alas, they had to compete only a handful of years later with the relics, real or not, of Saint Bartholomew, and consequently never really received the devotion that had been expected. Even though tradition had it that Saint Januarius had been the bishop of Benevento, he had very little hope of winning a contest with an apostle. Because of this, in the centuries to come every trace of those *sacra pignora* was lost.[29]

And then? Another *inventio*: in 1480, while tearing down an altar in the abbey church of Santa Maria Montevergine near Avellino, bones were found which were said to be those of Saint Januarius, together with relics that had probably come from Benevento. The whys and the wherefores of their arrival have engendered successive hypotheses, none of which have managed to convince the more thorough historiography.[30] Once again we must admit that we do not know. Negotiations for the return of the relics, which were now held to belong by right to Naples— where, as we shall see, the cult of the saint had proliferated during the previous century—were championed by Ferdinand I of Aragon, who had, however, to wait for one of the rare peaceful moments in his relationship with the pope to seek permission for the transfer.[31] The operation was not at all easy. On the contrary, the negotiations reached moments of high drama in the clash between the monks and the archbishop of Naples, Alessandro Carafa, brother of Cardinal Oliviero Carafa, the commendatory abbot of Montevergine: from then on, the history of the powerful family was intertwined with the story of the saint's relics. The monks barricaded themselves in the abbey, which was then put under siege. But some of them, "since the prior was missing, wanted to hide those sacred bodies; therefore [. . .] using a secret road inside the mountain they went to a thick forest, and there in a pit they hid them."[32] They certainly did not lack initiative.

It is almost as if we can still hear the monks' heavy breathing as they returned from hiding the relics, an act which had set them against not only the archbishop and the abbot, but also the king, who had requested the restitution, and the pope, who had authorised it. The situation would have quickly become worse had not the prior returned and made reverend fathers face reality. In consequence a delegation was sent to Alessandro Carafa, into whose hands the precious relics were finally delivered. Could they be trusted? The archbishop, requiring certainty, adopted a very circumspect attitude:

> The aforementioned archbishop immediately called for the celebration of a mass by one of the priests of his company, and before he held communion, made all the monks and friars come before him, and one after the other he made them swear on the Most Holy Sacrament that the body they had given him was the body of Saint Januarius. And when the mass was finished, to remove any suspicion, he ordered the sacred bones to be measured one to one: in other words

the right arm with the left arm, the right hand with the left, the right foot with the left, and so all the other parts.[33]

Despite these precautions, it seems that some relics remained in Montevergine[34] and that, conversely, Carafa took away with him bones that the scientific examination of 1964 demonstrated did not belong to the same subject as many of the others.[35] Be that as it may, most of the body of an individual identified as Saint Januarius could finally be translated to Naples, where the archbishop arrived "on Friday 13 January 1397, at one in the morning."[36] Unfortunately, the prelate and the holy bundle did not receive the solemn reception they had expected for the streets were deserted because of an outbreak of the plague, which made gatherings inadvisable. The bones were therefore taken by Alessandro Carafa himself, barefoot, into the cathedral or *duomo*, in which they would soon be given a final resting place. Between 1497 and 1508 the family had ordered the building of an elegant underground chapel in which to house them, known as the Succorpo, where they remain today.[37]

One might wonder which relics returned to Naples in 1497. Only a part of the skeleton, if it is true that the cranium, or rather what was left of it, had never left the city.[38] It is conjectured that for a long time the "head" remained in the Stefanìa, a basilica (named after bishop Stefano I, who had had it built) once situated in what is now the transept of the current cathedral. Then, with the latter's reconstruction, which began at the end of the thirteenth century, the relic was moved to a new location. We do not know why, between 1304 and 1305, King Charles II of Anjou had chosen Saint Januarius and generously paid for the gilded silver bust that still contains the cranial remains: the cathedral was dedicated to Mary and the remains of other saints could reasonably have aspired to acquire such a prestigious berth, which would have maximised their visibility and the devotion they received. For example, the mortal remains of the aforementioned Agrippinus were awaiting suitable enhancement, but even more so did those of Aspren, the first bishop of Naples. After the latter's translation into the Stefanìa a highly compelling hagiographic legend had grown up around him, according to which Aspren had been converted and consecrated by Peter himself on his journey to Rome. If the story had been appropriately corroborated, it would have made the local church an even older community than that of the Christian capital itself.[39]

Nevertheless, Charles II chose Saint Januarius, according to some because his decapitation may have allowed him to be seen as a local analogue of Saint Denis, whose cult was strongly supported by the Capetians. There are those who speculate that the bust, a veritable masterpiece of Gothic goldsmithing, was crafted for the millennial anniversary of the bishop's martyrdom. The hypothesis is quite fascinating and has the advantage of accounting for a suspicious temporal coincidence, but perhaps it requires better scrutiny since the medieval sources were

neither precise about dates nor in agreement about 305 being the year
of the saint's death, saying, in general terms, that it happened during
the "Great Persecution of Diocletian."[40] Be that as it may, at least from
1390 onwards the reliquary was housed in the so-called Old Treasury,
a rather narrow room carved out of the left tower of the cathedral and
corresponding to the current chapel of Santa Restituta dei Neri, which
was originally accessed by means of a slippery wooden spiral staircase. It
was nevertheless already in the hands of the archbishop when the bones
arrived.[41]

However, if anyone had declared that the new arrivals, at least because
of their number, would have gained a similar importance to the remains
of the martyr that were already venerated in Naples, he would have been
greatly mistaken. Despite the efforts of the Carafa, the bones of the rest of
the body were, on the contrary, destined to remain marginalised, in terms
of location, devotion and liturgy. With the forging of the anthropomor-
phic reliquary, the faithful had received confirmation of the impression of
possessing the entire and almost intact head of the saint, the *caput*—not a
mere *cranium*, which amongst other things was incomplete and perhaps
already partially fragmented—to which practically all the texts from the
Middle Ages onwards refer.

Perhaps the bones of Montevergine were not required, primarily
because from 1389 the sources had started to speak about something that
had never been mentioned in the preceding 1,000 years: the extraordinary blood of the martyr, which would liquefy only if it came into contact
with the head. The association between the latter and the holy fluid was
by then consolidated and the other parts of the body could do nothing
about it. It is claimed that when archbishop Carafa entered the cathedral
with the newly acquired bones, "the said body was placed by the head
and blood of the said saint, which liquefied."[42] After the certification of
the bones' authenticity had been notarised, the blood never interacted
with them again. The *corpus* had arrived too late to share or interfere
with the unique and exclusive rapport that in the meantime had been
forged between the *caput* and *sanguis*.

Saint Januarius the Mechanist

It is reasonable to conjecture that the first few times the Neapolitans
wished to venerate the *sanguis*, out of a sort of respect the bust of the
caput was also taken out and placed at one corner of the altar. And when
this was done the sacred blood, "placed in sight of the head" at the opposite corner changed state.[43] It required little for the two events, the appearance of the bust and the liquefaction of the blood, the one after the other,
to be linked, with the former being the cause of the latter.

The need for the head to be present so that the numen manifested itself
through the blood "normalised" the miracle and regulated its role as an

oracle: the blood no longer dissolved in an unpredictable and accidental way, but could instead be delayed until the encounter between the two parts could be staged. For the numen to speak a language understandable to men it was, however, necessary to define a "miraculous zero grade" that described, in fact prescribed, what normally happened, namely liquefaction at the moment of encounter between the two relics. Thus a "thaumaturgical rule" was established, which as such called for a generic positive conceptualisation, since it confirmed the balances achieved: this was the expression of the alliance between the saint and the city and, while being susceptible to decryptions that made the mystical symbolism explicit, did not require a new and precise interpretation to be undertaken on each occasion.

To put it more clearly: based on a hermeneutic economy principle, one would no longer ask why the blood liquified in the established conditions, but only why sometimes it did not. Only the deviations from the norm required clarification: those episodes, much less numerous, in which the blood did not behave as it should. Thus, while the miracle of 1389 was unexpected and had probably been conceptualised in a non-positive way, as the ritual took shape it would, on the contrary, have been the failures to liquefy that were charged with distressing semiotic power. In this way a binary code was placed in the hands of Saint Januarius—if the blood liquefied under the required conditions, yes; if it did not, no—with which he communicated with the Neapolitans for centuries.

On 22 February 1495, King Charles VIII of France, after having relentlessly cut through Italy, entered the city of Naples, whose throne he claimed as heir to the Anjou dynasty. Once in the city it was he who immediately offered thaumaturgical proof of his status: it is said that at least on a couple of occasions, in accordance with a tradition typical of the French kings and studied in depth by Marc Block, ceremonies were organised in which he healed scrofula sufferers simply by touching them.[44] But this was not enough for him to be accepted by the Neapolitans, and contrarily the most important miracle was one he had to be subjected to rather than perform. On 3 May he therefore went to the cathedral for the feast of Saint Januarius, where first he was brought the head then the blood, which, "hard as a stone," immediately began to liquefy. The patron saint had thereby blessed and wished prosperity on the new sovereign (who in reality would very quickly be expelled from the city and soon after die in France at less than 30 years of age). And this was possible because the numen had found a way to talk:

> And the lords of Naples, both of the church and of the city, said that thanks to the precious head and blood they had knowledge about the many requests they made to God, since if the prayers they said were good, the blood became soft. And if they did not make the right requests, it remained hard. Moreover, thanks to this blood they

had knowledge of their prince, and whether he should be their king or not.[45]

The search for meaning which had led to defining the language spoken by the saint through his own blood had arrived at a conclusion that modified in the constitutive elements the way in which the miracle had until then been understood. Expressions like *modo modo*, which had characterised the first voices, intent on giving an account of a haematic will, irreducible to any pattern or behavioural rhythm, gave way to *quoties*, "every time that" the head and the blood meet.[46] And it was at this juncture that a kind of supernatural determinism took form: a real "head-blood mechanism," whose development is all the more surprising if one considers that at the time the idea of mechanical action did not exist even in the conceptual toolbox of natural philosophy.[47]

The Miracle and the City

It is not known how often the status of the blood changed or who was allowed to witness the event in the Old Treasury, although it is conceivable that at some point there were, perhaps on the days dedicated to the saint, expositions of the blood through an internal window which, now reopened, faced the cathedral's left nave. Nonetheless, until the end of the fifteenth century these days would have seemed as almost insignificant with respect to blood activity. The fact of the miracle taking place on such or such a date was not yet perceived as the expression of a necessity dictated by the intrinsic rhythm of the phenomenon, but rather as the outcome of the dramatic-liturgical decision to stage ritual recognitions on significant dates.

Saint Januarius already had one important feast day in his honour, which was celebrated in the city in May, at the start of the hot season. This involved a procession of the "garlanded," so called because traditionally the clerics would walk "with crowns of roses and other flowers on their heads."[48] Whatever the festival's historical origins, which have been much debated by scholars, it had assumed a sort of fixed pattern. On the day before the first Sunday in May, a number of clerics took it in turns to carry the head of the saint into one of the city's main churches, a different one each year. The archbishop would later go to the church himself, and, together with the clergy, as well as, in some way, the rest of the urban community, would take the bust back to the cathedral in procession.

In the first half of the fourteenth century the blood, as is obvious, was never mentioned. Then, from the second half of the fifteenth, it became the undisputed protagonist of the event. It was enough for the archbishop to bring out the coagulated blood in the presence of the head for the recognition to be accomplished, and then the miracle too. Basically, it was then sufficient to reproduce on a wider stage and in front of a larger audience the already tested head-blood mechanism, which, now being performed the end of processions across the city, consolidated its dimension of "theatrical mystery," that is, of sacred representation understood as ritualising what at first had to appear as a sort of mystical wedding between the two relics.

The people flocked to watch the extraordinary show, so much so that at some point the churches could no longer contain them. This was the reason, or perhaps simply the pretext, for the proposal put forward in 1525 by the Eletto del Popolo (elected by the people), a post which, as Camillo Tutini explained, represented the demands of the non-nobles, but sometimes was held "due to virtues and riches very far from those of the plebeians."[49] Geronimo Pellegrino, for that was his name, asked the archbishop Vincenzo Carafa that "he concede the grace and honour of celebrating this solemnity in that year in his Piazza della Selleria."[50] For some decades the Popolo, with the agreement of the crown—first with Charles VIII, then with Frederick of Aragon, and finally with Ferdinand the Catholic—were endeavouring to restore balance in Naples between their prerogatives and those of the city's patriciate.[51] The Popolo was nevertheless, so to speak, a "seat without a seat": while it was one of the six institutions, known as "seats," that had access to power in the city and effectively divided it into the same number of districts (Capuana, Nido, Montagna, Porto and Portanuova, all noble, and Popolo), unlike the others it did not have one of the lodge-like buildings (also known as "seats") that served as meeting places for the district administrators and, primarily, as important markers of territory.

Because of this, on a few days of the year, the Popolo citizens were allowed to make amends for their political and architectural disadvantages by building in Piazza della Selleria a temporary "catafalque," which, recalling and exalting the structure of a seat, gave imaginative form to aspirations that in the main would remain no more than that. Since 1507 one of these frameworks had been erected for the feast of *Corpus Domini*, which we may surmise provided the inspiration for the request of 1525. In any case, as might have been expected, once the Popolo was allowed to host the procession, the archbishop had to do the same for the noble seats,[52] and it was decided that this would occur in rotation.[53] This ensured that none of the districts were excluded from organising the celebrations of Saint Januarius, as was happening with the celebration of the birth of Saint John the Baptist, which since 1522 had in a much clearer way seen the people become the undisputed main protagonists.[54]

Although at the time a public festival usually attended by the viceroy, the event was anything but a mere recreational opportunity. As John Marino has noted, during the viceroy's participation at these three feast days—that is, those of Saint Januarius, *Corpus Domini* and Saint John for which a catafalque would generally have been erected—he took his place in the ritual life of the city and promoted group solidarity in the Popolo, which reaffirmed rights and privileges that had for a long time been eroded because the new Spanish government deliberately operated a divide-and-conquer strategy among the local groups within the recently acquired kingdom.[55] Before 1525 the electors of the seats had been allowed only to support the poles of the pallium during the procession back to the cathedral. However, now that they assumed responsibility for the cost of organising the "solemnity," these ambitious institutions had a central role in managing the annual event, such as to foster over time the notion that the relics belonged to the city, rather than to the Curia.[56]

As it was, with the passing of the years the appearance of the blood in the procession eventually gave the impression that the "revivification" could take place only on that date, thereby compounding cause and effect: according to the first testimonies the public display was not in fact carried out *so that* the fluid of the saint would be alive for a day, but "*because* his head and living blood are [already] there in the Neapolitan cathedral."[57] And if that spring festival had not been held, perhaps it would have been left to carry out its miracle *quotidianum*. To put it briefly, the presence of the *caput* in the city had transformed a miraculous *quid* that originally consisted in being the *modo modo* of the blood, in other words sometimes liquefied and sometimes solid, into an action that took place *quoties*, every time that the relics came into contact with each other. And now the exhibition of that *quoties* in a processional context, punctuated by precise liturgical dates, transformed the miracle into an event that took place *quotannis*, annually.[58] The supranatural (or presumed supranatural) phenomenon was therefore "liquid," not only in the physical sense of the word, but also liquid in the sense written about by Zygmunt Bauman, that is to say, it took the form of the cultural containers in which it was placed. With the procession, it became definitively linked to a day in the calendar. In other words, to time. As many still believe.

Notes

1. Ennio Moscarella, "Considerazioni circa la più antica notizia conosciuta relativa alla reliquia ianuariana di sangue," *Ianuarius* 55 (1974): 367–73, in particular 369; Franco Strazzullo, "Introduzione," in *Il VI centenario del miracolo di S. Gennaro (1389–1989)* (Naples: Fondazione Pasquale Corsicato, 1989), 3–21. This contribution summarises and updates some of the suggestions contained in Francesco Paolo de Ceglia, *Il segreto di san Gennaro. Storia naturale di un miracolo napoletano* (Turin: Einaudi, 2016).
2. Luigi Pescatore, "Il 'miracolo' di S. Gennaro e il Chronicon Siculum. Osservazioni critico-diplomatiche," *Campania Sacra* 20 (1989): 179–209, in particular 18; Cf. Anon., *Chronicon Siculum*, ed. Giuseppe De Blasiis (Naples: Giannini, 1887), 85.
3. For the sake of simplicity I refer the reader to Caroline Walker Bynum, *Wonderful Blood: Theology and Practice in Late Medieval Northern Germany* (Philadelphia: University of Pennsylvania Press, 2007).

62   *Francesco Paolo de Ceglia*

4. Enea Silvio Piccolomini, *In libros Antonii Panormitae poetae* [. . .] (Basel: Hervag, 1538), 288–89.
5. Loise De Rosa, *Ricordi. Edizione critica del Ms. Ital. 913 della Bibliothèque Nationale di France* (Naples: Salerno, 1998), 660.
6. Matteo D'Afflitto, *In Utriusque Siciliae Neapolisque sanctiones et constitutiones novissima praelectio*, vol. 1 (Venice: Varisco & Co., 1580), 68v.
7. See Johann Elias Starck, *Dissertatio de prodigiis sanguinis* (Frankfurt an der Oder: Zeitler, 1676).
8. Giacomo Lubrani, "Il testamento militare del martire San Gennaro," in *Il fuoco sacro della divinità* [. . .] (Naples: Parrino & Muzio, 1694), 39.
9. There is, however, a tradition that considers the *cognomen* Ianuarius to have already become a *praenomen* in the lifetime of the protagonist. Antonio Caracciolo, *De sacris Ecclesiae Neapolitanae monumentis liber singularis* (Naples: Beltrano, 1645), 190–91.
10. Domenico Mallardo, "S. Gennaro e compagni nei più antichi testi e monumenti," *Rendiconti dell'Accademia di Archeologia, Lettere e Belle Arti* 20 (1940): 161–247; Domenico Ambrasi, "Gennaro, Vescovo di Benevento, e compagni, santi, martiri," in *Bibliotheca Sanctorum*, ed. Filippo Caraffa, vol. 6 (Rome: Città Nuova Editrice, 1965), 135–51; Gennaro Luongo, "Janvier, Saint," in *Dictionnaire d'histoire et géographie écclesiastiques*, vol. 26 (Paris: Letouzey et Ané, 1996), 274–80; Gennaro Luongo, "Gennaro," in *Il grande libro dei santi*, ed. Claudio Leonardi, Andrea Riccardi and Gabriella Zarri, vol. 2 (Cinisello Balsamo: San Paolo, 1998), 765–70.
11. I refer the reader to the classic Hippolyte Delehaye, *Le légendes hagiographiques* (Brussels: Bureau de la Société des Bollandistes, 1906).
12. Pio Franchi de' Cavalieri, "San Gennaro vescovo e martire," in *Note agiografiche*, vol. 4 (Rome: Tipografia Poliglotta Vaticana, 1912), 79–114.
13. Antonio Vuolo, "Rilettura del 'dossier' agiografico su San Gennaro e compagni," *Campania Sacra* 38, no. 1 (2007): 179–221.
14. Hans Achelis, *Die Katakomben von Neapel* (Leipzig: Hiersemann, 1936), 92.
15. Domenico Mallardo, "La via Antiniana e le memorie di S. Gennaro," *Rendiconti della Reale Accademia di Archeologia, Lettere e Belle Arti* 19 (1939): 303–65; Paul Arthur, *Naples, from Roman Town to City-State: An Archaeological Perspective* (London: British School at Rome, 2002), 85.
16. "Gesta episcoporum Neapolitanorum," in *Monumenta Germaniae Historica. Scriptores rerum Longobardicarum et Italicarumsaec, VI–IX*, ed. Georg Waitz (Hanover: Hahn, 1878), 406; Mallardo, "La via Antiniana"; Umberto M. Fasola, *Le Catacombe di S. Gennaro a Capodimonte* (Rome: Editalia, 1975). For an update, Nicola Ciavolino, "Scavi e scoperte di archeologia cristiana in Campania dal 1983 al 1993," in *1983–1993: Dieci anni di archeologia cristiana in Italia*, atti del VII congresso nazionale di archeologia cristiana. Cassino, 20–24 September 1993, ed. Eugenio Russo (Cassino: Edizioni dell'Università degli studi di Cassino, 2003), 615–69; Maria Amodio, "Riflessi monumentali del culto ianuariano. Le Catacombe di San Gennaro a Capodimonte. Dalla 'curiositas' degli eruditi alle indagini archeologiche," *Campania Sacra* 38, no. 1 (2007): 123–46; Danilo Mazzoleni, "Note e osservazioni sulle iscrizioni del complesso monumentale di San Gennaro," *Campania Sacra* 38, no. 1 (2007): 147–64; Fabrizio Bisconti, "Riflessi del culto di San Gennaro nel complesso catacombale di Capodimonte," *Campania Sacra* 38, no. 1 (2007): 165–78.
17. Mallardo, "S. Gennaro e compagni."
18. Domenico Mallardo, "La Campania e la crisi ariana," *Rivista di storia della Chiesa in Italia* 1, no. 2 (1947): 185–226, in particular 199–200.

19. Ibid., 354.
20. Achelis, *Die Katakomben*, 91–97. This interpretation is broadly shared by Hippolyte Delehaye, "Hagiographie napolitaine (II)," *Analecta Bollandiana* 59 (1941): 1–33, in particular 1–13.
21. Antonius Ferrua, ed., *Epigrammata Damasiana*, vol. 46, no. 4 (Vatican City: Pontificio Istituto di Archeologia Cristiana, 1942), 188.
22. Gennaro Luongo, "Neapolitanae urbis illustrat Ecclesiam (Uranio, *De Obitu Paulini* 3)," *Campania Sacra* 38, no. 1 (2007): 16–36, in particular 33.
23. Uranio, *De obitu Paulini ad Pacatum* 3 (*Patrologia Latina* 53, 861). This is the very first testimony, dated c. 432, of San Januarius's so-called biographic *dossier*.
24. Giorgio Otranto, *Per una storia dell'Italia tardoantica cristiana. Approcci regionali* (Bari: Edipuglia, 2010), 66–81.
25. André Vauchez, "Conclusioni," *Campania Sacra* 38, no. 2 (2007): 309–17, in particular 311.
26. *Vita et translatio S. Athanasii Neapolitani episcopi (BHL 735 e 737) sec. IX*, intr., critical edition and commentary by Antonio Vuolo (Rome: Istituto Storico Italiano per il Medioevo, 2001), 54.
27. Vinni Lucherini, *La cattedrale di Napoli. Storia, architettura, storiografia di un monumento medievale* (Rome: École française de Rome, 2009), 131–48.
28. Domenico Ambrasi, "Reichenau e S. Gennaro," *Ianuarius* 53 (1972): 454–63; Hubert Houben, "Benevento e Reichenau. Contatti tra l'Italia meridionale e l'Alamannia in epoca carolingia," in *Medioevo monastico meridionale* (Naples: 1987), 67–81. According to Gian Paolo Silicani the bones kept in Reichenau are those of another Saint Januarius, from Rome rather than Naples, one of the seven sons of Saint Felicity. Gian Paolo Silicani, "San Gennaro di Benevento-Napoli, Lotario I e Reichenau. Esame critico di una supposta traslazione," *Ianuarius* 11 (1989): 557–76.
29. The last attestation in Benevento dates back to 1129. Falcone di Benevento, "Chronicon Beneventanum," in *Chronicon Beneventanum. Città e feudi nell'Italia dei Normanni*, ed. Edoardo D'angelo (Florence: Sismel - Edizioni del Galluzzo, 1998), 105–7.
30. The hypotheses are examined by Amalia Galdi, "Da 'Sacra pignora' a oggetti d'arte: il tesoro di S. Maria di Montevergine," *Sanctorum* 2 (2005): 55–64.
31. Franco Strazzullo, "La politica di Ferrante I nei riflessi della traslazione delle ossa di San Gennaro," in *Quinto centenario della traslazione delle ossa di San Gennaro da Montevergine a Napoli. 1497–1997* (Naples: Edizioni Scientifiche Italiane, 1996), 9–31.
32. Camillo Tutini, *Memorie della vita, miracoli e culto di S. Gianuario martire, vescovo di Benevento e principal protettore della città di Napoli* (Naples: Paci, 1681), 54.
33. Ibid., 55.
34. In any case many churches in Naples and elsewhere have at various times claimed to have relics of Saint Januarius in their possession, including the saint's nerves. For example, Girolamo Maria Di Sant'Anna, *Istoria della vita, virtù e miracoli di S. Gennaro* [. . .] (Naples: Abbate, 1733), 431–42.
35. Aldo Caserta and Gastone Lambertini, *Storia e scienza di fronte al miracolo di San Gennaro* (Naples: D'Auria, 1968), 60; Pierluigi Baima Bollone, *San Gennaro e la scienza* (Turin: Sei, 1989), 166–67.
36. Paolo Garzilli, ed., *Cronica di Napoli di Notar Giacomo* (Naples: Stamperia Reale, 1845), 213; see Caracciolo, *De sacris*, 250–54. The questions posed by Vinni Lucherini on the identity of the bones brought to Naples by the Carafa are stimulating. Vinni Lucherini, "San Gennaro negato: il 'Chronicon

Sanctae Mariae de Principio' e le sue due redazioni (con qualche nota a margine sul 'San Gennaro vére' di Sándor Márai)," in *Tempi e forme dell'arte. Miscellanea di studi offerti a Pina Belli D'Elia*, ed. Luisa Derosa and Clara Gelao (Foggia: Grenzi, 2011), 204–15.

37. Bianca de Divitiis, *Architettura e committenza nella Napoli del Quattrocento* (Venice: Marsilio, 2007), 171–79. On the political and social dimension of the translation and the cult of the relics of Saint Januarius and the role of the Carafa family, see Maria Antonietta Visceglia, "Nobiltà, città, rituali religiosi," in *Identità sociali. La nobiltà napoletana nella prima età moderna* (Milan: Unicopli, 1998), 173–205; Charlotte Nichols, "Plague and Politics in Early Modern Naples: The Relics of San Gennaro," in *In Sickness and Health: Disease as Metaphor in Art and Popular Wisdom*, ed. Laurinda S. Dixon (Newark: University of Delaware Press, 2004), 23–44.

38. This is the hypothesis of the so-called "Acta S. Proculi o Acta Puteolana (BHL 4133)," *Acta Sanctorum* 6 (September): 872–74, in particular 874.

39. Lucherini, *La cattedrale di Napoli*, 74–75.

40. Vuolo, "Rilettura del 'dossier' agiografico," in particular 194–97.

41. It might be theorised, as Pierluigi Leone de Castris has done, that the bust was commissioned by Charles II of Anjou to mark the liberation of his son Philip. Pierluigi Leone de Castris, "Il busto-reliquiario di San Gennaro," in *San Gennaro patrono delle arti*, ed. Stefano Causa (Naples: Arte'm, 2008), 9–17; Jill Caskey, "The Look of Liturgy: Identity and ars sacra in Southern Italy," in *Ritual and Space in the Middle Ages*, Proceedings of the Harlaxton Symposium 2009, ed. Frances Andrews (Donington: Shaun Tyas, 2011), 108–29.

42. Garzilli, *Cronica di Napoli*, 213.

43. Cesare D'Engenio Caracciolo, *Napoli sacra* [. . .] (Naples: Beltrano, 1623), 9r.

44. Noemi Rubello, "Una bella et caritativa cosa. Episodes de thaumaturgie royale pendant la période des Guerres d'Italie," *Le Moyen Âge* 120 (2014): 53–77.

45. André de la Vigne, *Le voyage de Naples*, ed. Anna Slerca (Milan: Vita e Pensiero, 1981), 261–62.

46. Matteo Silvatico, *Pandectae medicinae* [. . .], ed. Angelo Catone (Naples: Arnaldo di Bruxelles, 1474), f. 3.

47. Peter Harrison, "The Development of the Concept of Laws of Nature," in *Creation: Law and Probability*, ed. Fraser N. Watts (Aldershot: Ashgate, 2008), 13–36.

48. As recited in section XXXVIII of the so-called "Constitutions," which in 1337 governed the procession. Luigi Parascandolo, *Memorie storiche-critiche-diplomatiche della Chiesa di Napoli*, vol. 3 (Naples: P. Tizzano, 1849), 133.

49. Camillo Tutini, *Del origine e fundatione de' seggi di Napoli* (Naples: Beltrano, 1644), 185.

50. *Ragioni incontrastabili dell'eminentissimo sig. cardinale Pignatelli arcivescovo di Napoli per chiarire la verità ed il gran torto che se gli farebbe se ancora si volesse persistere nella pretenzione mai più intesa intorno alla processione del glorioso San Gennaro*, 5.

51. John A. Marino, *Becoming Neapolitan: Citizen, Culture in Baroque Naples* (Baltimore: Johns Hopkins University Press, 2011), 92–94.

52. *Ragioni incontrastabili*, 5.

53. Caracciolo, *Napoli sacra*, 9r; Nicolò Carminio Falcone, *L'intera istoria della famiglia, vita, miracoli, traslazioni e culto del glorioso martire S. Gennaro* (Naples: Mosca, 1713), 507; Girolamo Maria di Sant'Anna, *Istoria della vita*, 387–89.

54. Gina Ianella, "Les fêtes de la Saint Jean à Naples, 1581–1632," in *Les fêtes urbaines en Italie à l'époque de la Renaissance: Vérone, Florence, Sienne, Naples*, ed. Françoise Descroisette and Michel Plaisance (Paris: Klincksieck, 1993), 131–85.
55. Marino, *Becoming Neapolitan*, 93.
56. On the origins of the Neapolitan seats, Monica Santangelo, "Preminenza aristocratica a Napoli nel tardo medioevo: i tocchi e il problema dell'origine dei sedili," *Archivio storico italiano* 171 (2013): 273–318. On the role of the representatives of the seats in the "Constitutions," Parascandolo, *Memorie*, 191–92.
57. D'Afflitto, *In Utriusque Siciliae Neapolisque sanctiones* (my italics), vol. 1, p. 68v.
58. Francesco Paolo de Ceglia, "Thinking with the Saint: The Neapolitan Miracle of Saint Januarius and Early Modern Science," *Early Science and Medicine* 19 (2014): 133–73; Francesco Paolo de Ceglia, "Playing God: Testing, Modelling and Imitating Blood Miracles in 18th-Century Europe," *Bulletin of the History of Medicine* 91 (2017): 391–419.

4　The Circulation of Roman Relics in the Savoy States

Dynamics of Devotion and Political Uses in the Modern and Contemporary Ages

Paolo Cozzo

Historians have long highlighted the legitimising role of relics on which, even in the modern age, states, dynasties, cities and territories founded their authority and propagated their prestige.[1] Many such relics were the object of intense circulation in distant times and places.[2] It is known, for instance, that the search for relics (or, more precisely, the "hunt" for them: an activity in which a wide variety of lay and ecclesiastical figures took an active part during the early modern era[3]) responded to a need that was especially widespread in lands still faithful to the Roman Church. And more than any other centre of Christianity, Rome—as a "subterranean civitas"[4]—was the most productive mine and forge of bodies of saints.[5]

Roman Relics, Civic Patronages and Local Identities in the Seventeenth and Eighteenth Centuries

Piedmont, in the sixteenth and eighteenth centuries, was the destination for many bodies extracted from the Roman catacombs, which, having reached subalpine territories, became the fulcrum of a form of worship that often conveyed a sense of identity. This is what occurred in local communities which, after having acquired relics of saints totally extraneous to their hagiographic tradition, unhesitatingly proclaimed them their new patrons or co-patrons.[6]

This was a pervasive phenomenon of the seventeenth and eighteenth centuries that concerned small (sometimes tiny) settlements (like those in Valsesia, where 30 or so communities were endowed with "Roman" co-patrons),[7] as well as in relatively large cities. Thus, while in 1663 Cavallerleone (then a rural village in the territory of Cuneo) welcomed as its patron the relics of an obscure Saint Romano from Rome, the same had happened years earlier in Giaveno with Antherus (1611), in Pinerolo with Leavio, in Collegno with Calocero, in Cherasco with Virginio and Euflamia (1623), in Palazzolo Vercellese with Caio and Faustina (1626), in Savigliano with Benedict, Giusto and Taddea (1630), and one could go on to arrive as far as Turin. In 1611 the city had received the remains of Saint Tigrino, which had been exhumed from the cemetery of Via Salaria, and these were kept and displayed for public veneration in the Church of the Holy Martyrs, while in the late 1620s another consign-ment of relics (of the martyrs Cristina, Elisabetta, Caterina, Margherita, Petronia, Emanuele, another Caterina *virgo et martyr cum sociis suis*) was delivered to Sardinia, to be placed by Archbishop Filiberto Milliet in the Cathedral of San Giovanni, where he had ordered "these holy bodies to be put on view for veneration."[8]

One could also cite the many relics taken from Roman cemeteries for the Confraternity of the Holy Cross (then given a new home in the Basil-ica of Saints Maurice and Lazarus, where they remain to this day)[9] or those of Saint Botonto, whose body—which we will refer to later—was taken from the cemetery of Nomentano to Turin in 1843, where it was greeted as a "celestial angel sent from the Metropolis of the Catholic world to spread its protective wings over august Turin."[10]

Although the dynamics that stimulated the relocation of sacred remains from Rome to Piedmont were varied, all responded to some common logic. The first was that of prestige, which local communities, large or small, tried to acquire (or boost) by bringing into play a hagiographic dimension which, as was usual in the modern age, expressed itself in a tangible form, of which relics were a preferred, albeit not the only, exam-ple. The demand for relics by Piedmont (and all corners of the Catholic world) met with a supply which swelled notably after the "discovery" in the mid-sixteenth century of the Roman catacombs. We know—though here is not the place to look into the subject—that the enormous quantity of remains extracted by the "arsenals of the faith"[11] presented the church with the serious challenge of identifying and, consequently, authenticat-ing them. Their arrival in the communities that had requested them was, however, hardly ever accompanied by reflections or debates on the his-torical validity of the martyrs of whom the relics were material testimony.

Hence it still needs to be explained how and why so many remains of saints whose genuineness, in almost all cases, the hagiographers of the Bollandist Society (and, before them, Cesare Baronio) must have doubted, reached Piedmont in such large numbers. The transfer of bodies was almost always made possible by the active involvement of church officials (preferably those based in Rome or who had contacts in the Curia) who were linked to Piedmontese communities through personal ties.

The best-known case is that of the relics recovered—often illicitly and fraudulently—by Giovanni Battista Cavagna, a controversial peronsality from Novara resident in Rome. Between the late sixteenth century and early seventeenth he orchestrated the transfer of more than 60 remains of saints to his home diocese,[12] and has been made known to the public by Sebas-tiano Vassalli's 1990 historical novel *La chimera*.[13] These relics (about which Baronio had strong reservations), after the initial wariness of the bishop

Carlo Bascapé (who tried in vain to have proof of their authenticity), were distributed to a large number of centres in the Novara diocese,[14] which immediately promoted the martyrs buried in Roman cemeteries as their new patrons or co-patrons.

The phenomenon, of particular relevance to Valsesia and other parts of the Novara diocese, which up to the early eighteenth century belonged to the State of Milan (and so benefited from considerable Lombard presence in the Curia, for example in the circles of Como-born Pope Innocent XI Odescalchi, 1676–89),[15] could also be found in Savoy territories (and lands that became such), and this depended equally on the dynamism of clergy of laity working in Rome. These, having come into possession of relics recovered by excavators or donated by influential members of the Curia, sent them to their communities of origin. Thus in Campertogno, in the Valsesia, which had passed under the control of the Savoy, the arrival in 1711 of the relics of the martyr Innocenzo came about through the good offices of Rocco Antonio Gianoli, a member of one of the country's most influential families, who, residing in Rome, had obtained them from Cardinal Gaspare Carpegna.[16]

The involvement of families in the translation of relics was even greater in cases involving members of the established nobility of the recipient villages and towns. This was so in the aforementioned case of Cavallerleone, where the arrival of the relics of Saint Romano in 1663 was the result of the direct involvement of the archbishop of Turin, Giulio Cesare Bergera, the eldest son of the count of Cavallerleone.[17] Or again, Cervignasco, a rural hamlet of Saluzzo, held by the Della Chiesa family, which in 1670 had acquired the relics of the martyr Vittorio through the Capuchin friar Vittorio Filippo, a member of the family; these were first translated to the Capuchin convent of Saluzzo, before being housed in the parish church of Cervignasco, which the Della Chiesa patronised.[18]

A similar procedure had been carried out in the early seventeenth century at Giaveno, the place of origin of the Claretta family, a member of which, Abbot Vincenzo, attended an exhumation carried out by Cavagna in the catacombs of Saint Callisto, and obtained no less a prize than the body of Saint Antherus, a third-century pope.[19] Taken to Giaveno, which immediately adopted him as its patron saint,[20] the remains of the pope-martyr were placed in the collegiate Church of San Lorenzo, in the chapel patronised by the Claretta family, where "for many years the descendants of the same family were buried."[21] The significance regarding identity taken on by the relics and the cult of Antherus was also reflected in the decision taken by Baron Gaudenzio Claretta (a key figure of nineteenth-century Piedmontese scholarship)[22] to evoke the martyr in the motto beneath the family coat of arms.[23]

At times the intermediary function was performed by a religious order, which saw the acquisition of Roman relics as an effective way of enhancing their presence in particular territories. In Savigliano the abbot of the ancient and powerful Benedictine Abbey of San Pietro[24] was responsible for obtaining from Rome the bodies of the saintly Benedict, Giusto and Taddea, which arrived in the town on 30 September 1629 and were greeted with grandiose "holy pomp."[25]

In Pinerolo, on the other hand, it was the Capuchins who acted as the link. Despite not having been present in the territory for long (they had arrived there in 1575),[26] in the early seventeenth century they safeguarded dozens of relics of martyrs brought from Rome thanks to the direct involvement of Cardinal Maurizio of Savoy. The cardinal attributed a clear anti-Protestant significance to these holy bodies, just as the Franciscan friars had done when promoting the devotion of relics "to invite the heretics around us to the worship of God and the despised veneration of the saints."[27] We know that these Roman saints, Leavio especially, were proclaimed co-patrons of the city, but their relics nevertheless continued to be kept and venerated in the Capuchin convent, despite repeated requests from the chapter of the collegiate Church of San Donato and the municipal authorities for them to be transferred to the cathedral and thus brought closer to the city's patron saint, Donato. The dispute between the mayors, the canons and the Capuchins was finally resolved in the mid-seventeenth century when, on the order of Louis XIV—after the Treaty of Cherasco Pinerolo had become a French city[28]—the relics of the co-patrons were transferred from the convent to the cathedral. There they became the focus of a civic ritual[29] which, surviving into the eighteenth century,[30] still attracted considerable interest in the second half of the nineteenth century, when the municipality participated officially in the procession in honour of its co-patron.[31]

This, then, is confirmation of how the identity-establishing use of the "allogeneic" holy bodies, in Piedmont as elsewhere, was maintained throughout the eighteenth century: a century of "regulated devotion" and of "aufklärung," during which, however, the extraction and consignment of Roman relics never ceased, but until at least the 1730s matched the levels reached in the seventeenth century.[32] While the situation in the second half of the eighteenth century changed significantly in general terms, in the same period Piedmont continued to request and obtain—using justifications and means not dissimilar to those used earlier—Roman relics on which to erect local cults of patron saints. This occurred, for instance at Scopa with Ammonisia (1755),[33] Trecate with Clemente (1758),[34] Cavour with Marziale (1761),[35] Fobello with Benedict (1766),[36] Lombardore with Giocondino (1770),[37] Caraglio with Dolcito (1779),[38] Rimella with Gioconda (1789)[39] and Montanaro with Aurelia.[40]

The trend endured, intermittently, into the nineteenth century. The body of Lupercilla, a child martyred in the third century, arrived in Crodo in 1819 to instantly become the community's co-patron. Her relics, placed in the high altar of the parish church, had been taken from the catacombs of San Callisto on the order of Cardinal Giuseppe Antonio Sala,[41] who had received a request from Francesco Guglielmi, a rich "businessman and landowner" from Crodo who had been living in Rome (where he drew up his will in 1832).[42] It was certainly no coincidence that Guglielmi was the brother of the Crodo parish priest, Don Giuseppe Guglielmi, who promoted the veneration of the new co-patron. As what had happened in past centuries, Saint Lupercilla helped to boost both local prestige and family honour. And this was by a no means a rare event, for, moving to Valsesia in the same diocese, we can observe the arrival of the sacred relics of Massimo to Cravagliana (1830), Benedict to Piana dei Monti-Madonna del Sasso (1832), Felice to Varallo (1845), Marcellino to Castagnola (1855) and Eugenia to Ferrera (1880).[43]

The Cult of Relics in Courts, Dynasties and States in the Nineteenth Century

In the nineteenth century, however, the translation of Roman relics to Piedmont changed circumstantially and indicatively. As has been rightly noted, the high value placed on the martyrs of late antiquity that characterised the first half of the nineteenth century should be construed as a means of strengthening the prestige of Rome and its bishop, in a historical phase which, after the Restoration, was increasingly perceived as a new season of martyrdom for the church.[44] It is not surprising, then, that in 1827 Pope Leo XII sent a relic of Saint Paul previously preserved in a column of the ancient Ostiense basilica to Carlo Felice, who placed it in the Castle of Agliè. The gift was an expression of the pope's indebtedness to the king of Sardinia who, like many other Catholic sovereigns, had contributed financially or materially to the reconstruction of the Basilica of St Paul Outside the Walls, which had nearly been destroyed by fire in 1823.[45] In addition to this significance there was the idea—clearly evident in the relations between the Roman Curia and the Savoy court[46]—of reinvigorating the primacy of Rome through the hagiographic and ideological power of its patrons, which the successor of Peter believed vital to propagate within the "society of the princes."

However, the apostolic see also used relics when trying to transmit messages to other social circles. Hence the body of Saint Botonto—a child martyred under Diocletian—which was taken from the cemetery of Sant'Agnese in Via Nomentana on 18 December 1841, was gifted by Gregory XVI to the Capuchin convent of Turin, the solemn translation taking place on 15 January 1843.[47] Political mediation had once again been essential: a Savoyard plenipotentiary minister, Federico Broglia di Mombello, had obtained the remains from the papal Curia before forwarding them to the Capuchins. These recognised that the sacred child-martyr had educational potential: parents would be inspired to teach their children "with brief, but vivid descriptions of the Roman Catacombs" about the "most horrible persecutions of the church and the triumphs of the martyrs."[48] Thus the image of innocent Botonto sacrificed by the cruel pagan emperors would prepare children for the hard challenges that the church would again be called upon to tackle. This reasoning seemed prophetic given that it anticipated a scenario—that of laicisation and secularisation—which liberal politics would bring to bear on Piedmont with great vigour only a few years later.

Here, however, in the pre-unification period, the Savoy monarchy was still pursuing a political strategy in which the religious dimension remained essential. At least it was so for Charles Albert, whose vision of relations between throne and altar naturally led (partly through a prodigious use of devotional practices)[49] to the exaltation of dynastic sanctitude. In this regard, while the sovereign's endeavours to obtain canonical recognition for the cult of his ancestors who had an aura of holiness is well known, as are his attempts to strengthen the symbolic value of family burials,[50] perhaps less well known is the attention he paid to relics, which he sought and celebrated not only to satisfy an intimate and personal need, but also for the public and political functions they served.

It is in this light that the arrival in Turin in 1840 of the relics of Saint Maurice, the ancient patron of the Savoy dynasty and states should be interpreted. The event dates back to the summer of that year, when the Piedmontese ambassador to Rome noticed that a fragment of the saint's head was held in the apostolic Quirinal Palace. "Thinking that His Majesty might be pleased to have in his royal dominions the very precious relic of the patron saint of the Savoy crown," the diplomat wrote, "I did my very best to obtain it as a gift from His Beatitude."[51] After a brief negotiation the relic, complete with authentication, was sent to Turin, where, however, it was received with a certain embarrassment. The court, which had for centuries been in possession of the main Mauritian relics (that came from Saint-Maurice d'Agaune in Turin on 15 January 1591),[52] in fact wished to verify the provenance of this new gift (a head "missing some teeth and the entire lower jaw") from Rome. It was clear, however, that "any difficulty that arose would cause harm to extremely delicate matters": raising doubts about the "genuineness" of the relic might be interpreted as an act of disrespect towards the Holy See, not to mention that "if the faithful were allowed to question the authenticity of the holy relic solemnly recognised by the church on the basis of due diligence, there is no doubt that such discussions would bring very serious problems."[53]

The issue of the "authenticity" of relics (to which Charles Albert, like his predecessors, showed unwavering devotion) seems to have been given increasing emphasis by the Savoy court from the middle of the century, as an episode concerning the relics of Saint Benedict confirms. On 27 February 1841 a wooden chest bearing the episcopal seals of Archbishop Alexis Billiet arrived in Turin, accompanied by Louis Rendu, a canon from the Cathedral of Chambéry. The chest contained a footless corpse "of masculine sex, European race, well-preserved in its natural state without the slightest sign of artificial work."[54] This was the body—wrote Luigi Fransoni, archbishop of Turin—"that is believed to be that of Saint Benedict, founder of the Benedictines," and which had arrived from the city most hostile to the cult of relics: Geneva. Rendu had in fact been ordered by Billiet to recover it from the city, and had also been charged with discovering—with the aid of the foreign minister of the Kingdom of Sardinia, Clemente Solaro della Margherita—what information about the holy body had been given to King Charels Albert by André Gosse, a Calvinist doctor.

Although no trace of the research commissioned by Rendu has survived, it is possible to piece together the history of the remains through an article published in 1863 in the *Bulletin de l'histoire du Protestantisme français*.[55] The story dates back to 1793, the year in which Gosse's father, Henri Albert, then a young pharmaceutical and medical student in Paris, where a campaign of de-Christianisation was being waged as part of the Reign of Terror, was informed of the exhumation of a body of Saint Benedict from the high altar of the cloistered church of the Monastery of Saint-Benoît-sur-Loire (which was destroyed in the nineteenth century). His interest piqued, the young Gosse acquired the remains by paying the monastery's guardian a small inducement and, on the completion of his studies, returned to Geneva in 1800 with the body in a chest on which he had written "objet d'histoire naturelle. Momie d'Egypte."[56] Very soon, however, a rumour that the mummy was actually all that remained of the body of the father of monasticism spread through the Calvinist city. This, on the one hand, heightened the reformers' ridicule of the cult of relics, but on the other intensified the devotion of many Catholics from neighbouring Savoy, who were not slow to knock on Gosse's door, requesting to see and touch Saint Benedict. After Gosse's death in 1816, the object was inherited by his son André, also a doctor. It was he, through the agency of della Margherita, who donated the body to Charles Albert who, in an accordance with his veneration of relics, arranged for it to be kept safe in the deposits of Turin Cathedral, in the chamber where Louise of Savoy's remains had been placed a few months earlier,[57] after the Holy See had officially approved the cult *ab immemorabili* in 1839.[58] This prestigious location made it appear that in the eyes of the sovereign the attribution of the remains to Saint Benedict on the basis of the donor's statements was regarded as plausible.

However, this was an opinion that, apparently, the Turinese ecclesiastical authorities did not fully share. This can be seen from the clarification made in curial circles that the seals of the archbishop of Turin on the chest now lying in the cathedral crypts were to be seen as "providential guarantees testifying to the identity of the said body brought here from Geneva, until it is legitimately demonstrated whether this body is or is not that of Saint Benedict."⁵⁹ The doubts about the true identity of this "fully mummified cadaver, with yellowish skin, 1.7 metres high, very well preserved, missing only the back three teeth of the upper jaw and the extremities of the feet, which appear to have been cut off in different times"⁶⁰ had arisen straight away, in both the Curia and the court. In the case of Saint Benedict, the negative conclusions eventually drawn following research on the true identity of the body sent to Turin certainly did not come with the same political and diplomatic problems as those in the case of the relics of Maurice: in the end there was a difference between a relic donated by the pope and one donated by a Calvinist doctor.

The problem nevertheless resurfaced in 1844, the year in which a new examination of the body was carried out. On this occasion, the ecclesiastical authorities were joined by Vincenzo Promis, the royal librarian and member of a dynasty of eminent intellectuals in service to the Savoy.⁶¹ His presence denoted a fresh, different approach to the question, which now appeared to be in all respects a responsibility of the court officials, who were just as concerned—if not more so—as the prelates to establish the merits of a cult about which the administration of the royal house now demanded clarification. Promis had been commissioned by the king, through his senior chaplain, to carry out all the investigations needed to establish the authenticity of the remains. Eventually there was an exchange of letters between the Bollandists and other scholars which determined that the body certainly could not have been that of the father of monasticism: "absolument sans fundament et risible" was how François Chamard, a Benedictine from Solesmes, had described the idea to Promis.⁶²

Once it had been proved that the mummified body was not that of Benedict of Norcia, it became imperative for the court to establish its real identity. One theory that gained traction—or, rather, was not ruled out—was that it might be the remains of his namesake, Benedict of Aniane.⁶³ This saint, a Benedictine monk who lived in the eighth and ninth centuries, had been an important reformer of the order and, for this reason, had himself earned the title of "patriarch" of Western monasticism.⁶⁴ However, this solution, which seemed a good compromise since it preserved, at least symbolically, a link to Saint Benedict, could not counter the measures taken in 1910, when Victor Emmanuel III asked for the remains to be transferred from their original site (where in the meantime the coffins of four Carignan princes who died in France in the early nineteenth century had been placed) to a cathedral crypt that had been set aside for the bodies of archbishops and canons.⁶⁵ With this move the ownership of the body was legally conveyed to the ecclesiastical authorities, deemed to be "the most suitable [entity] to have the deposit and most able to undertake its identification." Victor Emmanuel believed it inappropriate for rooms used as the burial chambers of the Savoy princes to be occupied by bodies unconnected to the dynastic sanctity or, as in this case, of uncertain origin. This had been made perfectly clear by the minister of the royal house, Alessandro Mattioli Pasqualini, in a letter to the senior chaplain, in which he said that "that body lacks any right to continue to still remain in the temporary deposit of the bodies of the princes of the House of Savoy."[66]

This indicated a sea change in attitude. Whereas for Charles Albert and his predecessors the arrival of relics (even those without official recognition) helped to reinforce the sanctitude of the court, for Victor Emmanuel III the dynasty's sacredness had in itself an autonomy and self-sufficiency that rendered the accumulation of relics in courtly spaces superfluous. Clearly at this point the sacred nature of the dynasty—which had elevated the mortal remains of princes of the royal house to the level of relics—now had connotations of a "lay" kind, compatible with the civil-national-state religion that emerged in the Risorgimento and proliferated in the post-unification era.[67] Moreover, the secularisation of the court's sacrality had begun at least half a century earlier, with Victor Emmanuel II's rise to the throne and the emergence of a policy characterised by the principle of state-church separateness, which had impacted on divisions of the court.[68]

Significant in this regard is what happened, on the eve of Italian unification, to the sword of Saint Maurice, a relic which, alongside the saint's bones and ring, had become one of the most celebrated symbols of dynastic power.[69] In 1858 it was moved with the king's consent from the Chapel of the Holy Shroud—where it had been placed alongside the martyr's remains—to the Royal Armoury.[70] This was a sign that the Savoy—now ready to leave Turin and project themselves onto the national stage where the legitimising force of the sacred had to assume new forms and move through different channels—were also preparing to manage their most illustrious relics in ways quite unlike those of the past. First of all, the Shroud, whose public expositions—already extremely rare in the nineteenth century—were no longer celebrated outdoors, but in the Turin cathedral, where "the clergy of the Metropolitana played a more important role than in previous centuries."[71]

Still with regard to Saint Maurice, it was the Turinese clergy and church who attempted to restore the devotion of the ancient martyr and patron of the state and royal lineage to its roots in a tradition that the court, now in Rome, seemed to have forgotten. The moment for this presented itself in 1891 with the third centenary of the translation of the Mauritian relics to Turin, when—through the senior chaplain—a request was made for the return of the sword as a "precious relic."[72] In making this request the Ministry of the Royal Household opposed the considerations of the director of the Royal Armoury, General Raffaele Cadorna, for whom since the "pious tradition, however respectable, that this sword belonged to Saint Maurice, who died in the early fourth century, has been historically refuted, since the precious heirloom is a work of the thirteenth century" it seemed right that the sword remained in the Royal Armoury "which is its appropriate home and where it is admired daily as a precious relic."[73]

What, then, was Saint Maurice's sword: a relic or an heirloom? Behind these different views of the same object one might see the gap between distant and in many ways opposite cultures, which the schism of the Risorgimento helped to make mutually hostile. In a climate of rupture and conflict between state and church, even holy bodies (starting from Roman times) that for centuries had been elements of political and social as well as religious cohesion within local communities, as well as in the courts, gradually lost their unifying function and, in some cases, actually became divisive. This is what occurred in Scopa, in Valsesia, where the co-patron Ammonisia, who since the middle of the eighteenth century had been invoked to placate the fury of the River Sesia, in the 1880s (the decade in which the statue of Giordano Bruno the "martyr of Freedom of thought" was erected in Rome's Campo de' Fiori)[74] became the favoured target of the anti-clerical controversies of the more radical liberal and masonic wings.[75] These saw the relic as the bones of an invented saint, fraudulently stolen from a Roman cemetery and furtively brought to Piedmont, as nothing more than concrete proof of a trade carried out by the clergy to delude the poor with macabre objects and superstitious rituals.

Yet despite becoming the target of fierce criticism, bitter disputes and, at times (as had already occurred at the late eighteenth century, in the France of the Terror, and as would occur at the start of the twentieth century in revolutionary Russia and civil war Spain), of destructive violence, the relics, including those that had arrived from Rome centuries earlier, nevertheless managed to continue to stimulate interest and attract attention, even in Piedmont which was rapidly moving down the road of secularisation. Whether treated as objects of devotion or as collectable heirlooms, venerated or contested, exalted or denigrated, the relics, with their intrinsic ability to connect with faraway places and bygone times, basically continued to be what, beyond their strictly cultic dimension, they had always been, which is to say powerful transmitters of "configurations historiques différentes."[76]

Notes

1. Philippe Boutry, Pierre-Antoine Fabre and Dominique Julia, eds., *Reliques modernes: cultes et usages chretiens des corps saints des réformes aux revolutions* (Paris: EEHESS, 2009).
2. Dominique Julia, "Reliques: le pouvoir du saint," in *L'Europe. Encyclopédie historique*, ed. Christophe Charle and Daniel Roche (Arles: Actes Sud Editions, 2018), 296–300.
3. Gianvittorio Signorotto, "Cercatori di reliquie," *Rivista di storia e letteratura religiosa* 3 (1985): 383–418.

4.   Massimiliano Ghilardi, *"Subterranea civitas"*. *Quattro studi sulle catacombe romane dal Medioevo all'età moderna* (Rome: Edizioni dell'Ateneo,2003).
5.   Stéphane Baciocchi and Christophe Duhamelle, eds., *Reliques romaines: invention et circulation des corps saints des catacombes à l'époque moderne* (Rome: École Française de Rome, 2016).
6.   Giorgio Cracco and Lellia Cracco Ruggini, "Cercatori di reliquie e parrocchia nell'Italia del Seicento: un caso significativo," in *Religione, cultura e politica nell'Europa dell'età moderna. Studi offerti a Mario Rosa dagli amici*, ed. Carlo Ossola, Marcello Verga and Maria Antonietta Visceglia (Florence: Olschki, 2003), 139–59.
7.   Paolo Cozzo, "Culti e spazi sacri nella Valsesia di età moderna: la dimensione devozionale del «mutamento di dominio»," in *Storia della Valsesia in età moderna*, ed. Edoardo Tortarolo (Vercelli: Gallo, 2015), 247–66, in particular 265.
8.   Paolo Cozzo, "Antichi santi, politica e diplomazia nella corte sabauda di età moderna," in *La mémoire des saints originels entre XVIe et XVIIIe siècle*, ed. Bernard Dompnier and Spefania Nanni (Rome: École Française de Rome, 2018), 429–45.
9.   Alberico Lo Faso di Serradifalco, Angelo Scordo and Maria Luisa Reviglio della Veneria, eds., *La Basilica Mauriziana: una chiesa torinese raccontata dai suoi antichi fedeli e frequentatori* (Collegno: Chiaramonte, 2009).
10.   Giuseppe Arnaud, "San Botonto," in *Il Cattolico. Giornale religioso-letterario* 19 (1842): 113–19, in particular 118–19.
11.   Massimiliano Ghilardi, *Gli arsenali della fede: tre saggi su apologia e propaganda delle catacombe romane (da Gregorio XIII a Pio XI)* (Rome: Aracne, 2006).
12.   Massimiliano Ghilardi, "Il pittore e le reliquie: Giovanni Angelo Santini e la Roma sotterranea nel primo Seicento," *Storia dell'arte*, new series 33 (2012): 5–24.
13.   Roberto Cicala and Giovanni Tesio, eds., *La chimera: storia e fortuna del romanzo di Sebastiano Vassalli* (Novara: Interlinea, 2003).
14.   A detailed list of these and other relics in the diocese of Novara is provided by the website of the Archdiocese of Novara, www.archiviodiocesanonovara.it/assets/santi-e-reliquie-nelle-parrocchie.pdf.
15.   Silvano Giordano, "Uomini e dinamiche di Curia durante il pontificato di Innocenzo XI," in *Innocenzo XI Odescalchi, papa, politico, committente*, ed. Richard Bösel et al. (Rome: Viella, 2014), 41–56.
16.   Damiano Pomi, "Il viaggio dei corpi santi dalle catacombe alla Valsesia," in *De Valle Sicida* 1 (2003): 85–132, in particular 113–15.
17.   Giovanni Maria Baravalle, *Conversione e martirio di S. Romano e traslazione delle sue reliquie in Cavallerleone* (Turin: Ferrando, 1863). On the archbishop of Turin, see Giuseppe Tuninetti, *Il cardinal Domenico Della Rovere, costruttore della cattedrale e gli arcivescovi di Torino dal 1515 al 2000. Stemmi, alberi genealogici e profili biografici* (Cantalupa: Effatà, 2000), 99–103.
18.   Aldo Ponso, ed., *Duemila anni di santità in Piemonte e Valle d'Aosta: i santi, i beati, i venerabili, i servi di Dio, le personalità distinte: guida completa dalle origini ai nostri giorni* (Cantalupa: Effatà, 2001), 43.
19.   Gaudenzio Claretta, *Cronistoria del Municipio di Giaveno dal secolo VIII al XIX: con molte notizie relative alla storia generale del Piemonte* (Turin: Civelli, 1875), 186–87; on Antherus see the entry by Federico Fatti, *Enciclopedia dei papi*, vol. I (Rome: Istituo dell'Enciclopedia Italiana, 2000), 263–65.
20.   Pier Giacinto Gallizia, *Vita di S. Antero papa, e martire, protettore di Giaveno* (Turin: Mairesse, 1724). The establishment of the cult of the patron

(of which in 1961 were held the *Solenni celebrazioni 350° anniversario traslazione s. reliquie sant'Antero, papa e martire, patrono di Giaveno: 1611– 1961* [Giaveno: 1961]) is testified by the announcements of the municipality relating to the saints day (www.comune.giaveno.to.it/wp-content/uploads/ 2018/06/Locandina-SantAntero-Papa-2018-.pdf) and the anniversary of his martyrdom (www.comune.giaveno.to.it/santantero-papa-copatrono-di-giaveno- domenica-8-dicembre-2016/locandina-di-santantero-2017/).

21. Gaudenzio Claretta, *Di Giaveno, Coazze, Valgioie cenni storici con anno- tazioni e documenti storici* (Turin: Favale, 1859), 45.

22. Isabella Ricci Massabò, "Claretta, Gaudenzio," in *Dizionario biografico degli Italiani*, vol. 26 (Rome: Istituto dell'Enciclopedia Italiana, 1982), 127–29.

23. Vittorio Spreti, *Enciclopedia storico-nobiliare italiana: famiglie nobili e tito- late viventi riconosciute dal R. governo d'Italia compresi: città, comunità, mense vescovili, abazie, parrocchie ed enti nobili e titolati riconosciuti*, vol. 2 (Milan: Carettoni, 1929), 479.

24. Alessandro Mortarotti, *L'abbazia benedettina di San Pietro in Savigliano* (Savigliano: L'Artistica, 1969).

25. *Sacre pompe saviglianesi nella traslatione de' santi martiri Benedetto, Giusto, e Tadea descritte dal P.D. Valeriano Castiglione milanese, monaco cassinense* (Turin: n.p., 1630).

26. Gabriele Ingegneri, *Storia dei cappuccini della Provincia di Torino* (Rome: Istituto Storico dei Cappuccini, 2008), 28.

27. Paolo Cozzo, " 'Per invitare gli eretici circonvicini al culto di Dio ed alla sprezzata venerazione dei santi'. Culto dei martiri e circolazione di reli- quie nel Pinerolese di prima età moderna," *Bollettino della Società di Studi Valdesi* 203, no. 2 (2008): 85–98.

28. Lucien Bély, "Le Piémont-Savoie au coeur des conflits européens," in *L'état, la cour et la ville. Le duché de Savoie au temps de Christine de France (1619– 1663)*, ed. Giuliano Ferretti (Paris: Classiques Garnier, 2017), 93–121, in particular, 102–5.

29. "Ordinato di Città, spesa per la processione di san Leavio a farsi ogni anno," Archive of the chapter of Pinerolo, Tit. 01, Cl. 2, fasc. 2, sr 23, 1654.

30. "Regolamento per la processione di san Leavio," ibid., Tit. 01, Cl. 30, sr. 35, 18 December 1754.

31. "Sindaco, processione di San Leavio," ibid., Tit. 03, Cl. 20, sr. 93, 14 April 1854; "Causa del capitolo di canonici della chiesa cattedrale di Pinerolo contro la città per l'annuale prestazione di cera a favore di quello nella pro- cessione di san Leavio e soci ed in altre funzioni," Tit. 01, Cl. 3, sr. 65/f, 1887–92.

32. Jean-Marc Ticchi, "Mgr. Sacriste et la distribution des reliques des cata- combes dans l'espace italien," in *Reliques romaines: invention et circulation des corps saints des catacombes à l'époque modern*, ed. Stéphane Baciocchi and Christophe Duhamelle (Rome: École Française de Rome, 2016), 175– 223, in particular 186–87.

33. Pomi, "Il viaggio dei corpi santi," 128–29.

34. Filippo Mittino, *1758–2008: San Clemente Martire. 250° anniversario dell'arrivo delle reliquie a Trecate* (Trecate: Parrocchia Beata Vergine Assunta di Trecate / Consulta dei Santi Cassiano e Clemente, 2009).

35. Ponso, *Duemila anni di santità*, 35.

36. Pomi, "Il viaggio dei corpi santi," 129–30.

37. Goffredo Casalis, *Dizionario geografico storico-statistico-commerciale degli Stati di S.M. il re di Sardegna*, vol. 9 (Turin: Maspero, 1841), 877. It is worth noting that in Lombardore (where the relics of Giocondino arrived in 1770 thanks to the involvement of Cardinal Vittorio Amedeo Delle Lanze) the

78   Paolo Cozzo

patron was already a Roman martyr, Agapito, of whom the village (which celebrated him with "a pompous feast on 18 August") preserved a relic "consisting of a tiny fragment of bone obtained at the start of this century," see Antonino Bertolotti, *Passeggiate nel Canavese* (Ivrea: Curbis, 1867), 38.

38. ·Ponso, *Duemila anni di santità*, 29.
39. Pomi, "Il viaggio dei corpi santi," 120–22.
40. Bertolotti, *Passeggiate nel Canavese*, 180.
41. Goffredo Casalis, *Dizionario geografico storico-statistico-commerciale degli Stati di S.M. il re di Sardegna*, vol. 5 (Turin: Maspero 1839), 664–65.
42. Filippo Bettini, *Giurisprudenza degli Stati sardi. Raccolta generale progressiva di giurisprudenza, legislazione e dottrina* (Turin: Pomba, 1857), 371.
43. Pomi, "Il viaggio dei copri santi," 122–28.
44. Tommaso Caliò, "Santità antiunitaria nella Roma di Pio IX," in *L'Italia e i santi. Agiografie, riti e devozioni nella costruzione dell'identità nazionale*, ed. Tommaso Caliò and Daniele Menozzi (Rome: Istituto dell'Enciclopedia Italiana, 2017), 243–67.
45. Paolo Cozzo, "Linguaggi del sacro fra Roma e i Savoia," in *Casa Savoia e curia romana dal Cinquecento al Risorgimento*, ed. Jean-François Chauvard, Andrea Merlotti and Maria Antonietta Visceglia (Rome: École Française de Rome, 2015), 19–36, in particular 19–20.
46. Pierangelo Gentile, "Questioni di etichetta. I rapporti tra i Savoia e Leone XII," in *La corte papale nell'età di Leone XII*, ed. Ilaria Fiumi Sermattei and Roberto Regoli (Ancona: Consiglio Regionale delle Marche, 2015), 83–92.
47. Arnaud, "San Botonto."
48. Ibid., 116.
49. Pierangelo Gentile, "Le pratiche devozionali alla corte di Carlo Alberto di Savoia," *Studi piemontesi* 38, no. 1 (2009): 173–82.
50. Sara Cabibbo, "Sovrane sante," in *Casa Savoia e curia romana dal Cinquecento al Risorgimento*, ed. Jean-François Chauvard, Andrea Merlotti and Maria Antonietta Visceglia (Rome: École Française de Rome, 2015), 37–53.
51. The story (whose documentary basis is represented by the diplomatic correspondence preserved in the Turin State Archives, Corte, Materie Ecclesiastiche, Materie Ecclesiastiche per categorie, 36, Reliquie, m. 1, not catalogued) is reconstructed in Cozzo, "Linguaggi del sacro," 20–23.
52. Cozzo, "Antichi santi, politica e diplomazia," 443–44.
53. Cozzo, "Linguaggi del sacro," 22–23.
54. "Corpo di San Benedetto (d'Aniane?) donato a Carlo Alberto e il 29 marzo 1910 traslato in un loculo del sotterraneo della metropolitana di Torino," in Archivio Centrale dello Stato (henceforth ACS), Real Casa, SS. Sudario, b. 43, fasc. 3, Rome.
55. "Saint Benoit sauvé par un genevois en 1793," *Bulletin de l'histoire du Protestantisme français* 12 (1863): 459–64.
56. Ibid., 461.
57. "Atto di aprimento e chiudimento della camera dei sotterranei della metropolitana per corpi degni di rispetto e venerazione," ACS, Real Casa, SS. Sudario, b. 43, fasc. 3, 1 March 1841.
58. Paolo Cozzo, "Savoia, Ludovica di, beata," in *Dizionario biografico degli Italiani*, vol. 91 (Rome: Istituto dell'Enciclopedia Italiana, 2018), 55–57.
59. "Atto di ricognizione di un corpo detto di San Benedetto," ACS, Real Casa, SS. Sudario, b. 43, fasc. 3, 1 March 1841.
60. Ibid., 10 July 1884.
61. On Vincenzo Promis and father Domenico Casimiro see the entries by Frédéric Ieva and Paolo Buffo, *Dizionario Biografico degli Italiani*, vol. 85 (Rome: Istituto dell'Enciclopedia Italiana, 2016).

62. "San Benedetto, Promis," ACS, Real Casa, SS. Sudario, b. 43, fasc. 3, letter of 17 March 1882.
63. "Letter by François Chamard," ibid., 6 March 1882.
64. Giancarlo Andenna and Cinzia Bonetti, eds., *Benedetto di Aniane: vita e riforma monastica* (Cinisello Balsamo: Edizioni Paoline, 1993).
65. "Verbale di consegna del corpo attribuito a san Benedetto esistente nei sotterranei della cattedrale di Torino," ACS, Real Casa, S. Sudario, b. 43, fasc. 3, 29 March 1910.
66. "Lettera del ministro della Real Casa," ibid.
67. Pierangelo Gentile, "Morte e apoteosi. Regolare i destini politici della nazione da Carlo Alberto a Umberto I," in *Regolare la politica. Norme, liturgie e rappresentazioni del potere fra tardoantico ed età contemporanea*, ed. Paolo Cozzo and Franco Motta (Rome: Viella, 2016), 273–92.
68. Pierangelo Gentile, *L'ombra del re. Vittorio Emanuele II e le politiche di corte* (Turin: Istituto per la storia del Risorgimento italiano, 2011), 53–76.
69. Andrea Merlotti and Paola Bianchi, *Storia deli Stati sabaudi (1416–1848)* (Brescia: Morcelliana, 2017), 52–53.
70. ACS, Real Casa, SS. Sudario, busta 4, fasc. 8.
71. In the second half of the nineteenth century two ostensions were celebrated solemnly, in 1868 and 1898. See Andrea Merlotti, "The Holy Shroud between the Court of Savoy and the City of Turin: The Ostensions in Seventeenth and Nineteenth Centuries (1630–1831)," in *The Shroud at Court. History, Usages, Places and Images of a Dynastic Relic*, ed. Paolo Cozzo, Andrea Merlotti and Andrea Nicolotti (Leiden: Brill, 2019), 124–66, in particular 165.
72. The high chaplain Valerio Anzino argued for his request by recalling how the sword "which, with little respect for the religious tradition of the Royal House of Savoy and due to the sole doubt that emerged on its authenticity, was moved among the objects of the Royal Armory, while due to the religious worship that it inspired over the centuries, and to the reference made in the authentications to the precious relic, it was transported in 1591 to Valais, and due to the use that the Dukes of Savoy made of it in the sacred functions of feudal institutions, it is a sacred object that must conveniently be preserved among the sacred precious relics of the chapel." See "Lettera del cappellano maggiore Anzino al ministro della Real Casa," ACS, Real Casa, SS. Sudario, b. 4, fasc. 8, 4 January 1891.
73. "Lettera del direttore della Reale Armeria al Ministro della Real Casa," ACS, Real Casa, SS. Sudario, b. 4, fasc. 8, 10 January 1891.
74. Vanni Candido Abele, *Giordano Bruno, martire della libertà del pensiero: sua vita dedicata al popolo* (Foligno: Cooperativa, 1891).
75. Pomi, "Il viaggio dei corpi santi," 118–19.
76. Julia, "Reliques," 297.

5 Jewish Intellectuals and the "Martyrdom" of Simon of Trent in Habsburg Restoration Italy

Anti-Semitism, Relics and Historical Criticism

Emanuele D'Antonio

The Legend of Simon of Trent: Jewish Responses in Habsburg Italy

In the age of the Restoration, Italian Jewry, which was in the process of gaining emancipation, witnessed with concern the revival of the cultural legitimacy of blood libel. A product of medieval theology, the stereotype of ritual murder derived from a negative anthropology of Judaism that projected onto the Jewish collective an image of mortal danger.[1] The Jews purportedly took part in (imaginary) religious rites in which young Christians were killed in an imitation of the Passion of Christ so that their blood could be used during the Passover feast. The diffusion of this anti-Semitic canard had in the past led to the ostracising and even to the destruction of Jewish groups under accusation.[2] Its re-emergence in the nineteenth century had its roots in the church's aversion to secular modernity, which disrupted the political and religious order of Christian society. This intransigent view of Jews, symbol of a secularisation that was liberating them from discrimination, became inflamed with hostility in the second half of the eighteenth century and throughout the nineteenth.[3] Catholic anti-Semitism, grounded in the stereotypes of Christian theology, was summed up in the capital charge of ritual murder.[4] Up to the age of Italian unification, the spread of this myth had direct repercussions on Italian Jewry, undermining its prospects and security. The propaganda against emancipation on the one hand used it as a weapon in the struggle against including a "dangerous" group within the political community.[5] On the other hand, in some local communities Jews were accused of monstrous crimes, and this led to unrest and, in extreme cases, assaults on the former ghettoes.[6]

The revival of the blood libel in Restoration Italy gained momentum in part from renewed interest in the legend of the "martyrdom" of Simon of Trent and the episode that had generated it. The Trent affair of 1475[7] ended with a judicial sentence against the accused Jews and the creation of a "saint" who, after initial opposition by the papacy had been overcome, was officially recognised by the church from 1588 until 1965. Over the centuries, the story of the alleged ritual murder retained its renown and authenticity thanks to the church's promotion of the cult connected to it. Relics of the so-called martyr formed the centrepiece of the devotion that was fuelled by the Tridentine church, and also bred the prejudice associated with the devotional, liturgical and ritual apparatus designed to demonstrate that he was both a saint and the cornerstone of Trent's identity. The transformation of the cult into a local phenomenon,[8] while curbing the use of relics, had little impact on the spread of the "martyr" legend. Up to the contemporary age, the main propaganda channel for this was hagiography, both of the popular kind and that of the historical erudition.[9] Nineteenth-century culture transposed the cultural production of the previous century, which had defended the devotion from the criticism of Protestant scholarship intent on freeing Christianity from superstitious beliefs.[10] The case of Trent was reaffirmed as the principal historical and explanatory "precedent" of ritual murder, evidencing, through the procedural acts reintroduced by hagiographers, the modus operandi and motive for the alleged religious criminality of the Jews.

This chapter focuses on the renascence of the legend of Simon's "martyrdom" during the Restoration from a different perspective, namely by examining the responses of the Jews who were close to being emancipated by Habsburg Italy.[11] At several times during the period of Austrian rule, blood libels threatened the "civil tolerance" that underpinned relations between the state, the social majority and the Jewish minority in Lombardy and Veneto. The Jewish world defended itself by securing the political protection of the sovereign power while working to refute the origins of the ritual murder.[12]

In this context the Hebraist Samuel David Luzzatto (also known by the acronym Shadal) and the historian Samuele Romanin, both authoritative intellectuals in Veneto, used the weapons of modern historical-philological critique to attack the pretexts of the Trent affair. The source of their texts was a Jewish recollection of the episode, wholly different to the dominant one, passed down over the centuries by counter-narratives of various literary genres[13] and taken up by the historical-rational apologetics that emerged in the late seventeenth century.[14] The rehabilitation of the Trentine Jews, innocent victims of fanaticism and unscrupulous powers, hinged on exposing the torture that had produced an unreliable legal and historical judgment. Shadal did this by drawing on an ancient Hebrew Jewish source, while Romanin built an argument by scrutinising the procedural acts used in the episode and, since these had previously been the exclusive preserve of the hagiographers, he therefore completed a pioneering exercise in critical historiography. The two thinkers'

rebuttals bolstered the defences of the Jewish world but, to avoid suc-
cumbing to the pressures of censorship and Catholic antagonism,[15] they
were not made public in Italy. This analysis will nonetheless place them in
the contexts in which they were generated and will illustrate their defence
strategies. The focus on the theme of relics—which in itself is foreign to
Judaism—sets a premise from which the anti-Jewish function of Simon's
remains could be inferred.

Simon of Trent and His Relics in Religious and Civil Life

The Trent affair exploded in the capital of the Prince-Bishopric led by
Johannes Hinderbach, during Easter 1475,[16] after the ground had been
prepared by the Lenten sermons of the Franciscan Bernardino da Feltre,
which had given rise to a climate of extreme anti-Jewish hostility. The
accusation of ritual murder spread after the death of Simon, an infant
of 29 months, whose body was found in the cellar of a Jew. After their
arrest, the Jews capitulated in court: torture forced them to confess to
the alleged crime, which was portrayed as a ritual murder. The subsequent cult of the "martyr," fuelled by popular emotion and prejudice
and encouraged by ecclesiastical authorities, was born in this setting.[17]
However, after the first executions the pope intervened at the behest of
other Jewish communities, calling into question the powers of Trent and
of the new "saint." After suspending the trials and banning the cult, Sixtus IV sent commissioner Battista de' Giudici to the city who, persuaded
that there was no case to answer, ordered the matter closed. However, the
bishop-prince regained the initiative by means of propaganda, political
pressure and diplomacy which, while failing to bring about the child's
canonisation, nevertheless enabled the resumption of trials. The Jewish
settlement was destroyed by a new wave of death sentences, expulsions
and forced conversions; Jews were thereupon banished from Trent until
the annexation of the Prince-Bishopric by Austria in 1803.[18]

The cult of Simon revolved around his relics—the body and the imple-
ments used to "martyr" him—which were kept in the parish Church of
Saints Peter and Paul.[19] At first the remains attracted crowds of believers
and pilgrims who sparked off a fanatical veneration that had miracle-
working as its goal.[20] From then on the "saint" became the protector of
the health of children and nursing mothers as well as a symbol of Trentine identity, a ubiquitous presence in the architecture and iconography
of the territory.[21] Being in harmony with the Counter-Reformation, the
cult was energised when granted "equivalent beatification" by Sixtus V
in 1588.[22] Simon's nomination as co-patron of the city and diocese was
reflected in the establishment of a collective ritual of citizenship based
on the public use of relics. From 1589 the Tridentine church celebrated
the annual feast—originally on 24 March, and from 1780 the third and

then the fourth Sunday of Easter—alongside a solemn and magnificent procession during which the "people," gathered around Simon's remains, paraded them through the city streets.[23] This practice was suppressed in the Napoleonic age, but the ecclesiastic institutions negotiated its reinstitution under the Austrian authorities. In 1816 the Confraternity of Saint Simon, now part of the Parish of Saint Peter,[24] resumed organising the procession, the frequency of which, before becoming decennial from 1875, changed several times.[25]

The cult of Simon, having been integrated into the anti-modern orientation of the Restoration church,[26] updated the anti-Jewish story origin. The adoration of the relics took place in the chapel devoted to the "martyr" in the Church of Saint Peter, which had been expanded and made brighter and more solemn by seventeenth-century refurbishments.[27] Visitors came to implore the saint for spiritual and earthly favours,[28] to take part in the confraternity's rituals or, in the case of foreigners, to satisfy touristic curiosity.[29] Visits to the "place of memory" of the "martyr"[30] did not leave them unmoved. It was difficult to see the infant's body since it was somewhat hidden by the urn and by the railing in front of the altar, but the story of his death was retold by iconography and information panels in the chapel. The pictorial cycle on the walls and the vault described Simon's "passion," which ended in triumph over the treacherous and superstitious Jews who had feasted on his blood. The gory scene

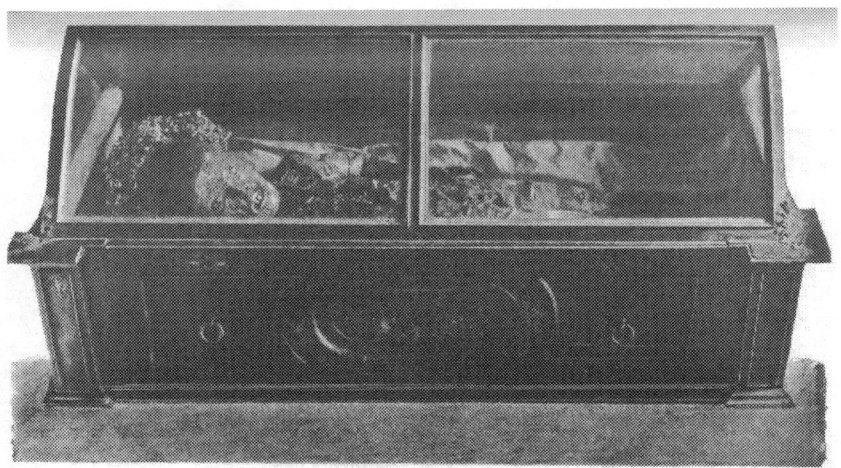

Figure 5.1 "Body of the blessed Simon preserved in a small urn," in *Storia del Beato Simone da Trento, compilata sui processi autentici istituiti contro gli ebrei e sopra altri documenti contemporanei,* ed. Giuseppe Divina, II (Trent: Artigianelli, 1902).

of "martyrdom," not on the canvasses, was depicted instead by other decorative elements and recounted in devotional leaflets.[31] Thus the visitors' feelings of anti-Jewish hostility and indignation were fomented, and their prejudices reproduced.

During the patronal festival, the church renewed the identity bond between the local community and Simon by promoting a collective legitimisation of the ritual murder story. This moveable event was advertised by pamphlets and popular calendars,[32] and during the triduum of adoration the people of Trent crowded into the Church of Saint Peter and huddled around the "little body" (*corpicciuolo*) clearly visible in the silver ark of the solemnity.[33] The anti-Jewish significance of the feast was made clear by the ceremonial of the "saint's" day. The priest officiating at the mass entrusted Trent to the co-patron, commemorating his "bitter death" that was followed by the bloody banquet of the Jews.[34] The procession, more sober than in the past, was well attended. The citizenry, assembled around the arks containing the relics, proceeded through the city space to the Palazzo Salvadori where they commemorated Simon in the place of his "martyrdom."[35] Depictions of the ritual murder were included among the iconography traditionally exhibited by the procession,[36] and echoes of the ceremony, conducted in profound solemnity, reverberated outside the city. In 1863 Simon's body, adored and carried in a procession, was part of the celebrations of the third centenary of the closing of the Council of Trent.[37] The press of the intransigent wing of the church, which paid some attention to the event, accentuated the anti-Semitic tone of the anti-modern propaganda.[38]

As well as being a wellspring of prejudice, the cult of Simon was also a danger to the safety of the Jews in Habsburg Italy.[39] The dominant cultures of the peninsula were familiar with the icon of the martyred body, which had been disseminated by long-established propaganda that entrenched—with or without the cult—the legend of the "martyrdom" outside Trent and sometimes also encouraged foreigners to show their devotion to him. The anti-Semitic potential of the myth is exemplified by a blood libel that provoked anti-Jewish unrest in Mantua in 1824.[40] The fuse was the discovery of a lacerated and bleeding girl near a property under Jewish ownership; the girl's body resembled that of the "martyr," in that both had been subjected to "innumerable stabbings [. . .] as if done by a needle,"[41] a factor which, taking advantage of a detail well-known to many Catholics,[42] proved persuasive. The cult of Simon, in part because of the presence of minor relics,[43] was widely known among the churches in and around Mantua, and, despite the fact that adoration of him had probably come to an end, paintings of his pitiful body still loomed over the faithful from church walls.[44] Hence disproving the story of ritual murder became, from a Jewish point of view, a task of considerable political and cultural importance.

Shadal and His Counter-Narrative of the "Martyrdom" (1840)

In September 1840 Samuel David Luzzatto wrote a work entitled *Intorno a San Simonin da Trento* published in German in the *Israelitische Annalen*.[45] Luzzatto, or Shadal, was born in Trieste in 1800 and died in Padua in 1865. He was professor at the Paduan Rabbinical College, a well-known Hebraist linked to the *Wissenschaft des Judenthums*, the European Jewish movement which, by means of scholarship and historical-philological criticism, promoted the rediscovery of the religious and historical-cultural heritage of Judaism.[46] His text emerged in the context of Jewish responses to the epochal crisis caused by the Damascus affair, when the purported ritual murder of a Sardinian Capuchin in the Syrian city triggered a political and diplomatic clash between European powers that caught the attention of the international press.[47] The resounding echoes of opinion about the Damascus incident, despite the fact that the defendants were acquitted, embedded the conception of blood libel in European culture.

Luzzatto's work was published just after the Syrian Jews were set free. With thanksgiving to God and the sovereigns and men of every faith who had worked to bring about that end, Shadal celebrated the universal triumph of "truth," noting that the only nation to oppose it had been Italy, still enraptured by the "public, solemn, pompous cult of lies." During the "feast of Saint Simon [San Simonin]" Trent commemorated an infant supposedly "martyred" by the Jews, at which time the "people" listened to the story in a church and filed out in a "great procession" into a city studded with artistic impressions of him, "monuments of infamy against the slandered wretches." After raising the idea of suppressing the festival in the name of tolerance, Luzzatto set about refuting the story of ritual murder that had brought it about in the first place. In the past months, the European press that supported the anti-Jewish cause—not that of Habsburg Italy, which sided with Austria in supporting the Syrian Jews' innocence[48]—had referred back to the case of Simon, considering it to be a "precedent" of the Damascus case.[49]

Luzzatto used the oldest Jewish counter-narrative of the case of Trent then known to challenge the story of Simon's "martyrdom." His target was the propagandist pamphlet, contemporary with the events in question, produced by Giovanni Mattia Tiberino[50] and widely accepted by the historical-erudite hagiography of the Counter-Reformation.[51] Historical-philological criticism proved it to be a malevolent falsehood. According to Tiberino, while killing the infant the Jews had recited an anti-Christian curse in Hebrew, but the formula, which in fact did not exist in Hebrew, was an invention aimed at "inspiring a horror of Jews." Moreover, the history of the "martyrdom," later legitimised by the church, had been rejected by authoritative Christians, contemporaries of Tiberino. Doge Pietro Mocenigo, for instance, had referred to it as malicious hearsay in an official document.[52] Having cleared the field of hostile sources, Shadal gave the word to the Franco-Piedmontese historian Yosef ha-Cohen, who had written on the subject in the then unpublished *Valley of Tears (Éméq ha-bacha,* 1558).[53] His narrative commemorated the "martyrdom" of the innocent Jews, giving voice to a conspiratorial interpretation of the case that was widespread in the Jewish world.[54] According to this, the "bishop" was the culprit, having been intent on enriching himself by confiscating the assets of the executed Jews and the proceeds of the new cult. The man hired to kill Simon, "evil Enzo," had ensured that the guilt fell on the Jews, whose brutal torture forced them to confess to a crime they had never committed. The pontifical commissioner investigating the case had uncovered the truth when "evil Enzo's" servant confessed the episcopal plot to him and the pope, thus halting Simon's canonisation. Resuming the narrative, Shadal celebrated the universalism of Jewish morality, a fount of benevolence to men of all faiths.

Although saying nothing about relics, Luzzatto's work did make reference to Simon's body. In the counter-narrative, ha-Cohen had insisted that this was a vital element of the investigation, explaining how the papal commissioner had seen behind the bishop's plot in part because he had been prevented from examining the body, which had been embalmed prematurely. The historian appears to give an inaccurate account of an incident that had taken place between the two ecclesiastics, the first act of their dispute.[55] In Trent, de' Giudici had gone to inspect the relic, but it had been left exposed without protection on an altar of the Church of Saint Peter. In consequence its "stench" had made him unwell, forcing him to go outside. The Dominican, horrified by the decomposing corpse, suggested that Hinderbach put it back in "a box." The inspection, however, had convinced him that the miracles which the bishop's entourage had bragged about were in fact non-existent: the "many sick people" who had pleaded for "the grace of health" had remained unsatisfied. The body of Simon, Shadal stated through ha-Cohen, had perhaps been a clue that could have exonerated the Jews; however, fate had united them as sacrificial victims of the unscrupulous episcopal plot.

Luzzatto's work produced echoes in European Jewish apologetics,[56] and also a revealing episode about the impact of the Damascus affair on Italian Catholic culture.[57] In 1843 the author sent the work to Alessandro Manzoni, asking him to speak out against blood libel.[58] In Habsburg Italy, ritual murder was a live and dangerous superstition that still led to "accusations against the Jews" of "child abduction." The authorities had unmasked the "fraud," but it was necessary to prevent new ones. Given that the Jews themselves were powerless, "authoritative Christians" ought to eradicate the sources of prejudice. The reconstruction of the Trent trials, for example, had overturned a guilty verdict extorted from the Jews by torture, and Shadal therefore hoped that he could count on the solidarity of the man of letters, the critic of the superstition of the artificial plague in his celebrated *Storia della Colonna infame* (*History of the Infamous Column*, 1840/42).[59] His telling of the trial held in Milan in 1631 had brought justice to the memory of the so-called *untori* (infectors) accused of deliberately spreading the plague, by delegitimising the judicial "truth" obtained through torture. Far from demonstrating the truth of crimes, torture nullified defendants, leaving them open to the "passions" of magistrates. However, Manzoni, uncertain about the "reality" or otherwise of ritual murder, did not respond to the appeal.[60]

Romanin and His Critical Reconstruction of the Trent Affair (1856)

In March 1856, Samuele Romanin handed over an unpublished memoir on the Trent case to the leaders of the Jewish community of Venice.[61] Romanin, who was born in Trieste in 1808, and died in Venice in 1861, was a famous historian who had written a *Storia documentata di Venezia* (*Documented History of Venice*, 1853–61) that had given new impetus to studies on the centuries-old story of the *Serenissima*.[62] His work concerned the Jewish response to a case of blood libel in Badia, which had led to the arrest of a Jewish citizen and to fresh anti-Jewish agitation in Habsburg Italy. Once the crisis had passed, the Jewish communities of Lombardy and Veneto promoted a pamphlet aimed at neutralising the prejudice of the dominant cultures, the rebuttal was to take the form of an account of the trial against the promoter of the blood libel, alongside a number of apologetic texts.[63] In the preparatory phase of the project the chief rabbi of Venice, Abraham Lattes, sharing the hope expressed by his teacher and mutual acquaintance Shadal,[64] commissioned Romanin to write a study that rehabilitated the Trentine Jews on the basis of sources found *in loco*.[65] The historian accepted the assignment, but declared himself against a public presentation of his research and also pessimistic about the possibility of producing new research on the subject. On the one hand, the Catholics would oppose any critique of Simon's sainthood. On the other, the transfer to Vienna and Innsbruck of the archives of the Prince-Bishopric[66] made it unlikely that there would be any useful documentation in Trent.

But Romanin's mission turned out to be more worthwhile than he had expected. In the nine days he spent in Trent, made warmly welcome by the local liberal intelligentsia,[67] he was in fact able to access the documentation he was interested in. Since the ecclesiastical archives had been broken up, his research concentrated on the new municipal library, whose director, Tommaso Gar, himself a renowned historian and anti-clerical critic of the ritual murder myth, enabled him to make an important discovery.[68] The collection left to the library by the magistrate Antonio

Mazzetti included an unknown seventeenth-century manuscript, which reproduced the declarations of six defendants of the "great trial."[69] As the first Jewish intellectual to see these records, albeit a late partial copy, the Venetian made a documentary criticism of them with a view to calling into question the historical-hagiographic narratives of Simon's "martyrdom." His main target was Benedetto Bonelli, an author apparently unknown to him, who had written—anonymously—an influential *Dissertazione apologetica* (1747).[70] A local Franciscan friar, Bonelli had defended Simon's sainthood from the rebuttal of the blood libel made by the Protestant scholars Johann-Christoph Wagenseil (1705) and Jacques Basnage (1706–1707),[71] reaffirming the ritual murder story by citing a substantial and at first sight authoritative documentary corpus, in keeping with the historical approach pioneered by Lodovico Antonio Muratori. In the first half of the nineteenth century Italian historians, having learned of Bonelli's text even through other hagiographers,[72] had given credence to his version of the case.[73] The Venetian, however, focused his examination on whether the trial had adhered to procedure, and found evidence of some interpretative distortions.

In his treatise, Romanin presented ample evidence in support of the innocence of the Trentine Jews. By means of a summary examination of the manuscript he was able to show, in disagreement with the *Dissertazione*, discrepancies in the confessions and irregularities in the trial process. Broken by torture, the defendants had initially given incompatible details about the infanticide, which were then brought into line by dint of further "horrendous torture." The interrogations had been made with "suggestive questions" and included "confessed answers," a practice prohibited in medieval jurisprudence.[74]

The Venetian then attacked what he considered the main witnesses who testified against the men. The first accuser to emerge from within the Jewish group was supposedly "Bolframo,"[75] a painter from Saxony who had converted to Christianity during the first part of the trial.[76] Discrediting him as a "thief" and "opportunist," Romanin considered his confessions to be contradictory and far-fetched. "Bolframo" had, among other things, declared himself a witness to the purchase of a boy to be vampirised in Brescia or Padua, a participant in a plot to poison Hinderbach and a custodian of the knowledge of the healthy virtues of human flesh. The Jews of Trent had been found guilty on the basis of a "story [that] lacked no extraordinary thing" and which could be understood only with the aid of superstition.

In his treatise, Romanin referred to the relics of Simon in a seminal historical-critical reconstruction of the Trent affair. The "highly important information" provided in the *Dissertazione* led him to identify the instigator as Bernardino da Feltre, who had been determined to break the "familiarity" between Christians and Jews.[77] Persuaded by the fanatical friar, the authorities in Trent had gone along with the "infamous

Figure 5.2 Augusto Benvenuti, *Bust of Samuele Romanin* (1896), part of the "Venetian Pantheon" of the Istituto Veneto di Scienze, Lettere ed Arti.

slander." Their conduct also revealed their "eagerness" to give the city "a saint to be proposed for the worship of the believers [in] great crowds." Hinderbach had sought the canonisation of the child, attempting to overcome papal opposition by forging alliances with political and religious third parties. His propaganda strategy, as documented by an eighteenth-century historical-ecclesiastical compendium,[78] called for the "gift [of]

relics." Fragments of Simon's body would reassure the Franciscan network of the "truth of the [martyrdom] and of the continuous miracles,"
and, in return, they would guarantee that the story would be a subject of
their sermons. In propounding this interpretation,[79] the Venetian appears
to restate on a new basis the traditional accusation of immorality levelled
at the prince-bishop by Jewish memorialism: Hinderbach's unscrupu-
lousness was demonstrated by his willingness to trade in the remains of a
child dead in tragic circumstances.

Romanin did not go to see the relics of Simon in the Church of Saint
Peter since an empirical observation of the corpse would not have provided any evidence in defence of the Jews. In 1705 Wagenseil had shed
doubt on the atrocious dynamics of the infanticide, as told by the hagiographers, on the basis of an inspection of the body,[80] but Bonelli had
countered by saying that the mummification of the body was so advanced
as to make the wounds and some of the organs indistinguishable.[81] The
Venetian was glad to spare himself the inspection, which would have
caused him great discomfort. The symbols of Simon strewn across the
city depressed him, as did a visit to the site of the "martyrdom" with
the abbot Giovanni a Prato. In Palazzo Salvadori the artistic impressions
of the "execrable action," despite the proximity of his host, oppressed
him, arousing in him a sense of "horror" and "very painful memories."
For Romanin, as for Shadal, the iconography constituted "monuments of
infamy," which, by encouraging a hostile memory, humiliated Jewry and
obstructed the path to tolerance. The relics, which dominated the public
space during the procession, fulfilled the same function, that of "keeping
alive in the people the memory of the event and thus animosity towards
the Jews."

Romanin's treatise was circulated among the leaders of the Jewish
communities of Lombardy-Veneto, influencing their decisions in respect
of the publication of the apologetic pamphlet. In his conclusions, the historian had hoped that its impact on the dominant cultures would be maximised, and the clamour provoked by the trial of the person behind the
Badia affair promised him a vast audience. The refutation of the blood
libel, disseminated in a "popular" format by a newspaper, could include
a "brief but juicy" documentary appendix to the judicial proceedings. In
that context, the treatise on the Trent affair, by virtue of its attack on the
"belief [. . .] unfortunately religious of the supposed Saint," would be
counterproductive. The church had resorted to censorship, and the work,
as long as it remained in circulation, would be rejected by the Catholics.
The Jewish leaders of the area agreed with his reasoning, acknowledg-
ing that the most effective strategy for overcoming prejudice entailed the
least possible conflict with the majority cultures. The apologetic offered
by the pamphlet put on record a generic account of the unreliability
of the judicial sentences based on the torture of the accused Jews. The
ritual murder was rejected on the basis of Christian sources, and the

contrast between the Talmudic-biblical norms and the nature of superstitious belief was highlighted. Despite the silence that fell on his research, however, Romanin had foreseen the critical historiography which, at the end of the century, would reopen the discussion on the truth behind the "martyrdom" of Simon of Trent.[82]

Notes

1. Furio Jesi, *L'accusa del sangue: la macchina mitologica antisemita*, introd. David Bidussa (Turin: Bollati Boringhieri, 2007).
2. Ruggero Taradel, *L'accusa del sangue. Storia politica di un mito antisemita* (Rome: Editori Riuniti, 2008).
3. Giovanni Miccoli, "Santa Sede, questione ebraica e antisemitismo tra Otto e Novecento," in *Gli ebrei in Italia. Storia d'Italia. Annali*, ed. Corrado Vivanti, vol. 11, no. 2 (Turin: Einaudi, 1997), 1369–574.
4. David I. Kertzer, *Il papi contro gli ebrei. Il ruolo del Vaticano nell'ascesa dell'antisemitismo moderno* (Milan: Rizzoli, 2001); Marina Caffiero, "Alle origini dell'antisemitismo politico. L'accusa di omicidio rituale nel Sei-Settecento tra autodifesa degli ebrei e pronunciamenti papali," in *Les racines chrétiennes de l'antisèmitisme politique (fin XIXe–XXe siècle)*, ed. Catherine Brice and Giovanni Miccoli (Rome: École française de Rome, 2003), 25–59; Marina Caffiero, *Battesimi forzati. Storie di ebrei, cristiani e convertiti nella Roma dei papi* (Rome: Viella, 2004), 43–60.
5. Gadi Luzzatto Voghera, *Il prezzo dell'eguaglianza. Il dibattito sull'emancipazione degli ebrei in Italia (1781–1848)* (Milan: Franco Angeli, 1998), 70–77.
6. Attilio Milano, *Storia degli ebrei in Italia* (Turin: Einaudi, 1963), 606; Simon Levis Sullam, "I critici e i nemici dell'emancipazione degli ebrei," in *Storia della Shoah in Italia. Vicende, memorie, rappresentazioni*, vol. 1, ed. Marcello Flores, Simon Levis Sullam, Marie-Anne Matard-Bonucci and Enzo Traverso (Turin: Utet, 2010), 47.
7. See Anna Esposito and Diego Quaglioni, eds., *Processi contro gli ebrei di Trento (1475–1478)*, vol. 1, *I processi del 1475*, vol. 2 (Padua: Cedam, 1990), *I processi alle donne (1475–1476)* (Padua: Cedam, 2008); Ronnie Po-Chia Hsia, *Trent 1475: Stories of a Ritual Murder Trial* (New Haven, CT: Yale University Press, 1992).
8. Anna Esposito, "Il culto del "beato" Simone e la sua prima diffusione in Italia," in *Il principe vescovo Johannes Hinderbach (1465–1486) fra tardo Medioevo e Umanesimo*, ed. Iginio Rogger and Marco Bellabarba (Bologna: EDB, 1986), 442.
9. Tommaso Caliò, *La leggenda dell'ebreo assassino. Percorsi di un mito anti-ebraico dal Medioevo a oggi* (Rome: Viella, 2007).
10. Nicola Cusumano, *Ebrei e accusa di omicidio rituale nel Settecento. Il carteggio tra Girolamo Tartarotti e Benedetto Bonelli (1740–1748)* (Milan: Unicopli, 2012).
11. On this, see Marino Berengo, "Gli ebrei nell'Italia asburgica nell'età della restaurazione," *Italia. Studi e ricerche sulla storia, la cultura e la letteratura degli ebrei d'Italia* 6 (1987): 62–103; Gabriella Cecchetto, "Gli ebrei a Venezia durante la III dominazione austriaca," *Ateneo Veneto* 13, no. 2 (1975): 83–104; Maurizio Bertolotti, "Introduzione," in Ippolito Nievo, *Drammi Giovanili. Emanuele. Gli ultimi anni di Galileo Galilei*, ed. Bertolotti (Venice: Marsilio, 2005), 9–58.

12. Emanuele D'Antonio, "Jewish Self-Defense Against the Blood Libel in Mid-Nineteenth Century Italy: The Badia Affair and the proceedings of the Castilliero Trial (1855–56)," *Quest. Issues in Contemporary Jewish History* 14 (2018): 23–47. On the "vertical alliance" with the sovereign power, see Yoseph Hayim Yerushalmi, '«*Servitori di re e non servitori di servitori'. Alcuni aspetti della storia politica degli ebrei* (Florence: Giuntina, 2013).

13. Emanuela Trevisan Semi, "Gli *Haruge Trient* (Gli assassinati di Trento) e lo *Herem* di Trento nella tradizione ebraica," in *Il principe vescovo Johannes Hinderbach*, ed. Iginio Rogger and Marco Bellabarba (Bologna: EDB, 1992), 407–16; Magda Teter, *Blood Libel: On the Trail of an Antisemitic Myth* (Cambridge, MA: Harvard University Press, forthcoming).

14. Cristiana Facchini, *Infamanti dicerie. La prima autodifesa ebraica dall'accusa del sangue* (Bologna: EDB, 2013).

15. On the Jewish approach to public opinion, see Luzzatto Voghera, *Il prezzo dell'eguaglianza*, 96; Piero Brunello, *Colpi di scena. La Rivoluzione del Quarantotto a Venezia* (Sommacampagna: Cierre, 2018), 191–92 and 412.

16. Esposito and Quaglioni, eds., *Processi contro gli ebrei*; Po-Chia Hsia, *Trent 1475*.

17. Esposito, "Il culto del 'beato' Simone," 429–30.

18. Trevisan Semi, "Gli *Haruge Trient*," 415.

19. Diego Quaglioni, "Il procedimento inquisitorio contro gli ebrei," in *Processi contro gli ebrei*, Esposito and Quaglioni, 33–34. See also Giuseppe Sava, *La chiesa di San Pietro in Trento* (Trent: Vita trentina, 2004).

20. Esposito, "Il culto del 'beato' Simone," 432–34.

21. Valentina Perini, *Il Simonino. Geografia di un culto inventato (1475–1588)* (Trent: Società di studi trentini di scienze storiche, 2012), 131–79.

22. Caliò, *La leggenda dell'ebreo assassino*, 24–25.

23. William Belli, "Forme della teatralità religiosa," in *Dilettando educa: attori, scene e pubblico nel mondo tridentino prima e dopo il Concilio. Storia e sociologia*, ed. Bruno Sanguanini (Trent: Arca, 1989), 56–60; William Belli, "'L'Adige festante': l'effimero a Trento al tempo dei Madruzzo," in *I Madruzzo e l'Europa. I principi vescovi di Trento tra Papato e Impero*, ed. Laura Dal Prà (Milan: Charta, 1993), 460–61 and 477–79.

24. See [Simone Weber,] *Memorie della Parrocchia di San Pietro* [1970], 47–49, 62–63, t-TCD 204, Biblioteca Comunale, Trent; Morena Bertoldi, ed., *Parrocchia dei Santi Pietro e Paolo. Inventario dell'archivio storico (1548–1947) e degli archivi aggregati (1577–1964)* (Trent: Provincia autonoma di Trento. Servizio beni librari e archivistici, 2000), 291 and 355.

25. Archivio Diocesano Tridentino, Libro B 188/313, 1817; 212/625, 1820; Giuseppe Divina, *Storia del Beato Simone. Compilata sui processi autentici istituiti contro gli ebrei e sopra altri documenti contemporanei*, vol. 2 (Trent: Artigianelli, 1902), 329; Caliò, *La leggenda dell'ebreo assassino*, 200.

26. On the local case Severino Vareschi, "Il nuovo regime della Chiesa di Trento nel secolo XIX," *Studi Trentini di Scienze storiche. Sezione 1* 73 (2004): 297–337.

27. Laura Dal Prà, "L'immagine di Simonino nell'arte trentina dal XV al XVIII secolo," in *Il principe vescovo Johannes Hinderbach (1465–1486) fra tardo Medioevo e Umanesimo*, ed. Iginio Rogger and Marco Bellabarba (Bologna: EDB, 1986), 469–75.

28. Domenica Primerano and Paolo Holzhauser, eds., *Il Calendario della Madonnina del Duomo. Immagini devozionali e testi di preghiera in un documento di religiosità popolare trentina* (Trent: Museo Diocesano Tridentino, 1986), 196.

29. N.P.T., *Guida del viaggiatore per la città e per li dintorni di Trento* (Trent: Monauni, 1837), 40–41; Carlo Perini, *Trento e suoi contorni. Guida del viaggiatore* (Trent: Seiser, 1859), 34.

30. Magda Teter, "The Sandomierz Paintings of Ritual Murder as *Lieux de Mèmoire*," in *Ritual Murder in Russia, Eastern Europe and Beyond: New Histories of an Old Accusation*, ed. Eugene M. Avrutin, Jonathan Deckel-Klein and Robert Weinberg (Bloomington: Indiana University Press, 2017), 253–77.

31. Divina, *Storia del Beato Simone*, 285 and 331; Dal Prà, "L'immagine di Simonino," 475.

32. *Almanacco trentino per l'anno 1843, compilato da Agostino Perini* (Trent: Giuseppe Marietti, 1843), XX–XXI.

33. Pietro Alessandrini, *Memorie urbane 1860–64*, 28 June 1863, ms BCT 1–2401, Biblioteca Comunale, Trent; Divina, *Storia del Beato Simone*, 294–95.

34. Marco Iacovella, "San Simonino da Trento. Un culto locale dall'antisemitismo politico al Concilio Vaticano II," *Rivista di Storia del Cristianesimo* 12 (2015): 383.

35. Divina, *Storia del Beato Simone*, 329. The Salvadori barons, whose palace included a chapel named after the "saint," were *magna pars* of his Confraternity, Archivio della Confraternita di San Simone, 7 b. 3, Parish Church of Saints Peter and Paul, Trent.

36. Dal Prà, "L'immagine di Simonino," 471–72.

37. On the celebration see Emanuele Curzel, "Il concilio e la città di Trento tra XIX e XX secolo," in *Ritornare a Trento. Tracce agostiniane sulle strade del concilio Tridentino*, ed. Stefano Zeni and Chiara Curzel (Bologna: EDB, 2016), 132–33.

38. Giacomo Margotti, *Le consolazioni del nostro Santo padre Pio IX nelle feste celebratesi in Trento dal 20 al 29 di giugno 1863 compiendosi il terzo secolo dopo la chiusura dell'ecumenico Concilio tridentino. Racconto* (Turin: Unione Tipografico-Editoriale, 1863), 59 and 80–81; *Delle feste in Trento commemorative della conclusione del Sacrosanto Concilio Tridentino. Cinque lettere del Canonico C.C.* (Brescia: Venturini, 1863), 19. For a scholarly example, see René François Rohrbacher, *Storia universale della Chiesa cattolica dal principio del mondo fino ai dì nostri. Prima traduzione italiana sopra la terza edizione francese*, vol. 11 (Turin: Giacinto Marietti, 1869), 707.

39. The prejudice had no concrete impact in Trent, which at the time did not have any Jewish residents, Trevisan Semi, "Gli *Haruge Trient*," 415–16.

40. Alessandro Novellini, "'Perseguitar li Ebrei a morte'. I tumulti contro il ghetto di Mantova nella prima metà dell'Ottocento," *Storia in Lombardia*, 22/1 (2002): 75–95.

41. Giovanni Arrivabene, *Compendio cronologico-critico della storia di Mantova dalla sua fondazione ai nostri giorni. A cura di Renato Giusti*, vol. 6 (Mantua: Accademia Virgiliana, 1975), 180.

42. Hillel Kieval, "Antisèmitisme ou savoir sociale? Sur la genèse du procès moderne pour meurtre rituel," *Annales* 49 (1994): 1091–105.

43. Raimondo Callegari, "Il Beato Simonino da Trento: un riconoscimento al Museo Civico di Padova," *Bollettino del Museo Civico di Padova* 81 (1992): 105.

44. Perini, *Il Simonino*, 312–24.

45. S[amuel] D[avid] L[uzzatto], "Nachrichten und Correspondenzen. Padua, 25. Sept.," *Israelitische Annalen* 2 (1840): 353–54. For the Italian text see Samuel David Luzzatto to Isaac Marcus Jost, 25 September 1840, *Epistolario*

italiano francese latino di Samuel David Luzzatto da Trieste pubblicato da' *suoi figli*, 2 vols. (Padua: Salmin, 1890), 380–85.

46. Maddalena Del Bianco Cotrozzi, *Il Collegio rabbinico di Padova (1824– 1871). Un'istituzione italiana sulla strada dell'emancipazione* (Florence: Olschki, 1995), 46–59 and 216–27; Luzzatto Voghera, *Il prezzo dell'eguaglianza*, 158–65; Gadi Luzzatto Voghera, "Samuel David Luzzatto," in *Dizionario biografico degli italiani*, vol. 66 (Rome: Istituto della Enciclopedia Italiana, 2006), 743–47.

47. Jonathan Frankel, *The Damascus Affair: "Ritual Murder", Politics and the Jews in 1840* (Cambridge: Cambridge University Press, 1997).

48. See for example "Inghilterra. Adunanza di banchieri per provveder agli Ebrei di Damasco," *Gazzetta privilegiata di Venezia*, 16 July 1840.

49. Frankel, *The Damascus Affair*, 204.

50. Stephan Bowd, ed., *'On Everyone Lips.' Humanist, Jews, and the Tale of Simon of Trent*. Latin Texts Edited and Translated by J. Donald Culligan (Tempe: Arizona Center for Medieval and Renaissance Studies, 2012), 21–22; Perini, *Il Simonino*, 95–97.

51. Caliò, *La leggenda dell'ebreo assassino*, 26.

52. For Shadal's source, see Isaac Cardoso, *Las excelencias de los Hebreos* (Amsterdam: David De Castro, 1679), 427–28. On this text, see Yoseph Hayim Yerushalmi, *Dalla Corte al ghetto. La vita le opere le peregrinazioni del marrano Cardoso nell'Europa del Seicento* (Milan: Garzanti, 1991), 384–91; Facchini, *Infamanti dicerie*.

53. Trevisan Semi, "Gli *Haruge Trient*," 407 and 41–12. On ha-Cohen see Alain Boyer and Maurice-Ruben Hayoun, *L'historiographie juive* (Paris: PUF, 2001), 33–34.

54. Daniela Rando, *Dai margini la memoria. Johannes Hinderbach (1418–1486)* (Bologna: Il Mulino, 2003), 478–79.

55. Anna Esposito, "La morte di un bambino e la nascita di un martire: Simonino da Trento," in *Bambini santi. Rappresentazioni dell'infanzia e modelli agiografici*, ed. Anna Benvenuti Papi and Elena Giannarelli (Turin: Rosenberg & Sellier, 1990), 107.

56. Lipman Hirsch Löwenstein, *Damascia. Die Judenverfolgung zu Damaskus und ihre Wirkungen auf die öffentliche Meinung, nebst Nachweisungen über die Ursprung der gegen die Juden wiederholten Beschuldigung* (Rödelheim: Lehrberger und Comp., 1840), 337. See Frankel, *The Damascus Affair*, 402–7.

57. Kertzer, *I papi contro gli ebrei*, 94–114; Caliò, *La leggenda dell'ebreo assassino*, 151–52.

58. Samuel David Luzzatto to Alessandro Manzoni, Padua 24 April 1843, *Epistolario italiano francese latino*, 417–20.

59. Paolo Preto, *Epidemia, paura e politica nell'Italia moderna* (Rome-Bari: Laterza, 1987), 105–8.

60. Luzzatto Voghera, *Il prezzo dell'eguaglianza*, 92.

61. Samuele Romanin, "Memoria," 26 March 1856, It Rov 360/7b, Jewish University of Rovigo, Central Archives for the History of the Jewish People, Jerusalem (henceforth CAHJP).

62. Gino Benzoni, "Dal rimpianto alla ricostruzione storiografica," in *Venezia e l'Austria*, ed. Gaetano Cozzi and Gino Benzoni (Venice: Marsilio, 1999), 364–69; Filippo Maria Paladini, "Civilizzazione europea, storia italiana e rigenerazione di Venezia," in *Ateneo Veneto 1812–2012. Un'istituzione per la città*, ed. Michele Gottardi, Marina Niero and Camillo Tonini (Venice: lineadacqua, Ateneo Veneto, 2012), 39–46; Giuseppe Trebbi, "Samuele Romanin," in *Dizionario biografico degli italiani*, vol. 88 (Rome: Istituto della Enciclopedia Italiana, 2017): 441–43.

63. *Processo Giuditta Castilliero. Supplimento al n. 641 dell'Eco dei Tribunali, Sezione prima* (Venice: Tipografia de "L'Eco dei Tribunali", 1856). See D'Antonio, "Jewish Self-Defense Against the Blood Libel."

64. Samuel David Luzzatto to Samuele Romanin, 09 August 1855, *Epistolario italiano francese latino*, 826.

65. Abraham Lattes to Abram Mainster, 19 December 1855, It Rov 360/7b, Jewish University of Rovigo, CAHJP.

66. Frumenzio Ghetta, "Documenti per la storia della Chiesa e del Principato tridentino nell'Archivio di Stato di Trento," in *Fonti per la storia del principato e della chiesa tridentina* (Trent: Provincia autonoma di Trento. Servizio beni librari e archivistici, 1995), 113 and 118.

67. Samuele Romanin to Tommaso Gar, 10 July 1857, Archivio Gar, E9/7, Fondazione per il Museo Storico Trentino, Trent. I thank Doctor Francesca Brunet, who told me about the letter.

68. Samuele Romanin to Tommaso Gar, 15 May 1856, ms BCT 1–2254/36, Biblioteca Comunale, Trent. On Gar and his critique of the Trent case, see Arnaldo Ganda, *Un bibliotecario e archivista moderno. Profilo biobibliografico di Tommaso Gar (1807–1871) con carteggi inediti. Presentazione di Marco Santoro* (Parma: Università degli Studi, 2001); *Annali del Principato ecclesiastico di Trento dal 1022 al 1540, compilati sui documenti da Francesco Felice degli Alberti vescovo e principe, reintegrati e annotati da Tommaso Gar* (Trent: Monauni, 1860), IV, 358 n.

69. Ms BCT 1–1591, Biblioteca Comunale, Trent. I wish to thank Doctor Silvano Groff for the assistance he provided to me.

70. Benedetto Bonelli, *Dissertazione apologetica sul martirio del Beato Simone nell'anno MCCCCLXXV dagli ebrei ucciso* (Trent: Gianbattista Parone, 1747).

71. Caliò, *La leggenda dell'ebreo assassino*, 94–97; Cusumano, *Ebrei e accusa di omicidio rituale*, 42–50.

72. Flaminio Corner, *De Cultu S. Simonis pueri Tridentini Martyris apud Venetos* (Trent: Monauni, 1753). See Caliò, *La leggenda dell'ebreo assassino*, 102; Cusumano, *Ebrei e accusa di omicidio rituale*, 75, 124 and 179.

73. Domenico Maria Federici, *Memorie trivigiane sulla tipografia del secolo XV per servire alla storia letteraria e delle belle arti d'Italia* (Venice: Andreola, 1805), 54, 913 and 187; Francesco Vigilio Barbacovi, *Memorie storiche della città e del territorio di Trento*, vol. 2 (Trent: Monauni, 1824), 77–78; Emmanuele Antonio Cicogna, *Inscrizioni veneziane*, vol. 1 (Venice: Giuseppe Orlandelli, 1824), 89, vol. 4 (Venice: Giuseppe Picotti, 1834), 557; Rawdon Brown, ed., *Itinerario di Marin Sanuto per la Terraferma veneta nell'anno MCCCCLXXXIII* (Padua: Tip. del Seminario, 1847), XLII n. 65; Carlo Perini and Carlo Lurati, *Illustrazione del Tirolo italiano e della Svizzera italiana. Sotto la direzione di Cesare Cantù* (Milan: Corona e Caimi, 1859), 99.

74. Giangiacomo Cresseri, *Ricerche storiche riguardanti l'autorità e la giurisdizione del Magistrato consolare trentino. Riordinate e annotate da Tommaso Gar* (Trent: Monauni, 1858), LXVII–LXVIII.

75. For this theory in the seventeenth-century Jewish historiography, see Heinrich Graetz, *History of the Jews from the Earliest Times to the Present Day. Specially Revised for the English Edition by the Author*, vol. 4 (London: Myers, 1904), 321.

76. On Wolfgang *olim* Israel of Brandenburg, see Po-chia Hsia, *Trent 1475*, 95–104.

77. Bonelli, *Dissertazione apologetica*, 152. For this thesis in Jewish historiography, see Graetz, *History of the Jews*, 320–21.

78. Baldassarre Ippoliti, *Compendium rerum tridentinarum ex Archiviis desumptarum*, ms, BCT 1–16, Biblioteca Comunale, Trent. See also Benedetto

Bonelli, *Monumenta Ecclesiae Tridentinae: voluminis tertii pars altera: in qua continetur Tridentinorum antistitum series universa commentario historico-diplomatico illustrata: accedunt catalogi decanorum, canonicorum, praepositorum* (Trent: Monauni, 1765).

79. For the current interpretation, see Anna Esposito, "Lo stereotipo dell'omicidio rituale," in *Processi contro gli ebrei*, Esposito and Quaglioni, vol. 1, 93.
80. Cusumano, *Ebrei e accusa di omicidio rituale*, 44–48.
81. Bonelli, *Dissertazione apologetica*, 108–9.
82. Iacovella, "San Simonino da Trento," 392–93.

6 Some Observations on the Itinerary of Don Bosco's Relics

Mauro Forno

During the past 90 years the mortal remains of Don Bosco have been the object of significant devotional manifestations and veneration, generally encouraged by the spiritual heirs of the Piedmontese priest who founded the Salesian congregation. Moreover, similar demonstrations have characterised the post-mortem stories of other notable figures of the Christian world and the church, which throughout their history have often shown considerable interest in the bodies of the saints and the beatified.[1]

If, however, the church has generally been inclined to interpret such forms of cult as homage paid to God for his mercy manifested through the life of a saint,[2] these practices have sometimes tended to assume, especially among the faithful, other meanings, thereby making relics, for example, an instrument to acquire the intercession of a saint, or a means by which to access mysterious healing powers, or an object with which to satisfy impulses of a fetishist kind.

For these same reasons, relics have often ended up encouraging the rise of markets of sacred objects, becoming something to sell, buy and even steal, as recently occurred to a piece of Don Bosco's brain matter, which was taken on 2 June 2017 from the lower church of the Basilica of Castelnuovo d'Asti, the saint's birthplace.

And again, for these same reasons, between 2012 and 2015 the Don Bosco urn—a plaster and resin sculpture decorated with the skeleton of the saint's hand—was the protagonist in a lengthy worldwide journey that took in a hundred or so countries and five continents.

This chapter will present a number of reflections on the use which, over the decades, has been made of Don Bosco's mortal remains, concluding with some general considerations.

Don Bosco's Burial in Valsalice

The leaders of the Salesian congregation confronted the problem of where to bury their founder's body even while he was still alive. They had hoped that by addressing the issue well in advance, they would be able to bury his remains in Valdocco, where his work had begun, or at least to avoid placing them in the anonymous city cemetery. Nevertheless, on 31 January 1888—the day of the Piedmontese priest's death—the civil authorities raised concerns about the initial plan given that public health laws forbade the burial of human remains within urban confines.[3]

In the ensuing days two Salesian priests did their best to find a solution: Cesare Cagliero (cousin of the bishop, later cardinal, Giovanni Cagliero), procurator of the Congregation to the Holy See, and Antonio Notario. Both attempted to plead the cause of the Salesians among members of the Royal household and senior members of government.[4] Francesco Crispi, the Prime Minister, took a particular interest, having been helped and hosted by the Salesians during his exile in Turin after the failure of the Sicilian revolution of 1848–49.

While being favourably disposed to the Salesians, in the end Crispi, not wishing to create dangerous precedents for the interpretation of health laws, opted to propose a compromise.[5] According to what can be read in a reconstruction signed by Don Notario, he suggested that Don Bosco's body be buried in Valsalice, the site of the Salesian seminary for foreign missions which was only a few hundred metres from the city limits. Burying him there, Crispi believed, would not require a new law, but merely the local prefect's authorisation.

The Prime Minister's solution seemed reasonable, seeing as on the one hand it ensured that the Salesians would not have to break the law and on the other it offered them a more than honourable way out. Don Bosco would in fact be a little farther from his house but would forever remain in a Salesian institution not far from the centre of Turin, where his followers would be able to honour his memory and nurture the cult.

From a later passage in the account by Don Notario we find other details about this episode, but it is somewhat difficult to evaluate their reliability:

> On 2 February, accompanied by Count Radicati [Talice di Passerano], the former Prefect of Turin, I went to the Prefect Count Lovera of Maria to obtain his signature on the request for internment in Valsalice. [. . .] "Please be so kind as to sign this request, which I presented in the name of Crispi." Having read it, he said drily; "I will not sign it." I was irritated and dared to say, "Excellency, if you do not sign it, tomorrow I will return to Rome and denounce you to Crispi and you will be removed as Prefect." And he in Piedmonese: "Chiel a la bun temp" ["you must have time to waste"]. I repeated the request insistently and he persisted in his refusal: "I will not sign."
>
> Don Cagliero and I went immediately to Crispi, who was very indignant, and quite disdainful, and had Commissioner Paliano called, to whom he said: Order Mayor Voli that Don Bosco be buried in Valsalice, and be quiet about it. Within 48 hours Lovera will no longer be Prefect of Turin. And so it was.[6]

There is no corroborating evidence that would allow a well-founded judgment to be made of this account. We do know, however, that prefect Lovera was not in fact removed, because on 4 February it was he who sent a letter to Cardinal Gaetano Alimonda, the archbishop of Turin, in which he said: "Excellency, I am pleased that the desire expressed by Your Excellency may be satisfied and I hasten to say that today the Decree will be signed, giving permission for the body of the late Don Giovanni Bosco to be buried in the precinct of the College he founded in Valsalice."[7] In the decree he also specified that the only condition was the use of "double coffins," one of which had to be metal.[8]

Therefore, despite the still delicate climate in relations between the state and the church due to the manner and period in which the process of national unification had taken place, at the moment of Don Bosco's passing, the attitude of the Italian government was not at all one of hostility towards the Salesians. And even at the level of public opinion the concession made by the government to a Catholic congregation was not interpreted as a dangerous yielding on the part of civil power to clerical demands.

Moreover, it should be remembered that the Salesians had often shown respect towards the secular authorities, from which they had generally received support for their initiatives, which in many cases were appreciated by people outside the Catholic world. Consider, for example, an atheist scholar like Cesare Lombroso, who in the second edition of his *Lezioni di medicina legale* (*Lessons on Forensic Medicine*), after deploring the state's inaction in the field of prevention and treatment of deviances, pointed to the work of the Salesians as a "colossal and cleverly organised model for preventing crime, in fact the only one to have been developed in Italy."[9]

Officially, Don Bosco's funeral took place on 2 February 1888, in the presence of no fewer than 100,000 people, while—for the reasons described earlier—the burial itself was delayed by two days.[10] It was in fact only on the afternoon of 4 February that the coffin was translated to Valsalice, "in a very private way," as Crispi had suggested. This happened in an atmosphere of raw emotion among the members of the congregation, as can be inferred from the actions of an elderly Salesian priest who, approaching the coffin, shouted "Look, he's being led away from the oratory!" and gave way to "such a burst of tears that he seemed to faint."[11]

The Salesians, however, never considered this move to be the final step. Of course, they did all they could to honour with dignity the remains deposited in that place ("those very stones will speak," Giovanni Cagliero affirmed after the translation ceremony; just as "the early Christians went to draw strength and courage from the tomb of the martyrs, so the brothers will come here from afar to restore their strength and to promise to preserve the spirit of the Congregation"). However, the Salesians also took immediate action to facilitate a resounding homecoming, having realised that the "forced" burial of Don Bosco outside of the city was the very thing that might open the way—once the political conditions and religious status of the body had improved—to a triumphal translation ceremony.

Particularly solemn words were uttered, during the Valsalice burial, by Don Michele Rua, Don Bosco's first successor: "We did not voluntarily give this precious pledge, only necessity forced it from us; but this desire to have him with us at [the Basilica of] Mary Help of Christians and the many efforts made to keep him there will serve to make known to you the value of the deposit."[12] Two days later the director of the Valsalice Institute, Giulio Barberis, together with another 122 Salesian priests and clerics, informed Don Rua that they were "greatly impressed" by the burial ceremony and therefore wished to work hard so that anyone leaving Valsalice could say that the house had become "the sanctuary of our dear congregation."

The promise was duly kept, and the institute soon became, to all effects, a place of worship, not only local, but international as well. Thus, as early as September 1891 a pilgrimage brought to Turin thousands of French Catholic workers, headed by Léon Harmel.[13] The need to cultivate forms of worship capable of giving substance to a reputation for sanctity that in those early stages seemed in some ways to be contested, especially at the level of local religious authorities, was keenly felt by the Salesians. In particular, they showed themselves to be aware that the case for canonisation, for which they straight away began to prepare, might have been compromised by the less than positive relations between Don Bosco and the archbishop of Turin, Lorenzo Gastaldi (1871–83). This very circumstance quickly led them to relate to the memory of their founder in terms of exceptionality, in line with an approach that the Piedmontese priest had been prone to use especially after the foundation in August 1877 of the "*Bollettino Salesiano*" (a free monthly, with a very large print-run and readership, focused on reporting the works created by the congregation).

The First Two Recognitions at the Tomb

On 15 August 1904 Rua sent the mayor of Turin a request for authorisation to carry out "some repair works" to the small crypt in which Don Bosco's remains had been preserved. He specified that in all likelihood some work on the coffin would also be necessary, so that "the human remains of a man so worthy of civil society" would be "preserved in the best state possible."[14] He added that he intended to proceed in a way that was "private and secret, avoiding any kind of publicity," in keeping with an approach that would be adhered to even in later years by the Salesian leadership: that of refraining from any act that might interfere with the

canonical process by attributing to Don Bosco's body supranatural qualities too prematurely, that is, before the acquisition of venerable status.

Two episodes appear to be especially emblematic in this regard: a blind
nun who, having approached the body of Don Bosco on the very day of
his funeral, shouting "I can see, I can see!" was immediately urged by the
Salesians to stay calm and quiet; and the claim of a parish priest from
Sardinia to having been healed of a serious eye disease by the intercession
of Don Bosco was immediately downplayed by Don Rua.[15]

Turning to the recognition of 1904, after having obtained the mayor's
authorisation, on 2 September Don Bosco's tomb was opened up amid
the intense emotions felt by his spiritual heirs.[16] According to the minutes
kept by the doctors, the body was still "fully intact," albeit "the facial
features were hardly recognisable." Clearly visible were "the sunken
eyes, the open mouth, the well-preserved hair, the arms outstretched with
fingers still all joined, the tip of the nose somewhat bent." Afterwards,
the body was chemically treated then covered with a large glass plate and
left to the "pious curiosity" of the priests and lay members in the Salesian
house.[17]

The second opening of the tomb was carried out in 1917, in accordance with the instructions given by the Sacred Congregation of Rites after
the closure of the apostolic process.[18] Once again a written account of the
important procedure is available to us, this time written by the appointed
expert, Pier Luigi Peynetti, from which we can deduce that any kind of
clamour or publicity (one should not forget that this occurred in the
midst of the First World War and on the eve of the "national drama" of
Caporetto) was again avoided.

On this occasion, however, the doctor in charge made, for the first
time, a reference suggestive of transcendence: "Finally, having completely removed the zinc cover, instead of the usual cadaveric stench, we
perceived a *sui generis* and not at all unwelcome perfume."[19] A sweet
effluvium, therefore, which in the Christian tradition of relic cults was
usually associated with the sanctity of the person to whom the remains
belonged.[20]

Exhumation and Canonical Recognition
on the Occasion of Beatification

The third recognition on the body of Don Bosco—that carried out in
May 1929, on the instruction of the Sacred Congregation of Rites at the
time of the Piedmontese priest's beatification—took place in a very different environment.

As already noted, until this time the Salesians had tried hard to avoid
the manifestations of devotion by the faithful going beyond what the
ecclesiastical institution appeared willing to tolerate, or degenerating into fanaticism. Moreover, they had waited for the declaration of

Figure 6.1 The podestà of Turin copies Cardinal Gamba's gesture of piety [and kisses Don Bosco's coffin during the 1929 exhumation] (Archivio Fotografico del *Bollettino Salesiano*, Rome).

"venerability," eventually accorded in July 1907, before publishing in the *Bollettino Salesiano* news about miraculous healings or other graces attributable to Don Bosco's intercession, limiting themselves to news that some of his "prophetic dreams" had come true. They allowed only flowers and candles to be left on the tomb in Valsalice and never other objects, such as candelabra, that might evoke forms of devotion reserved for saints and the blessed;[21] in addition, they kept well away from the sale of devotional objects to which miraculous powers might be attributed.[22]

In 1929, however, at the time of Bosco's "canonical recognition" (and the subsequent translation of his body from Valsalice to Valdocco, an operation anticipated by his devotees for over 40 years), all such constraints came to a dramatic end. What is more, the political climate had changed, as had, more importantly, the religious status of the body. Technological breakthroughs in radio, photography and film also made possible a worthy presentation of the event.

But above all, the Salesians showed themselves to be very attentive and aware of the importance acquired over the previous decades by the masses within political ritualism. They were also able to incorporate and build upon the new interests of the regime—following a post-unification phase in which the practices of celebrating the bodies of the heroes and martyrs of the nation had diminished—in this kind of cult. This allowed

Figure 6.2 Salesian priests of the Valsalice Institute carry the body of Don Bosco (Archivio Fotografico del *Bollettino Salesiano*, Rome).

Figure 6.3 In the main hall waiting for the opening of the Saint's coffin (Archivio Fotografico del *Bollettino Salesiano*, Rome).

them to maximise media interest in the event through an opportune mixture of archaic rites—namely those of the translation, celebration and veneration of the human remains—and a modern expressive sensitivity.

The solemn parade, surrounded by hundreds of thousands of people (and followed by four days of celebrations),[23] took place on 9 June, under the slogan "Don Bosco returns!" Representatives of religious, political, economic, social and cultural life took part: cardinals, bishops, parliamentary deputies, magistrates, the head of the polytechnic, the administrator of studies, the rector of the university, the president of the court of appeal, nobles, military personnel, the vice consul of France and the consuls of Hungary, Spain, Bolivia and Brazil. There was an enormous *festa del popolo* (party of the people), described in these terms by Eugenio Ceria: "The practice of transporting the bodies of saints from place to place with religious pomp is very ancient in the church [. . .]. Two causes always contributed to the grandiose celebration of these rituals: the veneration of the Servants of God and the prodigies taking place on their tombs." "In the case of Don Bosco both of these two causes acted powerfully."[24]

In all, 18 groups marched, interspersed with the same number of musical bands, ensuring not only that the newly blessed priest obtained the honour due to him, but also that Piedmont was showcased in full, since Don Bosco had been its illustrious son and the burgeoning automobile industry, led by Fiat, was now winning international recognition. Additionally, the whole ritual benefited from the new climate established between state and church sanctioned by the signing of the Lateran Pacts, which seemed to herald a brighter future for religious orders and congregations.[25]

However, despite their best efforts, the Salesians were faced with some disappointments in respect of the participation of the regime's leaders. By an unfortunate coincidence the solemn beatification ceremony in Saint Peter's Basilica, scheduled for 2 June 1929 fell right in the middle of the sensitive phases between the signing of the pacts on 11 February and their ratification on 7 June.

On 12 May 1929 Don Filippo Rinaldi, Don Bosco's third successor, wrote to Benito Mussolini to ask for the honour of his presence, which would have been "much appreciated in Italy and abroad" (and to confirm the convinced "closeness" of his congregation).[26] But the very next day the Fascist leader gave a harsh speech to the Chamber of Deputies, in which he strongly evoked the "Catholic" character of the state, but above all its "Fascist" character. Pius XI responded to this provocation a day later by highlighting the fundamental educational role played by the church within the state. On 25 May the Senate debate on the ratification of the Lateran Pacts concluded with discussions and arguments both inside and outside the chamber.

Mussolini's negative response reached the Salesians in the midst of this emotive atmosphere. The rejection was further expressed by the refusal to give Senator Eugenio Rebaudengo the right to say a few words to mark the event in the sitting of 5 June. The same decision was then extended to the President of the Senate Luigi Federzoni and all members of government.[27]

Turning now to the work carried out on the body of the saint, in the event the people admitted to the rite were only 40. But, even though the diocesan daily *Il Momento* felt it necessary to express the hope that the faithful would maintain their enthusiasm ("Catholic Turin must remain patient: the great day will come soon, and when it does the apotheosis will be even more moving and heartfelt"),[28] from the beginning many local and national newspapers unfailingly gave extensive coverage to the new recognition while also documenting the "uninterrupted pilgrimage" of the faithful to Valsalice.

Also interesting was the long and detailed *Cronaca della esumazione* authenticated by the Salesians with the notary Adolfo Baldioli on 8 June 1929.[29] From this chronicle we might deduce, among other things, the deep emotion that struck the three medical experts put in charge, Giovanni Battista Filipello, Luigi Peynetti and Eugenio Rocca. After having sworn the solemn oath and the formula of the rite "may God help me," they noted in their minutes:

> These were sublime moments of emotion and of faith. With a criterion that does not detract from the sacred moment and demonstrates the healthy understanding that the Salesian society has today, in the silence of the function the cameras shutters snap and the gears of the cinematographic machines hum. It will be by virtue of them that the world and posterity will have a precise view of what has been [. . .] described.

The technical work involved analysing the body meticulously, "treating" it to ensure a better preservation, splitting it up to obtain relics. With "utmost diligence" they collected the "the gown, the collar, the cassock dress, the stole," which were then "divided and placed in larger glass containers," while "the soft parts without flesh and bone" were placed "in smaller urns of absolute preservative security."

> Agreeing, in accordance with the desire expressed by the Postulator for the Cause in the name of the Major Chapter of the Pious Society of the Salesians, to see how to preserve as much as possible the mortal remains of the Rev. Servant of God, when asked by Prof. Giorgio Canuto [. . .] we have recommended the continuation of the conservation of the body by wrapping it with a bandage saturated with aromatic colloidal liquid [. . .] so that the trunk, pelvis and thighs might be preserved as a single piece. The other detached pieces were protected with a solution and with alcoholic paint made from lacquer or benzoin rubber.

[. . .] All the soft parts and all the pulverised residues of flesh and bone found and broken up during these operations have been diligently collected and enclosed in a glass jar with a frosted lid labelled with an appropriate plate.[30]

For his part, the general bursar of the Salesians prepared "thousands of little cases" in which to keep all the fragmented relics.[31] The removed parts were: the "seven cervical vertebrae" (in order to guarantee a better "composition of the body in the way established, with the waxwork face and the head placed on the chest");[32] the second and fourth right-side ribs (allocated for the "adoration of His Holiness Pope Pius XI and the Most Eminent Cardinals of the Curia"), and the first, fifth and sixth vertebrae (allocated to "the Congregation"), the third, seventh and eighth (left "free in packages"). As for the left ribs, the first was set aside to be sent "to Rome," the second, fifth and sixth were retained for the "Congregation," while the third and fourth were placed in a special "package." Fragments of "flesh" ("pulverised muscles and soft parts") were also removed.[33] The archbishop of Turin, Giuseppe Gamba, the parishes of the dioceses and the Salesian houses spread throughout the world received "the right clavicle," "the two kneecaps and as a *Reliquia insigne* the ulna cubitus of the right arm." The higher rector was given "two sealed ampoules containing ex-flesh and ex-bone fragments, a third ampoule containing the tongue, a fourth ampoule containing the right mummified lung, and a fifth containing the cartilages of the thyroid and larynx."

Great care was given to the preparation of the wax face mask. In particular, the sculptor in charge, Gaetano Cellini, was asked not to forget that Don Bosco would be venerated mostly by young people who, seeing his face, ought to be left with a "pleasant" impression.

In the meantime, outside the room in which the body was being given these treatments, the aforementioned collective rite was held, later being described in detail by Don Ceria in his *Memorie biografiche di San Giovanni Bosco (Biographical Memories of Saint John Bosco)*. Ceria recalled that from 24 May to 6 June Valsalice was host to "the most beautiful evidence of the attachment of Turin, and not only Turin" to Don Bosco. "The crowd that in these days has filed up to the modest little room on the second floor numbered more than 80,000 people." There were also countless expressions of genuine popular religious feeling:

Exhausted mothers with sick children went up to Valsalice so that Don Bosco might heal them. A blind child asked aloud, "Don Bosco let me see." A deaf-mute child asked for his voice. An unknown mother, sitting in pain, sent a sealed letter. She asked that this be allowed to touch the saint and then immediately destroyed, and her desire was respected. Weeping eyes accompanied trembling lips pleading for grace.

According to Don Ceria, the widespread coverage that the principal newspapers gave the event would not have even been "conceivable a few years earlier." "By the grace of God," the Salesian priest said, the advent of Fascism had "ended the irreligious and anti-religious politics of the past" and the newspapers had readily adapted "to the new situation."[34]

Some "Black Shirts" also honoured the body and,

> having placed a magnificent bouquet of flowers on the lid, filed past kissing the crystal and bringing with them, as a treasured memento, the withered flowers that were piled up here and there in the corners. Then it was the turn of the Piccole Italiane and members of the Balilla, who each passed by many times over.

Knowing that he was saying something that was only partly true, Ceria, referring back to the aforementioned manifestations of popular devotion, ended by observing: "In truth all of that public veneration was a little premature, but nobody had foreseen it, nor could the flow be stopped, so the Promoter of the Faith closed both his eyes to it."[35]

Being under a regime that made elements of celebration and especially those of the people a fundamental aspect of its activity, in June 1929 the Salesians did not therefore let slip the opportunity to glorify the body of their founder with exceptional splendour, at the same time re-emphasising publicly their position within the church and the society of the time.

> After such a spectacular triumph the prophesy made by Renan in *Etudes d'Histoire religieuse* came to mind: "There will be other saints canonised by Rome [. . .] but there will not be any canonised by the people." The pseudo-scientific oracle could not have received a more resounding rebuttal.[36]

From the day after the recognition the Salesians began to receive, from all over the world, urgent requests for relics, to the extent that on 2 June 1929 the general promoter of the faith, Carlo Salotti, found himself forced to authorise Don Rinaldi to "collect" other bones to distribute.[37]

The Canonisation (April 1934)

On 1 April 1934 Don Bosco was proclaimed a saint, an event that was celebrated anew with notable solemnity, particularly in Rome and in Turin, where the procession and display of the urn was held on 8 April.

The political climate, furthermore, appeared to be most favourable, since the controversies that followed the Concordat had died down and the Salesians' role within the state had become even stronger thanks chiefly to their strong presence in the field of education, charity and aid.

The man responsible for the celebrations in Rome was Don Francesco Tomasetti, the congregation's procurator general at the Holy See, who knew that he was working in the context of a consolidated and stabilised Fascism. The celebrations, despite being partially interrupted by rain, drew a huge number of participants. At the ceremony on 1 April the enormous basilica of Saint Peter's could not contain all the faithful. The event was celebrated by 86 bishops and 22 cardinals, demonstrating the full recognition of the Salesian charisma at the level of ecclesiastical hierarchy.

On 3 April around 30,000 members of the congregation had an audience with the pope. Don Bosco's "civil triumph" had been held the day before at the Capitol.[38] In the presence of Mussolini, the governor of Rome, the president of the Senate, the secretary of the Vatican City and another four cardinals, one of the quadrumvirs of the March on Rome and the ambassador of Italy to the Holy See, the Piedmontese Cesare Maria De Vecchi, gave the official oration, in which he attempted to place Don Bosco "within the framework of Fascism," interpreting his life as a historical synthesis of the "Italian Catholic saintliness":[39]

> Don Bosco is an Italian saint [. . .] and the most Italian of saints. An entire nation feels that he is theirs, and nevertheless the great spirit is present in all the world, so that this Italian perfection through him becomes Romanity. His religious glorification has occurred in a form of pomp and solemnity entirely new in the nineteen centuries of the church's history, and Italy has participated as never before. The fullness of divine magisterium today finds its extension in the honours of the Capitol, decreed by the Fascist government to this saint. His sanctity alone would today, for the character that distinguishes it, give him the right to be welcomed in this highest seat, but he would be a great Italian even without the attributes of saintliness; hence his citizenship on the Capitol.[40]

The notable success of the celebrations, the seal of a by now consolidated commonality of objectives between the civil and religious sphere, were indirectly mentioned a few weeks later by King Victor Emmanuel III at the opening of the 29th Parliamentary Legislature, in particular when— in recalling the "reinforced" agreement "between civil and religious authorities"—he took as an example the "recent great celebrations" organised in honour of Don Bosco.[41]

As for the celebrations in Turin, they for the most part took up the model of those held in 1929. On 8 April an impressive procession was organised, with an exhibition of the body, which took place among festive crowds. According to the statistics reported in the *Bollettino Salesiano*, over 300,000 people took part.[42] This new, grandiose collective rite was aimed both at reconfirming the image of Don Bosco as the saint of everyone and at reassuring the regime that—despite the unquestionable weight gained in the field and again confirmed in public form—the Salesians wanted to continue working for the benefit of the state.

In addition, and thanks especially to these collective solemn celebrations, it was therefore possible for the Salesians to reaffirm, during the 20 years of Fascism, their importance in public and civil life,[43] proving their ability to adapt to diverse political circumstances just as Don Bosco had done during his life as an active priest.

We should not forget, with regard to this, the strong support network that the Piedmontese priest had managed to establish with the political leaders of his time, from Urbano Rattazzi to Giovanni Lanza, Giovanni Nicotera, Giuseppe Zanardelli, and Agostino Depretis, as well as the aforementioned Francesco Crispi. Nor should we forget the willingness, readily displayed by the saint's spiritual heirs, to support the process of Turin's industrialisation in the early decades of the twentieth century. This support was never forgotten by the top management of Fiat who played a key role in the celebrations of 8 April, making available 20 limousines for the parade and, the following day, 30 cars and two coaches, so that bishops, cardinals and Salesian leaders could visit the large plant of Lingotto. During the visit to the Fiat factories, the company's founder, Senator Giovanni Agnelli, mentioned the contribution made by the Salesians in the selection of company personnel and expressed great esteem for the heirs of Don Bosco, noting that many of his workers came from Salesian schools.[44]

A New Intervention on Relics

Four years after the canonisation, on 7 June 1938, a second set of relics was extracted from the saint to help satisfy the ever-increasing requests from all parts of the world. Shortly afterwards the Salesian general chapter, held in September and October 1938, ruled that the *ex carne* and *ex ossibus* relics were to be reserved mainly for "churches, chapels, communities of religious houses, those who took particular care of the infirm, teachers in public schools that make praiseworthy propaganda for the Saint's devotion."

In accordance with these new provisions, relics were therefore not to be "distributed to individual persons for their private devotion," a few small exceptions perhaps being made for those who had "acquired special merits in the Salesians' field of action." The document produced by the chapter ended by saying: "The generous, widespread diffusion of these initial years means that in the future we have to be more careful and moderate in accommodating requests."[45]

In the ensuing years there were numerous other confirmations of the close attention which the Salesians gave to guarding the mortal remains of their founder, which had been transferred on 26 December 1942, in the middle of the Second World War, to Castelnuovo d'Asti, in order to be better protected "from the danger of enemy incursions."

In June 1955, after another survey, another 44 new types of remains were counted. By looking at these typologies, it is possible to understand what the Salesians saw as a relic and what kind of use they intended to make of it.[46] The list on the survey's minutes included the following: "powdery fragments of the pillow and mattress with probable fragments of flesh"; "debris of the contents in the second case taken during the search of the bones of the phalanges of the foot"; "swabs that touched the body during the recognition of the body"; "paper that contained the ends of the body and body fragments for several days"; "lead chloride foil"; "brush with which the bones were cleaned"; "swabs used by Don Bosco during his final illness"; "sawdust found in the case."[47]

Requests to the congregation for new relics did not cease even in the following decades, as we see, for instance, from a letter sent on 5 February 1961 by the parish priest of San Giovanni Bosco, Rome, to the general treasurer of the congregation, Don Fedele Giraudi:

> How can we have a feast worthy of the saint and ask the faithful to come in pilgrimage to his sanctuary without a distinguished relic? Everyone sought one, wanted one [. . .] In April, Saturday 8th, we will have the consecration of the Salesian bishop; on the 9th the consecration of twenty Salesian priests [. . .] Will it be possible by that date, or at least by the month of May, to have the long-awaited relics? Don Giraudi has to complete all this work [. . .] begun so well! Let me hope![48]

This was how Don Giraudi replied six days later, using, to say the least, eloquent words:

> In response to your letter of the fifth I can say, declare, assure that 32 years after the exhumation of the body of our dear saint no house of the congregation was sent a truly distinguished relic like the one you desire. I hasten to tell you immediately that the three churches that will be favoured are or will be the Temple of Don Bosco in Rome, the Church of PAS [Salesian Pontifical University] in construction, and The Temple of Don Bosco in the Hill close to the natal house of the saint.[49]

In conclusion, if starting from 1929 the term most often evoked by the press and Catholic journalism to refer to the cult of the body of Don Bosco was "apotheosis,"[50] prior to that moment veneration of the body tended to be kept secret. This was so to allow the saint's heirs to better direct the posthumous itinerary of their founder, in a historical period in which Catholic religiosity seemed to start to look not only to the saints and the blessed, but also to the servants of God (as in fact Don Bosco was until 1929) to enhance their own requests for intercession and grace.

Moreover, the canonical *iter* of Don Bosco also continued and evolved along a politically highly complex 40-year period marked by widespread anti-clerical sentiments, growing nationalistic impulses, imperialistic thrills and authoritarian political experiments. All phenomena that could have somehow influenced the consolidated "procedural praxis of canonisations" and the doctrinal systems that the church had developed during the last few centuries, in particular those between the Council of Trent and The First Vatican Council.[51]

As for relations with the public sphere, the Salesians were first able to moderate, then to channel and nourish—including by using the new media technologies—a perception of a *fama santitatis* that appeared essential to the success of the canonical process.

As regards Don Bosco's body, they were basically apt to borrow, in their outward forms, some of the sacralisation experiences of politics with which Fascism, in the practices of translating the bodies of its "martyrs," began to attempt at the start of the 1930s,[52] with moments of glorifying *squadrismo* expressed, for instance, in the spectacular collective inhumation of 53 *squadristi* at the Certosa cemetery in Bologna (22 and 23 October 1932); through the transfer to the crypt of Santa Croce, on 27 October 1934, of the bodies of 37 "martyrs" of Florence; through to the burial in Siena, on 27 November 1938, in the crypt of San Domenico, of ten local men who fell in the glorious "Fascist revolution."

Notes

1. It is impossible to consider here the numerous research works dedicated to the Christian cult of relics, starting from the analyses dedicated to the first centuries of Christianity by Peter Brown, *The Cult of the Saints* (Chicago: University of Chicago Press, 1981); *Society and the Holy in Late Antiquity* (London: Faber and Faber, 1982). On the means and times in which the Catholic Church welcomed, in its normative order, this kind of cult, see Nicole Herrmann-Mascard, *Les reliques des saints: formation coutumière d'un droit* (Paris: Klincksieck, 1975).
2. In particular after the Council of Trent, the church showed more determination to act with greater caution on such matters.
3. See *La salma di D. Bosco a Valsalice*, an unsigned manuscript account, in Archivio Salesiano Centrale (henceforth ASC), A 038, B 14001.
4. The minutes of the telegrams that were exchanged in these phases by Don Michele Rua—the first person to lead the congregation after Don Bosco—and Don Cagliero, also reveal some of the arguments to which the Salesians tried to appeal. See in particular the telegrams of 31 January, 13:14 ("As recommended by Correnti requested Crispi personally [.] Royal household informed [.] this evening will inform on outcome"); 31 January, 22:09 ("Almost impossible burial Oratory [.] possible Valsalice through prefecture [.] funeral delays"); 1 February, 18:30 ("Taken new steps Ministry uselessly [.] benevolent deputies tonight will solicit ministry"); 2 February, 19:40

(“Correnti consulted this morning Royal Minister without success [.] pro-poses temporary deposit continuing negotiations”); in ASC, A 038, B 14001.

5. Letter from Francesco Crispi to Ruggiero Bonghi, Rome, 15 February 1888, ibid.

6. “Relazione di don Notario sulla sepoltura di Don Bosco a Val Salice—Torino,” undated [but probably 16 March 1938], ibid.

7. Letter from Ottavio Lovera di Maria to Gaetano Alimonda, Turin, 4 February 1888, ibid.

8. Prefecture of the Province of Turin, Division II, n. 3289, Turin, 4 February 1888, ibid.

9. Cesare Lombroso, *Lezioni di medicina legale, raccolte da Virgilio Rossi* (Turin: F.lli Bocca, 1900), 190.

10. See, for example, Eugenio Ceria, *Memorie biografiche di San Giovanni Bosco. XIX. La glorificazione 1888–1938* (Turin: Società editrice internazionale, 1939), 141; Pietro Stella, *Don Bosco nella storia della religiosità cattolica. III. La canonizzazione 1888–1934* (Rome: Las, 1988), 7.

11. *La salma di D. Bosco a Valsalice.*

12. Ibid.

13. Bartolo Gariglio, *I cattolici dal Risorgimento a Benedetto XVI. Un percorso dal Piemonte all’Italia* (Brescia: Morcelliana, 2013), 65 ff.

14. Letter from Michele Rua to Secondo Frola, Turin, 15 August 1904, in ASC, A 038, B 14005.

15. Stella, *Don Bosco*, 144.

16. Letter from Secondo Frola to Michele Rua, Turin, 17 August 1904, in ASC, A 038, B 14005.

17. Michele Sorasio, Luigi Rocca, Stefano Trione and Bartolomeo Giuganino, “Ricognizione della Salma del Servo di Dio Don Giovanni Bosco,” Turin, 3 September 1904, ibid.

18. Letter from Filippo Rinaldi to Leopoldo Usseglio, Turin, 25 September 1917, ibid.

19. Pier Luigi Peynetti, “Copia del Certificato di perizia medica nella esumazione della Salma del Ven. Giovanni Bosco” Turin, 15 October 1917, ibid.

20. See for example Sofia Boesch Gajano, *La santità* (Rome-Bari: Laterza, 1999).

21. Stella, *Don Bosco*, 62–63.

22. Ibid., 143–47.

23. The programme was prepared by the general prefect of the congregation, Father Pietro Ricaldone, who established a male honorary committee chaired by the crown prince, seven princes of the House of Savoy, the archbishop and another 76 people chosen from aristocrats, dignitaries, high officials, parliamentarians, academics, industrialists, financiers. The committee of female honours was composed, among others, by Elena of France, Maria Bona of Savoy-Genoa, Maria Adelaide of Savoy-Genoa and Lydia d’Arenberg.

24. Ceria, *Memorie biografiche*, 167–68.

25. Some videos and photographs of the celebrations, which served as the setting for this solemn translation (and also of the celebrations that surrounded the subsequent canonisation of April 1934), are now available, having been created at the time by the Istituto Luce; see in www.archivioluce.com/archivio/.

26. Letter from Filippo Rinaldi to Benito Mussolini, Turin, 12 May 1929 and note by the head secretary of the prime minister, Guido Beer, 1 June 1929, in Archivio Centrale dello Stato (henceforth ACS), Pcm, 1928–30, 14.2.6597.

27. See “Appunto per il Capo del Governo,” Rome, 5 June 1929, on which the unequivocal “no” written in blue pencil by Mussolini appears, ibid.

28. A.C. “Il responso ufficiale dei periti medici in seguito al laborioso esame della Salma di Don Bosco,” *Il Momento*, 19 May 1929.

29. "Cronaca della esumazione constatazione e traslazione della Salma venerata del Beato Sacerdote Don Giovanni Bosco," Turin, 8 June 1929, in ASC, A 038, B 14005.
30. Pier Luigi Peynetti, Giovanni Battista Filipello, Eugenio Rocca, Edoardo Testera and Giorgio Canuto, "Relazione peritale collegiale dei medici," Turin, 20 May 1929, ibid.
31. Ceria, *Memorie biografiche*, 123.
32. "Dichiarazione di Fedele Giraudi," Valsalice, 22 May 1929, in ASC, A 038, B 14005.
33. Ibid.
34. Ceria, *Memorie biografiche*, 201.
35. Ibid., 128.
36. Ibid., 202.
37. Letter from Carlo Salotti to Filippo Rinaldi, Rome, 2 June 1929, and the approval letter from Don Rinaldi, Rome, 4 June 1929, in ASC, A 038, B 14005.
38. Letter from the under-secretary of state to the prime minister, Edmondo Rossoni, to Vittorio Solaro del Borgo, Rome, 28 February 1934, in ACS, Pcm, 1934–36, 3.2.2.380, b.1856.
39. Stella, *Don Bosco*, 265–66.
40. "Gli onori del Campidoglio," *Bollettino Salesiano* 6–7 (1934): 185.
41. Ibid., 186.
42. "Don Bosco Santo!" ibid, 162.
43. Stella, *Don Bosco*, 280–81.
44. Pietro Stella, "La canonizzazione di don Bosco tra fascismo e universalismo," in *Don Bosco nella storia della cultura popolare*, ed. Francesco Traniello (Turin: Sei, 1987), 362–67. One of these professional institutes had in fact been established thanks to money set aside by Giovanni Agnelli, with the aim of honouring the memory of his son Edoardo (who died in 1935 in an air accident).
45. See ASC, A 038, B 14005.
46. According to a well-established tradition, this kind of relic expressed a particularly extended conception of the body of the saint, such that it involved all the relations that he had had both in life and in death.
47. See "Reliquie di Don Bosco (Ricognizione Valsalice 1929—maggio; e 1955—giugno)," ASC, A 038, B 14005.
48. Letter from Pietro Garbin to Fedele Giraudi, Rome, 5 February 1961, ibid.
49. Letter from Fedele Giraudi to Pietro Garbin, Rome, 11 February 1961, ibid. The latter was in fact the relic stolen in June 2017 mentioned at the beginning of this chapter.
50. Stella, *Don Bosco*, 7.
51. Ibid., 9–11.
52. Regarding this see for example Emilio Gentile, *Il culto del littorio* (Rome-Bari: Laterza 1993), 301–15.

Part III
Collective Spaces of Death

7 Cemeteries and Villages in the Thirteenth-Century Countryside

Luigi Provero

An initial premise: in the late Middle Ages cemeteries were the scene of many different activities, including, among other things, even the burial of bodies. Above all, however, they were places in which people lived. Among the many well-attested cases of this custom is that of the Catalan *sagreras*, that is, the land encircling parish churches first occupied by cemeteries, then by small buildings and eventually by permanent dwellings. The word *sagrera*—that is, "sanctuary"—helps us to understand the process: the church's sacredness, and the right of asylum that this provided extended to the area surrounding the building, and this ability to provide protection attracted inhabitants.[1] More generally, in some places houses and storerooms were built in cemeteries, feast days were celebrated and ceremonies enacted in them, and major political acts and minor commercial agreements were signed in them.[2] But none of these uses should be seen as adulterations of the purpose of cemeteries as burial spaces, as in fact their pervasiveness demonstrates their structural and, I would say, inevitable nature.

A second premise: it was during the High Middle Ages that Europe first saw the formation of cemeteries not too dissimilar to those we know today.[3] Although I am obviously simplifying a very varied picture, it is true to say that the period saw the emergence of some easily recognisable tendencies: in around the eleventh century a model of collective cemeteries that were delimited, sacralised and directly associated to churches took form. This model was the culmination of a process that had begun in the early centuries of the Middle Ages after burials were moved from private sites to designated collective ones.

In the late Middle Ages, the living and the dead were in close proximity:[4] cemeteries became strictly linked to settlements and churches (above all parish churches), with the former usually organised both around sacred buildings and burial grounds.[5] The village-parish-cemetery triad is recognisable between the eleventh and twelfth centuries, and this is the context in which our analysis takes place: the relationship was by no means a standard structure nor an unchangeable reality, but certainly it was an important model of reference both for local practice and for episcopal and papal norms.

Third premise: in these cemeteries, the importance of individual identities and the marking of tombs diminished. There were few identification signs on the surface, and graves were frequently reworked, with bones being moved and new burials replacing or overlaying old ones. What mattered was not so much the individual remembrance of a family's dead as the collective remembrance of a community's dead.[6] Patrick Geary has explained this in somewhat extreme but effective terms as a phenomenon in which the dead constituted one of the "age classes" into which the local community was organised.[7]

But this does not mean that there were no longer any individual interments, particularly inside churches. Yet such events were exceptional and restricted to the privileged, marking the acceptance of the benefactors of monasteries into the spiritual protection offered by the monks' prayers and the saving grace of the relics and the altar.[8] Such tombs were placed hierarchically, and the closer an entombment was to the altar or relics, the more it expressed a special relationship with the church and offered hope of salvation.

I will not, however, be dealing here with the obsequies of the elites. Instead I intend to concentrate on collective and anonymous burial grounds, evaluating the significance and function they assumed for village communities. The value of sacred sites for the creation of a rural community's identity has often been stated yet only rarely has it been studied in depth, particularly with regard to parish and other local churches. My aim, then, is to use some examples from the western Alps in the late Middle Ages to assess the community value not of churches, but of the cemeteries linked to them. By doing so, I hope to shed light on three particularly evident processes: the construction of local political ritual, the delimitation of communities and the procedures of church building.

The Construction of Local Political Ritual

In 1228 Marquess Manfred III of Saluzzo, signed an agreement with the residents of Bersezio, in Valle Stura, which included a number of reciprocal guarantees and a commitment by the community to pay an annual tax of six *lire*. This act was ratified in the cemetery of San Marcellino di Demonte.[9] As we have seen, many activities took place in cemeteries, and these often included the most expressly political acts, the negotiation of agreements with feudal lords. However, the 1228 document presents a puzzle, for the agreement was negotiated between the marquess and the men of Bersezio, but the cemetery where the agreement was concluded was located in Demonte, farther down the valley. Why was this? In order to explain it, we must take account of political ritual, which needs to be analysed on the scale of the local territory, that of Valle Stura, from where around 20 acts of the thirteenth century have survived, all describing relationships between lords and communities.

The inhabitants of the valley's villages were periodically required to send representatives to the plains below to renew their oath of fealty to the marquess,[10] but there were many other occasions when the communities and the marquesses (or their deputies) met in the valley itself, for the most part in Demonte.[11] This village appears to have been a hub of the whole valley as well as being the pivot around which marquessate business revolved. It was in fact in Demonte, before the castle doors, that in 1231 Marquess Manfredo III, in a thorough and solemn act, recognised the customs governing his relations with the entire valley community.[12] The choice of location was not arbitrary: the castle of Demonte was the centre of the marquessate power over the valley, but they stood outside, in front of the door, in order to find an intermediate place acceptable to both the marquess and the community.

Demonte was also the site of an earlier investiture—this time under an elm tree, on the pastures—by Manfred II to the community, although this, as the valley's men recalled at the end of their declarations in 1231, was not officially written down on parchment.[13] The memory preserved of this investiture, which took place at least 20 years earlier, highlights how the drafting of the 1231 document should be inserted into a previous tradition of oral transmission and ceremonial promulgation of customs, but it also shows us the momentousness of the promulgations from the marquess's point of view. They were solemn moments that remained fixed in the local memory even as they evolved ceremonially.

Thus we see that Demonte appears to have been the dominant village of Valle Stura, and accordingly its churches and one of its cemeteries played an important role for the valley as a whole, as it did also for individual villages inside and outside of it: in 1284 some men from Valdieri (in Valle Gesso) swore their allegiance to the marquess in the church of San Giovanni di Demonte and the agreement between the marquess and the people of Bersezio was settled in the cemetery of San Marcellino in 1228.[14] These two acts were somewhat different: Valdieri was located outside the valley, but came under the control of the marquessate, while Bersezio was in the highest part of Valle Stura, under the jurisdiction of San Teofredo di Cervere and not the marquessate. The agreement with the marquesses of Saluzzo was therefore a pact of mutual protection that clarified certain economic mechanisms relating to tolls and pastures. The choice to sign it in San Marcellino made manifest the encounter between two powers since Demonte was the centre of the marquessate's activity in the lower valley (which it controlled) and San Marcellino was a priory dependent on San Teofredo, the seignorial authority of the upper valley, including Bersezio.[15]

The cemetery of San Marcellino di Demonte was thus a place that provided assurance for more than one reason: because of its sacredness, which protected its inhabitants, asylum seekers and the signatories of solemn agreements, and because of its dual association, namely that it belonged to a church of one lord and was situated in the main village of another one.

The Delimitation of Communities

The relationship between a cemetery and its village was at the centre of a brief series of acts relating to Chiomonte, Val di Susa. In the thirteenth century the village came under the control of the canons of San Lorenzo of Oulx, but was also the site of a hospital belonging to the Order of Knights of the Hospital of St John of Jerusalem, who served the needs of travellers using the Montgenèvre pass. Two very different religious entities thus shared a presence: Oulx, an ancient provostship, had full seignorial power over the community and the parish church, while the Hospitallers operated in a supra-local context and at the time had many benefactors.[16]

Two lawsuits in 1208 and 1229 granted the Hospitallers the right to have a cemetery for their monks and for patients and guests who died in their hospital, but prohibited them from interring inhabitants of the village. The fact that the legal process was repeated demonstrates that the Oulx provostship was trying hard to put an end to the villagers' preference for burial in the monks' cemetery. It seems that the villagers wanted to avail themselves of a more powerful spiritual protection and to that end were prepared to make donations in addition to paying their funeral dues.[17]

The struggle over the burials was therefore partly a financial matter, though it was also a struggle for control of the village, and this entailed distinguishing those who fully belonged to the community and those who were there temporarily. And tensions were heightened in a situation involving a constant flow of traffic, as was the case with the hospital.[18] It is not difficult, then, to understand the strenuous effort being made to draw the boundaries of the village, to keep inside the village cemetery those who belonged and who should belong to the local community.

To fully understand this conflict we must see it in its more general context, for setting and upholding community boundaries was a persistent source of strain in the thirteenth-century countryside, and cemeteries were but one factor to be considered in a process that involved the community, the local lord and individual residents. While in fact the word "inhabitant" (*habitator*) recurs frequently in acts of franchise, being used to identify recipients of the concession or to define who was in receipt of particular rights,[19] the precise meaning of this term and its implications are often elusive[20] and between the twelfth and thirteenth centuries were the object of specific tensions. Examples of this are numerous, and here I present just a few of the basic frictions and the methods used to manage them.

There are several cases of single individuals who, either by choice or compulsion, left their home village and later attempted to have their status as *habitatores* of their provenance reaffirmed legally, usually to retain access to community privileges, assets and benefits. This was the case in 1224 for the Crescenti family, originally from Rolasco near Casale Monferrato, who had come into conflict with a local aristocratic family. At the height of the clashes they had felt forced to relocate, an action that had the potential to exclude them from their birthplace and local social circles and, more precisely, to make them lose community entitlements. For this reason the Crescentis' move from Rolasco, its causes and the legal status of their living elsewhere were at the centre of their depositions to the judges. Their objective was to demonstrate that they had not chosen to move and, moreover, though they had been and still were somewhere else, they had never *inhabited* anywhere else.[21]

A similar case was that of a number of men who at the end of the twelfth century, despite not actually living in Bagnolo, a village near Tortona, claimed ancestral rights of access to its common land. The local community wanted to exclude them and obtained a favourable legal judgment on the basis that they were not fully inhabiting the village. The argument that repeatedly won the day was that no-one can claim to be a neighbour by hereditary right or in consequence of their ancestors' status, but only because they fulfilled the accepted social procedure of actually living in a place, which involved a series of steps that were self-evident to the eyes of contemporaries and the judges, even if they are not always so clear to us.[22]

This is not to say that the matter advanced along a clear path, but rather that two thirteenth-century tendencies converged, namely: the desire to preserve the effectiveness of land-based personal ties and the constitution of legally homogenous village communities. Ample use was made of the sacred—particularly of parishes—in these endeavours. For example, there is the case of the abbey of Santa Maria del Senatore in Pavia and its position within the territory of Voghera. At the end of the twelfth century the abbey built a church intended to become a parish to the people working the lands of the abbey on the opposite bank of the Stàffora river a few kilometres from Voghera. It then made a claim for its parochial status and independence from the parish church of Voghera. The process of building a community on patrimonial, seignorial, residential and ceremonial foundations should therefore be clear.[23] The struggle at Chiomonte was a case in point: a seignorial power (the provostship of Oulx) had seen the prestigious St John Hospital and its cemetery as a threat to the integrity of its control over the local community, and used ceremonial arguments to combat it.

However, there was another dimension in which the cemetery interfered with the processes of determining territorial demarcations, namely the mechanism of exclusion. Moving further ahead in time to a relatively disturbing case, in 1359 the Savoy clashed with the monks of San Michele della Chiusa over the boundaries between the villages of Avigliana and

Sant'Ambrogio, and especially over who had the authority—the count or the abbot—to pass judgement on people found guilty of murder.[24] As the two sides sought to establish their rights over the contested area, abbey witnesses told how, after ordering the drowning of an elderly woman,[25] the bailiff of Avigliana had had her buried outside of that area, on the Sant'Ambrogio side of the boundary, seemingly to affirm that the disputed territories belonged to Avigliana and were therefore under Savoy jurisdiction. On hearing this, Abbot Guglielmo ordered that the body be dug up and moved to the other side, at a place called "the gallow's rock." The bailiff thereupon took the body, and this time had it laid in front of the *maladeria* (presumably a leper colony) of Sant'Ambrogio and had it burned there, ordering that a stone "pro limite sive meta" (a limit or finishing stone) be placed on the site of the cremation and a cross carved on a nearby elm. At this point the abbot made a personal visit to the leper colony, where he had the body, "quasi combustum" (almost incinerated), taken back to the gallows of Avigliana and had the stone taken away and the elm uprooted. Obviously, both parties treated the body shamefully, as a worthless object to which no-one laid claim. The body did, however, take on an extraordinary political value when used to mark out territory, first to affirm and then to deny the right of the Avigliana officials to operate in the district claimed by the abbot. And the clear importance of the issue is shown by the personal intervention of the abbot, who moved the body and destroyed the boundary stone.

To my mind this is an interesting case in that it highlights two different ways of demarcating a community: the most evident is the dispute over boundary limits and hence the territorial limits of two communities, which becomes clear in part because the two villages depended on different lords—the counts of Savoy and the abbots of San Michele—both capable of acting forcefully from the jurisdictional and documentary point of view. The burial of the woman's body was used to affirm the extension of jurisdiction of the two lords, and not by chance was directly connected to the establishment of boundary limits.

But the other demarcation process concerns the woman's burial outside of a cemetery, which should also be considered as an exclusion from the community. In those centuries customs and doctrine merged to compose a category of the dead who could not be laid to rest in a cemetery. They included heretics, excommunicated people, and those who died while performing unlawful acts. And the exclusion was not limited to barring a burial, but could also involve the exhumation and expulsion from the cemetery of anyone whose guilt was verified after their burial.[26] Clearly, the woman from Avigliana had been found guilty of a crime and sentenced to death, for the text explicitly states that the bailiff had ordered her execution by drowning before her initial burial. We do not know what she had been found guilty of, and the sentence itself does not necessarily imply that she had perpetrated a serious crime: executions were not especially frequent, but we do know that a few decades earlier, not very far from Avigliana, some men had been hanged merely for having committed theft.[27] However, the manner in which the woman's body was subsequently treated leads to conjecture about excommunication, perhaps for heresy or witchcraft. What at least is certain is that the incident reveals the existence of two distinct processes, namely the delimitation of the village territory through the (conflictual) establishment of borders, and the delimitation of the community itself by means of inclusion or exclusion from the cemetery.

The Procedures of Church Building

The third issue is that of the dynamics involved in the construction of sacred buildings, which we will consider by examining a particular text. At the beginning of the thirteenth century, a group of neighbours living in Becetto, a small settlement in Val Varaita, built a church with an adjoining cemetery and then appealed to the bishop for these to be consecrated and given parochial status, but they obtained only the consecration of the cemetery. The church and cemetery had been founded on neighbourhood solidarity, consolidated ceremonially and, tellingly, some of Becetto's inhabitants, when called upon to testify, defined themselves collectively as both "neighbours" and "parishioners."[28] The purpose of this enterprise, clear and explicit, was to break away from the village of Sampeyre, to whose territory Becetto belonged. Probably at issue were such matters as access to common land and use of property, with the men of Becetto hoping to gain exclusive right to certain pastures. But it seems that this turn of events had been made possible by the peculiar circumstances of Val Varaita, where the homogenous power of the parental group of the lords of Verzuolo, Venasca and Brossasco had exposed deficiencies in the districting of individual villages.[29]

These events reveal how parishes were important for the creation of communities, but the point I wish to highlight is the bishop of Turin's decision to consecrate only the cemetery.[30] For the community of Becetto, who had hoped for more, this outcome must have seemed a partial failure, but for us it is of great importance as it demonstrates the fact that the cemetery had a definite status of its own even before the church was operational and consecrated, and that the requirements of the hamlet community could be centred upon it. This was not an isolated case: at the end of the eleventh century acts from the French region of Mayenne refer to the "parishioners of the cemetery." Thus we see that a burial ground was seen as an acceptable alternative to the parish church in terms of being a focal point that gave weight to collective identity.[31] To be sure, as a twelfth-century Breton document said, "a cemetery without a church isn't much use,"[32] and, indeed, its full potency as a centre of worship and identity was realised only when it became directly associated with a church. In Becetto this was achieved some years later when the construction of the church was concluded. The building then acquired region-wide religious prestige.[33] Nevertheless, even this did not bring about the creation of a new community because Becetto remained, and is still today, part of the municipality of Sampeyre.

The establishment of a cemetery can, however, be taken to mean something else: apart from having a role in acts of worship, political ceremonies and the determination of parish borders, a cemetery was also proof of a village community's ability to commission and construct. The direct commitment of villagers to each stage of construction is clear from early official records, as we can see from two examples, geographically distant but equally interesting because of their precocity. In the diocese of Urgell, in Pyrenean Catalonia, a rich series of documents gives an account of the foundation of local churches, schemes which in the ninth century were usually set in motion by the communities themselves before gradually giving way to initiatives driven by the lords. In Italy, one of the first franchises to have been documented is an agreement of 1058 between the Abbot of Nonantola and the local community, in which the people undertook to build three quarters of the curtain wall that would transform the village of Nonantola into a castle.[34]

Three things are immediately evident: that there was an early community commitment to the construction of key structures for the local society; that communities sometimes acted for themselves but at other times assisted their lords' projects; and that different types of buildings were involved.

This state of affairs continued into the following centuries but has yet to be studied in depth. However, the case of Dronero, near Cuneo, throws some light on the general situation. At the end of the Middle Ages, between the fourteenth and fifteenth centuries, the forces at work in the territory and on the ecclesiastical scene of the Valle Maira were in flux, but the communities played an important role in that changeable period by their ability and willingness to help with construction schemes. The context is different to what we have seen for Demonte and Valle Stura, which were only a few kilometres from Dronero: although Dronero was the marquessate's administrative centre in Valle Maira, its centrality was contested by other communities both in the whole valley and in the more restricted basin where Dronero was located. It was there that community dynamism was expressed through participation in the construction of religious buildings.[35]

Dronero was founded in around the middle of the thirteenth century, perhaps on the initiative of Cuneo, with the aim of uniting and absorbing the previous settlements of Ripoli and Surzana. As a result of this move, the church of Santi Andrea e Ponzio in Dronero (completed in 1315) was created, bringing together the dedications of the older churches of San Andrea in Ripoli and San Ponzio in Surzana. Community enterprise had until then been in the shade, but it gradually came to light, particularly on the ceremonial level. The first step was the constitution, during the fourteenth and fifteenth centuries, of the *Confraternita dei Disciplinati* (Confraternity of the Disciplined), which unified the earlier fraternities of Santo Spirito that had been active in various small settlements and parishes of the territory.[36]

The second step was building work on the local church. In June 1455 the municipality contracted a family of masons to construct a large entrance for the parish of Santi Andrea e Pozio. The payment of 260 florins over three years indicates that this was a major restoration, practically a total reconstruction. It is therefore unsurprising that in 1461 a memorial tablet was placed in the church to mark its rededication.[37] Interestingly, the registers of dues paid to the bishop of Turin show that in 1386 six churches of the territory of Dronero sent payments, and there was no reference to the Church of Santi Andrea e Ponzio; but in 1455 we find just a reference to the unified *cura* of Dronero.[38]

These changes did not, however, denote that the dynamics of local churches had waned: during the fifteenth century a community centred on the parish of Dronero did take form, but the end of the century saw the creation of other, vibrant religious centres on the periphery. Indeed, between 1477 and 1508, new churches were created in six of Dronero's hamlets.[39] That of San Michele di Tetti, a few kilometres above the centre of Dronero, is perhaps the prime example. Two acts of litigation—in 1503 and 1505—tell of rights of patronage exercised over the church by the men of the Tetti hamlet; their request (accepted) to transform the church into a parish; and their strong financial commitment, comprising an initial endowment of 500 florins and a pledge of a further 30 florins per annum. In effect, the people of Tetti were doing what the inhabitants of Dronero had done 50 years earlier: the ceremonial system and local churches had stuck fast to their function of constructing and shaping neighbourhood solidarity. In the same years when the oldest churches (those of Ripoli and Surzana) declined and the centrality of that of Dronero took root, local ecclesiastical structures continued to serve as flexible channels for the development of community identities that differed from the dominant image of districts and parishes, with Dronero and its church of Santi Andrea e Ponzio being a representative case.

But community involvement in construction programmes did not end with churches only: in 1428, 30 years before the restructuring of the parish, the municipality of Dronero paid a mason named Antonio 700 florins to build of a stone bridge over the Maira river (which is still in use today).[40] This created a vital link since it enabled the community to take advantage of several lucrative opportunities: in those years a fair had been set up at Dronero, the marquess of Saluzzo signed agreements for mine-working in Val Maira, and he had also negotiated an accord with all the valley communities for a road link with France.[41]

The case of Dronero demonstrates how, throughout the late Middle Ages, the foundation of cemeteries—as evidenced by patchy documentation—formed part of a vigorous construction endeavour by the communities. In the main this revolved around fortifications and religious buildings, but later it broadened to include completely different structures that helped to shape communal identities and ceremonial actions and also smoothed the path of commerce and trade.

In the mid-twelfth century, the bishop of Rennes, at the request of the monks of Marmoutiers, consecrated a cemetery by the chapel of Saint Aubert "only for the shelter of the living, not for the burial of the dead" ("ad refugium tantum vivorum non ad sepulturam mortuorum"). He observed that the chapel and cemetery lay within the parish of a church controlled by the abbey and thus prior permission from the monks would be required for burials.[42] From all appearances here was a conflict of interests similar to that of Chiomonte: an important abbey wanted to protect its prerogatives, which it exercised in part through control of the parish and authorisation of burials. Hence it asked the bishop to adjudicate. And his response brought a highly significant fact to notice, namely that cemeteries were used for many things not *in spite* of their being consecrated but *because of* this fact. The bishop's declaration was unambiguous on this point: "ad refugium tantum vivorum [. . .] quod-dam cimiterium benedixisse."

This text encourages me to conclude by reaffirming my initial point: that the uses of cemeteries which to us seem inappropriate, profane and unrelated to the burial of the dead, were in fact structural and necessary ones, directly connected to the nature of the place. Only after the area had been consecrated as a cemetery—and, as such, became an extension of the church's sacrosanct space—could it serve as a refuge for the living. This is surely the idea that encapsulates the analysis made above: consecration and the cemetery function gave the place the characteristics required for a variety of community activities, from hosting political ceremonies to facilitating the determination of communal boundaries.

Notes

1. On the *sagreras* see Pierre Bonnassie and Pierre Guichard, "Les communautés rurales en Catalogne et dans le pays Valencien (IX^c–milieu XIV^c siècle)," in *Les communautés villageoises en Europe occidentale du Moyen Age aux Temps modernes* (Auch: Centre culturel de l'Abbaye de Flaran, 1984), 87; in general, important observations are contained in Elizabeth Zadora-Rio, "Les cimetières habités en Anjou aux XI^c et XII^c siècles," in *La Normandie. Etudes archéologiques* (Paris: Comité des travaux historiques et scientifiques, 1983), 319–29. A fundamental contribution to this work was made by the Associate Research Directors Programme (DEA) of the Maison des Sciences de l'Homme, which allowed me to conduct research in Paris in Autumn 2018.
2. Anthony Perron, "The Medieval Cemetery as Ecclesiastical Community: Regulation, Conflict, and Expulsion, 1000–1215," in *Dealing with the*

Dead: Mortality and Community in Medieval and Early Modern Europe, ed. T. Tomaini (Leiden: Brill, 2018), 258–60.

3. For a general overview, Michel Lauwers, *Naissance du cimetière. Lieux sacrés et terre des morts dans l'Occident médiéval* (Paris: Aubier, 2005); Cécile Treffort, *L'Église carolingienne et la mort. Christianisme, rites funéraires et pratiques commémoratives* (Lyon: Presses Universitaires de Lyon, 1996).

4. Alain Dierkens and Cécile Treffort, "Le cimetière au village dans l'Europe médiévale et moderne: rapport introductive," in *Le cimetière au village dans l'Europe médiévale et modern*, ed. C. Treffort (Toulouse: Presses Universitaires du Midi, 2015), 7.

5. Lauwers, *Naissance du cimetière*, 206–8 and 269–76.

6. Ibid., 126–28; Michel Vovelle, *La mort et l'Occident de 1300 à nos jours* (Paris: Gallimard, 1983), 76.

7. Patrick J. Geary, *Living with the Dead in the Middle Ages* (Ithaca, NY: Cornell University Press, 1994), 6.

8. Among the many cases, see for example Paolo Cammarosano, *Abbadia a Isola. Un monastero toscano nell'età romanica. Con una edizione dei documenti 953–1215* (Castelfiorentin: Società storica della Valdelsa, 1993), 52 and 85.

9. Armando Tallone, Francesco Guasco di Bisio and Ferdinando Gabotto, *Cartari minori*, vol. III (Pinerolo: Società storica subalpina, 1912–23), 22.

10. For example: Armando Tallone, *Regesto dei marchesi di Saluzzo (1091–1340)* (Pinerolo: Società storica subalpina,1906), 493 and 497 ff.

11. Tallone, Guasco di Bisio and Gabotto, *Cartari minori*, vol. III, 13, 17, 19, 21, 29 and 34; Tallone, *Regesto dei marchesi di Saluzzo*, 371.

12. Tallone, Guasco di Bisio and Gabotto, *Cartari minori*, vol. III, 24–27; the act records and confirms the customs for "omnibus hominibus vallis Sturane, a Berzesio inferius" and thus excludes the higher part of the valley, which was headed by the village of Bersezio and under the dominion of San Teofredo of Cervere, and with which the marquess had agreed certain specific acts three years earlier (see below, n. 14).

13. They in fact swore that "dominus Maynfredus marchio, avus ipsius marchionis, dedit omnibus hominibus Valli Sturane, sub ulmo pascherii Demontis," these same customs in the presence of a series of listed witnesses: ibid., p. 26. The act can be dated to before 1215, the year of Manfredo II's death: Delfino Muletti, *Memorie storico-diplomatiche appartenenti alla città e ai marchesi di Saluzzo*, vol. II (Saluzzo: Lobetti-Bodoni, 1829–33), 187.

14. Tallone, Guasco di Bisio and Gabotto, *Cartari minori*, vol. III, 22 and 45.

15. On San Teofredo of Velay's presence in Piemonte and on the dependency of San Marcellino di Demonte: Frederi Arneodo, "L'abbazia di S. Teofredo e le dipendenze subalpine: la gradazione dei vincoli (secoli XI–XIII)," in *Attraverso le alpi: S. Michele, Novalesa, S. Teofredo e altre reti monastiche*, ed. Frederi Arneodo and Paola Guglielmotti (Bari: Edipuglia, 2008), 149–60, in particular 151 and 157. On the jurisdiction over Bersezio: Tallone, Guasco di Bisio and Gabotto, *Cartari minori*, vol. III, 6–11 and 48–51.

16. Piercarlo Pazé, "Lungo la strada di Provenza: i Gerosolimitani a Chiomonte," in *Luoghi di strada nel medioevo. Fra il Po, il mare e le Alpi occidentali*, ed. G. Sergi (Turin: Scriptorium, 1996), 179–212.

17. Giovanni Collino, *Le carte della Prevostura d'Oulx raccolte e riordinate cronologicamente fino al 1300* (Pinerolo: Società storica subalpina, 1908), 244 and 289.

18. Perron, "The Medieval Cemetery," 261.

19. For example (to remain in the same area) Maria Clotilde Daviso di Charvensod, "La carta di Tenda," *Bollettino storico-bibliografico subalpino* 47

(1949): 142; Francesco Cognasso, *Documenti inediti e sparsi sulla storia di Torino* (Pinerolo: Società storica subalpina, 1914), 37.

20. See Ennio Cortese, "Per la storia di una teoria dell'arcivescovo Mosé di Ravenna (m. 1154) sulla proprietà ecclesiastica," in *Proceedings of the Fifth International Congress of Medieval Canon Law*, ed. Stephan Kuttner and Kenneth Pennington (Vatican City: Biblioteca Apostolica Vaticana, 1980), 131–34; Yan Thomas, "L'extrême et l'ordinaire. Remarques sur le cas médiéval de la communauté disparue," in *Penser par cas*, ed. Jean-Claude Passeron and Jacques Revel (Paris: Ecole des Hautes Etudes en Sciences Sociales, 2005), 47–50 and 59–61; Susan Reynolds, *Kingdoms and Communities in Western Europe: 900–1300* (Oxford: Clarendon Press, 1984), 143 ff.

21. Ferdinando Gabotto and Ugo Fisso, *Le carte dell'Archivio capitolare di Casale Monferrato*, vol. I (Pinerolo: Società storica subalpina, 1907–1908), 174–86, in particular 175, 182 and 184 ff; on the overall question of the delimitation of communities, Luigi Provero, *Le parole dei sudditi. Azioni e scritture della politica contadina nel Duecento* (Spoleto: CISAM, 2012), 433–43.

22. Vincenzo Legé and Ferdinando Gabotto, *Documenti degli archivi tortonesi relativi alla storia di Voghera* (Pinerolo: Società storica subalpina, 1908), 56; Armando Tallone, *Le carte dell'Archivio comunale di Voghera fino al 1300* (Pinerolo: Società storica subalpina, 1918), 16.

23. Provero, *Le parole dei sudditi*, 354–59.

24. Patrizia Cancian and Giampietro Casiraghi, *Vicende, dipendenze e documenti dell'abbazia di S. Michele della Chiusa* (Turin: Deputazione Subalpina di Storia Patria, 1993), 337–95; a fuller analysis is provided in Provero, *Le parole dei sudditi*, 316–22.

25. Defined simply as a "vetula" (old woman), without any explanation about what had led to her being drowned by the bailiff.

26. See above all Perron, "The Medieval Cemetery," 262–70; Mathieu Vivas, "Prope aut iuxta cimiterium: un espace d'inhumation pour les 'mauvais morts' (XIᵉ–XVᵉ siècle)," in *Cimetière au village*, Treffort, 193–206; Lauwers, *Naissance du cimetière*, 166–76. The "shameless" nature of burials outside the cemetery is underlined by Treffort, *L'église carolingienne*, 157–63.

27. Luigi Provero, "Le forche del priore: giustizia e comunità nella Valle di Susa del Duecento," in *Una storia di rigore e di passione. Saggi per Livio Antonielli*, ed. Stefano Levati and Simona Mori (Milan: Franco Angeli, 2018), 13 ff. and 24.

28. The decisions taken by the residents of Becetto can be inferred above all from the testimonies collected and presented by the provost of the rectory of Rivalta against the abbey of Fruttuaria in 1211, in the dispute over the control of the church of Becetto: Edoardo Durando, "Alcune notizie sulla chiesa di santa Maria di Beceto," in *Miscellanea Saluzzese* (Pinerolo: Società storica subalpina, 1902), 143–53; on the episode as a whole see Luigi Provero, "Monasteri, chiese e poteri nel Saluzzese (secoli XI–XIII)," *Bollettino storico-bibliografico subalpino* 92 (1994): 462–66.

29. For the origins of the seignorial family in the eleventh century see Luigi Provero, "Aristocrazia d'ufficio e sviluppo di poteri signorili nel Piemonte sud-occidentale (secoli XI–XII)," *Studi medievali* 3a, no. 35 (1994): 597 ff; for the later period, see Tallone, *Regesto dei marchesi di Saluzzo*, 383 and 513 ff.

30. For the passages referring specifically to the cemetery, Durando, "Alcune notizie," 146, 148, 149 and 152.

31. Ernest Laurain, "Questions fabriciennes," *Bulletin de la Commission historique et archéologique de la Mayenne* 24 (1908): 348 ff.; see Michel

Lauwers, "Le cimetière au village ou le village au cimetière? Spatialisation et communautarisation des rapports sociaux dans l'Occident medieval," in *Le cimetière au village*, Treffort, 52.

32. Hubert Guillotel, "Du rôle des cimetières en Bretagne dans le renouveau du XI^c et de la première moitié du XII^c siècle," *Mémoires de la Société d'histoire et d'archéologie de Bretagne* 52 (1972–74): 11; see Lauwers, *Naissance du cimetière*, 117.

33. Benedetto Baudi di Vesme, Edoardo Durando and Ferdinando Gabotto, *Carte inedite o sparse dei signori e luoghi del Pinerolese fino al 1300* (Pinerolo: Società storica subalpina, 1909), 281.

34. On the diocese of Urgell see n. 1, above; on Nonantola see Ludovico Antonio Muratori, *Antiquitates Italicae Medii Aevi*, vol. III (Milan: 1738–42), 241.

35. On the entire matter, Luigi Provero, *Churches, Settlements and Resources in the Western Alps (11th–15th centuries)*, in *Economic History of the Alps in the Pre-Industrial Era*, ed. M.A. Denzel, vol. II (forthcoming).

36. Roberto Olivero, "Ripoli e Surzana: due villaggi scomparsi all'imbocco della Valle Maira," *Bollettino della Società per gli studi storici, artistici e archeologici della provincia di Cuneo* 145 (2011): 111–20; Roberto Olivero, *La Confraternita del Gonfalone a Dronero: secoli XIV–XVI* (Cuneo: Società per gli studi storici, artistici e archeologici della provincia di Cuneo, 2000), 29–61.

37. Giuseppe Manuel di San Giovanni, *Memorie storiche di Dronero e della Val Maira* (Turin: Marino e Gantin, 1868), I, 193–94.

38. Giampietro Casiraghi, *La diocesi di Torino nel Medioevo* (Turin: Deputazione Subalpina di Storia Patria, 1979), 215, 220, 226, 237, 242 and 248.

39. Elisabetta Giraudo, "Chiese e comunità nel Saluzzese medievale. Dall'XI secolo alla fondazione della diocesi (1511)," (Graduation thesis, University of Turin, 2010), 17–21 and 139–40.

40. Manuel di San Giovanni, *Memorie storiche*, 145–47.

41. Rinaldo Comba, *Per una storia economica del Piemonte medievale. Strade e mercati dell'area sud-occidentale* (Turin: Deputazione Subalpina di Storia Patria, 1984), 67 (fair); Teresa Mangione, "Allume, vetriolo e ferro: attività minerarie e metallurgiche nel marchesato di Saluzzo (secoli XIV–XVI)," in *Miniere, fucine e metallurgia nel Piemonte Medievale e moderno*, ed. Rinaldo Comba (Cuneo: Società per gli studi storici, artistici e archeologici della provincia di Cuneo, 1999), 80 (mines); Muletti, *Memorie storico-diplomatiche*, V, 281–85 (road).

42. Guillotel, "Du rôle des cimetières," 25.

8 Within, Beneath and Outside the City

The Space of the Dead in Early Modern Naples (Seventeenth to Nineteenth Centuries)

Diego Carnevale

The presence of human remains within spaces inhabited by the living was a characteristic of settlements in Western, Christian Europe from the late Middle Ages until the nineteenth century. This was largely due to ecclesiastical control over burials, which meant that the church participated fully in the dynamics of the construction, contention and manipulation of spaces within settlements. The actual concept of "burial" was not to be equated only with "a place of burial, but also an institutionalised funeral organisation, assuming inclusion and exclusion."[1] Tombs—and their contents—were the principal tangible manifestation of this institution, and the aim of this contribution is to understand how they helped to shape the relationship between inhabitants and the remains of their predecessors, particularly in large conurbations, where contacts between the living and the dead were more frequent. As regards this, the case of Naples during the early modern age is highly significant, since it was always among the most populous cities of the world.

In the mid-sixteenth century, Naples was, with over 200,000 residents, the most crowded urban centre of Christendom, although in subsequent decades that number was surpassed by Paris and London. In the next century, the plague of 1656 is estimated to have killed between a half and two thirds of a population that fluctuated between 360,000 and 400,000 people, and this disaster profoundly affected the culture and social structures of the entire kingdom. Nevertheless, at the start of the eighteenth century, when it had 220,000 inhabitants, Naples was once again Europe's third city. From that moment on the population grew steadily until it exceeded 400,000 at the start of the nineteenth century.[2]

With very few exceptions, at the beginning of the sixteenth century, burials in Naples took place in ecclesiastical structures. In the following century, however, an important change took place that made the sepulchral topography in Naples unique among the great European metropolises: that is, the near total disappearance of courtyards used for inhumation, there no longer being any churchyards. Even hospitals, where the level of mortality was obviously at its highest, had no such land. Most burials therefore took place in structures built within church buildings.

Research does not as yet allow us to determine the exact reasons for this transformation, which presumably came to pass in the course of the second half of the sixteenth century. Nevertheless, it is possible to identify certain factors that might have played a role in the phenomenon. First of all, the exceptional demographic growth of the city that occurred in the same period was matched by a reduction in land available for building. During the government of the Spanish Viceroy Pedro de Toledo (1532–53), Naples was the object of far-reaching urban regeneration, including the construction of new bastion fortifications that marked a clear separation between the city centre and the periphery. In order to defend the city more effectively, the government sought to limit the unregulated growth of new buildings in the suburbs with a series of restrictive measures issued during the 1560s.[3] Within the walls, on the other hand, noble and ecclesiastical properties expanded considerably, until all land suitable for development was filled. It is conceivable that in this phase it was the rectors of church buildings who chose to release their courtyards for other use.[4] Moreover, since this meant that thereafter interments would take place within the church building, it is quite likely that the rectors' decision met with the approval of the faithful, for whom the idea of being buried inside the holy space—thus *apud sanctos* (with the saints)—must have seemed attractive, given that this had previously been the prerogative of the privileged classes and the most affluent corporations. On the basis of the known data, the conversion of the Neapolitan funeral system must have been completed by the first years of the seventeenth century, when the diocesan synods began to refer to burials as operations that took place exclusively inside the churches.[5]

The Organisation of Urban Burials

There had been individual under-floor tombs in Neapolitan churches since at least the Middle Ages, but these were all exceptional cases, and the practice was regularly discouraged by order of the synods.[6] The dead were in fact generally laid to rest in burial pits: masonry structures under the pavement, of a size and depth dictated by circumstances, and left un-floored to enable soft tissues to disperse into the surrounding earth. The dead were lowered into the pits via a trap door and placed on top of each other, almost always without a coffin so as to save space. Even so, these mass graves often reached saturation point because their particular microclimatic conditions could slow down their occupants' decomposition or even assist their natural preservation.[7] The only known permitted way to accelerate their putrefaction artificially was to burn them by throwing quicklime in the pit. But even this method was risky, seeing as the lime frequently solidified before completing its work and consequently increased the difficulty of maintaining the pits.[8]

Another type of burial space was the family tomb of the aristocratic classes. This, too, was constructed under the level of the pavement, often beneath a chapel, using the same construction methods as the burial pits. On occasion, the tomb took the form of an underground chamber with masonry benches or housings dug into the walls. These resting places were seldom fully occupied, since they accommodated only a few corpses over the years.

The third and most interesting type of burial space present in Neapolitan churches was the hypogeum, which, while used in many other Italian and European cities, in Naples reached an extraordinary level of development. Hypogea were designed to house a large number of bodies buried next to each other, and their dimensions varied greatly: some were a small chamber of around 20 square metres while others were a replica of the churches above them. Internally they were organised around a central paved corridor to the side of which the ground level was lowered or raised by around half a metre and filled with soil. The soil was subdivided by means of wooden planks or small stone into rectangular plots known as *giardinetti* ("little gardens"), each one having room for one or two bodies. In the middle of the central corridor, or at the end of the crypt, there was a pit which was covered by a manhole and used as a repository for bones so that room could be made for new burials in the *giardinetti*: it was, in short, a sort of underground cemetery and in Naples took the name of *terrasanta* ("holy ground").[9] This compound of words was unusual, since all burial grounds were legally sacred, having been ritually blessed, but the adjective "santa" suggests a direct link with Christ and the saints. Very probably the name came from a new form of devotion practice that emerged in the years when the sixteenth century gave way to the seventeenth.

"Terra santa" was the also name given to the cemetery space within the basilica of San Felice in Cimitile, a small hamlet north of Nola (around 30 km northeast of Naples) that had become an important pilgrimage site in the High Middle Ages because it housed the tombs of Saint Felix and Saint Paulinus of Nola, as well as an indeterminate number of Christian martyrs of the Roman persecutions.[10] In 1644, as part of a promotional scheme, an apologia entitled *Del cemeterio nolano con le vite di alcuni santi, che vi furono sepeliti* was published, this being the work of Andrea Ferraro, canon of Nola Cathedral.[11] From it we glean valuable information about the system of beliefs that had made the site popular and about innovations introduced under the influence of Counter-Reformation teaching.

Extraordinary powers were attributed to the sanctuary because of the land on which it stood. Not only did this shelter the remains of two saints, but also those of hundreds of martyrs who, like Saint Felix, had been killed on the site, soaking the soil with their blood.[12] Moreover, unlike other cemeteries of martyrs, from that of "Nolano it is known that none had been transferred" so it had retained all its sacredness since ancient times.[13] The tangible proof of the powers of the *terra santa* of the cemetery of Cimitile was its ability to consume the remains of those buried there within 24 hours.

The miracle of the cemetery capable of decomposing bodies in a single day was known throughout Europe: a similar case was that of the Camposanto of Pisa whose soil, according to tradition, had been brought from Calvary by the crusaders on the order of bishop Ubaldo Lanfranchi in the middle of the twelfth century.[14] Michel De Montaigne wrote about the Pisa cemetery's miraculous power in his travel journal, recalling how there was another cemetery with similar properties in Rome.[15] At the start of the early modern age, the cult of the sanctuary of Cimitile was essentially localised, but canon Ferraro wrote about an important change that had occurred not long before:

> This virtue of this land, which they rightly call holy, has been admired by many religious men, many of whom, since the custom of building cemeteries under churches has been reintroduced, have come to Nola and obtained permission from the bishop and the chapter to fill sacks with that soil and, carrying it reverently away, have sprinkled their cemeteries with it. This was done by the Reverend Jesuit fathers for their church, called the Carminiello, near the Naples market, who took several sacks some years ago. So too did the Reverend Theatine fathers for the cemetery they have made under the church of the Santi Apostoli; the Reverend Dominican fathers for Santa Maria della Sanità and for the Rosario di Palazzo; the Reverend Discalced Augustinian fathers; the Reverend Reformed Order of Friars Minor and many others [. . .] not only the religious but also laymen for their oratories, who, not to be wordy, I omit.[16]

Ferraro thus gives credence to the hypothesis that cemetery courtyards gradually disappeared from Naples towards the end of the sixteenth century,[17] after which a direct link was forged between the *terresante* and the Cimitile sanctuary. The main espousers of the new practice appear to have been the regular orders, in particular those most sympathetic to the spiritual programme of the Counter-Reformation, but it must have quickly become more widespread since Ferraro said that others had started to take the sanctuary's soil "furtively," compelling the bishop of Nola to order "on pain of excommunication that without his licence it should not be taken and transported elsewhere."[18] In consequence of the ruling the partnership with Naples was regularised and the soil rationed and thereafter each allowance was placed in a small wooden casket doubly sealed by the notary of the Nolan diocese who, with the provost of the basilica, signed a certificate of authenticity. When a new *terrasanta* was blessed, a delegate from the Neapolitan curia opened the casket and emptied its contents into the burial ground, knowing that its effect would permeate the rest of the soil in the *giardinetto*.[19] The creation of the *terresante* was warmly encouraged by the authorities of the Neapolitan diocese partly because they helped to stem unlicensed burials on church land, but mainly because they provided a new place of devotion that complied with the spiritual programme implemented by the Counter-Reformation church.

A Macabre Report

Although the structural model of *terresante* was relatively standard-ised, different hypogea had been endowed with an architectural variant, namely a series of recesses along the perimeter of the underground chamber where corpses were suspended in an upright position and exposed to the air to continue their decomposition. This configuration was implemented in the *terresante* of several lay confraternities and was connected to a fundamental aspect of religious education promoted by the Counter-Reformation, often defined by Michel Vovelle as the "pedagogy of death."[20] This teaching method borrowed and renewed the traditional principle of the *memento mori*, merging it with an extreme conception of the artistic representation of the macabre. Human remains thus became the central feature of a *mise en scène* of life's end, the ultimate aim of which was to prepare people for death by raising their awareness of the precariousness of earthly things, primarily the human body.[21]

This practice was promoted by numerous religious orders born or reformed from the sixteenth century onwards, but also by clerical congregations such as the Lazarists, Oratorians and Redemptorists, in the name of the re-Catholicisation of European society. It was no coincidence that conventual burials were often characterised by unusual funerary scenes intended mainly for members of the community. In the south of Italy many hypogea were equipped with alcoves fitted with stone chairs where bodies of deceased members of the order were fixed in a sitting position. At the bottom of the alcove was a drainage channel through which the soft tissues passed into a container or cesspool.[22] Consequently, whenever other members of the order visited the crypt, they would witness the decomposition of the bodies of their departed brothers.[23]

Apart from the exhibition of the corpse, the practice of using human bones to decorate churches and the hypogea attached to them spread throughout Europe. The representation of the dead body had been an integral aspect of sacred art since at least the thirteenth century, as the famous *Dance of Death* and *The Triumph of Death* make clear. The renewed pedagogy of death made use of the progress in Renaissance art to depict bodies more realistically, not only in paintings, but also in sculpture, waxworks and, indeed, through the use of real human remains. Human skulls, often decorated with wigs or hats to denote specific social roles, were sometimes used by priests and missionaries during sermons.[24] As to theology, this macabre staging was closely connected to the cult of purgatory, the credibility of which needed restoring in the aftermath of fierce Protestant criticism.[25] The appeal for protection of souls in purgatory was crucially important in all cases of sudden or accidental death, that is when the lamented one had not had time to prepare for his passing. Such happenings, which were anything but rare, together with the alarmist preaching of the clergy, created the conditions for the emergence of confraternities that specialised in prayers for souls in purgatory and in dealing with unexpected departure from life.[26]

The Neapolitan *terresante* were therefore places imbued with symbolic meanings all of which were part of the pedagogy of death. Eighteenth-century sources throw some light on the way in which the faithful related to the hypogea. One significant episode attested by them occurred during the period of the Austrian Viceroyalty (1707–34). In May 1710, during an event dedicated to Saint Januarius, known as the feast of the "garlanded priests," the miraculously liquified blood of the saint was exhibited starting from the Saturday before the first Sunday of the month. An anonymous chronicler recounted how Viceroy Cardinal Vincenzo Grimani went to the cathedral to pay homage to the saint by kissing the ampoule of blood, which instantly changed colour:

> Appearing to have turned black, and so it remained for the next three days, without there appearing any space between the blood and the vial, making everyone afraid; whereupon processions of penitence were sent out of all the churches, carrying in their hands skulls of the dead, parched bones of the deceased, and also portions of the putrefied, freshly buried dead, which horrified those who saw them.[27]

The account suggests that the devotional manifestations were not spontaneous, but that in fact the processions "were sent out" for the purpose of penance because of the fear aroused in all by the alteration of the miracle.[28] In those years there was an ongoing political clash between the Holy See and Cardinal Grimani, and so the archbishop of Naples, Francesco Pignatelli, used the blood of the principal city patron to channel popular discontent against the viceroy, as had been done in the past. Nevertheless, it is possible that the parading of human remains in the processions had not been part of the archbishop's plans but was instead an excess on the part of the lower classes or the heads of the confraternities, perhaps inspired by particularly zealous priests. After all, as said earlier, skulls, bones and macabre representations were part of the arsenal of preachers and missionaries.

During the eighteenth century, the relationship between Neapolitans and the *terresante* drew the attention of the secular authorities. In 1734 the Kingdom of Naples regained autonomy under Charles of Bourbon, and the new dynasty promoted numerous absolutist political reforms as well as various development schemes in the city aimed at raising it to a level that could compete with other great European capitals. In November 1779 King Ferdinand IV, son of Charles, commissioned the health authorities to investigate urban burials in view of the possible creation of a major public cemetery *extra muros*. The five Neapolitan doctors charged with giving an opinion on the state of the burials aimed their main criticisms at the *terresante*:

> These are under the public churches, and some are not far below, others are on the same level as the street, to which they usually have an opening. Some of these openings are enclosed in glass, others only have an iron grate. In many small parterres [the *giardinetti*] the bodies are buried in ditches fashioned out of the soil, and the same earth covers them to a height of three or four palms [80 cm to 1 m]. The soil that covers the bodies is left loose and not even pressed down. On holy days a mass is said in these hypogea or *terresante*, with many people taking part. On All Souls' Day some of the common people follow the custom of going to visit their family and friends in the *terresante*, where they strip them of their rags and dress them again. After a few months the bodies are uncovered, and some are thrown into the burial pits, while others are placed as ornaments in the niches positioned around the same *terresante* and are left to continue their putrefaction (which, as mentioned, takes a long time), and to spread through the free air their deathly stench.[29]

Though writing from a highly critical perspective indicative of changed sensitivities, the Neapolitan doctors provided valuable information on the relationship between the people and the *terresante*. Some were used as places for weekly worship, while on 2 November visitors came to see their lamented loved ones.[30] The report does not make it clear whether the practice of changing the bodies' clothing concerned those who were still buried or those chosen for exhibition in the recesses, but it is likely that the doctors were referring to the latter. We should not forget that a direct relationship with the body of the deceased rarely lasted longer than a year or two, since at that point the remaining bones were gathered together and put into the *terrasanta*'s central pit. Nevertheless, the frequency of the faithful's visits to the hypogea is clear. The confraternities, which in Naples were made up entirely of lay people, played a fundamental role in this interaction, as the aforementioned doctors also revealed in their report:

> If one considers that most of the inhabitants of Naples are enrolled in some kind of confraternity, or join one when they are close to dying, and that each confraternity has its own *terrasanta*, it will be clearly understood that of the nine to ten thousand who die throughout the whole year about two thirds are buried in the *terresante*, in the manner described. Of the remaining third, many are buried in the parish

sepulchres, and in those of the churches of regulars. These burials are just as dangerous as the *terresante*, since they are in very busy churches.[31]

During the eighteenth century, the Neapolitan confraternities provided different types of mutual aid, often including the payment of medical care and always those relating to burial.[32] For this reason, many people who were not members of one of these burial clubs were enrolled by their family during the death throes or at the moment of their passing in order to have a dignified interment, limiting the risk of being considered destitute and therefore being given a dishonourable funeral.[33] It is therefore easy to understand why the possession of a *terrasanta* was of fundamental importance for the actual survival of this kind of confraternity.

Despite their greater availability of space, *terresante* could nevertheless still be filled to capacity. The presence of the ossuary, functionally similar to the French *charniers*, delayed the need for maintenance significantly, but at some point it was still necessary to take action. When the burial space of a church was no longer able to accept new bodies, the remains were "purged" and transported to the city's large mortuaries: the tuff caves of Fontanelle and Santa Maria del Pianto, respectively situated to the north-west and north-east of the capital, a few kilometres beyond the city walls.

Figure 8.1 The Fontanelle Cemetery, Naples (skulls boxed as ex-voto).

Source: Dominik Matus [CC BY-SA 4.0 (https://creativecommons.org/licenses/by-sa/4.0)], via Wikimedia Commons.

This habit of using the numerous caverns dug out over the centuries along the entire northern edge of Naples as funeral repositories dated back at least to the epidemics of the fourteenth century.[34] Starting with the 1656 plague, the two disused mines were pressed into service.[35] The work of transferring the bones was not accompanied by any ritual, but instead was handled by the city health authorities using a simple procedure: the remains were taken from the pits by gravediggers and loaded by night onto covered wagons, known as "carrettoni," and then taken to the caverns and placed in one of the galleries, which, once full, was walled up, after which the next one used, all at the expense of the owner of the pits being emptied.[36] This system of handling the mortal remains of Neapolitans started to fall into crisis in the mid-eighteenth century because of population growth and of the imposition of upgraded health and city planning policies by the new Bourbon dynasty.

The Expulsion of Urban Burials: Reform and Tradition

In the 1750s and 1760—in other words 20 years before the 1779 report on the state of the *terresante*—the Neapolitan monarchy had already intervened in the question of city burials, by taking care of people who died in the hospitals. From the mid-sixteenth century onwards these had been buried at the Ospedale degli Incurabili, the city's largest, in its so-called *piscina*, a vast space beneath the hospital, probably a quarry abandoned before the hospital's foundation in 1522.[37] But by the summer of 1755 the *piscina* had been filled up and the sovereign, through his secretary for ecclesiastical affairs, Gaetano Brancone, ordered the hospital governors "to think carefully about establishing and constructing at some distance from the inhabited quarters of the city a spacious cemetery suitable for the burial of the people who died in our great Ospedale degli Incurabili."[38] A commission made up of technicians, doctors and administrators was duly set up to identify a suitable site and formulate plans. After a long debate, in January 1762 the design and construction of the cemetery were assigned to Ferdinando Fuga, who had been in the service of the Neapolitan ruler for over a decade.

The complex designed by the Florentine architect, which is still in existence, was built on a square plot, with sides of 62.75 metres excluding the south-west facing entrance portico. Inside the court 360 burial pits were arranged in rows of 19 with one missing in the exact centre; six others were created in the portico, making a total of 366: one for each day of the year. The pits, built of masonry, were a little over six metres deep, and square, with the sides measuring 3.7 metres.[39] They were enclosed by a 70 cm square stone manhole each marked with its respective Arab numeral. Along the perimeter wall, which was a full six metres high so as "not to be scaled to commit acts of witchcraft or other excesses," were built a series of rectangular niches aligned with the pits. These spaces were used to house "the bones of the deceased already entirely without flesh and desiccated, in the event that after a very long time the aforementioned burial spaces needed to be emptied and cleaned out," in line with the system used by the French *charniers*.[40]

The burial technique proposed by Fuga was a development of the methods of allocating cemetery land suggested by the doctors who had addressed the problem. In fact, the idea of a "rotation of corpses" had been suggested by the commission charged with examining the Incurabili *piscina* in 1756.[41] Fuga himself had already built a similar sepulchre between 1740 and 1745 for the hospital of Santo Spirito in Sassia in Rome.[42]

Completed in three years, the *camposanto* of the Incurabili was in fact a veritable "funeral machine" designed to provide a self-sufficient system for the disposal of dead bodies over very long periods of time.[43] On 22 April 1762 judge Giuseppe Romano, the kingdom's general superintendent for public health, declared that the new cemetery was necessary despite its significant cost:

> The plans formulated by the Architect Fuga [are] too particular and regular for it to be possible to deviate from them even slightly. And although the expense has risen to twenty-five thousand five hundred ducats, there is no other way to repair it as long as the only plan that would make it possible to save this expense would be to burn the bodies. But this should not be attempted, because it would certainly bring forth the strong reaction and horror of this low-born, numerous population, and God knows what sinister effect this could lead to, since they have heard it said that this is usually practised elsewhere only with the corpses of those men who pass to the other life in the obstinacy of heresy and with enormous crimes, and we do not see this otherwise practised in any other Christian Kingdom or Province. This is because of the ancient first Christians, who instead wished to follow the Jewish custom of burying bodies, rather than the most praiseworthy custom of the Gentiles to burn them and preserve only the ashes and in so doing not only purge the stench from the heavily populated cities, as Rome was in its ancient greatness, but also avoid the excessive public expense of public burial spaces, which now we call *camposanti*.[44]

Romano alluded to one of the many cultural obstacles to reinstating the ancient practice of cremation: the association between heresy and death by burning was still very much alive in the collective imagination, despite such episodes having become rare. Having said that, even the removal of bodies from the city bounds presented difficulties of a cultural kind. In fact, people buried outside the physical limits of the urban area had in the past always been those who had died outside the communion of the church, such as suicides, sodomites and members of other religions.[45]

Hereupon the reform of Naples's cemeteries came to a standstill, for during the eighteenth century the social structures of the *ancien régime* and the scarcity of economic resources prevented any new attempts to move the urban graves from the city. But the advent of the Napoleonic age produced the political conditions for the launch of the project to build a large public cemetery away from the capital. On 1 September 1807, Joseph Bonaparte, having settled in Naples in March 1806, ordered that the poor should be buried in the *camposanto* of the Incurabili, while in September 1813, under the auspices of his successor Joachim Murat, work began on the new *camposanto* of Poggioreale, planned by the Neapolitan architect Francesco Maresca.[46] More than 20 years were needed for the completion of the structure, which was inaugurated in 1836 at the time of the cholera epidemic that swept through the Two Sicilies. During this period the health authorities intensified their supervision of urban burial plots, which were held responsible for the pollution of the air. Consequently, when the new cemetery was opened any kind of burial within the capital was strictly banned.

The "new *camposanto*" of Poggioreale was a hybrid structure divided into four distinguishable areas. The first three consisted of two rectangular courtyards within which were built a number of pits on the model of Fuga's cemetery: burial in these two areas was reserved for less well-off citizens, while a third, larger courtyard, located next to the previous two and alongside a church for funeral services, was used to house the sepulchral chapels of the confraternities. Each of these had its own burial plot in front and, inside, a crypt for the deposit of the mineralised remains. The peculiar design of the cemetery chapels of Poggioreale appears to have been a compromise between the Napoleonic legislation's insistence on interment being carried out in an open space and the traditional *terresante*, which resembled hypogea with an ossuary for human remains constructed beneath the chapels. The fourth area, which surrounded the three courtyards, was a vast space set aside for a garden (on the model of Paris's Père-Lachaise) in which families erected sepulchres, each with a recess for remains recovered from the ground.

The opening of the Poggioreale *camposanto* brought with it a clear categorisation of the dead based not on status but on economic means. As in the past, the city of the dead was a reflection of that of the living. Burial in the common grave had to be paid for, while the bodies of the poor and the sick—often one and the same—were still laid to rest in Ferdinando Fuga's Enlightenment cemetery machine. One can rightly ask oneself what effect this new approach had on Neapolitan society.

In May 1822, well before the inauguration of the new cemetery, the diocese received a request from some inhabitants of the parish of the Santissima Annunziata in Fonseca "in the Fontanelle district," who wanted permission to build, at their own expense, a church in the ossuary and to found a confraternity for the cult of the dead. The supplicants ended their letter by claiming how "truly necessary the aforementioned church in that deposit [is], following the example we see [. . .] in the *camposanto* of this capital." This probably referred to the chapel in the *camposanto* of the Incurabili, given that the church for worship in the new cemetery of Poggioreale was still being built.[47] Archbishop Luigi Ruffo Scilla wanted more information on the request and ordered Canon Ferdinando Panico, the secretary of the diocesan tribunal of the Santa Visita, to inspect the site in the presence of the petition's signatories, around ten people in all. According to them, the ossuary had been completely left to itself, to the extent that one often saw "dogs going out with a bone in their mouths." At the end of his visit secretary Panico submitted his report:

> I went to visit the place which is in the countryside, entirely separated from the inhabited area: here I found under a hill a kind of grotto, or cave, of a vast extension in terms of length and width. In the middle of it there is an altar made of masonry, where the devotees who met me there told me [the cult] had been celebrated in the past, and the parish priest of Fonseca attests the same. Walking through this cave you see here and there skeletons and pieces of bone of the dead, which, according to the devotees, had earlier been dumped in a heap and walked on, but which they had gathered together and placed in *giardinetti* that they had made as best they could. And to protect them from rain, which entered from the caves that partly surrounded the grotto, they had built small walls.[48]

It is not clear when and how these rituals had begun to be observed in the old ossuary, but it must have been a recent development given that at the end of 1817 the available documentation is unanimous on the fact that the caves had been used only to deposit human remains.[49] Canon Panico advised the bishop to establish a permanent rector to the Fontanelle and to sanction the creation of a place of worship, but in August the police informed the health authorities, who still had jurisdiction over the ossuary, leading to their sudden intervention and a prohibition on further meetings in the cave.[50]

What had prompted the request for the establishment of a cult of the dead in the Fontanelle ossuary? Perhaps the final transfer of all the bodies of the poor to the *camposanto* of the Incurabili had resulted in a considerable part of the population feeling an unduly sudden and traumatic detachment from their late loved ones. According to information collected by the local authority, in 1845 the hospitals had sent 4,064 bodies to the *camposanto* of the Incurabili and the parishes had sent 3,478 (presumably all poor), while there had been 4,897 burials in the *camposanto* of Poggioreale.[51] It should be remembered that the poor were only rarely outsiders, the majority being citizens who had fallen on hard times for one reason or another.[52] In Naples there was no lack of

Figure 8.2 The Fontanelle Cemetery, Naples (bones and skulls stacked behind a group of boxed skulls).

Source: Dominik Matus [CC BY-SA 4.0 (https://creativecommons.org/licenses/by-sa/4.0)], via Wikimedia Commons.

rootless vagabonds from the provinces and from the time of Charles of Bourbon a general hospice had been created for such as they: this was the Reale albergo dei poveri, which initially had its own burial arrangements but later made use of the Incurabili *camposanto*.[53] The 1835–37 cholera epidemic certainly contributed to the sudden detachment of families from their dead. More than 18,000 Neapolitans lost their lives on that occasion and were buried in groups in allocated land alongside the same *camposanto*. It is probably no coincidence that as early as 1838 the inhabitants of the Fontanelle district once again asked the government for permission to erect a place of worship near the caves.[54]

Direct interment in the Fuga cemetery and the lack of a meaningful setting on a par with a church or—more so—a *terrasanta*, might have driven many believers from the lower classes to call for a return to tradition. This desire appears to have been supported by the local clergy, always present in the petitions sent to the public authorities. Although intercessory rites did not require prayers to be said on the exact site of a person's remains, the custom of burying people in places of worship had led to this association. The age-old practice of burying the have-nots in the pits and *terresante* of parish churches and confraternities gave family members a place to go and pray over their loved ones' bodies, as well as the knowledge that they were in a special place.[55] To be sure, the graves would be emptied sooner or later, but in the *ancien régime* this occurred only when the situation had become unsustainable, presumably long after the end of the period of mourning.

After the closure and abandonment of urban burial plots in 1836, the Fontanelle ossuary was the only place in the city where it was possible to reproduce the macabre settings to which the people had been accustomed for over two centuries. On the basis of the available information, it does not appear that the caves were used as a place of devotion until the 1870s. However, in 1872, with the agreement of the lay and ecclesiastic authorities, the priest Gaetano Barbati oversaw the creation of a church and the organising of a local pilgrimage centred on the human remains present in the ossuary.[56]

In the years between the two World Wars, a new practice arose which involved adopting skulls and making reliquaries out of various materials (wood, marble or metal) in which to house them as an *ex-voto* for the souls in purgatory.[57] It is not clear whether this new devotional act was the fruit of an autonomous initiative taken by the faithful or if they once more had the clergy by their side: whatever the case, the practice was tolerated. In fact, after the Second World War, it extended to churches in both the centre and periphery of the city and these used their ancient *terresante* when observing the cult, exhibiting skulls that had not removed from the *giardinetti* after their closure of 1836.[58]

In 1969, Archbishop Corrado Ursi banned this new approach to the veneration of purgatory souls that it did not conform fully to church doctrine. By then, however, it was a marginal phenomenon, albeit one to which the inhabitants of the neighbourhoods where it had been practised still felt strongly attached, having come to see it as part of their identity. The new bourgeois attitudes with respect to the dead body had begun to hold sway as early as the mid-nineteenth century. This included the progressive hospitalisation of the corpse, which had the effect of taking its management out of the hands of families and the social organisations of the preindustrial age.[59] The renewed cult of the dead at the Fontanelle ossuary and other ancient Neapolitan burial grounds were thus little more than a holdover, the last vestige of a centuries-old Christian practice that mediated the relationship between the faithful and the bodily remains of their ancestors.

Notes

1. Michel Lauwers, "Sépulcre, sépulture, cimetière. Lexique, idéologie et pratiques sociales dans l'Occident medieval," in *Qu'est-ce qu'une sépulture? Humanités et systèmes funéraires de la Préhistoire à nos jours*, ed. Michel Lauwers and Aurélie Zemour (Antibes: Éditions APDCA, 2016), 95–111 and 109. More generally, see Michel Lauwers, *Naissance du cimetière. Lieux sacrés et terre des morts dans l'Occident médiéval* (Paris: Aubier, 2005). For reasons of space, questions relating to burial as a means of social exclusion

cannot be considered here; on this issue I refer the reader to two of my other works: Diego Carnevale, "La sépulture des non catholiques à Naples entre XVIIIe et XIXe siècle: règles et exceptions de l'intolérance," in *L'orchestration de la mort. Les funérailles des temps modernes à l'époque contemporaine*, ed. Élisabeth Belmas and Serenella Nonnis-Vigilante (Villeneuve d'Ascq: Presses Universitaires du Septentrion, 2017), 81–104; Diego Carnevale, "Il corpo dell'altro. Sepolture ebraiche e musulmane nella Napoli del Settecento," in *Napoli e il Mediterraneo nel Settecento. Scambi, immagini, istituzioni*, ed. Anna Maria Rao (Bari: Edipuglia, 2017), 161–74.

2. See Claudia Petraccone, *Napoli dal Cinquecento all'Ottocento, problemi di storia demografica e sociale* (Naples: Guida, 1974); Pasquale Villani, *Mezzogiorno tra riforme e rivoluzione* (Rome-Bari: Laterza, 1973).

3. See Franco Strazzullo, *Edilizia e urbanistica a Napoli dal Cinquecento al Settecento* (Naples: Arte tipografica, 1995). For a long-term perspective see Giuseppe Galasso, *Napoli capitale identità politica e identità cittadina studi e ricerche 1266–1860* (Naples: Electa, 2003).

4. Some examples of convents that in this period subsumed their cemetery courtyards are mentioned in Diego Carnevale, *L'affare dei morti. Mercato funerario, politica e gestione della sepoltura a Napoli (secoli XVII–XIX)* (Rome: École française de Rome, 2014), 61–63. Similar phenomena must also have been found in other Italian cities, but studies of this type are scarce. An early case appears to have been that of Florence, which between the thirteenth and fourteenth century developed similar vaulted rooms under the city's principal churches: Sharon T. Strocchia, "Burials in Renaissance Florence, 1350–1500" (PhD thesis, University of California, Berkeley, 1981), 359–68.

5. See *Constitutiones Dioecesanae Synodi Neapolitanae celebratae ab Illustriss. et Reverendiss. D.D. Octavio [. . .] Aquaviva [. . .] Anno Domini MDCVII* (Rome: 1608), 7–14.

6. Among the first attestations see ibid., 7.

7. See William D. Haglund and Marcella H. Sorg, eds., *Forensic Taphonomy: The Postmortem Fate of Human Remains* (Boca Raton: CRC Press, 1996).

8. Various examples of interventions by the municipal authorities are given in Archivio di Stato di Napoli (hereafter ASNa), *Supremo Magistrato e Soprintendenza Generale di Salute* (henceforth *Magistrato di salute*), 296–97.

9. On the use of the term "cemetery" see Lauwers, "Sépulcre, sépulture." In the texts produced by the Neapolitan synods the term *coemeterium* disappears during the course of the sixteenth century, being replaced by *sepultura* and more rarely *terra sancta*. As confirmation of the shift in meaning in common usage a significant document is decree X of the 1694 synod, entitled *De funeris, exequiis et sepulturis*, in which the writers cited a passage of the fourth provincial synod of Milan (1579) replacing the term "Coemeterium" with "Terra Sancta": see *Synodus Dioecesana [. . .] cardinali Cantelmo [. . .] Anno Domini MDCXCIV* (Rome: 1694), 136; *Acta Ecclesiae Mediolanensis [. . .] Carolus S. R. E. Cardinalis* (Mediolani: 1583), 189v. It is worth noting that one of the first references to burial hypogea is in *Constitutiones [. . .] Anno Domini MDCVII*, 7, where they are called "sepulchra testudineata" [vaulted burial places].

10. The same toponym highlights the cultural function of the place, as it is derived from *coemeterium*.

11. Andrea Ferraro, *Del cemeterio nolano con le vite di alcuni santi, che vi furono sepeliti* (Naples: 1644). I will quote from the critical edition, ed. Carlo Ebanista (Cicciano: Città futura, 1993). The chapter of Nola Cathedral managed the entire Cimitile complex between 1599 and 1675.

12. See ibid., 82.

13. Ibid., 14.
14. See Emilio Tolaini, *Campo Santo di Pisa—Progetto e cantiere* (Pisa: Edizioni ETS, 2008), 33–34.
15. See Michel De Montaigne, *Journal du voyage de Michel de Montaigne en Italie, par la Suisse et l'Allemagne en 1580 & 1581. Avec des notes par M. de Querlon*, 2 vols., vol. II (Rome: Le Jay, 1774), 349.
16. Ferraro, *Del cemeterio nolano*, 130.
17. The churches named by Ferraro were almost all built or renovated at the beginning of the seventeenth century: the Jesuits began work on the Church of Carminiello in 1612, the friars minor took over and renovated the Church of San Diego dell'Ospedaletto in 1595, the Theatines acquired Santi Apostoli in 1611, the Dominicans the Rosario di Palazzo in 1572 and Santa Maria della Sanità in 1602, and finally the discalced Augustinians renovated their church and convent starting from 1604: see respectively Italo Ferraro, *Napoli. Atlante città storica. Quartieri bassi e risanamento* (Naples: Clean Edizioni, 2003), 306 and 465; Italo Ferraro, *Napoli. Atlante città storica. Centro antico* (Naples: Clean Edizioni, 2002), 476; Italo Ferraro, *Napoli. Atlante città storica. Quartieri spagnoli e Rione Carità* (Naples: Oikos, 2004), 288; Italo Ferraro, *Napoli. Atlante città storica. Stella, Vergini, Sanità* (Naples: Oikos, 2007), 241 and 388.
18. Ferraro, *Del cemeterio nolano*, 130.
19. The procedure was described in the accounts produced by the vicar general of the diocese for the acts of the Tribunal of the Santa Visita, conserved, only starting from the eighteenth century, in the section *Cappelle sepolcrali* of the Archivio Storico Diocesano di Napoli (ASDN).
20. Michel Vovelle, *La morte e l'Occidente dal 1300 ai giorni nostri* (Rome-Bari: Laterza, 2000), 248.
21. Among the instruments used to spread this pedagogy there were innumerable manuals for the preparation for death, which contained frequent references to the transience of the body and its undoing, see Daniel Roche, " 'La mémoire de la mort': recherche sur la place des arts de mourir dans la librairie et la lecture en France aux XVIIe et XVIIIe siècles," *Annales E.S.C.* 31 (1976): 76–119; Roger Chartier, "Les arts de mourir, 1450–1600," ibid., 51–76.
22. See Pierroberto Scaramella, *Le Madonne del Purgatorio: iconografia e religione in Campania tra Rinascimento e Controriforma* (Genoa: Marietti, 1991), 281–99; Francesco Pezzini, "Doppie esequie e scolatura dei corpi nell'Italia meridionale d'età moderna," *Medicina nei secoli arte e scienza* 18, no. 3 (2006): 897–924.
23. It was Jean Delumeau who insisted so effectively on the fact that the first audience for the pedagogy of death was in fact made up of churchmen, who in turn were expected to pass this teaching onto the communities of the faithful: see Jean Delumeau, *Il peccato e la paura. L'idea di colpa in Occidente dal XIII al XVIII secolo* (Bologna: Il Mulino, 2006), 581–89.
24. On the situation in France, see ibid., 606; For the Kingdom of Naples see Alfonso Maria Di Nola, *La nera signora. Antropologia della morte e del lutto* (Rome: Newton and Compton, 2006), 362.
25. See Vovelle, *La morte e l'occidente*, 241–67; Delumeau, *Il peccato e la paura*, 197–99 and 704–17. On the artistic aspects see Michel Vovelle, *Les âmes du purgatoire ou le travail du deuil* (Paris: Gallimard, 1996); Alberto Tenenti, ed., *Humana fragilitas: i temi della morte in Europa tra Duecento e Settecento* (Clusone: Ferrari, 2000).
26. Delumeau, *Il peccato e la paura*, 662–69, but see also Maria Pia Donato, *Sudden Death: Medicine and Religion in Eighteenth-Century Rome* (Farnham: Ashgate, 2014). In Naples a confraternity for sudden death was founded

in 1665, Diego Carnevale, "Medicina e religione di fronte alla morte nella Napoli del XVIII secolo," in *Antropologia e scienze sociali a Napoli nell'età moderna*, ed. Roberto Mazzola (Rome: Aracne, 2012), 55–78 and 66.

27. Giovanni De Blasiis, ed., "Racconto di varie notizie accadute nella città di Napoli dall'anno 1700 al 1732," *Archivio storico per le province napoletane* 31 (1906): 430–508 and 446.

28. Soon after the middle of the century, the event was also recounted by the canon of the cathedral Giuseppe Sparano, who omitted the macabre details but confirmed the diocese's leadership role in these displays of piety, see Giuseppe Sparano, *Memorie istoriche per illustrare gli atti della S. Napoletana Chiesa e gli atti della Congregazione delle Appostoliche Missioni eretta nel Duomo della medesima*, 2 vols. (Naples: G. Raimondi, 1768), 292–93.

29. ASNa, *Magistrato di salute*, 286; *Relazione de' medici per l'abolizione delle terresante di Napoli*, 20 December 1779; this document was also cited by Scaramella, *Le madonne del purgatorio*; Pezzini, "Doppie esequie."

30. 2 November was also the day in which sermons on purgatory were delivered: see Delumeau, *Il peccato e la paura*, 697.

31. ASNa, *Magistrato di salute*, 286; *Relazione de' medici*.

32. On the organisation of confraternities in Naples and their social function, see Daniele Casanova, ed., *Mestieri e devozione* (Naples: La città del sole, 2005).

33. See Carnevale, *L'affare dei morti*, 167–76.

34. In this era one also finds ancient burial hypogea from antiquity, some of which were reused in later periods, see Carlo Ebanista, "Gli spazi funerari a Napoli tra antichità e tardo medioevo," in *Città, spazi pubblici e servizi sociali nel Mezzogiorno medievale*, ed. Giovanni Vitolo (Battipaglia: Laveglia Carlone Editore, 2016), 251–93.

35. See Pasquale Lopez, *Napoli e la peste 1464–1530. Politica, istituzioni, problemi sanitari* (Naples: Jovene, 1989), 33.

36. See ASNa, *Magistrato di salute*, 286; this was a recurrent procedure, at the end of which a report on the success of the operation was sent to the court.

37. All the other hospitals in the city sent their dead in covered carts to the pit in the Incurabili by night: Carnevale, *L'affare dei morti*, 76.

38. ASNa, *Segreteria e ministero per gli affari ecclesiastici*, espedienti di consiglio, 734, letter from the governor of the Incurabili, Giovanni Antonio Coppola, to secretary Brancone, 25 January 1756, which mentions the first letter sent by Brancone on 2 August 1755.

39. In fact Fuga had built 19 parallel galleries inside which were raised dividing walls in order to make the 360 pits. This construction technique had the dual advantage of reaching considerable depth while providing a solid foundation: see Paolo Giordano, *Il disegno dell'architettura funebre: Napoli Poggioreale, il Cimitero delle 366 fosse e il Sepolcreto dei Colerici* (Florence: Alinea, 2006), 111.

40. ASNa, *Segreteria di Stato d'azienda*, 1762, bound but unnumbered papers.

41. ASNa, *Segreteria e ministero per gli affari ecclesiastici*, espedienti di consiglio, 734. In Paris during the 1730s a similar technique for the management of the inhumation of bodies in the overcrowded cemetery of the Innocents was proposed, as illustrated by the anonymous memoranda of 1736 and in the report by the doctors and academics Louis Lemery, Joseph Haunault and Joseph Geoffroy: see Bibliothèque Nationale de France, coll. Joly de Fleury, ms. 1317, 50r–73v.

42. Roberto Pane, *Ferdinando Fuga* (Naples: ESI, 1956), 104, 129 and 198.

43. According to subsequent documentation the graves of the cemetery were not subject to any maintenance, certainly not until the inauguration of the new cemetery plant in 1836, but it is noteworthy that the work of Fuga

remained in operation until 1890. In 1788, Quatremère de Quincy described the *camposanto* of the Incurabili, issuing an invitation to imitate its structure and method of burial to those cities that "have an immense population that does not put any interest before that of its wholesomeness": Antoine Ch. Quatremère de Quincy, *Encyclopédie Méthodique. Architecture*, vol. I (Paris: Panckoucke, 1788), 681, quoted by Laura Bertolaccini, *Città e cimiteri. Dall'eredità medievale alla codificazione ottocentesca* (Rome: Kappa, 2004), 27.

44. ASNa, *Segreteria di Stato d'azienda*, 1762, bound papers but not numbered.
45. See Carnevale, "La sépulture des non catholiques."
46. See Carnevale, *L'affare dei morti*, 400–11.
47. ASDN, Pandetta 14, 91, n. 61, letter of 18 May 1822.
48. Ibid.
49. See Carnevale, *L'affare dei morti*, 401.
50. ASNa, *Magistrato di salute*, 289, report dated August 1822.
51. Carnevale, *L'affare dei morti*, 497–98.
52. See Robert Jütte, *Poverty and Deviance in Early Modern Europe* (Cambridge: Cambridge University Press, 1994).
53. Carnevale, *L'affare dei morti*, 314 and 469.
54. ASNA, *Intendenza di Napoli*, primo versamento, 856, n. 4937.
55. In 1835, Karl August Mayer testified in his travel journal that the Neapolitan *terresante* continued to be frequented in a similar way to that described by the doctors in 1779: see Karl August Mayer, *Neapel und die Neapolitaner oder Briefe aus Neapel in die Heimat*, 2 vols. (Oldenburg: Schulz 1842), 122–30.
56. See Italo Ferraro, *Napoli. Atlante città storica. Dallo Spirito Santo a Materdei* (Naples: Oikos, 2004), 491.
57. The practice has been studied from the anthropological point of view by Marino Niola and Stefano De Matteis, *Antropologia delle anime in pena* (Lecce: Argo, 1993); Marino Niola, *Il purgatorio a Napoli* (Rome: Meltemi, 2003); Stefano De Matteis, *Mezzogiorno di fede. Il rito tra esperienza, memoria e storia* (Naples: M. D'Auria, 2013).
58. See ibid., 170–71 and 185.
59. On bourgeois Naples in the nineteenth century, see Paolo Macry, *Ottocento: famiglia, élites e patrimoni a Napoli* (Bologna: Il Mulino, 1988); on the medicalisation of the body in the modern age see Anne Carol, *Les médecins et la mort, XIXe–XXe siècles* (Paris: Aubier, 2004).

9 Bodies "as Objects Preserved in Museums"[1]

The Capuchin Catacombs in Palermo

Natale Spineto

The Capuchin Cemetery in Palermo houses the biggest collection of natural and artificial mummies in the world.[2] They are located in a series of underground corridors which, by analogy with early Christian burial spaces, which still exist in and around Palermo and are in some ways similar structures, have come to be referred to as the Capuchin Catacombs. The catacombs contain around 2,000 corpses[3] arranged in various positions, most of them having undergone a drying process that preserves, in addition to their skeleton, their flesh and skin. The bodies are dressed according to the customs of their time and left on display for visitors.

History of the Capuchin Catacombs

Annexed to the church of Santa Maria della Pace, which was rebuilt after the Capuchins' arrival in Palermo in 1533,[4] a few years after the order's foundation, the cemetery passed into public ownership in 1621[5] and was made available for the committal of nobles, under licence from the General Fathers,[6] at first intermittently and then more and more frequently, in particular after circa 1670.[7] The earliest description of the place is of 1680, at which time it was already "famous" and "celebrated":

> One sees some compartments, like chapels [. . .] and in them the bodies stretched out, one on top of the other, with wooden partitions like bookshelves between them, or else standing, whole and desiccated with their beards and hair. They are placed in niches and above them are signs indicating their names and hometowns. In the lower part, in rooms off to one side, there are many corpses of princesses and Ladies, and on the other side, in other rooms, those of various titled gentlemen, and princes [. . .] wearing Capuchin habits or secular clothes, or else there are lay people in chests.[8]

The granting of the right to be laid to rest in the cemetery was a controversial topic that included discussions about the abundance of requests, the highly restrictive Capuchin rules and the possibility of exceptions and special dispensations.[9] All the same, the number of those who wanted to be buried on the site increased steadily, and if before licences were initially given only to benefactors and then to the nobility, at a certain point they were extended to everyone, with the peak being reached between the mid-eighteenth century and the middle of the nineteenth.

The affection in which Palermitans held the catacombs explains the failure of the civil authorities' attempts in the eighteenth century to ban the entombments on health grounds. A royal decree of 1710 that required the dead to be buried at least a mile from the city and outside of churches was disregarded. It remained a dead letter when it was issued again in 1743 and a further effort, in 1769, led to protests by nobles, ecclesiastics and the lower classes alike.[10] In 1781, in order to evade the prohibition, the catacombs were declared a place "for the preservation of skeletons more than for the burial of corpses."[11] In April 1783 an explicit ban on burying bodies was imposed on the Capuchins, but in July of the same year the friars themselves were exempted from the measure, which in 1785 was revoked altogether.[12] This arrangement can best be explained within the context of the policies of Viceroy Domenico Caracciolo, who had frequented Enlightenment circles in Paris and went on to promote reforms that brought him into conflict with the aristocracy and the clergy. There are in fact some traces of these events—and the cultural climate that inspired them—in written accounts from travellers: indeed, the abbot of Saint-Non, who had embraced Enlightenment ideas, praised Viceroy Caracciolo's willingness "to abolish the barbaric custom we talked about just now" and to build a large graveyard.[13] In 1787 the friars consecrated an area of their land to create a cemetery for burials, but in the same year Viceroy Francesco Maria Venanzio d'Aquino, Prince of Carmanico, allowed the catacombs to reopen.[14]

In the meantime, the site's exceptionalism had made it an international "tourist" destination. It was made a staging post on the Grand Tour, a substantial part of which usually took place in Sicily:[15] one of the "trailblazers"[16] who visited the site was John Dryden, who toured Sicily in 1700–1701.[17] From then on the cemetery became the subject of countless descriptions[18] in publications and grew in popularity not least for the fascination that its peculiar characteristics unfailingly inspired in visitors of the Romantic era.

The practice of drying and exhibiting corpses continued throughout the nineteenth century. A major cholera epidemic in 1837 quickly led to a tightening of burial regulations, but these did not cover the catacombs since they were "justly [. . .] very famous among nationals and foreigners."[19] In 1854, during another cholera epidemic, access to the catacombs during All Souls' Day was forbidden, and a year later an inspection led to the imposition of stringent laws on the friars for health reasons. The ensuing complaints resulted in a new inspection and in the end King Ferdinand II decided that the friars should be left alone. A report from 1859 speaks of the method used by the Capuchins as the "most suitable way of preserving corpses."[20]

Even with such a brief overview one can appreciate the appeal of a detailed historical investigation that highlights the implications of the debates that surrounded the events of the Capuchin cemetery in the various periods, taking into account the political and social circumstances and, in particular, the ecclesiastical, civil and health regulations and their application, which are particularly appropriate given that the catacombs often received special treatment. But, in view of the impossibility of carrying out such research, which would oblige us to select a single moment in the convent's history and therefore renounce a general view, which at this level of the investigation appears more useful, we must be content with noting that the above summary clearly indicates that the Capuchin hypogeum received a large and growing number of requests for places from all parts of Palermitan society right until its closure. All efforts to limit the demand and to contain or abolish the practice which, for one reason or another, involved from time to time the Capuchin, civil and health authorities, were consistently thwarted by protests that cut across social boundaries and were met with sympathy by the governing authorities—which were certainly not disinterested—and at a some point also took advantage of the site's international reputation. It is clear that securing a place among the Capuchins had significant social value.

An early crisis was triggered by the suppression of the religious corporations by the Italian government in 1866, which brought about the eviction of the Capuchins and the transformation of the catacombs into a municipal cemetery. But yet again the social importance of the site ensured that the mummification activities were allowed to carry on.[21]

However, there were changes of opinion: "the sight of decomposition and direct contact with corrupt corpses will no longer be acceptable for the new rational and hygienist sentiments that will impose a single admissible sepulchral form: cemeteries on the outskirts."[22] For example, in 1864 Francesco Finocchietti, prefect of Pavia and Siena and a future senator, opined that economic considerations lay behind the cemetery's existence and declared that "in times when public hygiene is supposed to be a primary concern of governors, so many corpses wrapped in miserable rags and kept in a humid atmosphere in a poorly ventilated place, to become, in the event of an epidemic, the source of more serious ills should not be tolerated."[23] Moreover, the social and religious values that had justified the continuity of the cemetery—about which more later—had weakened: Giuseppe Pitrè noted, in 1881, that "this spectacle proves the ostentation and not the sincerity of religious sentiment, which has become a plaything"[24] and in the same year a painting by Calcedonio Reina depicted two lovers kissing in corridors strewn with corpses.[25]

The desiccation process had been banned the year before, in 1880, by the municipal authorities (although the Capuchins were only notified

Figure 9.1 Calcedonio Reina, *Love and Death*, 1881, oil on canvas, Catania, Museo Civico Castello Ursino.

Source: [Public domain], via Wikimedia Commons.

in October 1881), but it continued until 1885,[26] albeit in a more toned-down way. Further corroboration of a change in attitude towards the display of embalmed corpses comes from Guy de Maupassant who, in 1885, wrote about the reactions of the city's residents when he told them that he wished to visit the catacombs: "Do not go to see that horror. It is a barbarous thing, which will soon disappear, thank goodness! However, no-one has been buried there for some years now."[27] Since then several cases had been recorded of chests of embalmed remains,[28] left in the corridors more or less temporarily, and some unusual cases of bodies exhibited in the catacombs for specific reasons, such as that of Rosalia Lombardo, who was treated with a different technique developed by the well-known embalmer Alfredo Salafia.[29]

Mummification and Christian Traditions

The history of the site briefly described was reconstructed, thanks mainly to two types of sources that differ from each other both in terms of character and point of view. The first provides us with the inside perspective of the Capuchin friars, who mentioned the catacombs in their reports or made them an object of scholarly research. The second comprises the annotations and diaries of travellers on the Grand Tour, who have left us with an image of the catacombs observed through the prism of expectations and sensibilities very different to those of the Sicilians.

The Capuchin authors were well aware of the exceptional interest in their site, but their records, which were always positive, focused on the general characteristics of the burials, on the sanctity of the friars, on the rules governing burials and the embalming techniques, surprisingly neglecting the issue of greatest interest to observers, namely the reasons behind a practice which they themselves most likely considered obvious and took for granted.

The tone of the travel reports, on the other hand, reflected the bizarre and unique character of a place that inspired horror (Jacques D'Orville used the Latin verb *exhorreo* to describe it)[30] and sometimes admiration, as well giving rise to irony, but never left anyone indifferent. Some even went so far as to declare it incompatible with Christian principles: "I could not believe," wrote William Fleury in 1903, "that a population of artists with Greek and Eastern blood could have maintained, without valid reason, as if it were completely natural, such a truly horrible tradition contrary to the ancient cult of the dead and also to the Christian idea of the resurrection of the dead which has so much poetry in it."[31]

Shock and consternation when faced with what appeared to be a picturesque curiosity to be photographed or written about in one's travel diary, were accompanied by incomprehension: a fundamental failure to understand, which left unanswered the question that everyone, more or less openly, asked themselves, and which Mario Praz expressed as follows in his *Travels in the East*: "what were these men thinking of to let themselves be 'buried' like this, with a sign bearing their name, like hanged criminals, pirates hung up in chains until the vultures and bad weather broke them up?"[32]

An effort of reflection is necessary to try to give an account, on the basis of the literature available to us and the sundry exchanges between insiders and outsiders, the significance of the custom and the reasons for its originality.

In a very general sense, it should immediately be said that the practices in question, while not violating orthodoxy, as Fleury claimed, constituted an anomaly with respect to Christian funeral customs. These, albeit with exceptions (for instance the many churches that contain collections of bones arranged in various poses, like Our Lady of the Conception of the Capuchins in Rome) and sometimes with local variations, can be said to have as their chief feature the removal of the body from the "sensorial satisfaction" of the living by means of inhumation. This creates a clear distinction with regard to other religious traditions, in which the body continues to be an object of perception (mostly involving sight and touch, but sometimes also smell and even taste)[33] for periods of varying lengths and in different ways.[34]

However, the general Christian principle does not apply, in the Catholic world, to the bodies of saints, whose relics, being objects of veneration, can be presented for viewing and manipulated on the strength of the particular status assigned to a saint: "the sacral value attached to the body of the saint, both in life and in death, is constituted in the background and on the basis of the esteem in which the body of the martyr is held, which in turn is founded on the example of the suffering body of Christ."[35] When the mortal remains of an individual are not subjected to the process of putrefaction, or at least are preserved for longer and in a better condition than is usually the case, that is considered a possible sign of sanctity and, when the processes of canonisation are formalised, becomes one of the factors taken into consideration. The recovery and recognition of bodies thus become, in these cases, habitual practices.

The saints show Christians the way, and become their exemplars, but the treatment of their bodies represents an exception to the norm, which remains that of interment. The Capuchin Catacombs housed simple, ordinary deceased people and the preservation of their bodies was not due to supernatural reasons but to specific methods of mummification. Nevertheless, the rationale behind the resistance to decay of the bodies of saints is not entirely unrelated to the case in hand: it is in fact present in the original, foundational and therefore particularly consequential phase in the life of the catacombs.

The burials began at the same time as the convent was established, in an area adjacent to the church. They continued there until the sixteenth century, when a new burial space was created inside Santa Maria della Pace and the already buried friars were exhumed and transferred there. Here is how the translation was presented by Father Gianmaria da Castelvetrano, provincial superior between 1600 and 1603 and then between 1609 and 1611, and therefore a contemporary of the events he described:

> In Palermo, in the year of our Lord 1599, the translation was made of the dead bodies from the outside graves [. . .] to the inside graves. And when unearthing those bone relics of the saintly friars, not only did we not smell a malodour, but rather there was a sweet odour. And 45 bodies of friars were found, all healthy and whole.[36]

The striking detail of this account is the insistence on the integrity and sweet smell of the bodies, both of which are signs of sanctity: Brother Serafino da Palermo appeared, for instance, "with his vermillion flesh, blond hair and red beard, and seemed not a dead man, but like one who slept, and he was one of the first to be buried there."[37] Forty of the 45 bodies were placed in "good order" in a separate, closed burial space.[38]

The matter did not end there, however. The years 1667–68 saw the start of enlargement works aimed at accommodating the many nobles who wished to be buried with the Capuchins. According to an account by Father Rosario da Palermo, written in 1737, the workers came across a wall that sounded hollow and made an opening in it and immediately became aware of a "a sweet odour they had never known before." A friar joined them and enlarged the opening: "A most beautiful spectacle opened to his eyes. He saw, and they all saw, standing in an immaculate room, with their habits in one piece, 40 dead Capuchins in a devout posture before an image of the great Mother of God."[39] These were the 40 friars who, having been found intact during the 1599 exhumation, had been placed on their feet in that room, which had subsequently been forgotten. Thus the miracle of 60 years earlier was repeated, as were the two signs of sanctity: their preserved bodies and their fragrance.[40]

Among the proofs of the saintliness of the 40 friars, whose remains were immediately the object of veneration, were their "nocturnal processions [. . .], especially when some scourge of God was imminent": in particular, during a severe drought in 1646–47 their appearance brought rain, and their reappearance was recorded on the occasion of the earthquake of September 1726.[41]

From our point of view it does not matter to what extent these tales reflect actual events, nor would it make sense to distinguish what is likely from what is not and to search for rebuttals of the testimonies concerning the rediscoveries. What counts, rather, is that happenings, beliefs and legends converged into a coherent story, which was connected to the origins of the Capuchin cemetery and which, as a primary event, took on fundamental value.

The friars' bodies were preserved because they were holy, and after their long concealment their reappearance made them the oldest nucleus of the catacombs. Their exhibition thus followed the logic of the display of relics (although they would normally have had to fully conform to a series of canons that regulated the form and character of such): "the burial place of the friars," Antonino da Castellammare wrote, "is, morally speaking, a *genuine reliquary of Saints*."[42]

Just as the exhibition of the remains of saints was covered by the canons, so placing the graves of ordinary people alongside relics was normal practice. From early Christianity there was a belief that being laid to rest next to the tomb of a martyr gave a better hope of salvation, since physical proximity was considered something that helped the deceased benefit from the virtues of the saint.[43] This principle was then transferred from the bodies of martyrs to those of confessors. The pressing and ever-increasing requests for burial in the catacombs—whose very name evoked early Christianity—responded at least at the beginning, to this need:

> from many [. . .] venerable religious people we know: being one day buried with them would bring the special esteem and maximum

honour of the Lord, and they recommended it to others so that thanks to the merits and intercession of the dear friends of God, their souls would receive support.[44]

The Capuchin burial site was therefore like the "real Christian catacombs":[45] not only for resembling hypogea or for certain architectural features, but also because it gave the faithful the chance to be laid to rest beside those who enjoyed eternal bliss.

The practices considered so far were not so very different from the most common customs. Rather, the uniqueness of the catacombs resided in the fact that the embalmed bodies belonged to common people and not the saints, and that the "mummies" on show were dressed in their everyday clothes.

The practice has been explained as a variant of the "double burial" phenomenon. Examined ethnologically following the aforementioned classic study by Robert Hertz, "double burial" and "double funerals" have recently been studied, in a Christian context, by Francesco Pezzini, who analysed evidence of them especially in Campania.[46] Leaving aside local variations and the many exceptions, the custom involved exhuming a body, cleaning the bones and then reburying them in a different location (or preserving some or all of the remains in the houses of relatives or elsewhere). The washing of skeletons had a special symbolic significance, since, by differentiating between the perishability of the soft tissues and the inalterability of the bones, it aimed to remove, through a cleaning operation that represented a form of purification, everything that was decomposable and subject to the wear of time, and thereby to extract the deceased from the human temporal dimension. Hertz contends that phenomena like embalmment and cremation, while apparently diverse, might also fit the same framework since they also have the aim of reducing the corpse to immutable elements no longer susceptible to degradation,[47] and of ritually managing the death of an individual—which might put the integrity of society at risk—to ensure that the deceased enters "into the peace of human community."[48]

Some of the characteristics of double burial are certainly similar to those of the catacombs: the manipulation and treatment of human remains in an attempt to save them from decay and give them a sort of social immortality connect the two practices. However, the insistence on making the dead resemble the living, the importance of exhibiting the corpses, and the reference to the unaltered bodies of saints (which introduces a point that is indissolubly linked to Catholic theology), are elements of the treatment of the Capuchin dead that induce us to combine Hertz's interpretations with those of other sources.

More than once the sources provide details of the Capuchins' drying methods, which have recently been studied from a scientific and physico-anthropological angle,[49] consistently underlining how the knowledge put into practice managed to preserve the elasticity and complexion of the skin. The summit arrived at by the applied technical knowledge of the embalmers was the preservation of the body of Rosalia Lombardo, which was placed in the catacombs over 30 years after the practice of mummification had ended. Given a different treatment than those of Capuchin tradition, the child does not seem dead at all. Thus the destructive force of nature is challenged both by the miracle of the virtuous life of 45 monks and by the miracle produced by arts and science, and as the former— and the first friars—faded away into oblivion, the second advanced, ultimately triumphing after the centuries-long history of the catacombs had reached its endgame. Supranatural interventions and human artistry did, however, share the same aim, that of evading the very processes that the practice of double burial generally made more complete and quick; in other words preserving soft tissue, the colour of the flesh, and the skin and hair.

Processes for desiccating bodies can be found in various parts of southern Italy, mostly Campania and Sicily, where the practice was most common.[50] Both regions came under Spanish influence, and it is noteworthy that Mario Praz has recognised in the catacombs "the same carnal feeling that is at the root of the mysticism and obsession with death that are proper to Spain."[51] For his part, Antonio Fornaciari has put forward the hypothesis that the system of mummification "was, so to speak, developed by the order of the Capuchins towards the end of the sixteenth century, and only later extended to other sections of the Sicilian clergy and to certain confraternities."[52] Be that as it may, even when compared to the rest of Sicily, the situation in Palermo was unique, as noted by Friedrich Münter, who travelled in the island between 1786 and 1788: "The Capuchins have equal regulations in different parts of Sicily; but those burials are the largest and most famous in the whole island."[53] The results of an investigation that has tried to inventory the "Sicilian mummies," while still provisional, demonstrates this clearly: compared to the 3,000 bodies in the catacombs, those in the rest of western Sicily total around 170 and those in the east around 150.[54]

This concentration in Sicily and especially Palermo leads us to wonder whether the custom of exhibiting embalmed corpses was related to Sicilian traditions concerning man's relationship with death. This is a delicate subject, and addressing it requires us to take into account a huge and extremely varied literature and to sidestep the temptation of simplistically fixing a human group into a historically and anthropologically fragile series of generic identity categories. It is nevertheless difficult to avoid seeing in Sicilian customs relating to the 2nd of November (and not only)[55] indications that there existed a particular proximity between the world of the living and that of the dead,[56] which, as Ignazio Buttitta has written, had its roots in an agrarian way of life that "must maintain a continuous circuit of exchange (primarily nutritional) with the 'dead' to make future harvests prosperous and bring wellbeing to the family."[57]

This proximity was evident to visitors of the catacombs: Ippolito Pindemonte, in 1807, in response to Ugo Foscolo's *Sepolcri*, presented the Capuchin cemetery as a case in point in which "a small gap divides the two Worlds, and life and death were never so united and joined in friendship."[58] And apropos of the same, Alexandre Dumas père, in his visit of 1835, underscored the cultural distance between the northern countries from where he had come and what happened in Sicily, where his friend and companion Arami, after having guided him through the corridors of the catacombs ate a hearty dinner as if nothing had happened, obviously considering the spectacle he had just seen to be normal and habitual.[59]

From this point of view the judgment of Carlo Levi is eloquent. Writing more than 100 years later, when the catacombs had become a sort of museum, he said: "There are also cemeteries of this type in other parts of Italy, even in Rome, but here in Sicily this familiarity with the dead, with their presence, seems more natural and does not provoke terror."[60] And Jean Baudrillard saw the site as emblematic of a past way of conceiving death in which the cemetery became "a place of Sunday walks for the family and friends of the deceased, who came to see them, to recognise them, to show them to their children, with a living familiarity; a Sunday-ality of death similar to that of the mass and the theatre."[61]

Returning now to the justifications for the practice of mummification, it must be recognised that a consequence of the desire to preserve some soft tissues of the body to ensure the permanence of the characteristics of the living even after death is that of bringing the deceased commoner closer to the saint. At the root of the practice of mummification there is therefore always the broadly shared idea of the benefits that the dead can derive from being near to relics, which in this case was actually emphasised and heightened to the point that proximity also became similarity. Assimilation to those who enjoy eternal bliss no longer occurred only on a moral level, but also on a physical one, with everyone involved sharing the characteristics which, during canonical recognitions, are considered signs of holiness. Thus the catacombs contained the symbols of a diffuse sanctity such that when the French traveller Auguste de Forbin visited the site, the friar serving as a guide showed him corpses which "on holidays gave off the sweetest smells, and others that had the property of curing fevers when they were touched or approached."[62]

The Display of the Bodies

What we have considered so far helps us to understand the significance of mummification within a framework—the Christian one—which does not treat it as a common practice and to grasp the set of ideas underlying the customs of the Capuchin convent in Palermo. But we have not yet touched on the peculiarity that most characterises the complex, even when compared to similar situations found elsewhere: the permanent display of corpses, usually in an upright position, dressed as they would have been in life. This is what provoked the reactions of greatest astonishment or horror on the part of visitors.

Here again, the starting point for submitting an interpretation are the texts produced within the Capuchin order itself, together with the accounts of travellers. The initial key is, as might be guessed, the idea of the *memento mori*: bones and skeletons have always figured in the Christian imagination as reminders of the vanity of life. This is underlined several times both by the Capuchin authors (such as Antonino Mongitore)[63] and the travellers, like Patrick Brydone, the author of a widely read travel narrative: "it might be made of very considerable utility to society; and that these dumb orators could give the most pathetic lectures upon pride and vanity. Whenever a fellow began to strut [. . .] or to affect the haughty supercilious air, he should be sent to converse with his friends in the gallery."[64]

While the deteriorating flesh, with the deformation of the faces and signs of time's erosive power, remind us of the inevitability of death, the sumptuous clothes, the symbols of status and profession, demonstrate the emptiness and inanity of the objects with which we surround ourselves and will no longer need. As a sonnet by Ferdinando Miraglia Termini states:

> The Duke, the Prince, the titled, the strong,
> have their foolish pride debunked here
> The same fate will be yours one day!
> Observe in the man every vanished beauty [. . .]
> death [. . .] magnificent, holds very strongly by the foot
> togas, purple cloth, mitres and crowns.[65]

These images evoke those of the *danses macabres*[66] or the "triumphs of death" and "carnivals of the dead."[67]

The theme of the vanity of earthly glories is linked to that of death as a leveller, as an event that eliminates all social distinctions to make everyone equal; the same poet quoted above wrote in another composition:

> Look! . . . The King, the Cardinal, the great
> are united with the weak and the strong.[68]

The corpses, as many witnesses pointed out, beginning with D'Orville, are in fact dressed in the monastic habit, which makes them all uniform and which, moreover, is a symbol of penitence.

These two justifications for the display of corpses, both of which accentuate the moral value of the practice and certainly have their merits insofar as every representation of death is a reminder of the transience of existence, are, however, insufficient. Indeed, many of the surviving testimonies appear to draw quite opposite conclusions.

The first idea, that of the *memento mori*, which stresses that the disintegrating bodies symbolise the futility and emptiness of earthly life, runs counter to the appreciation expressed throughout the literature generated by the catacombs for the preservation of the remains and the freshness of the mummies, which "seem alive," as well as being at odds with the admiration shown for the face of Rosalia, who appears to be asleep.

The catacombs appear to be even less evocative of the idea of death as a "leveller": for example, the German Johann Heinrich Bartels, who visited them in 1786, noted, like D'Orville, that "they are almost all dressed in the habits of the Capuchins," but added that:

> Princes, counts, and marquis present themselves with their own clothes. But since destiny wants them to bend the nape of their necks under the heavy hood and appear in the deepest humiliation, so they easily subject themselves, but in death still cannot deny their character. On the card that each of them presents to you in their stiff, dry hand, we read in large letters: I am the Prince, the Marquis, the Count—as if even now they want to force you to pay homage.[69]

Furthermore, the sources contain several references to the practice of dressing the bodies on 2nd November, "in their finery, their uniforms, in all the pomp that death thought he had robbed them of forever,"[70] at least from the early decades of the nineteenth century. At a certain point the custom of dressing those who had not been friars in their habits appears to have ended:

> Everyone is dressed in the clothes which they wore in life, according to their position, and therefore we see the poor and rough habit of the friar alongside the silk skirt of the young lady, and this next to the velvet dress embroidered with gold and silver of the duke and the marquis, or the military uniform of the general.[71]

Thus, far from bringing to mind thoughts of equality, humility and humiliation, the display of the bodies of the catacombs expresses, to Bartels's mind, "a great desire for glory"; "the Palermitan wants to be seen for the great man that he is, he sits to show the exuberance of his gold, and to be admired: as he showed everything in life, so he does in death."[72] De Forbin, for his part, noted that in the catacombs, "the societies, the habits of this life, seem to have been observed and respected."[73] What is more, although the most humble were not excluded from the area housing the Capuchins, they were not to be seen among those whose remains were on display, being placed in graves instead:[74] in other words, even they were in their rightful place. Cemeteries, from the Middle Ages onwards, were intended to convey the identity of a community, and the same could be said of the catacombs, in which Palermitan society was represented in microcosm: "we have here, under our eyes, a part of Palermitan society."[75]

The catacombs, therefore, did not render invalid, but, on the contrary, appear to have perpetuated Sicilian social hierarchies, taking them away from time. They exposed them to the view and admiration of everyone, and renovated them every time a new mummy was added or when people visited the galleries, on the day of the dead and other occasions. The spiritual benefit of being close to a saint was therefore accompanied by the social benefit of having a place in what in some ways was a showcase of Palermitan society.[76] Naturally, as in all exhibitions representing social structures, the reproduction was not strictly accurate, but an idealisation and a methodical rearrangement carried out, in this case, in a classifying exercise designed to make clear the distinctions between representatives of the professions and those of the low-skilled, between laymen and ecclesiastics, between friars, nobles and non-nobles, and between women, men and children. Ultimately, the practice of the catacombs was fully a part of those strategies of manipulation of bodies that aimed to resolve the conflict between "the inexorability of individual deaths" and "the continuation of social life."[77]

It is therefore possible to identify a religious aspect in the practice of exhibiting mummies, which involves the desire to preserve and not remove from "sensorial satisfaction" the corpses of common people in the context of their assimilation to saints, and to identify also a "lay" aspect, which involves an affirmation and a systematising of the social order and its hierarchies beyond the death of the individual. Yet these two aspects of the Palermo experience are not, in hindsight, antithetical or in tension. The consecrated space of the cemetery provided the conditions for the lay ritual, which mostly took place during the (religious) festival of the dead. Or to put it another way, the religious context was the precondition of the social event, even after the latter became autonomous. The saints lying in their cases served as a model for the nobles lying in the ossuary or standing by the walls with signs indicating their status, while the sacred space of the cemetery complex provided the framework in which to realise the desire to perpetuate hierarchies of power. These were hierarchies that, intending to go beyond the boundaries of life, could do no other than move within the ideological system of the institution that traditionally controlled the rituals, practices and imagery that accompanied death and relations with the eternal. After the system itself disintegrated, the symbols remained, having new functions.

The same reasoning helps us interpret the treatment of the corpses of illustrious people not known for any attachment to the church, such as that of Francesco Crispi, which was embalmed by the same hands that took care of the body of Rosalia Lombardo before being passed to the Capuchins and laid to rest in a sumptuous chapel in the Palermitan church of San Domenico.[78] Then there is Angelo Nicolao,[79] who Crispi called a "patriot with many merits,"[80] who was stabbed to death in 1861[81] and is now resting in the first corridor of the catacombs. Yet another occupant of the catacombs is the one of the most widely discussed protagonists of the Sicilian Risorgimento, the Garibaldian general Giovanni Corrao, who was assassinated in 1863: "among the white linens of his shroud, that idealistic and decisive face, that Garibaldian beard, were much more alive than a history book, and reopened with their physical presence, in our eyes, a time already consigned to memory."[82] It is no coincidence that the body of the general, whose exploits have been closely linked to the feelings and spirit of the popular classes, found space in a place so emotionally charged and significant for the Palermitans.

The protagonist in these cases was not the religion of the clergy, but that of the homeland, which had its own martyrs and saints and which borrowed from the imagery of sacred practices, rituals, terminology and rhetoric. This was not, ultimately, just about what Katherine Verdery, when writing about other themes, called the "political lives of dead bodies,"[83] but primarily an example of "secular religion" phenomena, which consist in the attribution of the prestige and perpetuity normally accorded to sacred things to objects that do not belong to the religious sphere.[84]

The sensations inspired by the sight of the body of Giovanni Corrao, whose facial features and resemblance to Garibaldi so struck Levi, are as far as anything can be from the ideology of the *memento mori* but nevertheless cannot be separated, as we have tried to show, from the overall system of meanings that the catacombs encompass. In essence, there is no break in the continuity between the sanctified Capuchin whose body was miraculously preserved, the benefactor of the convent who arranged to be buried alongside the holy friars, the devout whose desire was to rest in the catacombs, the poor and the rich, the men and the women who aimed to maintain their social position post-mortem, or the public personage whose body was to be exhibited, long- or short-term, to the public. Indeed, the first and the last perhaps constitute two extreme cases among a single range of possibilities. And it is precisely this intertwining of social and religious functions, set in the anthropological background of the proximity between the living and the dead that appears typical of many Sicilian traditions, which explains the strenuous resistance of the practice of the catacombs' burial system to religious, civic and hygiene rules.

By the time that Carlo Levi described this system it was already in crisis and the only characteristic that apparently survived, from among the intermix of meanings of the catacombs, is that which had ensured since the eighteenth century the success of the site in the Grand Tour journeys: its spectacularity. After the loss of its social function, and changes to the terms of its religious one, the catacombs still remain a Wunderkammer or, even more prosaically, a "waxwork museum."[85] For the study of its dynamics, other concepts become indispensable, those dear to present-day anthropology, such as spectacularisation, museification and patrimonialisation.

Notes

1. "Ils resteront éternellement alignés sous ces voûtes sombres, à la façon des objets qu'on garde dans les musées": Guy de Maupassant, *La Sicile* (travel notebooks from 1885 published for the first time in 1886 in a magazine) (Paris: République des Lettres, 2018), 20.
2. In accordance with the usage that has become widespread among scholars and in particular among paleopathologists, which differs from the one in common use, I use the term "mummies" to refer to corpses whose soft tissues have been preserved either by intentional human methods or not: see Dario Piombino-Mascali, *Le catacombe dei Cappuccini. Guida storico-scientifica* (Palermo: Kalós, 2018), 36.
3. The authors who wrote about the site gave very different estimates of the number of corpses. Piombino-Mascali, based on the most recent cataloguing, speaks about at least 1,949 bodies (*Le catacombe dei Cappuccini*, 22).
4. See Antonio Mongitore, *Dell'Istoria Sagra di tutte le Chiese, Conventi, Monasterj, Spedali, et altri luoghi pii della città di Palermò, le Chiese e le Case dei Regolari*, First Part (undated but completed in 1742), transcription and critical ed. Francesco Lo Piccolo, *Storia delle chiese di Palermo. I conventi*, vol. 1 (Palermo: CRICD, 2009), 445.
5. Antonino da Castellammare, *Le catacombe ossia la grande sepoltura dei Cappuccini in Palermo* (Palermo: Fiamma Serafica, 1938), 30.
6. *Libro in cui si registrano le licenze concesse da nostri Superiori Maggiori a Secolari di potersi sepelire nella Sepoltura di questa nostra Chiesa del Convento di Palermo*, www.archivumdoc.it/registro-dei-morti-delle-catacombe/.
7. Flaviano D. Farella, *Cenni storici della chiesa e delle catacombe dei Cappuccini di Palermo* (Palermo: Fiamma Serafica, 1982), 84.
8. P. Benedetto Sambenedetti da Milano (although the attribution is contested: see Piombino-Mascali, *Le Catacombe dei Cappuccini*, 36), *Vita del Venerabile Servo di Dio Fra Bernardo da Corleone, siciliano, religioso laico dei Cappuccini della Provincia di Palermo* (Palermo: Pietro d'Isola, 1680), quoted in da Castellammare, *Le catacombe ossia la grande sepoltura dei Cappuccini in Palermo*, 44.
9. Farella, *Cenni storici della chiesa e delle catacombe dei Cappuccini di Palermo*, 74–75.
10. Ibid., 84–85.
11. Ibid., 86.
12. Ibid.
13. Jean-Claude-Richard de Saint-Non, *Voyage pittoresque, ou description des royaumes de Naples et de Sicile*, tome 4, first part (Paris: Clousier, 1785), 152.
14. Farella, *Cenni storici della chiesa e delle catacombe dei Cappuccini di Palermo*, 86–87.
15. Atanasio Morzillo, "Il viaggio in Sicilia," in *La frontiera del Grand Tour. Viaggi e viaggiatori nel Mezzogiorno borbonico* (Naples: Liguori, 1992), 253–324.
16. The term belongs to Piombino-Mascali, *Le catacombe dei Cappuccini*, 37.
17. *A Voyage to Sicily and Malta, written by Mr. John Dryden, Junior, When He Accompanied Mr. Cecill in That Expedition, in the Years 1700 and 1701* (London: for J. Bew, in Pater-Noster-Row, 1776).
18. Giuseppe Pitrè has collected the accounts of travellers to Sicily. The scholar's notes are published in Giuseppe Pitrè, *Viaggiatori italiani e stranieri in Sicilia*, 3 vols. in 5 tomes (Comiso: Documenta, 2000). On the descriptions of

the Catacombs I refer the reader to the university thesis by Rebecca Sabatini, "Le Catacombe dei Cappuccini di Palermo: riflessi letterari" (University of Turin, history degree, academic year 2017–2018, viva held in 2019). I thank the author for the information she gave me on the subject.

19. Farella, *Cenni storici della chiesa e delle catacombe dei Cappuccini di Palermo*, 87.
20. Ibid., 87–88. For a more detailed reconstruction of the discussions and events relating to the prohibitions of the nineteenth century I refer the reader to Piombino-Mascali, *Le catacombe dei Cappuccini*, 46–49.
21. Farella, *Cenni storici della chiesa e delle catacombe dei Cappuccini di Palermo*, 88.
22. Francesco Pezzini, "Trattamento dei cadaveri nel Mezzogiorno preunitario," a section in "Processi di tanatometamorfosi: pratiche di scolatura dei corpi e mummificazione nel Regno delle Due Sicilie," ed. Antonio Fornaciari, Valentina Giuffra and Francesco Pezzini, *Archeologia postmedievale*, 11 (2007), 8–18. The quote is on page 17.
23. Francesco Finocchietti, *Ricordi di un viaggio a Napoli e in Sicilia* (Pisa: Citi, 1864), 69.
24. Giuseppe Pitrè, "I morti," in *Spettacoli e feste popolari siciliane, descritte da Giuseppe Pitrè* (Palermo: Pedone Lauriel, 1881), 394.
25. The painting *Love and Death* (Catania, Castello Ursino Civic Museum), shows two lovers in a pose recalling that of Francesco Hayez's *Kiss*.
26. Farella, *Cenni storici della chiesa e delle catacombe dei Cappuccini di Palermo*, 88 and 100.
27. de Maupassant, *La Sicile*, 18–20.
28. Piombino-Mascali, *Le catacombe dei Cappuccini*, 34.
29. Farella, *Cenni storici della chiesa e delle catacombe dei Cappuccini di Palermo*, 101. On Salafia see the study by Dario Piombino-Mascali, *Il maestro del sonno eterno* (Palermo: La Zisa, 2009).
30. Pitrè, *Viaggiatori italiani e stranieri in Sicilia*, vol. 1, tome 1, 112.
31. A. Dry (pseudonym of William Fleury), *Trinacria, Promenades et impressions siciliennes* (Paris: Plon-Nourrit, 1903), 147.
32. Mario Praz, *Viaggi in Occidente* (Florence: Sansoni, 1955), 396–97.
33. As in the cases of endocannibalism, in which families ritually consume the flesh of their dead relatives: Robert Hertz, "A Contribution to the Study of the Collective Representation of Death," in *Death and the Right Hand*, ed. Robert Hertz (Glencoe, IL: The Free Press, 1960).
34. See ibid. For an anthropological definition of the methods of the treatment of the corpse after death, see Adriano Favole, *Resti di umanità. Vita sociale del corpo dopo la morte* (Rome-Bari: Laterza, 2003); Francesco Remotti, "Tanato-metamòrfosi," in *Morte e trasformazione dei corpi. Interventi di tanatometamòrfosi*, ed. Francesco Remotti (Milan: B. Mondadori, 2006), 1–34; Francesco Remotti, "Categorie mortuarie: 'ciò che scompare', 'ciò che rimane', 'ciò che riemerge'," in *Antropologia e archeologia a confronto: archeologia e antropologia della morte. 1 La regola dell'eccezione*, ed. Valentino Nizzo (Rome: E.S.S., 2018), 69–99.
35. Giovanni Filoramo, "La sacralità del corpo," *Humanitas* 62, no. 3 (2007): 563–75. The quote is on page 571.
36. Gianmaria da Castelvetrano's report, dating back to around 1610, can be found in the provincial Capuchin archive of Bologna, Cl. I, Ser. V, Bust. VII, n. 2. His transcription is in da Castellammare, *Le catacombe ossia la grande sepoltura dei Cappuccini in Palermo*, 14–17. The quote is on page 15.
37. Ibid.
38. Rosario da Palermo, cit. in da Castellammare, *Le catacombe ossia la grande sepoltura dei Cappuccini in Palermo*, 22.
39. Rosario da Palermo, ibid., 34.

40. For later events involving the bodies, da Castellammare, *Le catacombe ossia la grande sepoltura dei Cappuccini in Palermo*, 50–52.
41. Ibid., 36–37.
42. Ibid., 53.
43. Between the fifth and sixth century the idea spread that being buried along-side the tomb of a saint means finding oneself next to him on the day of resurrection: Peter Brown, *The Rise of Western Christendom: Triumph and Diversity 200–1000 AD* (Malden: Blackwell, 2013), ch. 11, par. 8.
44. Rosario da Palermo, cit. in da Castellammare, *Le catacombe ossia la grande sepoltura dei Cappuccini in Palermo*, 55.
45. Ibid.
46. See Pezzini, "Trattamento dei cadaveri nel Mezzogiorno preunitario"; Pezzini, "Doppie esequie e scolatura dei corpi nell'Italia Meridionale d'età moderna," www.paleopatologia.it/articoli/aticolo.php?recordID=2. The idea that Capuchin funerary practices are a variant of "double burial" is taken up again by D. Piombino-Mascali et al., "The Catacomb Mummies of Sicily. A State-of-the-Art Report (2007–2011)," *Antrocom Online Journal of Anthropology* 8, no. 2 (2012): 341–52 and 343; Piombino-Mascali, *Le catacombe dei Cappuccini*, 53–54.
47. Hertz, *Sulla rappresentazione collettiva della morte*, (Rome: Savelli, 1978), 51–53.
48. Ibid., 87.
49. I refer mainly to the work of Dario Piombino-Mascali, founder and director of the "Sicilian mummy project" (www.paleopatologia.it/Live/Savoca/index.php). See Piombino-Mascali et al., "The Catacomb Mummies of Sicily."
50. "Under the church it is bizarre, since it is common in Sicily to see numerous dried bodies of various people": Jeanine Power Villepreux, *Guida per la Sicilia* (Naples: Cirelli, 1842), 229.
51. Praz, *Viaggi in Occidente*, 397.
52. Antonio Fornaciari, "I luoghi della pratica funeraria: le strutture materiali," in "Processi di tanatometamorfosi," ed. Fornaciari, Giuffra and Pezzini, 32.
53. *Viaggio in Sicilia di Federico Münter* (Palermo: Abbate, 1823), cit. in Pitrè, *Viaggiatori Stranieri in Sicilia*, vol. 2, tome 2, 245.
54. Valentina Giuffra, "Le mummie come documento storico e biologico," in "Processi di tanatometamorfosi," ed. Fornaciari, Giuffra and Pezzini, 42. I refer to the same article for a provisional census of the sites. It should be noted that the most recent catalogue, provided by D. Piombino-Mascali and cited above, has downgraded the number of corpses in Palermo, which nev-ertheless remains much bigger than the number held elsewhere.
55. On this subject see: Pitrè, "I morti," 393–408; Giuseppe Pitrè, "I morti e la Vecchia strina," in *Usi, costumi, credenze e pregiudizi del popolo sicilia-no*, vol. 4 (Palermo: Pedone Lauriel, 1889), 58–62; Antonino Buttitta, "Ritorno dei morti e rifondazione della vita," in *Babbo Natale suppliziato*, ed. Claude Lévi-Strauss (Palermo: Sellerio, 1995), 8–42; Antonino Butt-itta, "La festa dei morti," in *Dei segni e dei miti. Una introduzione alla antropologia simbolica* (Palermo: Sellerio, 1996), 245–55; Valerio Petrarca, "La festa dei morti in Sicilia," in *Le tentazioni e altri saggi di antropologia* (Rome: Borla, 1990); Ignazio Buttitta, *I morti e il grano. Tempi del lavoro e ritmi della festa* (Rome: Meltemi, 2006), 91–94.
56. It may be in relationship with this proximity that we might understand the use of preserving, as a memory of past family members, not only their pho-tographs in life, but also those taken after their death. On the subject of the relationship between photography and death in Sicily, see Rosario Perri-cone, "Death and Rebirth: Images of Death in Sicily," *Visual Antrhropology*

29 (2016): 1–21; Perricone, *Oralità dell'immagine. Etnografia visiva nelle comunità rurali siciliane* (Palermo: Sellerio, 2018), 168–99.

57. Buttitta, *Il morti e il grano*, 110.
58. Ippolito Pindemonte, "I Sepolcri," in *Poesie di Ugo Foscolo d'Ippolito Pindemonte e di Giovanni Torti* (Milan: Silvestri, 1822), 33. The writer visited the catacombs in 1779.
59. A. Dumas, *Le speronare* (Bruxelles: Hauman, 1842), online edition, www.quandletigrelit.fr/images/Alexandre-Dumas-Le-Speronare.pdf, 248. The journey was made in 1835.
60. Carlo Levi, *Le parole sono pietre* (Turin: Einaudi, 2016), 61, first published 1955.
61. Jean Baudrillard, *Lo scambio simbolico e la morte* (Milan: Feltrinelli, 1979), 202.
62. Auguste de Forbin, *Souvenirs de la Sicile* (Paris: Imprimerie Royale, 1823), 46. Forbin's travels in Italy took place between 1821 and 1822.
63. Mongitore, *Dell'Istoria Sagra di tutte le Chiese*, 453–54.
64. Patrick Brydone, *A Tour Through Sicily and Malta* (London: Printed for W. Strahan; and T. Cadell, in the Strand, 1774) quoted in Pitrè, *Viaggiatori italiani e stranieri in Sicilia*, vol. 1, tome 1, 130; see also, for example, William Henry Thompson, *Sicily and Its Inhabitants: Observations During a Residence in That Country in the Years 1809 and 1810* (London: Clarke, 1813), 146–47; Fanny Lewald, *Italienisches Bilderbuch* (Berlin: Neuauflage, 1847).
65. Ferdinando Miraglia Termini, "Sonetto" (2 November 1867), quoted in Farella, *Cenni storici della chiesa e delle catacombe dei Cappuccini di Palermo*, 119–21.
66. Baudrillard refers to these directly when writing about the Catacombs: *Lo scambio simbolico e la morte*, 202.
67. de Maupassant, *La Sicile*, 26.
68. Ferdinando Miraglia Termini, "Il giorno dei morti. Elegia" (1903), quoted in Farella, *Cenni storici della chiesa e delle catacombe dei Cappuccini di Palermo*, 123–25. The quote is on page 124.
69. Johann Heinrich Bartels, *Briefe über Kalabrien und Sizilien*, vol. 2 (Göttingen: Johann Christian Dietrich, 1791), 631.
70. Fedor de Karaczay, *Manuel du voyageur en Sicile* (Stuttgart: Cotta, 1826), 89–90.
71. The testimony is from the Tuscan nobleman Felice Carrone di San Tommaso, "Le catacombe dei conventi de' Cappuccini di Roma e di Palermo," *Prose e poesie inedite o rare di italiani viventi*, vol. 5 (Bologna: Nobili, 1836), 154–60. The quote is on page 158.
72. Pitrè, *Viaggiatori Stranieri in Sicilia*, vol. 1, tome 1, respectively 250 and 251.
73. de Forbin, *Souvenirs de la Sicile*, 46.
74. See Piombino-Mascali, *Le catacombe dei Cappuccini*, 33.
75. René Bazin, *Sicile. Croquis italiens* (Paris: Calmann-Lévy, 1893), 131.
76. "The elites considered the display of the mummified body as a way to preserve the physical individuality of the deceased and to display his social status beyond death" (Pezzini, "Trattamento dei cadaveri nel Mezzogiorno preunitario," 17).
77. Remotti, "Categorie mortuarie," 69.
78. This is mentioned, among others, by Fleury, *Trinacria, passeggiate ed impressioni siciliane*, 148.
79. Piombino-Mascali, *Le catacombe dei Cappuccini*, 29.
80. Chamber of deputies, session of 1661–62, session of 25 April 1863, 6537.
81. Other protagonists of the Sicilian Risorgimento buried among the Capuchins are Filippo Salafia, father of Alfredo Salafia, and Giulio Ascanio Enea (Piombino-Mascali, *Le catacombe dei Cappuccini*, 76).

82. Levi, *Le parole sono pietre*, 58. In the biography, fictionalised but nevertheless founded on extensive documentary research, which he dedicated to Corrao, Matteo Collura wrote that, after his embalmment by the Capuchins, a friar hid the body, which would then be found only by chance after a wall was knocked down, around 70 years later and in poor condition: *Qualcuno ha ucciso il generale* (Milan: 2006), 147. Alfredo Salafia, in a manuscript written between 1927 and 1933, nevertheless found the overall state of the body to be good (Piombino-Mascali, *Le catacombe dei Cappuccini*, 75), and Levi, in the early 1950s, saw the patriot in much better condition than that described by Collure; in 1960 the body was photographed before being interred in the cloister belonging to the church of San Domenico (*Qualcuno ha ucciso il generale*, 155; Piombino-Mascali, *Le catacombe dei Cappuccini*, 75).

83. *The Political Lives of Dead Bodies: Reburial and Postsocialist Change* (New York: Columbia University Press, 1999). Among the cases mentioned by the scholar is that of the Romanian patriot and "friend of Garibaldi" Nicolae Bălcescu (150, n. 50), also mentioned by Thomas W. Laqueur, *The Work of the Dead. A Cultural History of Mortal Remains* (Princeton: Princeton University Press, 2015), 22–23 and n. 26, 564, whose remains, buried in a pit close to the Capuchins, have been sought by his compatriots on several occasions. On this subject see Farella, *Cenni storici della chiesa e delle catacombe dei Cappuccini di Palermo*, 96–99.

84. Taking up the concept of lay (or secular) religion from E. Gentile, *Le religioni della politica fra democrazie e totalitarismi* (Rome-Bari: Laterza, 2001), 3–4.

85. Baudrillard, *Lo scambio simbolico e la morte*, 202.

Part IV

Public Uses of Human Remains Between Politics, Religion and Science

10 "Roasted and Eaten"

The Neapolitan Counter-Revolution of 1799 and the Use of Jacobin Remains

Luca Addante

The counter-revolution that swept through the Neapolitan Republic in 1799 is a classic example, never fully investigated, of the use of human remains. And yet, as far back as 1986 Anna Maria Rao had called for "an organic study of the insurgency" that would take into "account every element of the conflict—social, political, cultural—between Jacobins and *Sanfedisti* in 1799, including the rituals relating to the 'Jacobin dead'."[1] This work is dedicated to those "Jacobin dead."

"Neapolitan Anarchy"

The counter-revolution began in February 1799, when Cardinal Fabrizio Ruffo landed in Calabria from Sicily to form a counter-revolutionary movement, organising the "Armata cristiana e reale" (Christian and royal army), better known as the *Sanfedisti*. Within four months Ruffo had reached Naples with support from local insurgencies, and countless episodes of brutal violence marked the reconquest of the Bourbon kingdom. Since the sheer scale of events makes it necessary to limit the scope of this study, I will concentrate my analysis on the capital in the aftermath of the fall of the Republic on 13 June 1799.

Having bested the republicans at the Ponte della Maddalena, on the outskirts of Naples, on 14 June the *Sanfedisti* hordes—an advance guard entered during the night—swept into the city to the accompaniment of tocsins, with ecclesiastics "preaching the massacre of the patriots"[2] while clerics yelled out slogans: "Long live the King! Long live the Faith! Death to the Jacobins!"[3] This, then, was the start of a genuine holocaust, described by everyone, whether royalist or republican, as a "horror": Ruffo himself was not insensitive to it,[4] and neither were other members of his army.[5] Without waiting to differentiate between real or presumed Jacobins, the Neapolitan *lazzari* (the city's lowest class) and the *Sanfedisti* from the provinces launched into an orgy of blood: "The streets and the squares of Naples were covered with bodies, with blood, with skulls and limbs scattered here and there."[6] The liberty trees were uprooted, while

> a large number of victims [. . .] arrived [. . .] and one after the other were all shot at the foot of the tree. [. . .] This done, without the villains bothering to kill them, or let them expire entirely, they cut off their heads, parts of which were carried in procession on top of long poles while others were used for fun, being rolled on the ground as if they were balls.[7]

Those who survived were arrested and led through the middle of the crowd—many naked, amid insults, mockery, spitting and blows—as far as the Ponte della Maddalena, where in the nearby Granili (granary) building Ruffo had set up his headquarters and into which the prisoners were crammed: a real, living hell.[8]

The worst violence started on 14 June and continued for months. The terror imposed by the rampant *lazzari* and *Sanfedisti* held sway over the streets, despite the cardinal having issued an edict ordering that force be reserved for those who resisted, forbidding its use against the rest on pain of "the most severe penalties, to extend [. . .] even to the death penalty."[9] Localised military operations continued against some patriots and a French patrol, mostly barricaded in three castles, who held out, but otherwise Ruffo called for "peace." It was a waste of breath: as his collaborators remarked, "the cardinal's orders to curb the abuses of the masses and of the people were not respected"[10] and "the rabble, taking little notice [of the edict], became increasingly infuriated."[11]

A week after his arrival in Naples, Ruffo wrote to Prime Minister John Acton:

> I am so crushed and destroyed that I do not see how I will be able to survive if such a state continues for another three days. The need to govern, or more to the point, to contain a vast population grown accustomed to the most determined anarchy; the need to govern a score of uneducated and insubordinate leaders of light troops, all dedicated to continuing the looting, massacres and violence, is so terrible and complicated that it is absolutely beyond my strength. They have brought me 1,300 Jacobins, who I do not know where to keep in safety, and I keep in the granaries by the bridge. They must have slaughtered or shot at least 50 of them in my presence without my being able to prevent them, and wounded at least 200, who they had dragged here naked.[12]

A day later the legitimist Carlo De Nicola noted in his diary: "Despite continuous edicts prohibiting arrests and looting, the people, united to the Calabrians, continue to arrest and plunder. [. . .] Around Naples we have seen arrested people being dragged around by the hundreds every day, and on its own that would have been nothing; but they were lacerated, injured, mutilated and killed, their heads being carried on poles."[13] On 12 July De Nicola expressed the hope that the "plague" would not break out "given the quantity of corpses."[14]

To make matters even worse, the *lazzari* and *Sanfedisti* soon became disillusioned with the cardinal: as early as 2 July De Nicola had written that: "They complain about Ruffo's clemency,"[15] and at the end of August the situation had deteriorated: "The people [. . .] go around saying that Cardinal Ruffo and his ministers are all Jacobins!"[16] In the meantime, the battle in Naples had raged for a month, in particular against those holed up in the Nuovo, Ovo and Sant'Elmo castles. After Ruffo's offer of an honourable surrender, the first two castles surrendered between 19 and 21 June, while the French and the other patriots in Sant'Elmo resisted until, between 11 and 12 July, they also capitulated.[17] This, however, did not mark the end of the disorder. Once again, on 3 September, the king came under pressure from the governing junta— established by him to support Ruffo—to issue an edict to enforce an end to the violence.[18]

The edict was emanated on 12 September, and it prescribed death by shooting for those who "smeared others as Jacobins" and "slaughtered and looted under this pretext." But on 24 September the chronicler Diomede Marinelli commented: "If not backed up by force this law is of little value."[19] And in fact, the pillaging, thieving and murders continued, "nor did these violences cease [. . .]. The *crocesegnati* [the *Sanfedisti*] stayed in Naples for months, and in this time their brutality never once slowed down."[20]

Meanwhile, between June and July the death penalties endorsed by the Bourbon authorities had been set in motion. In spite of the protests of Ruffo, who risked arrest,[21] the terms of surrender were broken, and on 29 June Admiral Francesco Caracciolo[22] was hanged on the orders of Horatio Nelson who had been sent to Naples by the Bourbon.[23] The subsequent arrival of Ferdinand IV into the Bay of Naples saw the start of the "bloodbath"[24] of patriots, with dozens and dozens of executions by hanging being handed down through the arbitrary procedures of the king's junta. A procession of condemned were sent to the gallows— lines of "hung cheeses" as the king, even before his arrival,[25] described them[26]—and from 20 August onwards the real sequence of "massacres" by the "junta of butchers,"[27] as the faithful royalist De Nicola called them, carried on into the next year.

The spectacular return to the scene by monarchic power had, however, to contend with the *lazzari* and the *Sanfedisti*. On the occasion of the eight hangings carried out on 20 August before an immense crowd, the people, "upon every execution shouted 'Long live the King!'." The last to mount the scaffold was Eleonora de Fonseca Pimentel: when she appeared the people "wanted to shout, but on the signal of the [Confraternity of the] *Bianchi* they quietened; when she fell, however, the cries rose to the stars."[28] Since she, the editor of the *Monitore napoletano*, was not a Neapolitan citizen, her body remained suspended from the gibbet alongside four others until the day after, and it is said that in front of her dangling body the people sang merrily:

> Where has she gone, Donna Eleonora,
> who danced in the theatre,
> and now dances in the Market?
> She couldn't dance anymore!
> Traitors gone down.[29]

But as the death sentences were carried out the crowds did much more than make cruel jokes: on 29 August six people were hanged, and one body, that of the Puglian soldier Nicola Fiani, was not taken down. According to Marinelli, "the people were upon him, tearing into the body and leaving almost only the bones. It was reduced to pieces by the carnivorous plebs. Maybe everything was roasted and eaten. I know that the liver was cooked and eaten in the same market by the vile *Sanfedista* plebs. A *lazzaro* who refused to eat was killed."[30]

Eating the Jacobins

At this point it is appropriate to break off from recounting the facts. For we must confront the unimaginable. Not only were the remains torn to pieces and defiled, but they were actually eaten. And yet, clearly, we cannot trust one source alone: when addressing oneself to an issue like anthropophagy, it is always necessary to proceed with extreme methodological circumspection. Without being excessively sceptical,[31] one must keep in mind the power of cannibalism as a myth. It is therefore possible that the sources exaggerated what really occurred for political reasons. A good way of ensuring that we are dealing with an authentic happening, then, is to use accounts from both sides of the conflict, making certain they are of eyewitnesses.

In Marinelli's story, this is not clear, whereas we can be sure that De Nicola was reporting the matter second hand.[32] However, full confirmation of the happening is given by an account of the Confraternity of the Bianchi della Giustizia (Whites of Justice), who were delegated to comfort the condemned and accompany them to the gallows, and were certainly not suspected (like De Nicola) of harbouring Jacobin sympathies. In this account the Bianchi noted that:

> the unfortunate Fiano, [. . .] not being Neapolitan, had to remain hanging, to be buried the morning after. Now in the day, being

suspended, a great crowd began to tear at him, to pull him, to toss him around; and they stripped him naked and began to cut him into pieces with knives, which left nothing but the bones. And, with the pieces of meat on the tips of their knives, the *lazzari* began to go through the city, shouting, almost selling the meat: *Who wants to see Jacobin meat and liver!*, carrying pieces of meat also on the tips of pikes; and there were those who ate the liver fried.[33]

That at least Fiani's liver was eaten is hereby confirmed. And further indirect confirmation comes from the fact that this was not the only incident of cannibalism. As another eyewitness wrote, on 14 June

there was no corner of the city where there was not a bonfire into which the drunken mob threw [. . .], still palpitating, the victims they sacrificed; I who write saw some of this infamous rabble devour with cannibalistic anger the roasted limbs of the hapless victims, and then boast about it.[34]

Furthermore, Vincenzo Cuoco and Amodio Ricciardi gave accounts of cannibalistic episodes in the early days,[35] while other cases of early July were also verified. On 2 July "mass troops united with the people began to agitate" suspecting that "certain officials" were cheating them when issuing ammunition,

they were thus taken [. . .] three loyal officials, they were dragged, and one of them was quartered towards the end of Toledo [Street] [. . .] and half of him was burned, while the other half, which was roasted was taken for sale in the squares of Naples, reduced to small pieces for those who bought and ate a little. His genitals were attached to a long staff and carried in triumph around Naples. Something unbelievable but true, and which I saw myself. Such scenes of horror and revulsion were not rare.[36]

In this instance Marinelli made clear that he had been an eyewitness, and he was quite right in saying that cases of cannibalism were not rare. Another one had in fact occurred on the same day. On 3 July De Nicola recorded a resurgence "of the fury of the people: the arrests and pillaging have restarted," adding:

It is worthy of note that something was seen yesterday, horrible to say but which tells us what man is. Having burned the bodies of two Jacobins, the furious and angry people broke off pieces of their roasted meat and ate them, offering them to one another, even to boys. Here we are in the midst of a city of cannibal anthropophagists who eat their enemies.[37]

The diarist was speaking at second hand but stated that what he related had come from eyewitnesses who, as we know, were not lacking, a sign that the phenomenon was widespread. The republican Nicasio de Mase, in a manuscript poem, recalled:

> Near to me [. . .]
> there was an insane group of thugs,
> addicted to roasting on the fire,
> without any disgust, human flesh.[38]

Similar recollections were made by an anonymous chronicler, who wrote "that the supporters of Ferdinand [IV] and Jesus, like so many cannibals and anthropophagous, ate their neighbours roasted: they devoured their limbs, sold human flesh."[39] It was a picture also described by Marquis Filippo Malaspina, Ruffo's aide-de-camp: "There are those who have even seen roasted the human flesh of those who that horde of cannibals killed [. . .], and have seen on the Strada dei Ventaglieri [fan-maker's street] human limbs nailed to the wall."[40] Malaspina himself reported the case of a royalist officer who "was also killed, and his heart torn out of him with teeth."[41]

Episodes of cannibalism were also registered in the provinces. In Teramo a French soldier was killed by a crowd and "his heart was extracted, roasted and eaten."[42] While in Montesano (now Montesano sulla Marcellana), the president of the municipality, Nicola Cestari, was killed on 17 February, after which his genitals were cut off (and pocketed by someone) and his head was severed, raised on a pike, and carried in procession to where the tree of liberty had been erected: the pole with the head on top was put in its place. Then there began a dance "to the sound of guitars and drums" and later, "night having fallen, a bonfire was lit and, while the macabre dance continued [. . .] Andrea Montemurro, Nicola Cafaro and Tommaso Barbella cut a piece of cheek from Cestari's head, roasted it on the fire and ate it."[43]

Western Cannibalism

In short, there is no doubt that the violence of the counter-revolution frequently sank to the level of cannibalism, a fact which poses an enormous historical and anthropological problem. It was, in fact, something that went well beyond mutilating and burning defiled cadavers, or putting heads on spikes or rolling them along the streets. These are signs of a level of violence inconceivable to us, but which is an age-old phenomenon equivalent to what happened during other European crises of the period, such as the French Revolution. Moreover, the spectacle of torture was a classic demonstration of political power. It is true that the spread of Enlightenment culture had induced European governments to tone down the theatricality of capital punishment that had typified the six-teenth and seventeenth centuries. But when politics were involved (as in the crime of lese majesty), the states continued to employ the most brutal violence. Hence the famous case of Robert-François Damiens (1757) in Paris, recalled by Michel Foucault, and what took place in Naples shortly before the revolution.

On 11 May 1794, shortly after the failed Jacobin conspiracy to kill the royal family, a mass was held in the Church of Carmine during which:

> A certain man from Messina named Tomaso d'Amato [. . .] stood before the high altar rail and began to bellow such words as: "I am a Jacobin for life, long live the most holy Assembly of France, long live freedom!" Then, still in a high voice, he used sacrilegious words to rail against God, the Virgin, the Prince and others.

The man was promptly arrested and punished by execution, staged as a violent rite:

> The aforementioned patient emerged [. . .] to be executed on a large table, dragged out by a bridle with a block in his mouth so that the people would not hear [his] loathsome words [. . .]. Arriving at the gallows, he was more obstinate than ever, and wished to die unre-pentant [. . .] and the executioner carried out the sentence. Then he severed his head, tore out his tongue, showing it to the huge crowd, and threw it into the fire that had been readied, and then also cut off his hands and feet, and threw the rest of the body into the fire, scat-tering the ashes on the air.[44]

Dragging, hanging, beheading, dismembering, burning and scattering the remains. The violence of the punishment dispensed by justice "from above" was in many ways akin to that meted out "from below." Nev-ertheless, while some acts carried out by the *lazzari* and *Sanfedisti* might have been inspired by practices of the state repression apparatus, others—primarily cannibalism—certainly were not.[45] In it, therefore, we can detect profound attitudes within the popular culture, independent of the customs of secular and religious elites, such as to challenge one of their supreme taboos.

In truth, the question is too complex to be adequately addressed in an essay. Nonetheless, we need to at least draft an analysis lest we reduce everything to a *Grand-Guignolesque* ethnography of events. That being so, it is timely to reiterate that cannibalism has always been one of Europe's cardinal taboos, in both the Greco-Roman and Judeo-Christian traditions. Furthermore, at least from the time of Herodotus, if not of Homer's Lestrygonians, in Europe (and not only)[46] cannibals were syn-onymous with the other, barbarians, savages. This association was in fact emphasised to justify the colonisation of America: for Europeans, once the cannibalistic practices of the Aztecs, the Tupinambá, the Iroquois, the Hurons and so on had been discovered, those races were seen as savages so beyond the human as to give grounds for the harsh methods used in their subjugation and conversion to Christianity.

This prejudice was still strong in the eighteenth century, even though Montaigne had two centuries earlier posited the subject on an advanced basis in his essay *On the Cannibals*,[47] where he asked who were the real barbarians: the cannibals or the Europeans who slaughtered each other in religious wars.

Such reasoning animated the entry "Cannibals" in Voltaire's *Dictionnaire philosophique*, which nevertheless attributed the custom of eating human flesh to Native Americans, not to civilised Europeans. Still, Voltaire knew very well that this had occurred in Europe in the relatively recent past, since in the entry "Atheist," speaking of Spinoza, he observed: "It was certainly not him who tore to pieces the two brothers De Witt and ate them on the grill." He was referring to the killing of the Pensionary of Holland, Johan De Witt, and his brother Cornelis, who were cooked and eaten in The Hague in 1672.[48] This ought to have been included in the entry "Cannibals," which ended by denouncing a European episode from Cromwell's time in which corpses had been not eaten but used to make candles. We might therefore wonder why Voltaire did not mention the De Witt brothers when writing about cannibalism. Perhaps his silence is evidence of a European's bad conscience, which inclined him, as a minimum, not to overplay the thing but to conceal it in other places, such as the entry "Resurrection," where he declared: "it has been said that we have all been cannibals."[49] Being the ultimate taboo and an identifying criterion of otherness since antiquity, cannibalism at home was an issue to be handled with the greatest discretion, and this was also linked to the more general European process of interiorising and containing aggressive impulses that Norbert Elias writes about in *The Civilizing Process*.[50]

This reticence might also explain why most of the testimonies on cannibalism in Naples were in manuscript form, although at the time there was news of the facts. Notably the protests were made in the House of Commons by the Whig leader Charles James Fox, who denounced Nelson's behaviour in Naples and the atrocities that had given rise to cannibalism.[51]

To be honest, it is also true that in 1729 Jonathan Swift had proposed selling the tender flesh of one-year-old babies, and that in 1789 Jean-Paul Marat declared cannibalism legitimate in a pamphlet outlining a plan for the declaration of the rights of man.[52] These, however, had been absurd arguments brandished by the two authors while championing other things entirely. Marat held that cannibalism was acceptable in a state of nature so that he could claim the right to subsistence in the civil state, while Swift used sarcasm to denounce British tyranny in Ireland and the great landowners who exploited rural populations.

Essentially, in Europe cannibalism was (and is) such a taboo that it was difficult to talk about it, at least from the time of Plato: when in the *Republic* he characterised the tyrant as an expression of maximum "folly," defining him as incestuous and cannibalistic, he wrote unambiguously about the first attribute ("[he] has no hesitation in attempting sexual intercourse with a mother") while in the second case he stopped short of being explicit ("[there is] no meat it will not eat").[53]

The documented cases of cannibalism cited here inevitably cause a sense of displacement: we are not in 1799 BCE but in CE, we are not among American "savages" but in a principal capital of civilised Europe. Nonetheless, the horror was not something that had never been seen before, and the torture of the De Witts shows how it was a practice that Naples shared with others. Several cases of cannibalism had also emerged in sixteenth-century France during the Wars of Religion and during the French Revolution.[54] Although we still know relatively little about the matter, it is a fact that cannibalism survived for a long time in Europe, before it became confined to the pathology of serial killers.

However, if the eating of human remains in 1799 was not unique in Europe, neither were such episodes unprecedented in Naples itself, at least one having taken place in 1585, when the people's elected representative, Giovan Vincenzo Starace, was first tortured and killed in a popular riot, then dragged along in procession "through all the streets of the city, and in every street a piece of him was cut off: there were some who took a breast in their hand, others the heart, and others the brain." The crowd "tore him into many pieces, some cutting off a hand and a foot, others a piece of leg or arm, others the ears, others the nose, others a limb, and something else. Then they took out his guts, his heart, and the other entrails, which were reduced to small pieces that they divided greedily among themselves." Then "someone in the crowd said he wanted to cook the brain and eat it, and another ate the heart, [. . .] and another drank the blood."[55]

The fact that cannibalism was a taboo broken on several occasions in Naples and modern Europe brings into question its significance: what did this extreme, ostentatious display of violence—bragged about in 1585 and repeated in 1799—mean? The copious literature on the phenomenon may help us arrive at an answer.[56] And we may start by excluding one of the standard interpretations, that of subsistence cannibalism. The idea that people cannibalised because they were ravenous is to be precluded since we know that in the great Naples famine of 1764 there were riots, but no cases of cannibalism. Furthermore, if the events of 1799 had been the result of starvation, the cases would have been more numerous, without all that waste of meat left out in the open.

We must also rule out class struggle as a cause. The long-dominant postulation that the counter-revolution is to be interpreted through a socio-economic lens has now been refuted by empirical findings.[57] To be exact, something of the kind did emerge—on a primitive level devoid of class consciousness—during the constant looting of the counter-revolution. Sources from all sides mention the fact that during the looting, and the concurrent arrests, torture and murder, the *lazzari* and *Sanfedisti* cared little about who was a real or a presumed Jacobin. The poor's hatred of the rich certainly helped to fuel the violence both in Naples and the provinces, but this was politically blind, the sole objective being robbery, and the attacks on the houses of the rich was pure common sense: having been given licence to plunder, why choose the homes of the poor who had nothing worth stealing? But none of what happened can be used to draw a connection between class struggle and cannibalism.

Of greater relevance is another classic analytical key used by anthropologists to explain cannibalism: that of revenge. There are even links to be found in Western tradition: from Achilles, who threatened Hector to "eat you raw," to Hecuba, who longed to devour the heart of Pelide.[58] On a local level, revenge could impact on the factional clashes underlying those of revolution and counter-revolution.[59] In Naples, on the other hand, counter-revolutionary propaganda which could trigger retaliatory desires probably played the more decisive role. This propaganda had obsessively and extensively promoted the image of the "Jacobin cannibals,"[60] the "French cannibals"[61] and the "horrendous cannibals" referred to even in post-Thermidor France, in the *Réveil du peuple*.[62] In Italy counter-revolutionary literature, the press and sermons from the pulpit had pounded away at the population, presenting the French revolutionaries as monsters: atheists, regicidists and, of course, cannibals. In Naples itself, "anti-Jacobin propaganda had had all the time necessary to spread its demonic images of revolutionaries as 'blood suckers,' in the literal and figurative sense."[63] One of the republicans' problems was therefore that of "dissipating the frightening diffidence felt towards the French, who for years and years had been painted from the pulpits as cannibals."[64] Indeed, in an attempt to dispel the stigma during the formal announcements of the proclamation of the Republic, republican counter-propaganda had warned the "good but seduced and misled Neapolitans" that "from the beginning of the happy French Revolution they have always depicted the inhabitants of that great nation as cannibals, atheists and enemies of the Catholic faith."[65]

Vernacular songs circulating during the months of the counter-revolution made some mention of this kind of retaliation. In one, the question "What has equality done for us?" was answered with: "it has squeezed us, plucked us, stripped us to the bone."[66] This probably referred to the heavy contributions levied by the French Directorate,[67] and the final phrase therefore seems to evoke a theme that calls for reprisal: stripped to the bone like the scapegoat Fiani. Food-related revenge featured in another song that described the plight of the population during the Republic, starving while the Jacobins and a favoured few filled their bellies at patriotic banquets. Thus, the song demanded retribution from the hangman:

> [. . .] preparing a banquet,
> [the Jacobin] knew how to stuff themselves;
> and for everyone else?
> there is no equality and freedom.
> Millstone merchant!
> what did he spend out of his own pocket?
> our blood, which the executioner
> must now make him shit out.[68]

It is therefore reasonable to think that works such as these fuelled the unrestrained violence, while something similar would also explain the slaughter of the royalist officers eaten in July: a sign of revenge for assumed treason. Treason that in general was key to the way in which the protagonists construed things,[69] and which is invoked in various songs:

> Majesty, we're hanging those who betrayed you,
> priests, monks and nobles!
> More of them here, more of them there,
> kicking freedom in the face![70]

The hanging of traitors was again the leitmotif of the ditty sung while the body of Eleonora de Fonseca Pimentel swung from the scaffold. Both that and the song about banquets contains another clue, both being parodies of republican rites, like theatre parties and banquets. Such lampooning was also on display in the ceremonies that accompanied the removal of the liberty trees.[71] Ritual elements, therefore, emerged from beneath the apparent total confusion. To some extent, these bear resemblance to the *charivari* or *rough music*,[72] rituals which involved noisy, mock parades that expressed disapproval of certain remarried widowers and widows, or others deemed guilty of violating the community order, like husbands beaten by their wives, adulterers and so forth. In Naples the parade involving second marriages was called the *ciambelleria* (or *ciambellaria*). This involved making noise at night under the houses of the people in question and was widespread in other parts of the kingdom, under different names (*scampanacciata*, *scurdia*). In 1540 the Viceroy Pedro de Toledo strictly prohibited the *ciambellerie*, which were the cause of "fights, disputes, injuries and deaths,"[73] but at the end of the eighteenth century "in other parts of the kingdom there was no lack of such abuses,"[74] and in reality it was attested in Naples and elsewhere until at least the late the nineteenth century, albeit in a domesticated form.[75]

Some variations of these manifestations of "ritualised hostility"[76] emerge from the stories of arrestees led naked to prison, amid the noise of the crowd, the music, the gross humiliations and the "malignant roaring laughter"[77] of irrepressible celebratory joy. However, to concentrate on rituals, there were also other types of insult and mockery, like the *macriate*, a custom that involved soiling the door of betrayed spouses, as well as the example *par excellence*, that of the carnival. In eighteenth-century Naples the high point of the carnival was the *Cuccagna*, a game which took place in the piazza of the royal palace up to 1773, before being banned in 1779.[78] The event was staged for four consecutive Sundays, and in it thousands of *lazzari* were goaded to compete in a ferocious game, often marked by death and injury. Against a backcloth of complex theatrical scenes representing the mythical land of Bengodi, they were given licence to loot all kinds of prizes distributed in "machines" brim-full of obstacles. The game was managed by the authorities: the king oversaw its organisation, and he signalled the start of the *agone* in which the *lazzari* fought, tooth and nail, for the best pieces. In a certain sense, we might construe the series of events that began on 14 June as a giant *Cuccagna*. After all, it was Ruffo who, after winning the battle, gave the go-ahead for the looting, which then got completely out of hand. In the *Cuccagna*, any form of violence was allowed in the battle for trophies, and sometimes that game, too, got out of hand, degenerating into riot. Moreover, since food was the most sought-after prize, pieces of meat and animals were scattered the *Cuccagna*, bearing a resemblance to scenes of 1799.

In short, it is probable that this rite and others played a role in the cannibalism, which seems confirmed by the episode in which a *lazzaro* was killed for refusing to eat his share of Fiani's remains, as well as by the ritual staged in the Cestari case. Nevertheless, cannibalism is not a self-explanatory ritual, and in seeking its motives it would seem unwise to place the accent on the defence of the faith, as in the case of the French religious wars. For here we are in a completely different context, and the studies and sources, beginning with Ruffo, show that it was not injured faith that roused the masses in the counter-revolution. What is more, for Christianity cannibalism is an act against nature, which violates the divine order.

Rather, it may be that the *lazzari* and the *Sanfedisti* were under the illusion that they had religious sanction for their actions. After all, they were in an army led by Ruffo, a cardinal, who fought under the banner of the "Holy Faith" of Christianity. And again, the clergy was at the forefront of anti-Jacobin propaganda: we have seen how on 14 June preachers had entered the city, stirring up the carnage to the sound of tocsins. In the following months there followed an unbroken succession of feasts, bonfires, illuminations and processions, often organised by churches, at which the same bells often rang out. All of this inevitably helped to create a heady, befuddling climate in which the overconsumption of wine was an unsurprising feature; indeed, I think it would be a mistake to underestimate the part that drunkenness played in the violence.[79]

If the defence of faith does not throw light on the cannibalism of 1799,[80] it might be more profitable to give thought to the widespread magical beliefs in Naples, seeing that "in the cases of mutilation and destruction of corpses, ancient sacrificial and magical-propitiatory practices linked to violent death also seemed to re-emerge."[81] These are practices which anthropologists have shown us can be connected—as in the case of the Tupinambá—to revenge, which, in turn, is intimately linked to the political dimension.

And politics, in fact, can provide a strong lead to follow in the quest for an understanding of European cannibalism.[82] Basically, what was the cannibalism of Cronus, who devoured his children so as not to lose the throne of king of the Titans, if not a political act?[83] And did not Plato link cannibalism to tyranny, the worst political crime of all? If we look at the more than 15 cases of cannibalism in Italy in the early Middle Ages and the early modern age, documented by Angelica Montanari, we find that the majority are linked by a thread in which politics is central, being connected to clashes between factions, conspiracies, revolts, tyrannies, attacks on the lord, and resisting invasion.[84] Moreover, it is difficult not to see the centrality of politics in the cases of Starace and De Witt, as well as in the destruction of the remains of the assassin of Henry IV, François Ravaillac (1610)[85] and of the favourite of the Regent of France, Concino Concini (1617).[86] In short, it seems arguable that in Europe cannibalism represented the ultimate form of contempt, of popular infamy, especially in the political dimension, with the victim being treated as a beast to be butchered and his violated cadaver, reduced to excrement, being denied burial.

Nonetheless, placing politics at the heart of the 1799 events requires great caution, since we might be led to imagine that the people's actions sprang from a pronounced loyalty to the monarchy. In fact, this idea is confuted by the royalist sources themselves, not least the man who knew the masses best: Fabrizio Ruffo. He, writing to the king, warned:

> His Majesty believes that the people are the defenders of the Throne, and I have shown that I believe this, but I am not persuaded. For them all parties are the same, as long as they can steal. Now the people are marking the houses of royalists in order to loot them if, as some hope, the republicans return. In the meantime, around 6,000 of my men fled with the booty [. . .]. In a word I saw the whole army desert, a phenomenon I met in Cotrone, Cosenza, Paola and Altamura, where pillaging had to be allowed.[87]

Writing to the king, the government junta also denounced the "spirit of robbery that thrives in the plebeians":

> This [mob], which knows its strength, has no goal other than its private interests, which it obtains with the most vile and wicked means.

It applauds the august name of [Your Majesty], but with the cheers of the lower people. [. . .] The plebs [. . .] cover their fierce rapacity with a cloak of zeal and allegiance to the crown, and seek to make themselves and the others believe that robbery is a consequence of the destruction of the rebels and not in fact the main objective behind their actions.[88]

Even more significant are some of the notes that De Nicola added to his diary on 12 October:

What pains me is to see this murderous and drunken mass claiming credit for being the only ones loyal to the king, and with its songs maligning all the classes, for example by singing *Maiestà chi t'ha tradute/Muonece, prievete e cavaliere/Te volevano prigioniere* [Majesty, who betrayed you/monks, priests and nobles/wanted you imprisoned] and the like. It looks with ostility at all gentlemen, and almost claims that it has restored the kingdom to the king. When we, who have been in the midst of this horrendous catastrophe, know that the very ones who went about shouting *long live the King*, shouted *long live Freedom* around Championnet [. . .]. The same ones who were singing the songs mentioned above, went singing the *Marseilleise* and the [. . .] *Carmagnola*. The same people who ran to cut down the [liberty] trees, ran to celebrate when they were planted. The same who boasted about being adherents of the Sovereigns, deafened our ears by shouting in the streets *The Escape of the Tyrant, the New Song of Caroline, the Freedom of the monks and priests*, and similar wickedness that made me tremble. [. . .] Now they are the faithful, we are the traitors, after we were assassinated and demoralised by the French, and then looted by the populace.[89]

Bitter reflections, which speak volumes about the monarchic sentiments of the *lazzari* and *Sanfedisti*. Certainly, a *lazzarone* king, as Ferdinando was called, was more congenial to them than a Republic which lasted only a few months and which they had understood little and benefited from even less. Even so, that same king had fled a month before the French reached Naples, abandoning his people, and only after the counter-revolution had he returned to the capital for about a month, albeit taking care to stay at a safe distance, on board a ship. Defence of the monarchy was not therefore the motive for the cannibalistic violence. Rather, what we seem to see is the deployment of substitutive people power—as described by Edward P. Thompson and Natalie Zemon Davis—in a moment of crisis which the ruling power had failed to address satisfactorily.[90]

However, it is also true that the Fiani episode took place when the monarchy had returned, when the surrender agreement was broken, and the trials and the death sentences were under way. A further step forward, then, can be attempted by reflecting on the term used by all the sources to describe the phase that began on 14 June: "Anarchy." This definition reveals the inability of the higher classes to understand and legitimise popular dynamics. There was not, in fact, an absence of power in Naples, but rather, faced with the "empty throne,"[91] the people took up the sceptre and imposed their own rules, their rituals, their beliefs: anarchy, then, not in the sense of a power vacuum, but in the sense of an absence of power from above and the ignition of power from below. This throws light on the Fiani case, which occurred when the monarchy was attempting to resume control: beside and beyond it were the people, who decided what would be done with the corpse of the condemned. In the counter-revolution of 1799, there was no power that could guarantee public order, indeed the only credible force on the streets were the armed *Sanfedisti* and *lazzari* who could dispense their own brand of justice to the very end: "They thought they had the right to do whatever they thought."[92]

According to Marc Augé, "in a certain sense, cannibalism may appear to be the apex of social reversal, and even of inversion in general."[93] Following the great anthropologist, in the cannibalism practised in 1799 we see the culmination of political inversion, with the people appropriating the prerogatives of supreme power: of arrest, of life and death, of the administration of death and of the post-mortem.[94] But the right to arrest, to condemn to death and to decide what would happen to the body of the executed, and the right to inflict justice pertains to the sovereign: it is the ultimate power of the sword. Ruthless and publicly displayed torture was an essential expression of it: "It is a ceremonial by which a momentarily injured sovereignty is reconstituted. It restores that sovereignty by manifesting it at its most spectacular [. . .] The ceremony of punishment, then, is an exercise of 'terror'."[95]

If this is true of official power, then the brazen practice of cannibalism during the Neapolitan "anarchy" can better be understood. It was the symbolic proclamation of justice, of power, in the hands of the people. It was, however, an ephemeral power, given that it lacked a sense of direction that could make the people aware of their own strength and lead to a political future. In fact, as the monarchy gradually regained control, especially after the departure of the *Sanfedisti* masses and the return of the royals, the popular "anarchy" retreated and all memories of its violence were allowed to fade into oblivion.[96]

Notes

1. Anna Maria Rao, "La Repubblica napoletana del 1799," in *Storia del Mezzogiorno*, ed. Giuseppe Galasso and Rosario Romeo, vol. 4, t. II (Rome: Edizioni del sole, 1986), 535.
2. "Compendio istorico della rivoluzione e controrivoluzione di Napoli," in *La Repubblica Napoletana. Diari, memorie, racconti*, ed. Mario Battaglini, vol. 2 (Milan: Guerini e Associati, 2000), 65.

184 *Luca Addante*

3. Francesco Apa, *Brieve dettaglio di alcuni particolari avvenimenti accaduti nel corso della campagna nella spedizione dell'eminentissimo D. Fabrizio Ruffo [. . .]* (Naples: Vincenzo Manfredi, 1800), 38; Carlo De Nicola, *Diario napoletano*, vol. 1 (Naples: Luigi Regina, 1999), 187.
4. Domenico Sacchinelli, *Memorie storiche sulla vita del cardinale Fabrizio Ruffo* (Naples: Cataneo, 1836), 219.
5. Ibid., 218–19; Antonino Cimbalo, *Itinerario di tutto ciò ch'è avvenuto nella spedizione dell'eminentissimo signor D[on] Fabrizio cardinal Ruffo [. . .]* (Naples: Vincenzo Manfredi, 1799), 48; Domenico Petromasi, *Storia della spedizione dell'eminentissimo cardinale D. Fabrizio Ruffo [. . .]* (Naples: Vincenzo Manfredi, 1801), 68.
6. "Compendio istorico," 66.
7. Giuseppe De Lorenzo, *Memorie*, ed. Paola Russo (Naples: Vivarium, 1999), 25.
8. See ibid., 35 ff.; *Racconti storici di Gaetano Rodinò ad Aristide suo figlio*, ed. Benedetto Maresca (Bologna: Forni, n.d.), 495 ff.; Filippo Malaspina, *Occupazione de' francesi del Regno di Napoli dell'anno 1799 [. . .] e l'impresa intrapresa dal cardinale Don Fabrizio Ruffo di Baranello di cacciare i francesi dal Regno di Napoli [. . .]* (Paris: Dondey-Dupré, 1846), 105–6.
9. *Leggi, atti, proclami ed altri documenti della Repubblica napoletana*, ed. Mario Battaglini and Augusto Placanica, vol. 2 (Cava de' Tirreni: Di Mauro, 2000), 600.
10. Malaspina, *Occupazione*, 109.
11. Sacchinelli, *Memorie*, 240.
12. Ruffo to Acton, 21 June 1799, in *La riconquista del Regno di Napoli nel 1799*, ed. Benedetto Croce (Bari: Laterza, 1943), 227–29.
13. De Nicola, *Diario*, 208, 22 June. The term "Calabrians" is used to refer to the *Sanfedisti* in general.
14. Ibid., 239.
15. Ibid., 223.
16. Ibid., 295, 28 August. See also Giuseppe M. Galanti, *Memorie storiche del mio tempo*, ed. Augusto Placanica (Cava de' Tirreni: Di Mauro, 1996), 214.
17. Battaglini and Placanica, *Leggi*, 604–12; De Nicola, *Diario*, 202–4, 237–38 and 110–11.
18. Alfonso Sansone, *Gli avvenimenti del 1799 nelle Due Sicilie* (Palermo: Era Nova, 1901), 172.
19. Diomede Marinelli, *I giornali*, in Battaglini, *La Repubblica Napoletana*, vol. 1, 120.
20. "Compendio istorico," 66.
21. Battaglini and Placanica, *Leggi*, 624–25.
22. Marinelli, *I giornali*, 110.
23. See documents and letters edited in *Nelson and the Neapolitan Jacobins: Documents Relating to the Suppression of the Jacobin Revolution at Naples*, ed. Harold Cooke Gutteridge (London: The Navy Records Society, 1903), 251, 276–79, 287–91 and 293–94; Croce, *La riconquista*, 221–23; Battaglini and Placanica, *Leggi*, 617–33.
24. De Nicola, *Diario*, 287 and 350.
25. On the sentences: Luigi Conforti, *Napoli nel 1799. Critica e documenti inediti* (Naples: Anfossi, 1889), 144 ff.; Vittorio Spinazzola, *Gli avvenimenti del 1799 in Napoli da nuove ricerche e documenti inediti del Museo Nazionale di S. Martino* (Naples: Pierro, 1899), 120 ff.
26. Croce, *La riconquista*, 11 and 267.
27. De Nicola, *Diario*, 322.
28. Ibid., 287.

29. Benedetto Croce, "Canti politici del popolo napoletano," in *Un paradiso abitato da diavoli,* ed. Giuseppe Galasso (Milan: Adelphi, 2006), 136. Another version of the verse is in Benedetto Croce, *La rivoluzione napoletana del 1799,* ed. Cinzia Cassiani (Naples: Bibliopolis, 1998), 79.
30. Marinelli, *I giornali,* 117.
31. Like William Arens, *The Man-Eating Myth: Anthropology and Anthropophagy* (New York: Oxford University Press, 1979).
32. De Nicola, *Diario,* 296–97 and 323.
33. *Cronache de' Condannati,* quoted in Giustino Fortunato, *I Napoletani del 1799* (Florence: Barbera, 1884), 27–28. See also Onofrio Fiani, *Carattere de' Napolitani. Quadro istorico-politico scritto in Francia dopo la controrivoluzione di Napoli,* ed. Anna Maria Rao and Lidia Membrini (Naples: Vivarium, 2005), 94.
34. Emanuele Palermo, *"Colpo d'occhio su la condotta de' patrioti durante la Repubblica Napoletana [. . .],"* ms. quoted in Battaglini, *La Repubblica,* vol. 1, 147.
35. Vincenzo Cuoco, *Saggio storico sulla rivoluzione di Napoli,* ed. Antonino De Francesco (Rome-Bari: Laterza, 2014), 211, recalled "those fires in which the limbs of the unfortunate killed were cooked, which the people ate"; Amodio Ricciardi, *Napoli 1799. Memoria sugli avvenimenti,* ed. Silvana Musella (Sorrento: Di Mauro, 1994), 80: "Their flesh was also eaten out of an excessive religious and moral zeal."
36. Marinelli, *I giornali,* 110.
37. De Nicola, *Diario,* 224.
38. *Il Nicasio. Vicende politiche del '99 divise in sentimenti poetici,* quoted in Spinazzola, *Gli avvenimenti,* 89.
39. "Compendio istorico," 66–67.
40. Malaspina, *Occupazione,* 107.
41. Ibid., 108.
42. Uomobono delle Bocache, "Cronaca degli Abruzzi," in *L'invasione francese negli Abruzzi,* ed. Luigi Coppa Zuccari, vol. 1 (L'Aquila: Vecchioni, 1928), 35.
43. Leopoldo Cassese, "Giacobini e realisti nel Vallo di Diano," *Rassegna storica salernitana* X (1949): 92–93.
44. *Cronistoria del Real Convento del Carmine Maggiore di Napoli,* ms. quoted in *I giornali di Diomede Marinelli,* ed. Alfonso Fiordelisi (Naples: Ricc. Marghieri di Gius., 1901), 2. The same Marinelli reported the episode (ibid.); see also Attilio Simioni, *Le origini del Risorgimento politico dell'Italia meridionale,* vol. 2 (Messina: Principato, 1930), 99 ff.
45. The difference between forms of violence induced by customs of justice from above and anthropophagy Rao, "La Repubblica," 503; Angelica A. Montanari, *Il fiero pasto. Antropofagie medievali* (Bologna: Il Mulino, 2015), 63.
46. The Europeans were not the only ones who saw cannibals everywhere except amongst themselves. "The belief in real cannibalism is widespread in Black Africa, even if it always concerns others," including Europeans, given, that, for example, the Germans in Rwanda were believed to have been cannibals: "It is always the other, the ruler or the distant, who is suspected of inhumanity," see Marc Augé, *Genio del paganesimo* (Turin: Bollati Boringhieri, 2002), 221–22. In the same way, at the end of the sixteenth century the Chinese believed the Portuguese to be cannibals: Alessandro Pastore, "Antropofagia in chiave storica: prospettive a confronto," *Storica* 66 (2016): 151.
47. Michel de Montaigne, "On the Cannibals," in *The Complete Essays,* trans. M.A. Screech (London: Penguin, 2003), 228–41.

186   *Luca Addante*

48. See below.
49. Voltaire, *Philosophical Dictionary* (London: Penguin, 1979).
50. As noted in Alain Corbin, *Un villaggio di cannibali nella Francia dell'Ottocento* (Rome-Bari: Laterza, 1991), 126; see Norbert Elias, *The Civilizing Process* (Oxford: Blackwell, 1994).
51. *The Speech of [. . .] Charles James Fox, in the House of Commons, on Monday, the 3d of February 1800 [. . .]* (London: A. Wilson, n.d. [1800]), 44.
52. Jonathan Swift, *A Modest Proposal for Preventing the Children of Poor People from Being a Burthen to Their Parents, or the Country, and for Making Them Beneficial to the Publick* (Dublin: n.p., 1729); Jean-Paul Marat, *La Constitution, ou projet de Déclaration des droits de l'homme et du citoyen, suivi d'un plan de Constitution [. . .]* (Paris: Buisson, 1789), 8 and 14.
53. Plato, *The Republic*, ed. G.R.F. Ferrai, trans. Tom Griffin (Cambridge: Cambridge University Press, 2000), Book 9, 571d, p. 286.
54. Emmanuel Le Roy Ladurie, *Les paysans de Languedoc*, vol. 1 (Paris: S.E.V.P.E.N., 1966), 398; Natalie Zemon Davis, "The Rites of Violence: Religious Riot in Sixteenth-Century France," *Past and Present* 59 (1973): 83; See Corbin, *Un villaggio*, 132; Paolo Viola, *Il trono vuoto. La transizione della sovranità nella rivoluzione francese* (Turin: Einaudi, 1989), 129–48.
55. On this riot see Rosario Villari, *La rivolta antispagnola a Napoli. Le origini* (Rome-Bari: Laterza, 1994), 42 ff. The testimonies on violence in the text are quoted in Luca Addante, "Starace, Giovan Vincenzo," in *Dizionario biografico degli Italiani*, vol. 94 (Rome: Istituto della Enciclopedia italiana, 2019), 43.
56. In order not to overload the notes, I point out some more recent studies on cannibalism in Europe: Merrall L. Price, *Consuming Passions: The Uses of Cannibalism in Late Medieval and Early Modern Europe* (New York: Taylor & Francis, 2003); Cătălin Avramescu, *An Intellectual History of Cannibalism* (Princeton: Princeton University Press, 2009); Agnès A. Nagy, *Qui a peur du cannibale? Récits antiques d'anthropophages aux frontières de l'humanité* (Turnhout: Brepols, 2009); Vincent Valdenberg, *De chair et de sang. Images et pratiques du cannibalisme de l'Antiquité au Moyen Âge* (Rennes: PUR-Presses universitaires François Rabelais, 2014); Giuseppe Mandalà, "Antropofagia nella Sicilia medievale: un tema culturale tra cronaca e rappresentazione," *Bullettino dell'Istituto storico italiano per il Medio Evo* 119 (2017): 1–107; Silvio Leydi, "'O Facinus Inauditum' (O Horrendous Crime): Anthropophagy in Renaissance Milan," in *Murder in Renaissance Italy*, ed. Trevor Dean and K.J.P. Lowe (Cambridge: Cambridge University Press, 2017), 144–63; Michel Perret, "Le cannibalisme: l'absolu interdit, le fantasme extreme," in *La cuisine est un langage*, ed. Michel Perret (Paris: L'Harmattan, 2017), 9–24.
57. Luca Addante, *Repubblica e controrivoluzione. Il 1799 nella Calabria cosentina* (Naples: Vivarium, 2005); Nello Ronga, *La Repubblica napoletana del 1799 nell'agro acerrano* (Naples: Istituto italiano per gli studi filosofici, 2006).
58. Homer, *Iliad*, XXII, v. 345; XXIV, vv. 265–70.
59. On factions and cannibalism: Montanari, *Il fiero pasto*, 57 and 61 and *passim*. On factional clashes as a factor of violence: Francesco Benigno, *Words in Time. A Plea for Historical Re-thinking* (London: Routledge, 2017), 25 and 28 ff. and *passim*; on the importance of clashes between local factions in 1799: Gaetano Cingari, *Giacobini e sanfedisti in Calabria nel 1799* (Reggio-Calabria: Casa del libro, 1978), 41 ff. and *passim*.
60. L.A. Baudy, *Causes particulières de la Révolution française [. . .]* (Frankfurt: Esslinger, 1793), 201.
61. Quoted in Luciano Guerci, *Uno spettacolo non mai più veduto nel mondo. La Rivoluzione francese come unicità e rovesciamento negli scrittori*

controrivoluzionari italiani (Turin: Utet, 2008), 108, but see the whole of ch. 4, "I 'cannibali della Francia'," 81–119. See also Vittorio E. Giuntella, ed., *Le dolci catene. Testi della controrivoluzione cattolica in Italia*, (Rome: Istituto per la storia del Risorgimento italiano, 1988); Marco Cuaz, *Le nuove di Francia. L'immagine della rivoluzione francese nella stampa periodica italiana* (Turin: Albert Meynier, 1990); Marina Formica and Luca Lorenzetti, eds., *Il Misogallo romano*, (Rome: Bulzoni, 1999).

62. Quoted in Francesco Benigno, *Terrore e terrorismo. Saggio storico sulla violenza politica* (Turin: Einaudi, 2018), 20.

63. Rao, "La Repubblica," 515. See also Rao, "Napoli e la rivoluzione (1789–1794)," *Prospettive settanta* 7 (1985): 403–76; Rao, "La Rivoluzione francese nella stampa periodica napoletana," ibid., 11 (1989): 44–61.

64. Benedetto Croce, *Vite di avventure di fede e di passione*, ed. Giuseppe Galasso (Milan: Adelphi, 2002), 414–15.

65. See the Antonio Brunner, "Proclama patriottico," in *Leggi*, ed. Battaglini and Placanica, vol. 3, 9–10.

66. Quoted in Rosa Troiano, "Codici linguistici e tecniche retoriche nei canti giacobini e sanfedisti," in *Novantanove in idea. Linguaggi, miti, memorie*, ed. Augusto Placanica and Maria Rosaria Pelizzari (Naples: ESI, 2002), 206.

67. Ibid.

68. Quoted ibid.

69. Luca Addante, " 'Vipere arrabbiate'. Variazioni moralistiche sui traditori tra storici e pseudo-storici," in *Novantanove in idea*, ed. Placanica and Pelizzari, 503–28.

70. Croce, *Canti*, 135.

71. Rao, "La Repubblica," 502; see also *supra*.

72. See Natalie Zemon Davis, "The Reason of Misrule: Youth Groups and Charivaris in Sixteenth-Century France," *Past and Present* 50 (1971): 41–75; Edward P. Thompson, " 'Rough Music': le charivari anglais," *Annales E.S.C.* 27 (1972): 285–312; Jacques Le Goff and Jean-Claude Schmitt, eds., *Le charivari*, (Paris: EHESS-Mouton, 1981); Franco Castelli, ed., *Charivari: mascherate di vivi e di morti* (Alessandria: Edizioni dell'Orso, 2004).

73. Giovanni Antonio Summonte, *Dell'historia della Città e Regno di Napoli*, vol. 4 (Naples: Antonio Bulifon, 1675), 86.

74. Francesco De Jorio, *Introduzione allo studio delle prammatiche del Regno di Napoli [. . .]*, vol. 1 (Naples: Nella Stamperia Simoniana, 1777), 389.

75. Antonio De Nino, *Usi abruzzesi*, vol. 1 (Florence: Barbera, 1879), 101–3; Francesco Brandileone, "Come si maritano le vedove," *Giambattista Basile. Archivio di letteratura popolare* 2 (1884): 11–12; Gaetano Amalfi, "Disapprovazione popolare," ibid., 5 (1892): 40; Berengario G. Amorosa, *Riccia nella storia e nel folk-lore* (Casalbordino: Arcangelis, 1903), 308.

76. Thompson, " 'Rough Music'," 286 and 288.

77. Rodinò, *Racconti*, 494.

78. See Laura Barletta, *La regolata licenza. Il carnevale a Napoli* (Messina: D'Anna, 1978); Barletta, *Il carnevale del 1764 a Napoli. Protesta e integrazione in uno spazio urbano* (Naples: Società editrice napoletana, 1981); Domenico Scafoglio, *La maschera della cuccagna. Spreco, rivolta e sacrificio nel carnevale napoletano del 1764* (Naples: Colonnese, 1981); Scafoglio, *Il carnevale napoletano* (Rome: Newton Compton, 1997).

79. On wine as a factor in violence: Yves-Marie Bercé, *Croquant et nu-pieds* (Paris: Gallimard, 1991), 101–2; Yves-Marie Bercé, *Fête et révolte* (Paris: Hachette, 1994), 14.

80. As Ricciardi, quoted above, appears to indicate.

81. Rao, "La Repubblica," 503.

82. On the link between anthropophagy and politics: Montanari, *Il fiero pasto*, 57 ff. and *passim*. More generally, on rituals of violence intended to place "the main focus on politics," Benigno, *Words*, 26 and *passim*.
83. Esiod, *Theogony*, vv. 459–67.
84. Montanari, *Il fiero pasto*, 56 ff.
85. Orest Ranum, "The French Ritual of Tyrannicide in the Late Sixteenth Century," *The Sixteenth Century Journal* 11 (1980): 72.
86. Sergio Bertelli, *Il corpo del re. Sacralità del potere nell'Europa medievale e moderna* (Florence: Ponte alle Grazie, 1995), 219–23.
87. Ruffo to Ferdinando IV, 28 June, in *Leggi*, ed. Battaglini and Placanina, 629.
88. Sansone, *Gli avvenimenti*, 171–72.
89. De Nicola, *Diario*, 341–42. On the tranformism of the *lazzari* in 1799, see Eric J. Hobsbawm, *Primitive Rebels* (Manchester: Manchester University Press, 1971), 120–21.
90. Edward P. Thompson, "The Moral Economy of the English Crowd in the Eighteenth Century," *Past and Present* 50 (1971): 88 and 110 and *passim*; Zemon Davis, "The Rites of Violence," 61 ff.
91. The reference, by extension, is to Viola, *Il trono vuoto*.
92. Galanti, *Memorie*, 214.
93. Augé, *Genio*, 220.
94. Obviously, religious power was also at stake in the *post-mortem*. For Napoli see Diego Carnevale, *L'affare dei morti. Mercato funerario, politica e gestione della sepoltura a Napoli* (Rome: École française de Rome, 2014), 42 ff., 77 ff. and *passim*.
95. Michel Foucault, *Discipline and Punish: The Birth of the Prison* (New York: Pantheon, 1977), 48–49 and *passim*.
96. Piero Pieri, "Il Regno di Napoli dal luglio 1799 al marzo 1806," *Archivio storico per le province napoletane* 51–52 (1926–27): 5–163 and 136–286; Anna Maria Rao, "La prima restaurazione borbonica," in *Storia del Mezzogiorno*, ed. Galasso and Romeo, 543–74.

11 "You Can Tell a Man From His Head"

The Study and Preservation of the Skulls of Celebrated Italians in the Nineteenth Century

Simone Baral

In 1874, when the tomb of Gaetano Donizetti was opened in readiness for the translation of his body from the Valtesse cemetery to Bergamo's Basilica of Santa Maria Maggiore, those present were surprised to find that "the upper segment of the skull was missing."[1] Subsequent investigations led to Girolamo Carchen, a doctor in the city's military hospital, being identified as the thief: he had been excluded from the group that carried out the composer's autopsy after his death in 1848, and so lost out on the opportunity to observe the "highly developed gyri corresponding to the parts of the brain responsible for music, idealism and wondrousness."[2] Offended by the perceived insult, Carchen decided to enter the Valtesse cemetery at night to remove Donizetti's skullcap, being driven by an "excessive passion for the science of phrenology."[3]

The Donizetti theft was not an isolated incident: in the same century a similar fate befell, for example, the skulls of the Austrian composer Joseph Haydn, the Spanish painter Francisco Goya and the Italian writer Giacomo Leopardi.[4] At the time of an often under-regulated market,[5] this phenomenon was the morbid expression of an interest in the bodies of the great, but not until the nineteenth century had it reached such a scale. Originating in both the romantic attitude towards the nature of genius[6] and the positivist rigour of measuring traits outside the norm, it led to many studies, investigations and publications,[7] all mainly the work of doctors, who had the highest level of expertise in the field of anatomy and the functioning of the body.[8]

Craniological Analyses of Great Italians

In recent years renewed historiographical interest has been displayed in anatomical research carried out on people of note,[9] and this has led to the publication of a number of Italian studies. These, though often limited to particular individuals[10] or institutions,[11] have begun to reveal how such practices and debates in nineteenth-century Italy deserve broader and lengthier analysis. To this end, this chapter will offer a "map" of the various craniological analyses carried out on the heads of famous Italians during the nineteenth century, in an attempt to suggest certain lines of enquiry that bind together the history of scientific thought, culture and society of that period. The corpus utilised is composed of around 60 analyses of skulls belonging to famous Italians,[12] which, while certainly not exhaustive,[13] can nonetheless provide an initial overview of the phenomenon, as well as a guide for future studies.

The phenomenon peaked twice in the nineteenth century, the two high points corresponding to distinct attempts to affirm certain knowledge about man. The first, which occurred during the 1830s,[14] was the international golden age of a theory known as phrenology—the irresistible scientific passion that drove Carchen to theft—and which, in the Italian peninsula, endeavoured to obtrude into scientific debate,[15] especially in the meetings held periodically between 1839 and 1847[16] in the absence of other forums for the scientists of the pre-unification states. Among the different interpretative approaches used to link the physical form and the inner nature of individuals, for half a century phrenology constituted the most convincing scientific proposal, bringing to the anatomical table the idea, widespread since the eighteenth century, that the brain was the "custodian" of the human personality, and the skull, by inference, was the "constant symbolic signification of the intellectual faculties."[17]

According to phrenological theories, first formulated by the Viennese anatomist Franz Joseph Gall, the brain was made up of organs, each performing a specific function. That being the case, by studying the structure of the brain and skull—the latter faithfully reproducing the characteristics of the former—it was possible to reconstruct the character of single individuals.[18] It followed, then, that the size—and consequently the strength—of a single organ distinguished people with talent from those less gifted, and dictated their actions and justified their reputation. As Giovanni Mayer, one of the first authors to bring the ideas of phrenology to Italy put it,[19] "an organ that is very developed, and rules over all the others, whose functions are subjected to it, is what makes the man of genius. [. . .] Therefore, from a particular formation of the head we can infer the presence of a dominant organ: for example, from parallel temples we can deduce mechanical talent."[20] As a result of the epistemological nature of this theory, the heads of exceptional individuals—be they politicians, scientists, artists, but also criminals and madmen—constituted, at the same time, the material for the creation of the science and the proof of its veracity. While for Gall the structure of the brain, and accordingly the personality of its owner, was innate, some of those who continued his studies, like Caspar Spurzheim and George Combe, would later attenuate this fixation on individuality by allowing for a possibility of change both in behaviour and in the head itself due to "environmental" circumstances, such as education and habit.[21] At the same time specialists began to take greater account of the impulses originating

Table 11.1 Craniological analyses carried out on famous Italians during the nineteenth century

Subject	First known analysis	Later analyses
Raphael (Raffaello Sanzio) (1483–1520)	[*1800, Vienna, F.J. Gall][1]	[*1825, Edinburgh, W. Scott] 1833, Rome, A. Trasmondo *1833, Rome, R. Verity *1835, Rome, G.G. Belli #*1833–35, Milan, P. Molossi *1844, Rome, G. Combe *1882, Rome, H. Schaaffhausen[2]
Bartolomeo Sestini (1792–1822)	(*1822, Paris, G.A.L. Fossati)[3]	
Guido Reni (1575–1642)	1825, Bologna, G.A.L. Fossati[4]	
Andrea Palladio (1508–80)	1831, Vicenza, G. Grabner Maraschini[5]	
Antonio Scarpa (1752–1832)	1832, Pavia, C. Beolchini[6]	1878, Pavia, G. Zoja[7]
Vincenzo Bellini (1801–35)	(*1835, Paris, G.A.L. Fossati)[8]	1876, Catania, C. Federici *1882, Naples, B.G. Miraglia 1886, Turin, A. Gamba[9]
Gian Domenico Romegnosi (1761–1835)	1835, Milan, P. Molossi[10]	(*1835–38, Paris, G.A.L. Fossati) (*1835–38, Paris, C. Broussais)[11] (*1835–38, Paris, C. Broussais)[13]
Giovanni Paolo Olini (1773–1835)	1835, Paris, G.A.L. Fossati[12]	
Luigi Sacco (1796–1836)	1836, Milan, G, Polli[14]	1837, Milan, G. Polli[16] (Bergamo, G. Carchen) (1874, Bergamo, M. Galli) 1887, Bergamo, Capelli[18]
Giovanni Rasori (1766–1837)	1837, Milan, P. Molossi[15]	
Gaetano Donizzetti (1797–1848)	1848, Bergamo, Novati et al.[17]	
Medicean skeletons	1857, Florence, L. Paganucci and Tarugi[19]	1875, Florence, L. Paganucci and A. Foresi[20]
Leonardo da Vinci (1452–1519)	1863, Amboise, A. Houssaye[21]	#1866, Naples, G. Nicolucci #1866, Modena, P. Gaddi #1866, Turin, A. Garbiglietti #1866, Paris, P. Broca #1867, Halle, H. Welcker[23]
Dante Alighieri (1265–1321)	1865, Ravenna, G. Puglioli and C. Bertozzi[22]	

(Continued)

Table 11.1 (Continued)

Subject	First known analysis	Later analyses
Giovanni Battista Niccolini (1782–1861)	1865, Florence, L. Paganucci and P. Betti[24]	
Ugo Foscolo (1778–1827)	1871, Florence, P. Mategazza[25]	
Ambrosian skeletons	1871, Milan, E. Cornalia[26]	
Goffredo Mameli (1827–49)	(1872, Rome, A. Bertani)[27]	
Petrarch (Francesco Petrarca) (1304–74)	1873, Padua, G. Canestrini[28]	
Giovanni Maria Bussedi (1802–69)	1873, Pavia, G. Zoja[29]	
Vincenzo Brunacci (1768–1818)	1874, Pavia, G. Zoja[30]	
Alessandro Volta (1745–1827)	1874, Como, C. Lombroso, E. Cornalia and A. Verga[31]	#1879, Naples, B.G. Miraglia[32]
Ambrogio Fusinieri (1775–1853)	1875, Vicenza, G. Canestrini[33]	
Antonio Lodovico Muratori (1672–1750)	1876, Modena, E. Giovanardi[34]	
Sebastiano Valfré (1629–1710)	*1878, Turin, G. De Lorenzi[35]	
Bartolomeo Panizza (1785–1867)	1879, Pavia, G. Zoja[36]	
Pasquale Massacra (1819–49)	1882, Pavia, G. Zoja[37]	
Antonio Bordoni (1788–1860)	1883, Pavia, G. Zoja[38]	
Defendente Sacchi (1796–1840)	1887, Milan, G. Zoja[39]	
Gerolamo Ramorino (1792–1849)	1889, Turin, A. Gamba[40]	
Vincenzo Monti (1754–1828)	1891, Milan, A. Verga[41]	1891, Milan, C. Lombroso, G. Romiti and G. Amadei[42]
Gian Galeazzo Visconti (1351–1402)	1895, Milan, G. Zoja[43]	
Camillo Benso (1810–61)	*1897, Turin, A. Gamba[44]	
Paolo Emilio Demi (1798–1863)	1898, Livorno, A. Mochi[45]	
Carlo Giacomini (1840–98)	1898, Turin, G. Sperino[46]	

1 Franz Joseph Gall, Organologie ou exposition des instincts, des penchans, des sentimens et des talens, ou des qualités morales et des facultés intellectuelles fondamentales de l'homme et des animaux, et du siege de leurs organes, vol. 5 (Paris: Boucher, 1825), 177–78.

2 William Scott, "Remarks on the cerebral development of Raffael d'Urbino, compared with the accounts given of his character and genius," The Phrenological Journal and Miscellany 7 (1825): 327–60; Antonio Trasmondo, "Discorso," in Istoria del ritrovamento delle spoglie mortali di Raffaello Sanzio

da Urbino, ed. Pietro Odescalchi (Rome: Boulzaler, 1833), 22–30; "Raphael's Skull," The Phrenological Journal 9 (1834–36): 93–94; Marcello Teodonio, "'Sor Carlo mio'. Giuseppe Gioachino Belli e Carlo Maggiorani," in Carlo Maggiorani: politica e medicina nel Risorgimento, ed. Claudio Canonici and Giuseppe Monsagati (Rome: Gangemi, 2004), 68–69; Pietro Molossi, Studi frenologici. Parte polemica (Milan: Guglielmini e Radaelli, 1840), 17–19; George Combe, "On the Cerebral Development and Moral and Intellectual Character of Raphael Sanzio d'Urbino," The Phrenological Journal and Magazine for Moral Science 19 (1846): 42–56; Hermann Schaaffhausen, Der Schädel Raphaels. Zur 400järigen geburstagfeier Raphael Santi's (Bonn: Verlag von Max Cohen & Sohn (Fr. Cohen), 1883).

3 See Giovanni Antonio Lorenzo Fossati, Manuel pratique de phrénologie: ou, Physiologie de cerveau d'après les doctrines de Gall, de Spurzheim, de Combe et des autres phrénologistes (Paris: Baillière, 1845), 380.

4 Giovanni Antonio Lorenzo Fossati, De l'influence de la physiologie intellectuelle sur les sciences, la littérature et les arts; discours pour l'ouverture d'un cours de phrénologie, suivi d'un rapport sur a phrénologie en Italie, fait à la Société Phrénologique d'Edimbourg; avec des notes (Paris: Bechet J, E, Sautelet, 1828), 45–46.

5 See Antonio Magrini, Memorie intorno la vita e le opere di Andrea Palladio pubblicate nell'inaugurazione del suo monumento in Vicenza li 19 agosto 1845 (Padua: Tipografia del Siminario, 1845), 341.

6 Carlo Beolchini, "Necroscopia del defunto Cav. Antonio Scarpa, con alcuni brevi cenni sulla malattia che lo condusse alla tomba," Annali universali di medicina 65 (1833): 211–24.

7 Giovanni Zoja, "La testa di Scarpa," Archivio per l'antropologia e l'etnologia 8 (1878): 443–50.

8 See Biagio Gioacchino Miraglia, "Parere frenologico su Vincenzo Bellini," in Questioni filosofiche, sociali, mediche e medico-forensi trattate coi principii della fisiologia del cervello, Biagio Gioacchino Miraglia (Naples: Iride, 1883), 268.

9 Cesare Federici, "Lettera al Direttore del giornale Lo Statuto, riguardante lo "scoprimento della salma dell'immortale Bellini, e lo studio di quel capo che fu sede dell'altissimo intelletto musicale," in Bellini: Memorie e lettere, ed. Francesco Florimo (Florence: G. Barbèra 1882), 262–64; Miraglia, "Parere frenologico su Vincenzo Bellini," 259–75; Gamba, "Presentazione della maschera della faccia e del cranio di Vincenzo Bellini," 748–57.

10 Pietro Molossi, "Osservazioni frenologiche sulla testa di Gian Domenico Romegnosi," Annali universali di medicina 78 (1836): 250–328.

11 See Giuseppe Canziani, "Note," in Notizie sulla vita pubblica e privata del principe Talleyrand di Périgord con l'esame frenologico del suo cranio e con l'elogio sul del barone di Barante (Milan: vedova di A.F. Stella e Giacomo figlio, 1838), 104; Casimir Broussais, "Compte-rendu des travaux de la Société phrénologique de Paris pendant l'année 1834–1835," Journal de la Société Phrénologique de Paris 3 (1835): 481–82.

12 See ibid, 482.

13 See ibid.

14 Giovanni Polli, Saggio di fisiognomonia e patognomonia ossia dei mezzi di conoscere le interne facoltà e le malattie degli uomini dalle loro esterne apparenze (Milan: Paolo Andrea Molina, 1837), 170–75.

15 Pietro Molossi, Saggio della recente opera col titolo: An introduction to phrenology del signor Roberto Macbnish membro della Facoltà medica e chirurgica di Glasgow, ecc. Traduzione dall'Inglese con note (Milan: Molina, 1838), 67.

16 Polli, Saggio di fisiognomonia e patognomonia, 170–75.

17 See Alborghetti and Galli, Gaetano Donizetti e G. Simone Mayr, 135–36.

18 Ibid, 137–38; Gino Cappelli, "La calotta cranica di Donizetti," Archivio italiano per le malattie nervose 24 (1887): 135–53.

(Continued)

Table 11.1 (Continued)

19 Guido Sommi Picenardi, "Esumazione e ricognizione delle Ceneri dei Principi Medicei fatta nell'anno 1857. Processo verbale e note," *Archivio Storico Italiano* 165 (1888): 333–60.

20 Alessandro Foresi, *La tomba di Lorenzo e d'Alessandro de' Medici aperta il 1° di marzo 1875* (Florence: Tipografia del Vocabolario, 1875).

21 Arséne Houssaye, *Histoire de Léonard De Vinci* (Paris: Didier et C., 1869), 315–16.

22 See Municipio di Ravenna, ed., *Della scoperta delle ossa di Dante. Relazione con documenti* (Ravenna: G. Angeletti, 1870), xi–xii.

23 Giustiniano Nicolucci, *Il cranio di Dante Alighieri. Lettera all'illustre antropologo sig. dr. F. Pruner-Bey di Paris* (Naples: Stamperia del Fibreno, 1866); Paolo Gaddi, "Intorno al cranio di Dante Alighieri. Nota antropologica," *Memorie della Regia Accademia di scienze, lettere ed arti in Modena* 7 (1866): 29–46; Antonio Garbiglietti, *Sopra alcuni recenti scritti di craniologia etnografica de' Dottori Giustiniano Nicolucci e G. Bernardo Davis* (Turin: G. Favale, 1866), 33–40; Paul Broca, "Sur le crâne de Dante Alighieri," *Bulletin de la Société d'Anthropologie de Paris* 1 (1866): 206–10; Hermann Welcker, "On the skull of Dante. A letter to Dr. J. Barnard Davis," *The Anthropological Review* 5 (1867): 56–71.

24 Luigi Paganucci, "Lettera," *Gazzetta del Popolo*, 25 May 1865.

25 Paolo Mantegazza, "Il cranio di Ugo Foscolo," *Archivio per l'antropologia e l'etnologia* 1 (1871): 301–6.

26 Emilio Cornalia, "Gli scheletri Sant'Ambrosiani scoperti nel 1871 in Milan," *Archivio per l'antropologia e l'etnologia* 3 (1873): 233–52.

27 See Gino Carocci, "Mameli dalla Chiesa delle Stimate alla gloria del Colle Garibaldino," *Camicia Rossa: Rassegna mensile di pensiero e di azione* 17 (1941): 202.

28 Giovanni Canestrini, "Le ossa di Francesco Petrarca. Studio antropologico," *Atti della Società veneto-trentina di scienze naturali residente in Padua* 3 (1874): 65–142.

29 See Giovanni Zoja, "Nota sul teschio di Antonio Bordoni, matematico pavese," *Memorie del Reale Istituto lombardo di scienze e lettere. Classe di scienze matematiche e naturali* 15 (1883): 97.

30 See ibid, 96.

31 Cesare Lombroso, "Craniologia. Relazione sul cranio di Volta con osservazioni dei MM. EE. Cornalia e Verga," *Rendiconti del Reale Istituto lombardo di Scienze e Lettere* 11 (1878): 331–41.

32 Biagio Gioacchino Miraglia, "Sul cranio di Alessandro Volta. Considerazioni frenologiche," in *Questioni filosofiche*, ed. Miraglia, 48–64; Biagio Gioacchino Miraglia, "Ulteriori considerazioni frenologiche sul cranio di Alessandro Volta," in ibid., 241–58.

33 Giovanni Canestrini, "Il cranio di Ambrogio Fusinieri. Studio antropologico," *Atti del Reale Istituto veneto di scienze, lettere ad arti* 1 (1874–75): 963–84.

34 See *Relazione ufficiale del riconoscimento e del trasporto delle ossa di Lodovico Antonio Muratori. XI ottobre MDCCCLXXII* (Modena: Cappelli, 1872), 7–8.

35 Giovanni De Lorenzi, "Misure craniane e facciali del cranio del beato teologo Valfré ed altre della testa del famigerato assassino Vincenzo Artusio," *Giornale della R. Accademia di Medicina di Turin* 10 (1871): 518–20.

36 Giovanni Zoja, "Cenni sulla testa di Bartolomeo Panizza," *Bollettino scientifico* 1 (1879): 17–20 and 37–40.

37 Giovanni Zoja, "Del teschio di Pasquale Massacra, pittore pavese," *Memorie del Reale Istituto lombardo di scienze e di lettere. Classe di scienze matematiche e naturali* 1 (1882): 1–11.

38 See Zoja, *Nota sul teschio di Antonio Bordoni*, 91–98.

39 See Giovanni Zoja, "Nota su la salma di Isabella Valois," *Rendiconti del Reale Istituto lombardo di Scienze e Lettere* 31 (1898): 702–3.

40 Alberto Gamba, "Il cranio del Generale Ramorino," *Giornale della R. Accademia di Medicina di Turin* 37 (1889): 617–19.

41 Andrea Verga, "Un cranio controverso. Memoria," *Archivio per l'antropologia e la etnologia* 21 (1891): 315–25.

42 See ibid., 325.

43 Giovanni Zoja, "Nota intorno alle ossa di Giovanni Galeazzo Visconti," *Bollettino scientifico* 17 (1895): 1–13.

44 Alberto Gamba, "Presentazione di una maschera di Camillo Cavour, getto in gesso del Prof. Vela," *Giornale della R. Accademia di Medicina di Turin* 60 (1897): 517–18.

45 Aldobrandino Mochi, "Le ossa di Paolo Emilio Demi, scultore Livornese," *Archivio per l'antropologia e la etnologia* 28 (1898): 439–45.

46 Giuseppe Sperino, "Descrizione morfologica dell'encefalo del professore Carlo Giacomini," *Giornale della R. Accademia di Medicina di Turin* 63 (1900): 737–805.

Figure 11.1 Phrenological notes by B.G. Miraglia on the skull of Alessandro Volta, in Biagio Miraglia, *Sul cranio di Alessandro Volta. Considerazioni frenologiche* (Naples: Enrico Detken, 1870), 245.

from the cerebral organs more comprehensively: thus any dominance of a particular function over others would increasingly come to be seen as evidence of mental imbalance.[22] This new approach came to influence the pathological analysis of genius, which began in France with the works of Louis Fraînçisque Lélut,[23] who ironically was one of phrenology's most ferocious opponents.[24]

The emergence of a similar, even greater, interest in the skulls of the famous had to wait until the 1870s:[25] the abrupt reduction in craniological analysis after the 1840s[26] must in fact be read principally in the light of the decline of phrenological thought internationally,[27] which had been refuted on an anatomical basis by new physiologists, attacked by the Catholic world which considered it materialistic,[28] and, in Italy, deserted by its supporters, who were otherwise engaged in the political upheavals of the Risorgimento.[29]

The resumption of the analysis was probably triggered by certain processes involving the scientific world of the time, first, the post-unification development of a national scientific community,[30] albeit one without a real centre of elaboration and dissemination, a role played by Paris in the French context. And the needs of the new Italy—especially after the rise to power of the Historical Left—made the heads and bodies of the famous double targets. On the one hand, such human remains became subject to celebrations and initiatives promoted by national and local authorities to give a boost to the forming of a civic religion.[31] Corpses and remains began to be treated, exhumed, transported and exhibited as never before in the history of the peninsula. On the other hand, different political actors gradually began to appropriate the church's prerogative over the definition and use of relics in order to stage ceremonies and exhibitions endowed with strong symbolic and identity value around bodies of personalities of the recent past.[32] In this context, doctors and public authorities sometimes found themselves on opposite fronts, as demonstrated by the ban in 1887 on "carrying out a craniological study of the immortal master" Gioacchino Rossini, which shows the persistence, at the height of the positivist period, of what Mantegazza called "elements that fight against the light because they are afraid of it and feel a real and I would say foolish dismay for any positive research carried out to explain the functioning of the human brain."[33]

At the same time, however, the two sides were allies in a common cause. One thinks for example of how, in the nineteenth and twentieth centuries, the imperialist and nationalist political ambitions of Europe were reflected in the struggle between scientific theories that propounded alternative and competing hierarchical scales between races,[34] beginning with the conformation of "national crania."[35] In attempting to establish physical characteristics specific to regions, such as those of a refined and anthropological "Italianness,"[36] the skulls of the great proved to be of little use: the head of the Livornese sculptor Paolo Emilio Demi, for instance, did not match "the normal Tuscan type,"[37] while that of Petrarch "did not have the rounded, almost spherical shape of the majority of Italian skulls."[38] Moreover, the features of genius, being by definition "outside the norm," could not respect the anatomical criteria of common men.

But anthropological study was not the only driver of the rediscovery of famous skulls, since it was burgeoning new disciplines, like psychiatry[39] and neurophysiology, which, while seeking to disown their ties to the conceptual substratum of phrenology, continued to treat the brain and skull as special objects of analysis. From Cesare Lombroso's *Genio e follia*[40] to the "patographies of geniuses"[41] of the late nineteenth and early twentieth centuries, the pathological explanation of genius continued to consider possible cranial and cerebral anomalies of famous men as the origin of their greatness, while the localisationist paradigm once again began to assign single mental functions to particular parts of the human brain.[42] In any case, whatever was the door of entry to cranial observation, skulls continued to be investigated as part of the search for a physical confirmation of the defining talents that their owners were known for, invariably ending up finding "those usual indications of an extraordinary development of the intellectual faculties, which," as Giosuè Carducci pointed out ironically, "all well-behaved skulls give when they have the honour of having been part of the body of a great man."[43]

In the absence of valid shared scientific alternatives on which to base discourse and research on the skulls and brains of famous men,[44] the language of phrenology continued to be a descriptive and interpretative option for some time to come, showing how, rather than the skull itself, it was the gaze of its observers that was "well-behaved." In this regard it may be useful to reflect for a moment on the doubts of the Turin doctor Alberto Gamba, who, when handling a plaster cast of the skull of Vincenzo Bellini, revealed his discomfort with modern craniology, saying that, according to those who emphasised the importance of the volume of the brain, Bellini "would be classified among mediocre men,"[45] while according to those who impugned the cephalic index (the breadth to length ratio of the skull) the composer's head merely indicated an "average intelligence."[46] In order to justify anatomically the greatness of the composer, Gamba, like many of his colleagues,[47] had no choice but to defer to the antiquated phrenological theories: with the detection of the "moderate protrusion of the supraorbital and superciliary arches" and the "markedly pronounced frontal side drafts, and high vertical forehead" it was possible to observe "the imprint of ideality, [. . .] faculty [that] predominates over reflection and perceptibility [. . .]. This was evident in Vincenzo Bellini."[48]

Thus despite the fact that knowledge of this field had changed significantly, orienting towards anthropometric criteria such as volume or cephalic index, even as late as 1880 the Florentine anthropologist Paolo Mantegazza felt the need for a "craniological reform" that would dispense with the sterile accumulation of "measures upon measures, angles over angles, horizontal planes over vertical plains,"[49] and proposed a new descriptive taxonomy in the Linnean mould.[50] In short, "between the big-headed anthropologist and the small-headed anthropologists,"[51] phrenology had the potential to continue being one of the possible bases on which to establish a medical and expert discourse about the brain and its container, above all because, in contrast to other theories, it provided a more malleable and versatile series of case studies capable of combining talents, defects and character propensities, that promised to describe the "essence" of every individual.

The Study of Celebrated Men: The Circulation of Ideas

While this was the landscape on which scientific thought progressed, analyses of skulls remained for a long time the engines of very different movements. The quest for the secret of the greatness of famous men led some amateur enthusiasts, as well as men of science, to go on pilgrimages in search of the physical features of history-makers, like those reproduced on the marble bust of Kant in Köninsberg,[52] or the skull of Raphael, which attracted devotees for over half a century. At the same time, the artisan market of those years seized the opportunity to meet the demand for famous skulls, as we see from that attributed to Raphael, of which from the closing years of the eighteenth century "everyone wanted [. . .] a cast, and an endless stream of them was sent throughout Europe, and wooden models, illustrations and engravings were taken from it."[53] Looking again at the analyses listed in the table above, one might note how only two thirds were carried out directly on skulls, while the rest studied the annotations and measurements compiled by other scientists, or else funeral casts and masks. Another symptom of this epistemic equivalence between the original and its copy can be traced in the behaviour of the scientists gathered together for the embalming of the corpse of Alessandro Manzoni, when "no note was made of the most important cranial measurements, thinking that this could be done more easily using a plaster cast."[54]

The international circulation of this type of study material passed through a wide range of channels. In the first phase the main conduits used for sharing information on famous skulls were *The Phrenological Journal and Miscellany*,[55] published in Edinburgh, and the *Journal de la Société phrénologique de Paris*,[56] both produced by their cities' respective phrenological societies. The importance of the Parisian society explains the high number of analyses of "Italian" skulls conducted in the French capital (seven in total), where the opportunity to lay hands on the skulls of political or artistic exiles was not wasted.

In the Italian peninsula, however, the absence of a centralised phrenological institution severely limited the production of printed works on the subject, prompting phrenologists on that side of the Alps to communicate privately,[57] sometimes even sending each other casts for the comparison of observations.[58] In Italy, therefore, articles on famous heads only became an editorial phenomenon in the second half of the century, thanks to the proliferation of numerous journals of international importance, as demonstrated by the many critical reviews of the craniological report on the *Dantis ossa*, not to mention by the frequent comparisons made with the anthropometric data on other famous Italians that accompanied every new investigation.

Still, the ease of transmission of information and materials for study cannot obscure the fact that interest in the subject varied from place to place. While the investigations completed in Rome related almost exclusively to "Raphaelite skulls," among the areas with the biggest concentration of analyses was Turin,[59] where curators of the Academy of Medicine managed to combine the psychiatric and criminological focus of early nineteenth-century Savoy phrenology with anthropological research of a much wider spectrum.[60] But the territory that interacted most with these particular scientific practices was Lombardy-Veneto, in which almost half of the surveyed analyses took place.[61] From the 1830s onwards phrenology in Milan progressed from being a matter of private discussion to a theme of public debate: in the absence of complete acceptance from the official scientific community, Gall's Milanese followers used the examination of these famous heads to obtain another form of legitimacy, that of the public, which was more drawn to the idea of understanding the anatomical foundation of genius than to spending time and energy on statistical frameworks of measurements carried out on collections of anonymous "scientifically valid" individuals. In other words, phrenology helped to make the skulls of people famous for either their good or bad deeds not only the object of scientific research, but also a topic capable of attracting the interest and curiosity of a most varied audience.[62]

The case of Pavia, where the Cabinet of Anatomy boasted a long tradition of the preservation of human remains belonging to the university's professors, was different.[63] Following the wishes of "maestro" Panizza

I TESCHI DEL BEATO VALFRÉ, DEL FOSCOLO, DI GIOVANNI DALLE BANDE NERE, DEL VOLTA E DI UN IDIOTA.

Figure 11.2 The skulls of Beato Valfré, Foscolo, Giovanni dalle Bande Nere, Volta and an idiot [display in the Museo Nazionale di Antropologia e Etnologia, Florence], in Matteo Pierotti, "Il Museo delle passioni umane," *Emporium. Rivista mensile illustrata d'arte, letteratura, scienza e varietà* XX, 120 (December 1904): 448.

(according to whom "you can tell a man from his head. [. . .] The heads of great men [. . .] should always be preserved [and] with such relics should be used to create a Pantheon, a new sanctuary or speaking monument of instruction to the nations and of the honour and veneration to the benefactors of humanity"),[64] his pupil Giovanni Zoja launched an intense campaign of craniological analyses:

> knowing that in the old cemetery there were the graves of many worthy individuals and well-known scientists, and therefore wanting to save those precious remains from oblivion and destruction, he asked the local authorities for permission to remove them from those old mounds and under careful custody place them in a sacred scientific space that also held the mortal remains of other personages, like Scarpa, Volta, Brunacci, Bordoni, the painter Massacra and others.[65]

Collections of this kind were then spreading throughout Europe[66] and even various scientific institutes in the Italian peninsula had in the meantime started such work:[67] heads and casts of scientists, composers, writers, men of state and of the Church, patriots and painters were studied and exhibited so that, as Andrea Verga recalled of his donation of a part of the Galliana collection to the Civic Museum of Milan:[68]

> Every scientist, every friend of humanity must feel a fervent desire to know what particularities distinguish the head of the first despot of our times from that of Abbot Grégoire who spent all his life publicly defending the civil rights of man, [. . .] the heads of Mirabeau and Benjamin Constant, both famed for their eloquence, from that of Newton, a solitary thinker who in all the time he sat in the English Parliament [. . .] did not open his mouth except once to ask for a window that was bothering him to be closed. [. . .] There will then be a very natural and common desire to establish comparisons between the heads of Voltaire, Sestini, Broussais and those living individuals already known for satirical zest, for tender verses and for serious medical works.[69]

Scientists themselves, then, were not indifferent to the cultural climate of the century, intent on identifying and celebrating the great men of the nation, an atmosphere that had led to the creation of pantheons like that of Canova[70] and of the Pincian Hill,[71] even though the finds that they housed prevented them from assembling logically planned "Olympuses" since they were the result of fortuitous and contingent exhumations.

Having come to the end of this mapping of anthropometric studies on great Italians, it remains only to highlight a significant absence in this "cranial pantheon": women.[72] After all, the female gender, as the anthropologist Giuseppe Sergi stated as late as 1893, "cannot be geniuses" but "can be mothers of geniuses," simple "vehicles for the hereditary transmission of characteristics that they do not possess."[73] We should therefore not be surprised by the attitude of Zoja when, a few months before his death, he faced the first Italian study dedicated to the body of a famous woman, Isabella di Valois,[74] the wife of Gian Galeazzo Visconti, analysed a little earlier. The Pavian scientist spared Isabella's skull only a few brief words,[75] focusing his attention and almost all of his text on a completely different part of her anatomy, because "the facts that here draw the attention of the scholar to this body are those relating to the considerable reduction of the walls of the uterus and the notable dilation of the vagina."[76] While the scientists of the time believed that "you can tell a man from his head," the nature and secrets of a woman were evidently to be sought elsewhere.

Notes

1. Federico Alborghetti and Michelangelo Galli, *Gaetano Donizetti e G. Simone Mayr. Notizie e documenti* (Bergamo: Garuffi e Gatti, 1875), 137.
2. Ibid., 135–36.
3. Ibid., 137.
4. See Colin Dickey, *Cranioklepty. Grave robbing and the search for genius* (Denver: Unbridled Books, 2009).
5. See Antonie M. Luyendijk-Elshout, "Opening Address: The Magic of the Skull. 'Commercium craniorum' in the Nineteenth Century," *International Journal of Osteoarchaeology* 7 (1997): 571–74.
6. See Darrin M. McMahon, *Divine Fury: A History of Genius* (New York: Basic Books, 2013), 113–88; Ann Jefferson, *Genius in France: An Idea and Its Uses* (Princeton: Princeton University Press, 2015), 45–122.
7. See Peppino Ortoleva, "Vite geniali: sulle biografe aneddotiche degli inventori," in *Le biografie scientifiche, Intersezioni. Rivista di storia delle idee* 1 (1995): 41–61. For an examination of the relationship between the concept of genius and that of famous men, see Laura C. Ball, "The Genius in History. Historiographical Explorations," in *The Wiley Handbook of Genius*, ed. Dean Keith Simonton (Chichester: Wiley, 2014), 1–19.
8. See David Le Breton, *La chair à vif. De la leçon d'anatomie aux greffes d'organes* (Paris: Editions A.M. Métailié, 2008).
9. See Michael Hagner, "Skulls, Brains, and Memorial Culture: On Cerebral Biographies of Scientists in the Nineteenth Century," *Science in Context* 16 (2003): 195–218; Michael Hagner, *Des cerveaux de génie. Une histoire de la recherche sur les cerveaux d'élite* (Paris: Editions de la Maison des sciences de l'homme, 2008); Frances Larson, *Teste mozze. Storia di decapitazioni, reliquie, trofei, souvenir e crani illustri* (Novara: UTET, 2016).
10. On the "skulls" of Raphael, see Anna Lisa Genovese, *La tomba del divino Raffaello* (Rome: Gangemi, 2016); Simone Baral, "Il cranio dei grandi. Indagini scientifiche ottocentesche sui corpi di italiani illustri," *Il Risorgimento* 2 (2017): 5–36. On the analyses on the skull and casts of Vincenzo Bellini, see Simone Baral, "Un''armonica e magnifica fronte'. La persistenza della frenologia nei discorsi medici italiani intorno al genio musicale," in *Musique italienne et Sciences médicales au XIXᵉ siècle, Laboratoire italien. Politique et société* 20 (2017), http://journals.openedition.org/laboratoireit alien/1619. On the skull of Alessandro Volta, see Gianfrancesco Venturini,

"La follia dell'uomo di genio: il calco del cranio di Alessandro Volta," in *Il Museo di Antropologia criminale Cesare Lombroso dell'Università di Torino*, ed. Silvano Montaldo (Cinisello Balsamo: Silvana, 2015), 179–82. On the heads of Dante and Petrarch, see the contributions by Roberto Balzani, "Dante's Remains and the Politics of Mystery in 19th Century Italy," and Nicola Carrara "Giovanni Canestrini (1835–1900) and the Strange Case of Petrarca's Skull," for the conference "The great laboratory of humanity— Collection, patrimony and the repatriation of human remains" (Padua 30 May–1 June 2016), whose proceedings will be published shortly.

11. See Valentina Cani, "Pavia's Relics of Notable Scientists. A Journey Between Science and Scientific Mythology," in *Savant Relics. Brains and Remains of Scientists*, ed. Marco Beretta, Maria Conforti and Paolo Mazzarello (Sagamore Beach: Watson Publishing International, 2016), 133–56; Silvano Montaldo, "The Relics of Two 19th-Century Scientists: Carlo Giacomini e Cesare Lombroso," in *Savants Relics*, Beretta, Conforti and Mazzarello, 183–99.

12. See the included table, with the following legend:

* Examinations carried out on casts of the original skull
\# Examinations carried out using data collected by other scholars
() Examinations based only on indirect testimonies
[] Examinations on skulls whose attribution changed during the course of the century. Regarding the skull that was supposed to have been that of Raphael, and later attributed to Desiderio d'Adiutorio (1481–1546), see Baral, "Il cranio dei grandi." On the skull claimed to have been that of Leonardo da Vinci, see Gustavo Uzielli, *Ricerche intorno a Leonardo da Vinci* (Florence: Pellas, 1872), 47–49.

13. See Cani, "Pavia's Relics of Notable Scientists," 153.

14. Fifteen analyses were carried out in the 1830s, around 25 percent of the total.

15. See Barbara Maffiodo, *La "medicina delle passioni" nel Piemonte ottocentesco (1815–1859)* (Santena: Fondazione Camillo Cavour, 1986).

16. See Carlo Fumian, "Il senno delle nazioni. I congressi degli scienziati italiani dell'Ottocento: una prospettiva comparata," *Meridiana* 24 (1995): 95–124; Maria Pia Casalena, *Per lo Stato, per la Nazione: i congressi degli scienziati in Francia e in Italia, 1830–1914* (Rome: Carocci, 2007); Marco Meriggi, "Prove di comunità. Sui congressi preunitari degli scienziati italiani," in *Storia d'Italia. Annali 26: Scienza e cultura dell'Italia unita*, ed. Francesco Cassata and Claudio Pogliano (Turin: Einaudi, 2011), 7–35.

17. Alberto Gamba, "Presentazione della maschera della faccia e del cranio di Vincenzo Bellini per la raccolta frenologica del Museo Craniologico della R. Accademia di Medicina di Torino," *Giornale della R. Accademia di Medicina di Torino* 49 (1886): 756. See Marc Renneville, *Le langage des crânes. Une histoire de la phrénologie* (Paris: Institut d'edition Sanofi-Synthelabo, 2000).

18. See Georges Lanteri-Laura, *Histoire de la phrénologie. L'homme et son cerveu selon F. J. Gall* (Paris: Presses Universitaires de France, 1970).

19. On the penetration of Gall's ideas on the Italian peninsula in the early nineteenth century, see Ugo D'Orazio, "Gall e la prima diffusione della frenologia in Italia," *Sanità scienza e storia* 2 (1991): 79–124.

20. Giovanni Mayer, *Esposizione della dottrina di Gall sul cranio, e sull'encefalo* (Italy: n.p., 1808), 114.

21. See Renneville, *Le langage des crânes*, 197–205.

22. See Simone Baral, "Il frenologo in tribunale. Nota per una ricerca sul caso italiano," *Criminocorpus. Histoire de la justice, des crimes et des peines* (2014), http://journals.openedition.org/criminocorpus/3283.

23. See François Lélut, *Du démon de Socrate, specimen d'une application de la science psychologique à celle de l'histoire* (Paris: Trinquart, 1836); François Lélut, *L'amulette de Pascal pour servir à l'histoire des hallucinations* (Paris: J.B. Baillière, 1846).

24. See Renneville, *Le langage des crânes*, 262–64.

25. The majority of the craniological investigations were carried out in the final three decades of the century: a full 31 (50 percent of the total) of which in the 1870s, eight in the 1880s and six in the 1890s.

26. Only ten analyses were carried out in the 30 years from 1840 to 1869.

27. See Renneville, *Le langage des crânes*, 239–92.

28. The Catholic judgment of phrenology was in fact more complex than has traditionally been argued, see Fernanda Alfieri, "The Weight of the Brain: The Catholic Church in the Face of Physiology and Phrenology (First Half of the Nineteenth Century)," *Annali dell'Istituto storico italo-germanico / Jahrbuch des italienisch-deutschen historischen Instituts in Trient* 2 (2017): 57–93; Fernanda Alfieri, "L'anima o il cervello? Sant'Uffizio, Civiltà Cattolica e teologia morale di fronte alla teoria frenologica," in *"In unum corpus coalescerent". La Compagnia dei Gesù dalla Soppressione (1773) alla Restaurazione (1814)*, ed. Pierre-Antoine Fabre, Martin Morales and Patrick Goujon (forthcoming).

29. See for example the personal stories of Giovanni Stefano Bonacossa, Luigi Ferrarese and Biagio Gioacchino Miraglia, see Baral, "Il frenologo in tribunale."

30. See Pietro Redondi, "Cultura e scienza dall'illuminismo al positivismo," in *Storia d'Italia. Annali 3: Scienza e tecnica nella cultura e nella società dal Rinascimento a oggi*, dir. G. Micheli (Turin: Einaudi, 1980), 679–811.

31. See Catherine Brice, "La religion civile dans l'Italie libérale: petits et grands rituels politiques," in *Le destin des rituels: faire corps dans l'espace urbain, Italie-France-Allemagne*, ed. Ilaria Taddei and Gilles Bertrand (Rome: École française de Rome, 2008), 309–40.

32. See Umberto Levra, *Fare gli italiani. Memoria e celebrazione del Risorgimento* (Turin: Comitato di Torino dell'Istituto per la storia del Risorgimento italiano, 1992), 3–40; Erminia Irace, *Itale Glorie* (Bologna: Il Mulino, 2003), 150–64; Dino Mengozzi, *Garibaldi taumaturgo. Reliquie laiche e politica nell'Ottocento italiano* (Manduria: Lacaita, 2010); Sergio Luzzatto, *La mummia della repubblica. Storia di Mazzini imbalsamato* (Turin: Einaudi, 2011).

33. Paolo Mantegazza, "Sul divieto di studiare il cranio di Rossini," *Archivio per l'antropologia e l'etnologia* 17 (1887): 426.

34. On the relationship between phrenology and racial theories, see Loïc Rignol, "La phrénologie et le déchiffrement des races: savoir, pouvoir et progrès de l'Humanité," in *L'idée de "race" dans les sciences humaines et la littérature (XVIIIᵉ–XIXᵉ siècles): actes du colloque international de Lyon, (16–18 novembre 2000)*, ed. Sarga Moussa (Paris: Harmattan, 2003), 225–38.

35. See Carole Reynaud-Paligot, *De l'identité nationale. Science, race et politique en Europe et aux Etats-Unis XIXᵉ–XXᵉ siècle* (Paris: Presses Universitaires de France, 2011).

36. See Antonino De Francesco, *The Antiquity of the Italian Nation: The Cultural Origins of a Political Myth in Modern Italy (1776–1943)* (Oxford: Oxford University Press, 2013); Fedra Pizzato, "Per una storia antropologica della nazione. Mito mediterraneo e costruzione nazionale in Giuseppe Sergi (1880–1919)," *Storia del pensiero politico* 1 (2015): 25–51.

37. Aldobrandino Mochi, "Le ossa di Paolo Emilio Demi, scultore Livornese," *Archivio per l'antropologia e la etnologia* 28 (1898): 445.

38. Giovanni Canestrini, "Le ossa di Francesco Petrarca. Studio antropologico," *Atti della Società veneto-trentina di scienze naturali residente in Padua* 3 (1874): 95–96.

39. Patrizia Guarnieri, *L'ammazzabambini. Legge e scienza in un processo di fine Ottocento* (Turin: Einaudi, 1988); Maria Ferro, ed., *Passioni della mente e della storia. Protagonisti, teorie e vicende della psichiatria italiana tra '800 e '900* (Milan: Vita e Pensiero, 1989).

40. Cesare Lombroso, *Genio e follia* (Milan: Giuseppe Chiusi, 1864). See Francesco Cassata, "Dall'Uomo di genio all'eugenica," in *Cesare Lombroso cento anni dopo*, ed. Silvano Montaldo and Paolo Tappero (Turin: UTET, 2009), 175–84.

41. See Maria Conforti, "The Poet Who Lost His Head: Giacomo Leopardi's pathographies," in *Littérature et médecine. Approches et perspecives (XVIᵉ– XIXᵉ siècles)*, ed. Andrea Carlino and Alexandre Wagner (Geneva: Droz, 2007), 135–55; Gianfranco Venturini, "Tra Leopardi e Zola: le patobiografie degli scrittori," in *Cesare Lombroso e la cultura francese. Dibattiti, contrasti e collaborazioni*, ed. Silvano Montaldo and Michel Porret (forthcoming).

42. See Lorenzo Lorusso et al., "Filippo Lussana (1820–1897): From Medical Practitioner to Neuroscience," *Neurological Sciences* 3 (2012): 703–8; Claudio Pogliano, *Storie di cervelli. Dall'antichità al Novecento* (Milan: Editrice bibliografica, 2017), 145–60.

43. Giosuè Carducci, "Il secondo centenario dalla nascita di Ludovico Antonio Muratori," in *Bozzetti critici e discorsi letterari*, ed. Carducci (Livorno: Franc. Vigo, 1876), 290.

44. See Claudio Pogliano, "Il cranio e il corpo," in *Misura d'uomo. Strumenti, teorie e pratiche dell'antropometria e della psicologia sperimentale tra '800 e '900*, ed. Giulio Barsanti et al. (Florence: Istituto e Museo di storia della scienza, 1986), 51–76.

45. Gamba, "Presentazione della maschera della faccia e del cranio di Vincenzo Bellini," 751.

46. Ibid., 454.

47. When analysing the skull of Gian Galeazzo Visconti, the Pavian Giovanni Zoja saw the following as standing out: "the clear signs of destructiveness, of the desire to have, of numbers, of wit, of firmness, of self-love; and even more those of order, calculation and individuality; less so those of comparison, benevolence, figural love and physical love" (Giovanni Zoja, "Nota intorno alle ossa di Giovanni Galeazzo Visconti," *Bollettino scientifico* 17 (1895)). As for the recovered skull of Gaetano Donizetti, Capelli appreciated the signs "of the rich imagination and robust genius of the composer" (Alberto Gamba, "Il cranio del Generale Ramorino," *Giornale della R. Accademia di Medicina di Turin* 37 (1889): 619), while Lombroso noted "how no part of Volta's skull jutted out considerably, except for that portion of the temporal bone where those alchemists of cerebral physiology would place acquisitiveness and others the instinct for stealing and fighting" (Cesare Lombroso, "Craniologia. Relazione sul cranio di Volta con osservazioni dei MM. EE. Cornalia e Verga," *Rendiconti del Reale Istituto lombardo di Scienze e Lettere* 11 (1878): 341).

48. Gamba, "Presentazione della maschera della faccia e del cranio di Vincenzo Bellini," 756.

49. Paolo Mantegazza, "La riforma craniologica. Studi critici," *Archivio per l'antropologia e l'etnologia* 10 (1880): 118.

50. Giulio Barsanti and Mariangela Landi, "Fra antropologia, etnologia e psicologia comparata: il museo della 'storia naturale dell'uomo'. Paolo Mantegazza

e Aldobrandino Mochi," in *Il Museo di Storia naturale dell'Università degli Studi di Firenze. V: Le collezioni antropologiche ed etnologiche*, ed. Jacopo Moggi Cecchi and Roscoe Stanyon (Florence: Firenze University Press, 2014), 10–15.

51. Andrea Verga, "Del volume del cranio. Suo significato," in *Studi anatomici psicologici e freniatrici sul cranio e sull'encefalo. I: Parte anatomica*, ed. Verga (Milan: Stab. Tip. Ditta F. Manini-Wiget, 1896), 79.

52. See Marco Duichin, "Tra frenologia e criticismo: Vincenzo Mantovani e la prima traduzione europea della "Critica della ragion pura" (1820–1822)," *Studi Kantiani* 20 (2007): 117–31.

53. Giuseppe Del Chiappa, "Lettera a Defendente Sacchi sullo scoprimento delle ceneri di Raffaello Sanzio," *Il Nuovo Ricoglitore* 9 (1833): 623.

54. Luigi Bono et al., "Verbale del processo d'imbalsamazione della salma di Alessandro Manzoni," in *Onoranze funebri ad Alessandro Manzoni. 29 maggio 1873* (n.p.: n.p, n.d), 16.

55. See Terry M. Parssinen, "Popular Science and Society: The Phrenology Movement in Early Victorian Britain," *Journal of Social History* 1 (1974): 1–20.

56. See Renneville, *Le langage des crânes*, 129–41.

57. On the importance of epistolary writing for the phrenology movement, see James Poskett, "Phrenology, Correspondence, and the Global Politics of Reform, 1815–1848," *Historical Journal* 2 (2017): 409–42.

58. See Giuseppe Canziani, "Note," in *Notizie sulla vita pubblica e privata del principe Talleyrand di Périgord con l'esame frenologico del suo cranio e con l'elogio sul del barone di Barante* (Milan: vedova di A.F. Stella e Giacomo figlio, 1838), 104.

59. There were six analyses, carried out from the 1860s onwards.

60. See Simone Baral, "Crani su misura. La frenologia in Piemonte," *Studi Piemontesi* 2 (2014): 419–26.

61. 25, of which 10 in Milan, seven in Pavia, four in Bergamo, two in Vicenza and one each in Como and Padua.

62. See Pogliano, "Localizzazione delle facoltà e quantificazione: frenologia e statistica medico-psichiatrica," in *Follia psichiatria e società. Istituzioni manicomiali, scienza psichiatrica e classi sociali nell'Italia moderna e contemporanea*, ed. Alberto De Bernardi (Milan: Franco Angeli, 1982), 346–49; Giorgio Cosmacini, "Cattaneo, Gall e la frenologia," in *Carlo Cattaneo e il Politecnico*, ed. Arturo Colombo and Carlo Monteleone (Milan: Franco Angeli, 1993), 267–74.

63. See Cani, "Pavia's Relics of Notable Scientists."

64. Giovanni Zoja, "La testa di Scarpa," *Archivio per l'antropologia e l'etnologia* 8 (1878): 444.

65. Angelo Maestri, "Cenni sul Cimitero di Pavia," *Il Patriotta. Giornale della città e provincia di Pavia* 136 (1883).

66. See Erwin Heinz Ackerknecht, "P. M. A. Dumoutier et la collection phrénologique du Musée de l'Homme," *Bulletins et Mémoires de la Société d'anthropologie de Paris* 5–6 (1956): 289–308; Christine Quigley, *Skulls and Skeletons: Human Bone Collections and Accumulations* (Jefferson-London: McFarland, 2001); Nélia Dias, "Nineteenth-Century French Collections of Skulls and the Cult of Bones," in *Immortal Bodies, Nuncius* 2 (2012): 330–47.

67. See Giacomo Giacobini, Cristina Cilli and Giancarla Malerba, "Il Museo di Anatomia umana," in *La memoria della scienza. Musei e collezioni dell'Università di Torino*, ed. Giacomo Giacobini (Turin: UTET, 2003), 143–54.

68. See Paola Livi, "La storia naturale dell'uomo nella Milano dell'Ottocento. Un viaggio attraverso le raccolte del Museo Civico di Storia Naturale,"

Atti della Società italiana di Scienze naturali del Museo civico di Storia naturale in Milano» 2 (2008): 273–92.

69. Andrea Verga, "Il cranio. Introduzione al corso di craniologia dato nell'Ospitale maggiore di Milano la primavera del 1881," *Archivio italiano per le malattie nervose* 12 (1882): 94–95.
70. See Eveline G. Bouwers, "Il culto degli italiani illustri nella Roma pre-risorgimentale," *Memoria e ricerca* 45 (2014): 128–55.
71. See Alessandro Cremona, ed., *Il giardino della memoria. I Busti dei Grandi italiani al Pincio* (Rome: Artemide, 1999).
72. See Rachel Malane, *Sex in Mind. The Gendered Brain in Nineteenth-Century Literature and Mental Science* (New York: Peter Lang, 2005); Rob Boddice, "The Mainly Mind? Revisiting the Victorian 'Sex in Brain' Debate," *Gender & History* 2 (2011): 321–40; Lucy Delap, " 'Genius Must Do the Scullery Work of the World': New Women, Feminists, and Genius, Circa 1880–1920," in *Genealogies of Genius*, ed. Joyce Chaplin and Darrin McMahon (Basingstoke: Palgrave Macmillan, 2016), 97–113.
73. Giuseppe Sergi, "Se vi sono donne di genio," *Atti della Società italiana di Antropologia* 1 (1893): 167 and 178. See Alessandro Volpone and Giovanni Destro Bisol, eds., *Se vi sono donne di genio: appunti di viaggio nell'Antropologia dall'Unità d'Italia a oggi* (Rome: Casa editrice Università La Sapienza, 2011).
74. Giovanni Zoja, "Nota su la salma di Isabella di Valois," *Rendiconti del Reale Istituto lombardo di Scienze e Lettere* 31 (1898): 695–705. This analysis was not included in the table as it was of a skull belonging to a person born in Vincennes, near Paris.
75. "We find that the skull of Valois has a cephalic index of 85.71 but was nevertheless decidedly brachiocephalic; that its capacity can be calculated at 1,440cc, thus higher than the average of Parisian women. According to the Manouvrier formula Valois's brain weighed 1,252 grammes," ibid., 698.
76. Ibid., 701.

12 The Remains of the Vanquished

Bodies and Martyrs of the Roman Republic From the Risorgimento to Fascism

Silvia Cavicchioli

Towards the Janiculum Ossuary

With the capture of Rome on 20 September 1870 and the end of the temporal power of the pope, the democrats, having lost out to the monarchists with the creation of the Kingdom of Italy, had their first opportunity to retrieve the remains of the patriots of the Roman Republic of 1849 and in doing so to recover the historical memory of their autonomous and in many ways decisive experience within the nationalist uprising.

However, they had to wait until the death of their leader, Giuseppe Mazzini, in 1872 to realise the first symbolic recovery, that of the body of Goffredo Mameli, the poet-soldier who gave his life for the 1849 Republic. Agostino Bertani, the Garibaldian doctor who had embalmed and hidden Mameli's body in Rome, along with a republican and masonic committee chaired by Giuseppe Avezzana, took charge of translating the remains and, during a carefully controlled ceremony, had them laid to rest in a modest tomb in the cemetery of Campo Verano.[1]

A few years later, the rise to power of the Historical Left led to a change of direction in Italian domestic and foreign policy, and the martyrs of the Roman Republic once more became the centre of attention of the historical memory of the democrats, which was minor and subordinate to the official dynastic and moderate version.

On 28 April 1876, a month after the fall of the Historical Right and the swearing-in as prime minister of Agostino Depretis, leader of the Left, Bertani presented a bill to parliament aimed at extending "the rights to a military pension to the injured, the widows and the families of those who died for the liberation of Rome from 1849 to 20 September 1870, and for the defence of Venice in 1849." The intention was to ensure that volunteer soldiers were accorded the status of combatants of the nationalist military campaigns. Garibaldi, who throughout his life and writings insisted on the need to remember and celebrate his fallen comrades and to retrieve their forgotten remains, supported the bill by launching a public petition.[2]

Having already been proposed, in vain, by Bertani four years earlier, this first, important step towards granting material and memorial compensation for the martyrs of 1849 was approved in July 1876. A subsequent step was facilitated by political conditions even more favourable to the democrats, with the rise to the government in March 1878 of Benedetto Cairoli, leader of the Dissident Left, who was sympathetic, in part for family reasons, to the memory of the fallen Garibaldini.

There were thereafter two engines driving forward the initiative: Garibaldi himself and the Giuseppe Garibaldi Society for Mutual Aid to Veterans, formerly the Society for the Veterans of the Patriotic Battles, which was established in Rome on 8 June 1871 with the general's first son, Menotti, as president.

For some time Garibaldi and his son had been working to give the remains of the fallen of the 1849 Republic a worthy mausoleum. From the early 1870s the Hero of the Two Worlds had deplored their state of abandonment: in 1874 he published in Turin *I Mille*, a book in which he shared a twofold vision: that of a group of Romans intent on demolishing the "mausoleum of damnation," that is, the monument dedicated to the French fallen of the siege of '49; and that of other Romans "busy digging up the bones of our martyrs and, on the ruins of the cursed mausoleum, building a tomb" engraved with the names of the heroes who fell for Rome.[3]

The turning point in Garibaldi's initiative came with the tenth anniversary of the Battle of Mentana (1867) and with the 30th anniversary of the Roman Republic, leading in just over three years after the inauguration of the Altar of Mentana (which, built with the help of the Freemasons, contained the remains of the fallen and was inaugurated with solemn ceremony on 25 November 1877)[4] to the ossuary on the Janiculum and to the Milanese monument to Mentana (inaugurated on 3 November 1880 in the presence of Garibaldi). Despite the country's change of political direction, the reframing of the experience of the Risorgimento as a unified and conciliatory vision and of the image of the national unification process as a *concordia discors* was yet to come. And this was all the more true for "partisan" initiatives such as those of the commemorations of Mentana and of 1849 which, by evoking the Republic and the great name of Mazzini, were feared by the royal and liberal-moderate establishment.[5] It was still necessary, then, to wait until the memory of those events ceased to be the exclusive property of the Democratic Left and was subsumed in the official narrative, gradually shedding its original oppositional character,[6] but not without causing internal divisions within democratic circles.

For this reason, the municipal authorities remained non-committal about the idea of a city ossuary for the fallen of the Roman Republic, as had been proposed by the Garibaldini following the erection of the Altar of Mentana, and were probably minded to support only an epigraphic commemoration. Nevertheless, in 1877 a "Central Committee to eternalise with a monument on the Janiculum the national glory of the defence of Rome in 1849" was set up under the presidency of the

Freemason Giuseppe Mazzoni. Thus, as in 1872 during the translation of the remains of Mameli, the Freemasons continued to be one of the bulwarks of the democratic memorialisation of the Risorgimento. The monument was to be built on the part of the Janiculum known as the "Colle del Pino," where in 1941 the mausoleum that we will talk about later was raised, and on 30 April 1877 the mayor of Rome, Pietro Venturi, in the presence of the government ministers Giovanni Nicotera and Giuseppe Zanardelli, laid the first stone of what was meant to be a simple monument memorialising the defence of the city.[7]

"Ciceruacchio Has Come Back"

The initiative to create a real ossuary actually came from below, being launched by the Society of Garibaldini Veterans, which established a committee chaired by Menotti Garibaldi and supported by his father. At the end of 1878—the year that began with the solemn funerals of King Victor Emmanuel II, the dynastic symbol of national unity, and of General Alfonso La Marmora, the uniformed emblem of moderate and military power—this committee promoted a bill for the exhumation and translation of the remains of the patriots of 1849, the most politically advanced moment of the revolutionary biennium. The plan for the ossuary, "which would constitute the first sacred space of national, popular and Garibaldian monumentality,"[8] in its original form had one main objective, that of recovering the bones "of the popular hero Angelo Brunetti and of his son."[9] After abandoning Rome to follow Garibaldi in July 1849, Ciceruacchio (as Brunetti was nicknamed), his two sons[10] and some other companions were shot a month later in Ca' Tiepolo when desperately trying to reach Venice.

Immediately after 1870 there had already been attempts by the Democratic Left in Rome to commemorate Ciceruacchio, and in 1871 a rally in his memory had been banned by the authorities, which were fearful of triggering republican and anti-French demonstrations.[11]

But the principal objective in 1878 was that of celebrating not only the memory of the major figures of republican martyrdom, but also the contribution made by many anonymous fighters and the sacrifice of ordinary Romans. After the individual action to honour Mameli, it was time to take care of all the others, abandoned in the crypts of churches, buried in mass graves or neglected in the embankments of the city walls. The centre of gravity of the celebration shifted towards the issue of popular participation: the contribution of the Roman people, whose tribune, Ciceruacchio, had been their greatest representative.

The task was to overturn the popish and more generally anti-republican portrayal of a hostile and passive Roman population, that had remained loyal to the pontiff in 1849.[12] The focus on Ciceruacchio in the 1878–79 project that is, the enhancement of the emblem of popular participation and of the combative and democratic element of the city, was an important part of the response to this distorted representation. At the same time, it became charged with irredentist symbolism, since Ciceruacchio and his companions had been executed by the Austrians when going to the aid of Venice: this aspect was demonstrated by the activism of Avezzana, a leading light in the commission for the monumental ossuary and president of the Pro-Italy Irredentist Association, as well as by the decision to recover also the remains of Giacomo Venezian, the Trieste-born hero of the Medici Legion, through whose martyrdom the association tried to sublimate its Italianness.[13]

What is more, the honours paid to Ciceruacchio in Rome reverberated among those intellectuals, writers and journalists working in the anti-government press and actively engaged in the construction of a new republican martyrology, initiated by the late Mazzini with the figure of Pietro Barsanti.[14]

Due to anti-republican fears, the parliamentary process of the law was strongly opposed, mainly because of anxiety felt in the upper chamber. On 16 June 1879 the bill, which was in fact sponsored by Cairoli (who had resigned as Prime Minister at the end of 1878 following an attempt by an anarchist to assassinate the King), went to the House of Deputies for discussion, and was ratified on 28 June 1879:

> The Government of the King is authorised to grant that on the Janiculum, at the precise spot where the first stone of the monument was laid, be collected the bones of those who died fighting for the defence of Rome in 1849, or, becoming refugees after taking part in the defence, were called to arms after the surrender of the city, or fell during its liberation in 1870.[15]

Recognising the Janiculum as a place of conservation, from December 1878 the Society of Veterans had turned to the municipal Central Committee, established in 1877, in the hope of promoting together the idea of the ossuary becoming "almost the base of the monument" that would contain "not only the bones of Ciceruacchio and his son, but instead all the mortal remains of those who fell in defence of Rome [. . .], which were found long ago in the Campo Verano Cemetery, and which would be transported on April 30."

The work was not completed for the deadline of the 30th anniversary of Garibaldi's victory over the French because of the delays in the bill's passage through parliament, the resistance of the moderates and the bureaucratic issues involved in exhuming the remains of Ciceruacchio and his martyred comrades. As said, the official establishment's support for a public celebration was lacking throughout the operation due to a growing fear of having to face vociferous demands of irredentist forces, and the impasse was unblocked only in July 1879, with the return of

Cairoli to the government, after which the date of the inauguration was set for the autumn.

In the meantime, the search had begun to locate the victims of 1849, many of whom had been buried in two large tombs in the cemetery of Campo Verano[16] (including the remains of Francesco Daverio, translated in 1854 from the Roman church of San Carlo ai Catinari).[17] Efforts were likewise made to recover those fallen in the capture of Rome in 1870, who had also been buried in the Campo Verano cemetery or in Santa Agnese.

As an aside that attests to the many plot-lines and ideas connected to this subject, it may be worth noting that in September 1880 Adriano Lemmi purchased from the Rome municipality a burial plot in the Verano to be reserved for Freemasons. This became the so-called pantheon of the Grand Masters and Grand Dignitaries of the Order, in other words the funeral chapel of the Grand Orient lodge, and the first ashes to be placed within it were those of Mazzoni,[18] who had been president of the citizens' committee for the erection of the monument on the Janiculum.

Returning to the ossuary, which was far from being "monumental" as had been the intention of its proponents, the modest sepulchre, named the "Monument to the Fallen for the Cause of Italian Rome," was ultimately built, in a divergence from the original plans, at the entrance of the small piazza of San Pietro in Montorio, a symbolic site of 1849. The ossuary was quite unexceptional, smaller than planned and above all scarcely visible, leaning against the boundary wall, set down a few metres in depth, and crowned by a simple tombstone.[19]

The burials in the Janiculum sepulchre took place in a solemn opening ceremony on 12 October 1879. The boycotts and fears of the authorities had diminished what had been conceived as a great celebration of national reconciliation, even though from the chapel located at the Termini railway station to San Pietro in Montorio the funeral procession was escorted for six kilometres by a crowd so huge that it stopped the city traffic.[20] Six wagons transported the mortal remains. On the first of these was the wooden chest containing the remains of Ciceruacchio, his sons and companions, followed by one symbolising the irredentists' contribution to the national cause and carrying the zinc urn containing the 118 pieces of the skeleton of Venezian, exhumed from the ancient Jewish cemetery. Then came the wagons carrying three large chests containing around 300 skulls still whole and the fragments of others together with bones only partly identified (for example, those of Andrea Aguyar, the black slave who became a follower of Garibaldi). The procession terminated with a wagon bearing the remains of 26 casualties from 1870.[21]

Ciceruacchio's heirs were given a prominent position in the procession, which passed by Via Ripetta to honour the folk hero's birthplace.

In the presence of Cairoli and other ministers, the mayor, Emanuele Ruspoli, delivered the official speech, his words leaving many, in particular Menotti Garibaldi and Avezzana, with the impression that the occasion had been hijacked at the last minute.[22] The speech sent by the president of the Pro-Italy Irredentist Association, who was away in Naples, was not read out since the popular celebration had been turned "into an official shindy that took over the function and did not let anyone except the mayor speak."[23]

An exceptional witness, an English writer with a passion for the Italian Risorgimento, Evelyn Carrington Martinengo Cesaresco, had found herself on 10 October 1879 on the railway convoy that carried Ciceruacchio's remains from Rovigo to Rome, and at the station of Bologna saw a crowd of 4,000 people gathered to salute its passage. Arriving at Rome Evelyn took part in another large popular event, and perhaps nothing better than her comment can describe to us of today the sense of those rituals, as well as their pedagogic potential: "Ciceruacchio had come back, and who should say that he was entirely dead? This was the thought uppermost in the minds of all."[24]

Many years later the Fascist regime would make use of the persuasive force of funeral liturgies when re-appropriating the many symbols of the history of the homeland, thus making these remains the object of renewed political attention.[25]

In 1884 more remains were added to the ossuary, namely those belonging to the martyrs of the Polish Legion and those who fell in the Parioli neighbourhood of Rome and were buried in the garden of Villa Borghese. Once again the initiative had been taken by the Garibaldini veterans headed by Menotti Garibaldi, the same who, a few months before, had joined the national pilgrimage to the tomb of Victor Emanuel II, who—according to the title of the manifesto prepared by the veterans—had crowned "the edifice of Italian Unity." Other veterans, members of a democratic association led by the parliamentary deputy Achille Majocchi, chose not to attend and instead organised a separate ceremony. "The funeral of the dead, who had already been suitably located and were dug up from the Villa Borghese and Villa Giustiniani to be reburied in the Janiculum as an insult to the Pope," as the *Civiltà Cattolica* described it, was observed solemnly by the Roman municipality, by Garibaldini in their red shirts and presided over, with speeches, by the Garibaldian general Ernesto Haug, as well as by Francesco Crispi. This was the future prime minister's effort to bring conciliation by seeking consensus around the new unitary state based in part on the construction and diffusion of a unified public memory. For the 40th anniversary of the Roman Republic, Crispi also acknowledged the need to honour Mameli with a worthy tomb and solemnly inaugurated a new monument in the Campo Verano cemetery in 1891. But always alongside this project there were the profound fractures within the diverse world of the veterans and the Left, which reflected, in the issues they raised and the forms that they assumed, the fractures and antagonisms produced during the Risorgimento process.[26]

In the meantime, with the passing of the years the Janiculum ossuary, owing to its position and lack of grandeur, became forgotten and ended up in a state of total abandonment that would last until the Fascist period. In 1926 an initial expression of interest in the little sepulchre came from the Governorate of Rome, established that year, but this did not result in a concrete intervention.[27] Another decade was to elapse before a series of conditions made possible the recovery of the shrine and its insertion in a new political and propagandist project.

This was the umpteenth chapter in the history of the preservation of the remains of the Roman Republic, which had at its centre Ezio Garibaldi and the Roman Committee of the Institution for the History of the Risorgimento (henceforth the Roman Committee).

Garibaldini Martyrs for the Duce

It is well known that Mussolini could not avoid engaging with the memory of the Risorgimento: the appropriation of events and protagonists of the unification process and of Italy's foundation myths, including the Garibaldi tradition, proved useful to the regime's narrative rhetoric and to Fascism's identification with nation. They were vital for reinterpreting the history of the homeland with the regime portrayed as heir while simultaneously being the initiator of a new era.

In this sense, 1932 served as a primary test case for the regime, committed as it was to celebrating the tenth anniversary of the March on Rome and the 50th anniversary of the death of the Hero of the Two Worlds. The Garibaldi exhibition in Rome and the inauguration of the monument to Anita Garibaldi on the Janiculum, as well as the translation of her ashes from Nice to the Italian capital, were the culminating moments.[28] Yet there is no doubt that many similar translations of Risorgimento martyrs carried out or repeated during the Fascist period were also effective instruments used by the regime to establish its complex relationship with the legacy of the Risorgimento and to present itself as the crowning moment of the nationalisation of the Italians.[29] Through them the propagandist use of the nation's foundation history was also pressed into service at the local level, allowing the Fascist hierarchies to enhance their political reputation within the municipalities. This is the context in which the translations of remains that had already been exhumed and moved during the nineteenth century, such as those of the martyrs of Belfiore (1925) and of Ciro Menotti (1929), should be understood.

Such operations placed at the centre those martyrs who had given their lives for the greater good of the nation, that is, the volunteers and men of action ready for anything: an example for the youth of the Fascist nation to follow. The operations were made possible by the involvement of the local committees of the Risorgimento Institute, which proposed and carried out the translations. Such suggestions were then supported by scholars, journalists and those involved in preserving the cultural heritage, many of whom were veterans and ready to establish networks and collaborate. This was true, for example, in the case of the great tribute paid in 1937 in Cosenza by the Fascists to the martyrs of the massacre of 15 March 1844 of the Calabrian patriots whose uprising preceded the raid by the Bandiera brothers: ten chests with the remains of the city's ten patriots were entombed in a monument in the cathedral. Just as the organisers of that translation of remains were members of the Cosenza committee of the Risorgimento Institute, in Rimini members of the institute's provincial committee, led by its vice president Paolo Mastri, took charge of the repatriation of the body of Giovanni Venerucci, the Rimini patriot executed by firing squad alongside the Bandiera brothers.[30] It was much the same in the case of the new translation of the remains of those who fell for Rome from 1849 to 1870, an operation that best allows us to grasp the implications and the manoeuvring mentioned above.

To have a better understanding of this episode and its political import, we must pause to consider one of the protagonists, General Ezio Garibaldi (son of Ricciotti and grandson of the Hero of the Two Worlds), who had already directed the celebrations for the 50th anniversary of his grandfather's death in 1932, when Mussolini had found in him an effective foothold by which to exploit the influence of the Garibaldi legend.

After the assassination of Giacomo Matteotti in 1924, the broad church of Garibaldinism had been divided between those who opposed Fascism in the name of liberty, universalism and democracy, and those who instead believed it possible that the legacy of the Garibaldi tradition could coexist with the ranks of Mussolini's loyalists. Ezio Garibaldi, who in that year launched the Italian Federation of Garibaldini Volunteers, then became the reference point for Fascist Garibaldinism, whose manifesto, based on the idea of a continuity between the red shirts and black shirts, was expressed in his work *Fascismo garibaldino* (1928).

Despite his firm adherence to the regime, Ezio Garibaldi tried to find spaces that gave him room to manoeuvre, as well as a specific place within the regime, to which end he used the columns of *Camicia Rossa*, the periodical that he founded in 1925.

The idea of being at once a devotee of Garibaldinism and Fascism was, however, impossible, at least without sacrificing the deepest meaning of the actions that had moved those who, from Dijon to Greece to the Argonne, had fought in the name of a voluntary intervention in the causes of the oppressed.[31] The incompatibility became increasingly evident with the passing of time, and particularly acute in 1937 with the hostility of the most intransigent hierarchs of the party, who could not tolerate the resistance of the Garibaldinism personified by Ezio Garibaldi to a full identification with Fascism, nor his freedom of action and his openly pro-French stance. They also reproached him for failing to take a clear position against those who fought in the Spanish Civil war under the banner of the Garibaldi Brigades. Equally embarrassing for Ezio was the position taken by his brother Sante, who, as an anti-Fascist, had fled to France and in June 1937 had founded an anti-totalitarian Garibaldian *Fédération*. In the same year Ezio's fiercest enemy, the Fascist leader Roberto Farinacci, sought to portray him in an even worse light by publishing a series of articles in the newspaper *Regime Fascista*.

It was evident that in order to continue to maintain his Garibaldinism in the orbit of Fascism, making it an essential and active component of the regime, Ezio needed to relaunch his initiative and cultivate new projects that would show how much his movement served the regime in terms of popular involvement and as a link between the Garibaldi tradition, rooted in a pulsating unification story, and the modernity of the Fascist revolution.

His first project, in May 1937, was the proposal, approved by parliament, for an Institute of Garibaldi Studies in Rome. His second was an ambitious undertaking aimed at exalting—on the basis of an appeal to patriotism and voluntarism, and of the bond between Fascism and the myth of Rome—those who died for the liberation of the city between 1849 and 20 September 1870.

It was in fact in the pages of *Camicia Rossa* that—still in May 1937—Antonio Reggiani drew attention to the abandoned ossuary of Garibaldini forces on the Janiculum.[32] As the editor of the monthly magazine, he was also responsible for the propaganda section of Garibaldian History of the Garibaldi Veteran Mutual Aid Society, and he would go on to play a central role in the new translation of the Roman martyrs. Alongside him was Giuseppe Ceccarelli, the Romanist *Ceccarius* who served as president of the Roman Committee. It was Ceccarelli who, a few months later, would set in motion the initial act of symbolism that brought back into focus the Janiculum ossuary when he arranged for the 25th National Congress of the Risorgimento Institute to conclude on the Janiculum, right in front of the Ossuary of San Pietro in Montorio. Thus on the afternoon of 15 October, in the presence of Ezio Garibaldi and the directorship of the Federation of Garibaldini Volunteers, a laurel wreath was placed on the now illegible tombstone, after, in the morning, a wreath had been placed on the tomb of the Unknown Soldier and at the Altar of the Fallen Fascists on the Capitoline.[33] This was the first official acknowledgement of the monument after years of oblivion and abandonment.

Three days later and 27 kilometres away, another place of Garibaldian memory was saved from indifference and the ravages of time. The Altar of Mentana had for some time been remembered only by a few nostalgic Garibaldini who left sad bunches of flowers there, while the last significant commemoration had taken place in 1920 for the 50th anniversary of Rome as capital. Even this, though, had been a divisive occasion involving separate processions. This time those intending to return the site to the centre of the patriotic agenda were members of the Society of

Garibaldini Veterans, led by Ezio Garibaldi and governed by the prefec-
tural commissioner Arnaldo Belli, a veteran of the Argonne campaign.
Belli was responsible for the altar's conservation and since 1934 had
equipped the vault of its crypt with a votive lamp, and in 1937 had begun
to redevelop the nearby Garibaldian Museum. However, water infiltra-
tion was then putting the remains of the fallen at risk, so on 18 October
alterations were made and the tomb was given a new zinc lining and a
crystal covering, while the bones were cleaned.[34] After the final closure of
the altar-ossuary, on Sunday 7 November, the solemn commemoration of
the 70th anniversary of the Battle of Mentana was held in the presence
of Ezio Garibaldi and the veterans of the Greek and Argonne campaigns.

Once again, therefore, as in 1877–78, part of the task of identifying and caring for the remains of the Garibaldini took place in Rome
between the Janiculum, the area of the city subjected to the 1849 siege,
and—as we shall see—the Campo Verano cemetery. Another part of this
operation also took place at other sites linked to the heroism of the Garibaldi forces and to attempts to liberate Rome, starting with the symbolic
location of Mentana, in the territory of the Ager Romanus.

What is more, the initiative could once more count on the contribution
"from below" of the Garibaldian associations, represented in this case
by the Society of Garibaldini Veterans and the pro-Fascist Italian Federation of Garibaldini Volunteers, both of which were led by Ezio Garibaldi,
who was involved in the political and propagandist aspects of the entire
operation. This time, however, a convergence was achieved with the
authority of the historical-scientific wing in the form of the Roman Committee, and these two entities coexisted, but not always harmoniously.

The initial phase was thus promoted and moved forward, with some
hitches and arguments, by a group of people whose roles intersected both
the Garibaldian world (with Ezio Garibaldi at the head), and that of
Risorgimento history. In addition to those already mentioned, there were
Mario Lizzani, secretary of the Roman Committee, and Giuseppe Fonterossi, a committee member and close collaborator of Ezio Garibaldi, as
well as co-director of *Camicia Rossa*.

Revealed in advance in an article by Ceccarelli, the Roman Committee,
in a meeting of 13 December 1937, voted for a more dignified arrangement of the shrine:

> The Rome Council of the Royal Institute for the History of the Risor-
> gimento, in consideration of the dilapidated state of the so-called
> Janiculum Ossuary situated in front of the church of San Pietro in
> Montorio, and taking into account that in the said Ossuary are kept
> the glorious remains of some of the martyrs of independence and
> of the fallen in Rome in 1849 and in 1870, so as to constitute a
> sacred place for the religion of the homeland and be therefore worthy
> of better arrangement, hopes that Your Excellency the Governor of

Rome will examine the possibility of removing and transferring the
Ossuary from its current site to the lawn of the Janiculum Park [. . .]
where on 30 June 1849 were placed the final batteries in defence of
Rome, and thus to locate it in a worthy place where it can be deco-
rously safeguarded and honoured.[35]

It was Fonterossi who proposed that the new Janiculum monument-
ossuary should also house the ashes of the officers Valenziani, Bosi and
Ripa, who fell during the liberation of Rome in 1870, and those of the
common people who died gloriously in the slaughter of Casa Ajani during the Roman insurrection of 1867. As in 1879 and in the additions of
1884, the martyrs of the 1849 Roman Republic were joined by those
who fell during the capture of Rome, thereby confirming the historical
continuity of those events.

At this point the governor of Rome, Prince Piero Colonna, entered the
scene. Ceccarelli, who had a close relationship with him, advised him to
build a memorial, and obtained permission to carry out an examination
of the remains in the ossuary.

On the morning of 12 January 1938, the long recovery operation of
the remains began: those in zinc chests were fairly well preserved, while
in the deteriorating wooden chests were found only shapeless clusters
of earth and ash. Of the more than 300 skulls deposited in 1879 only
around 20 were salvaged. The work continued the next day and all the
bones in the rotten chests were placed in special urns. Together with the
others, they were wrapped in the tricolour and placed temporarily in
the Campo Verano cemetery, in the crypt of the war memorial, to await
further instructions.[36]

Apart from officials of the Rome governorate and others, those who
took part in the re-exhumation were Ceccarelli, Lizzani, Fonterossi, Reggiani and Belli, the latter as representative of Ezio Garibaldi and the
federation he headed. On that occasion, the Roman Committee and the
Federation of Garibaldini Volunteers repeated the call for the Ossuary of
San Pietro in Montorio to be transferred to the so-called "Colle del Pino"
and for "the remains of all the other fallen for the freedom of Rome" to
be placed "in a single Ossuary."[37]

The latter hope, which alluded to a further search yet to be started, and
the temporary placing in the Verano, were together a key factor of the
story. These in fact made necessary a wide-ranging operation, which from
then on would proceed in parallel with the creation of the new ossuary on
the Janiculum. The research, examination and inventory of the remains
of those fallen in Rome became a project in itself, not simply something
secondary to the relocation of the remains, and Reggiani worked assidu-
ously on it in the years to come. In a sense, he continued the effort of
Bertani, who between 1849 and 1851 had worked to produce a census
of the fallen, editing and publishing a *Register of the fallen and injured*

(which Reggiani had copied by staff of the Risorgimento Museum in Milan where it was kept) with the idea of carrying out a "compilation of a genuine Catalogue" for which "it was necessary to start again from the beginning."[38] Reggiani began immediately, with the identification of the group of Ciceruacchio, made possible by information that he had collected on the translations of 1878 to 1884, and in the following days, in the office of the inspector of the Campo Verano cemetery, Pietro Ascenzi, he opened a tin urn and found the remains of Daverio, which had initially been mistaken for those of Colomba Antonietti Porzi. Daverio was killed in 1849 and buried in the chapel of Santa Cecilia in the church of San Carlo ai Catinari, but all traces of him had been lost.[39]

While at first Reggiani's research was aimed at documenting the profiles of the fallen of 1849, 1867 and 1870 (in order to compile as precise a list as possible for the engraving of names on the walls of the new ossuary and to justify the choice of the hill for its reconstruction), his work expanded like a blot of ink, since he also wanted to include the events of Aspromonte (1862), Mentana, Casa Ajani and even the decapitations of Giuseppe Monti and Gaetano Tognetti (1868), within a clearly anticlerical interpretation of history.

Ceccarelli had been very adept at somehow forcing the governor's hand and confronting him with the fait accompli of the temporary location of the remains at the Verano and securing from him the promise that the new ossuary would indeed be created.[40] The support of Prince Colonna, who had already made other interventions relating to monuments, such as the refurbishment of the Mausoleum of Augustus and the reconstruction of the Ara Pacis, was decisive; and the presence as his representative on the executive committee—of which more below—of Antonio Muñoz, director of Antiquity and Fine Arts for the governorate and a protagonist in the transformations of the monuments of Fascist Rome, was in keeping with this commitment.[41]

The Fascist Regime Re-Exhumes Mameli

On 4 August 1938 Ezio Garibaldi and Fonterossi brought the mausoleum project to the attention of Mussolini, who approved it, declaring that 30 April 1939, the 90th anniversary of the "heroic resistance against the troops commanded by Oudinot," would be the date of inauguration.[42]

The project thus passed from its proponents to the direct control of the regime, whose management of it was reinforced by the fact that in April 1938 the Federation of Garibaldini Volunteers (soon to be renamed the Garibaldi Legion) became included among the organisations directly subsidiary to the Fascist Party. The following year the Duce granted the financing required to execute the work, which was entrusted to the technical office of the governorate, using funds under Mussolini's control.

In this way the regime, procuring the legacy of Italian homeland history, showed itself to be animated by an authentic cult of the nation and its heroes and to have intervened where Liberal Italy had allowed things to fall into oblivion and abandonment.[43] As for the mausoleum, this became, in that particular historical moment, on the eve of Italy's entry into the war against France, the material symbol of a cycle that was closing and that brought all of Garibaldian history into the purview of Fascism.

Not only this, for the regime also managed to appropriate even more knowingly the political and pedagogical aspects of the project, performing a symbolic twist when Giuseppe Bottai, the education minister, acting in concert with Ceccarelli, proposed that the ashes of Mameli, which from 1872 had laid in the Verano, be translated to the new ossuary, and even be allocated a privileged position there. The centre of gravity of the media and popular effort thus shifted to the powerful, individual and celebrated symbol of Mameli, finally bringing together in a single monumental place the remains of the bard of Giovine Italia and those of the fallen of the Roman Republic, gathered in 1879 at the behest of Giuseppe and Menotti Garibaldi.

Figure 12.1 Translation of the remains of Goffredo Mameli from the Campo Verano cemetery to the Crypt of the Unknown Soldier [15 September 1941; on the right: Antonio Reggiani, wearing the uniform of the Giuseppe Garibaldi Society for Mutual Aid to Veterans, holding the coffin] (Archivio Storico Istituto Luce Cinecittà, Rome).

An initiative initially conceived as a collective commemoration was therefore relinquished in favour of a celebration of a symbol that Fascists, from Giovanni Gentile to Bottai, had exalted for his patriotic charisma; meanwhile, from 1927, on the centenary of Mameli's birth, the writers Alessandro Luzio and Egilberto Martire had freed his memory from the masonic legacy, projecting the Christian nature of the moment of his death onto the whole of the poet-soldier's short life. Thus, just as the Italian Social Republic presented the myth of Mameli as the epitome not only of sacrifice for the homeland, but also of youth ready to die for the nation, his Christian death could now also be turned to account in support of the conciliation reached between the church and the Fascist regime in 1929.[44]

For Bottai, who a year earlier had opened the celebrations of the bimillennium of Augustus's birth with the *Mostra della romanità* promoted by the Institute of Roman Studies, celebrating the attempts by the Garibaldini to make Rome Italian was another way to keep alive the cult of the myth of Rome in support of historical continuity.[45] Reggiani had made a similar effort to emphasise the continuity between the Risorgimento, the Great War and the Fascist regime by recommending to Bottai that the remains of Mameli be temporarily transferred to the Crypt of the Unknown Soldier at the Altar of the Fatherland.[46]

As to the mausoleum, an executive committee had been formed with Ezio Garibaldi as president and Ceccarelli as vice president. The architect Giovanni Jacobucci was responsible for carrying out the work while Reggiani—not without some friction—was in charge of the epigraphs, the decorations and the symbols of the regime, in tune with the most effective Fascist mysticism.

In the meantime, however, in 1939 the campaign against Ezio Garibaldi reached its peak and, having been accused of not renewing his membership of the Fascist Party in 1929, the undisputed leader of Fascist Garibaldinism was removed as commander of the Legion and forced to suspend *Camicia Rossa*. His momentary disgrace was certainly a reason for the slowdown of the works that led to the inauguration slipping first to 1940 and then to 1941, although the project did progress thanks in part to the operational continuity guaranteed by Reggiani, who was the general secretary of the executive committee and the overseer of the work, personally appointed by the Duce.[47] Thus on 3 January 1940 the first stone was laid on the "Colle del Pino."

During all this Reggiani had persevered with his research on the fallen, setting himself the ambitious target of bringing to light the names of all who had died for the ideal: "We have given an honourable burial to the mortal remains of those glorious fallen scattered a bit everywhere, in churches, cellars, in the open countryside, undeservingly and indecently forgotten."[48] To give just two examples, thanks to him the remains of two fusiliers from the Manara Legion who fell at Monte Porzio Catone and the remains of the fallen of Casa Ajani in 1867 were recovered. Reggiani was thwarted only in the case of the remains of Monti and Tognetti, who had been condemned by the papal power and beheaded in 1868, because their bodies had been thrown into one of the wells of the cloister of the church of San Giovanni Decollato, and thereby mixed up with those of common criminals.[49] Reggiani's work notes—contrary to what he stated many years later—testify to a truly meticulous research and survey effort conducted in libraries and archives with the collaboration of 600 Italian municipalities and 1,300 people, and with the help of EIAR (the public service broadcaster of the Fascist regime), which sent out appeals for documentary evidence.[50]

The result of the three years of investigation was the publication of a *Catalogo dei caduti* (*Catalogue of the Fallen*), which listed over a thousand names. This was included in the book *Ai caduti per Roma* (*To the Fallen for Rome*), which appeared in time for the inauguration. In this, the Roman Committee and the Giuseppe Garibaldi Society, thanks to Reggiani (a member of the former and vice president of the latter), were able to describe the various stages of the construction of the mausoleum with a certain degree of autonomy. I am thinking in particular of the apparent anti-clerical tones of the main compiler, who had had a significant past in Freemasonry and in the Giordano Bruno association: he called the Casa Ajani incident "a real massacre perpetrated by the pontifical soldiers" while elsewhere praising the ecclesiastics who had been in favour of the 1849 Roman Republic.[51]

The book proudly conveyed an exaltation of all the deeds of the Garibaldian epic, with repeated references to the Risorgimento, the figures of Garibaldi, Ciceruacchio, Mazzini and Ugo Bassi, but it also enabled the memory of more common people, like Marta Della Vedova, and the names of many obscure heroes to be restored to the pages of history. Everybody involved contributed to remembering the "heroic phalanx" and "the personal dedication of volunteers, martyrs and apostles to the great ideal of Italian Rome." For Ezio Garibaldi "to create around the symbols of the Garibaldian efforts on the Janiculum Hill an atmosphere of sanctity and faith, in which the Roman of yesterday passed the baton to the Italian of today, was the best thing that could have been done."[52]

In this way the historical and ideal continuity with the Garibaldi legacy—the principle of Garibaldinism precursor of Fascism—was confirmed. As Reggiani wrote to Ceccarelli two months before the inauguration of the ossuary, the ceremony would achieve the goal of "glorifying the Risorgimento through its martyr forerunners who wanted *Rome*."[53]

The narrative included the greatness of ancient Rome, to which the nineteenth-century martyrs laid claim. Compared to this historical exaltation linking the myth of ancient Rome to the Risorgimento epic, the references to Fascism appeared more nuanced, except perhaps in the reporting of some official speeches in Reggiani's conclusion.

Every page was filled with references to patriotic exploits, to voluntary sacrifice and heroic death, from the first republican martyr, Paolo Narducci, to another Roman, the infantry lieutenant Augusto Valenziani, who fell on 20 September. For their part the martyrs of Aspromonte, who were not translated but nevertheless were included in the catalogue, were compared in the book to the legionnaires who lost their lives in the Fiume campaign of 1919–20, considered forerunners of Fascism.

The book was produced by the ATENA publishing house, which belonged to Ezio Garibaldi, who in the meantime had been pardoned by Mussolini and welcomed back into the ranks of the regime with a new mission, that of championing the cause of Nicoise irredentism. This was closely linked to the name of the Hero of the Two Worlds, who was born in Nice, which had been ceded to France in 1860. As early as 1940 Ezio Garibaldi had founded the Gruppi di Azione Nizzarda (GAN), to which the reborn *Camicia Rossa* gave copious prominence, supporting the annexationist line of Fascism in the face of the Vichy government. The explicit references to current events, especially the ongoing war, and to the anti-French policy of the Mussolini regime would be manifested in all their symbolic strength on the opening day, bringing Fascism and its mission to the fore.

The Inauguration of the Mausoleum-Ossuary, 3 November 1941

Every minute detail of the choreography and the succession of ritual moments was studied closely in order to celebrate first of all the Fascist revolution.

A few days before the inauguration, on 28 October 1941, the anniversary of the March on Rome and the start of the 20th year of the Fascist era, the Memorial to the Fallen of the Revolution in the Foro Mussolini (now the Foro Italico) was inaugurated, and it was from there that early in the morning of 3 November, with a laying of wreaths by the Garibaldi Legion and Ezio Garibaldi's GAN, the inauguration day of the new ossuary on the Janiculum began. The emphasis on voluntarism and the cult of heroic death was reaffirmed in the next two stages of the event, with a similar ritual being performed at the tomb of the Unknown Soldier and the Altar of the Fascist Fallen on the Capitoline Hill. The fusing together of the two epics of recent history reached its highest point in the procession that accompanied the coffin of Mameli from the Vittoriano to the Janiculum, which included soldiers singing the *Inno* (for which he wrote the words and which is now Italy's national anthem) and *Giovinezza* (the most popular song of the Fascist regime), and in the inauguration of the ossuary, in which Mussolini himself—making one of his last public appearances—took part.[54]

Figure 12.2 The Garibaldian Ossuary Mausoleum on the Janiculum, Sovrintendenza Capitolina ai Beni Culturali, Rome (exterior).

Source: Photo by Silvia Cavicchioli.

The link with the Risorgimento tradition was evoked by the new date chosen for the event, 3 November, which was the anniversary of the Battle of Mentana and also the eve of victory in the First World War; as well by the votive crowns placed prominently on the initiative of the new governor of Rome, Prince Gian Giacomo Borghese, in the places where the 1849 siege had taken place; and also by the Garibaldian motto at the top of the structure, *Roma o morte*.

Alongside the regime's attempt to highlight the link with the Risorgimento tradition was the desire to solemnly reaffirm the innovation and originality of the political and social experiment of the Fascist revolution. In fact, the most salient feature of the work lay in the final design of the monument: in the austere quadrangle constructed from travertine, inspired by rationalist architecture and decorated by symbols of Fascist mysticism; in the literary references, particularly to Gabriele D'Annunzio; in the motto of Fascist mysticism "Believe, Obey, Fight"; and finally in the bronze braziers at the four corners of the perimeter for ritual fires to be lit during commemorations, an ideal proscenium for the funeral liturgy so dear to the regime.

In the official speeches of the inauguration and in press reports of the event, the anti-French interpretation of the facts of 1849 and 1867 became apparent, reaching from the Risorgimento to the present:

> After ninety years, those who defended this Garibaldian Hill with outstanding valour and desperate tenacity during the Roman Republic of 1849 return to it. They return to the climate of the Black Shirt Revolution, surrounded by the love of the Italian people.

The French enemy, in Mussolini's words, was identified as the party responsible for much of the martyrdom: "Republican rifles those of 1849; imperial rifles those of 1867. [. . .] But both came from the same frontier. [. . .] We do not forget!" The threatening and bellicose rhetoric of the Duce resounded once again in the afternoon when it was broadcast on the radio, and it also echoed in the cinema news programme *Luce* on 6 November, and finally was included in the book *Ai caduti per Roma*.

The consecration of the mausoleum, which took place in front of the coffin of Mameli carried by the Fascist avant-garde alone, was sublimated in the invocation of the name of the martyr by Mussolini, to whom all those in attendance responded in chorus "Present!" in accordance with the roll-call ritual staged in public commemorations.

The coffin descended into the twilight of the hypogeum, surrounded by large mother-of-pearl crosses, by D'Annunzian inscriptions in praise of heroic vigour, and by the names of the fallen crowned by the words of Mussolini: "May the names of those who died fighting to make the homeland greater and more beautiful remain permanently engraved in our hearts." To complete the picture of symbolic references, the sacellum made out of polished porphyry that received the urn containing the ashes of the hero was engraved with the words of Mameli's mother that gave expression to the collective mourning of all the nation's mothers.[55] On the entrance portal an inscription informed visitors that the martyrs were "not dead but eternally alive in the future."

But the Fascist mausoleum, surrounded, as said, by braziers that would have been lit during the ceremonies to celebrate the cult of the martyrs of the Fascist era rather than those of the past, served its propagandistic purpose for only a few years and then fell into decline with the defeat of Mussolini's Italy, eventually closing itself in its remote position that still sets it apart today.

Figure 12.3 The Garibaldian Ossuary Mausoleum on the Janiculum, Sovrintendenza Capitolina ai Beni Culturali, Rome (interior with the sarcophagus in porphyry containing the remains of Goffredo Mameli).

Source: Photo by Silvia Cavicchioli.

After the liberation of Rome by the allies, Reggiani took care to chisel
out the more compromising epigraphs from the walls of the mausoleum,
those echoing his Fascist faith, which he repudiated in a document with
the significant title *Prefazione in tempo di libertà* (*Preface in a time of
freedom*) given to the press on 3 July 1944, but later reaffirmed in a
memoir-confession published at the age of 70, in 1951.[56] Two years earlier, on 14 October 1949, in his role as superintendent of the Garibaldian
mausoleum, he had welcomed the delegates of the 28th Congress of the

History of the Risorgimento. In his vibrant re-enactment of the last episode of the defence of 1849, he transmitted the idea of a republican continuity between the nineteenth and twentieth centuries, expunging the interruption of the Fascist dictatorship from history.

Notes

1. On the history of the remains of the martyrs of the Roman Republic up to 1879 and on the work of Bertani, I refer the reader to Silvia Cavicchioli, "I resti dei vinti. I martiri della Repubblica romana (1849–1879)," *Il Risorgimento. Rivista di storia del Risorgimento e di storia contemporanea* 2 (2017): 37–84.
2. *Garibaldi in Parlamento* (Rome: Camera dei Deputati, 2007); Archivio del Museo del Risorgimento di Milano, *Carte Bertani*, cart. 52, pl. XLI, n. 11, notes on the presentation of the bill in the Chamber of Deputies.
3. Giuseppe Garibaldi, *I Mille* (Bologna: Cappelli, 1933), 347–48.
4. Ulisse Bacci, *Il libro del massone italiano* (Rome: Tipografia fratelli Centenari, 1908), 352–54.
5. Sergio La Salvia, "Tra irredentismo ed ebraismo. L'«invenzione» del corpo di un martire della patria: Giacomo Venezian e la costruzione del primo ossario al Gianicolo," in *Per Carlo Ghisalberti. Miscellanea di studi*, ed. Ester Capuzzo and Ennio Maserati (Naples: Edizioni Scientifiche Italiane, 2003), 397.
6. Fulvio Conti, *Italia immaginata. Sentimenti, memorie e politica fra Otto e Novecento* (Pisa: Pacini, 2017), 169–78.
7. Alfredo Comandini, *L'Italia nei cento anni del secolo XIX (1801–1900), giorno per giorno illustrata. 1871–1900* (Milan: Vallardi, 1879), 582–83.
8. La Salvia, "Tra irredentismo ed ebraismo," 398.
9. Antonio Reggiani, "Come vennero ritrovate nel 1879 le ceneri dei difensori della Repubblica Romana," *Camicia Rossa* 11 (1937): 238.
10. At the time it was still thought that only one of Brunetti's sons was put to death with him, instead of two. Silvia Cavicchioli, *Anita. Storia e mito di Anita Garibaldi* (Turin: Einaudi, 2017), 112–13.
11. Comandini, *L'Italia nei cento anni*, 44.
12. Giuseppe Monsagrati, *Roma senza il Papa. La Repubblica romana del 1849* (Rome-Bari: Laterza, 2014), 149–52.
13. La Salvia, "Tra irredentismo ed ebraismo," 399–406.
14. This is the case with the radical newspaper *Gazzettino Rosa*, which in 1879 offered its readers a portrait of Ciceruacchio in the series entitled "Galleria dei Martiri."
15. *Atti parlamentari, Camera dei Deputati, Sessione del 1878–79, Discussioni, 1.a tornata del 16 giugno 1879* (Rome: Tipografia Camera dei Deputati, 1880), 7498–99. The Senate vote, held in secret, resulted in 27 votes against and 52 in favour.
16. Carlo Arrigoni, "La morte di Goffredo Mameli," *Minerva Medica* 7 (1949): 5–48.
17. Ermanno Loevinson, "La tomba di Francesco Daverio," *Rassegna Storica del Risorgimento*, vol. I–II (January–April 1916): 696–99.
18. Bacci, *Il libro del massone italiano*, 365–67.
19. Luigi Huetter, *Iscrizioni della città di Roma dal 1871 al 1920*, vol. III (Rome: Istituto di Studi Romani, 1962), 359.
20. Comandini, *L'Italia nei cento anni*, 830.
21. "Vita dell'Istituto," *Rassegna Storica del Risorgimento*, vol. I (January 1938): 288–90.

22. *Ai caduti per Roma. 1849–1870*, [ed. Antonio Reggiani] (Rome: ATENA, 1941), 28.
23. Letter from Giuseppe Avezzana to Menotti Garibaldi, quoted in La Salvia, "Tra irredentismo ed ebraismo," 410.
24. Evelyn Martinengo Cesaresco, *Italian Characters in the Epoch of Unification* (London: T.F. Unwin, 1890), 237–38.
25. Gino Carocci, "Goffredo Mameli dalla chiesa delle Stimmate alla gloria del Gianicolo," *Camicia Rossa* 9–12 (September–December 1941): 200–9.
26. Massimo Baioni, "I rituali del fascismo e la controversa eredità del Risorgimento," in *Rituali civili. Storie nazionali e memorie pubbliche nell'Europa contemporanea*, ed. Maurizio Ridolfi (Rome: Gangemi, 2006), 179.
27. Giovanni Di Peio, "L'ultimo omaggio di Mussolini a Garibaldi. Il Monumento ai Caduti per la causa di Roma italiana (1849–70)," *Nuova Storia Contemporanea* 5 (September–October 2008): 51–53.
28. Cavicchioli, *Anita*, 203–27; Claudio Fogu, "Fascism and Historic Representation. The 1932 Garibaldian Celebrations," *Journal of Contemporary History* 2 (1996): 317–45.
29. Silvia Cavicchioli, "The Translations of the Remains of Martyred Patriots in Risorgimento Italy," in *The Great Laboratory of Humanity: Collection, Patrimony and the Repatriation of Human Remains*, ed. Maria Teresa Milicia (Padua: Cleup, 2019), 81–92; Baioni, "I rituali del fascismo," 181.
30. *I martiri cosentini del 15 Marzo 1844. Celebrazione ad iniziativa della consulta del comitato cosentino del Regio Istituto di storia del Risorgimento italiano: 15 marzo 1937* (Cosenza: SCAT, 1937).
31. On Ezio Garibaldi see Alberto Malfitano, "Ezio Garibaldi," in *Garibaldi. Due secoli di interpretazioni*, ed. Lauro Rossi (Rome: Gangemi, 2010), 174–77; Annita Garibaldi Jallet, *Ritratti di famiglia* (Imola: Santerno, 1989), 25.
32. Antonio Reggiani, "L'Ossario del Gianicolo," *Camicia Rossa* 5 (May 1937), 117.
33. "Vita dell'Istituto," *Rassegna Storica del Risorgimento* XI (November 1937): 1841–47.
34. Antonio Reggiani, "Storia dell'Ara di Mentana," *Camicia Rossa* 10–11 (October–November 1937): 219–21.
35. "Vita dell'Istituto," 288.
36. Antonio Reggiani, "L'esumazione delle salme dei Caduti nel 1849 e nel 1870," *Camicia Rossa* 1 (January 1938): 18–19; Antonio Reggiani, "I difensori di Roma. Il rinvenimento dei resti mortali di Ciceruacchio e dei suoi compagni," *Corriere della Sera* (13 January 1938); Arrigoni, "La morte di Goffredo Mameli," 41–42.
37. "Vita dell'Istituto," 288.
38. *Catalogo dei caduti per Roma dal 1849 al 1870*, [ed. Antonio Reggiani] (Rome: ATENA, 1942), 98.
39. *Ai caduti per Roma*, 41–42; Reggiani, "L'esumazione delle salme," 18–19.
40. This was announced by Reggiani at the start of a series of conferences promoted by the Committee. Ibid.
41. Alessandra Argenio, "Il mito della romanità nel ventennio fascista," in *Il mondo classico nell'immaginario contemporaneo*, ed. Benedetto Coccia (Rome: Apes, 2008), 138.
42. *Ai caduti per Roma*, 28.
43. In some documents explicit reference was made to the fact that by the will of Mussolini "the aforementioned law of 22 June 1879 was executed with the creation, on the Holy Janiculum Hill of a Monumental Ossuary." Museo Centrale del Risorgimento, Rome (henceforth MCRR), b. 602 16, *Minutes of the Exhumation of the Bodies of Two Fallen Soldiers from the Manara Legion* (21 June 1939).

44. On the 95th anniversary of his death, a manifesto was published in the form of a free postcard given to the Republican Armed Forces: *Lo spirito di Goffredo Mameli difenderà la Repubblica Sociale.* This showed the Genoese Mameli at the head of a force of Red Shirts and Black Shirts united under the Italian tricolour.

45. Argenio, "Il mito della romanità," 81–178; Giuseppe Bottai, *Roma e fascismo* (Rome: Istituto di Studi Romani, 1937).

46. A very similar solution was found in Bologna in 1940 for the remains of Ugo Bassi, *Bologna in camicia nera* (Bologna: Pendragon, 2006).

47. Antonio Reggiani, *Confessioni* (n.p.: n.p., 1951), 13.

48. *Ai caduti per Roma*, 334.

49. Ibid., 44–45.

50. MCRR, NA 18, Various notes by Antonio Reggiani.

51. *Ai caduti per Roma*, 332–35.

52. Ibid., 7–9.

53. Letter from Reggiani to Ceccarelli, 11 September 1941, quoted in Di Peio, "L'ultimo omaggio di Mussolini," 83.

54. Bruno Tobia, *Salve o popolo di eroi . . . La monumentalità fascista nelle fotografie dell'Istituto Luce* (Rome: Editori Riuniti-Istituto Luce, 2002).

55. *Ai caduti per Roma*, 322–28.

56. MCRR, NA 18, Antonio Reggiani, *Prefazione in tempo di libertà*; Reggiani, *Confessioni*, 7.

13 The Medicalisation of the Corpse in Liberal Italy
National Legislation and the Case of Turin

Silvano Montaldo

Anatomy in Pre-Unification Italy: A Glorious Past, a Difficult Present

Historiography has by now assimilated the fact that during the nineteenth century and the first decades of the 20th medical personnel assumed an increasingly significant role at the bedside of the dying, while that of the clergy slowly diminished.[1] A result of changed attitudes towards illness and of the diffusion of treatments to the lower classes, this process of the "medicalisation of death" coincided with the public authorities taking responsibility for dead bodies and their management, in line with the principles of the French Revolution.[2] In Italy, too, the creation of the office of the civil state, the unfolding "revolution of cemeteries" and the establishment of municipal funeral transport services, which started in the Napoleonic era, triggered growing tension over the management of death and corpses with the Catholic Church, which during the *ancien régime* had had absolute control over such matters.[3] Somewhat less studied, however, has been the medicalisation of post-mortems, another facet of the secularisation of death. The following pages therefore propose to reconstruct the essential elements of the legal picture and some aspects of the practices that structured the management of the corpse in the middle of the positivist age. Special attention will be given to the role that teaching, research and museum collections played in imparting, together with the imperatives of science, a new order of values.

In recent years numerous studies have brought to light the experimental dimension of anatomy in the *ancien régime*, its importance in the field of natural philosophy and its correspondence to the dominant ethical-religious system. Although the persistence of humoral theories impeded the birth of a systematised knowledge in the sphere of pathology, autopsies were by no means rare, for a number of reasons only partly connected with a desire for knowledge on the part of scholars. On the one hand, the governing authorities ordered post-mortem investigations in the course of judicial trials or during epidemic emergencies, while on the other hand families themselves requested autopsies of their relatives in

order to rebut slanderous accusations, to seek reassurance about hereditary disease, to exalt the spiritual qualities of those who died in odour of
sanctity, to receive an explanation that might ease their pain of sudden
loss and for many more reasons.[4]

Autopsies and anatomical observations were also frequently carried
out in hospitals on the bodies of dead patients. Some of the leading hospitals in eighteenth-century Italy, owing to university reforms that imposed
regular periods of hospital practice by students, became equipped with
anatomical theatres in order to avoid recovering patients seeing dissections which were normally carried out in the wards.[5] While Paris was by
then the seat of the main institutions promoting research on the human
body, it was still in Bologna and Padua—where centuries earlier a sort
of modern anatomy had emerged—that the premises of the new pathological anatomy were laid, whose foundation then took place in France
in the years of the Revolution and the empire with Xavier Bichat and
Jean-Nicolas Corvisart, through the construction of a new conceptual
framework able to relate diseases, symptoms and injuries.[6]

However, wherever such studies were carried out, the problem of the
provision of bodies remained: anatomists were forced to use bodies eco-
nomically and invent techniques for preserving their remains. Anatomical waxworks, which were conceived in the eighteenth century, were part
of an attempt to respond to the decay of remains and the difficulties of
procuring bodies for teaching. Even Giovanni Battista Morgagni, one of
the major scientific celebrities of his time, who taught anatomy at Padua
from 1717 to 1771, occasionally lamented the lack of bodies for his lessons. The universities' hunger for human flesh had certainly increased.
The old anatomical theatres, seats of the ritualised anatomies of the
ancien régime, were by then unsuited to the new requirements of the discipline: the French were the first to have understood that students had to
be given the opportunity to practise directly on bodies, and this obviously
made the need more pressing.

In 1742 Maria Teresa of Austria promulgated a decree authorising the
professor of anatomy at the University of Vienna to use the bodies of
criminals for his demonstrations. A few years later this was extended to
cover the bodies of the poor who died in hospitals, and was reaffirmed in
1787 when her son Joseph II issued a new penal code to impose limits on
the death penalty. The effect of these measures was felt in Britain half a
century later: the 1832 *Anatomy Act* and the 1834 *Poor Law* guaranteed
a supply to the schools of anatomy after the abolition of the *Bloody Code*
in 1823 had reduced the number of capital punishments, thereby provok-
ing a rise in the illegal acquisition of cadavers.[7] The desire to ensure a
dignified funeral for oneself or one's family, avoiding anatomical dissection and the mass grave where deceased welfare recipients were buried, in
compliance with the principle that public expenditure should be repaid,
was a problem that often occurred in the patronage relations within

English communities.[8] Hence many of the difficulties faced by Oxford in securing an efficient and low-cost supply system of corpses for its anatomical school, which ended with a crisis in teaching at that university in the late Victorian era. By contrast, the rival Cambridge was able to secure a constant provision of corpses at lower costs, and thus took the lead in the field of anatomical studies.[9]

And what of Italy? Here the division between the states probably determined the survival of local agreements at city level, without there being a precise normative definition on the part of governments. Moreover, the crisis of Italian science in the early nineteenth century, caused by unfavourable political and cultural circumstances, led to the continuation of antiquated systems. In those decades, being without large anatomical and pathological institutes based in hospitals and of museums dedicated to the subject, pathological anatomy was still an essentially theoretical discipline that had little connection to clinical practice, in contrast to the position in the German-speaking world, France and Britain.[10]

The same was true of forensic medicine.[11] In Turin, in the 1850s by means of an agreement with the management of a number of hospitals, hospices and prisons, municipal undertakers provided cadavers to the section head of the university for autopsies and dissections. The number of these could vary from one to five a day. Dissection, which took place from 20 November through all of March, used up to three a day. In that decade there was an annual average of 340 students enrolled in medicine, with around 59 graduating, but both figures were in slight decline.[12] Before delivering the bodies to the anatomical theatre, the undertakers checked that they had not putrefied or been damaged by illness, in order to avoid the dissectors' certain rejection.

Other welfare organisations in Turin had, however, refused to be involved in this agreement, and so the bodies of their beneficiaries were not used by the school of anatomy.[13] Furthermore, supply costs were high due to fraud perpetrated by the undertakers, who avoided delivering to the university bodies from the city-owned San Giovanni Hospital, for which they received a lower payment. Instead they favoured bodies from other hospitals. For example, in 1853, 191 patients died in San Giovanni. The proportion of hospital deaths was decidedly low: in Turin in the decade from 1828 to 1837, for which we have date, it was just over three percent.[14] At this time, in Italy as everywhere in the world, people almost always died at home and only those who did not have a bed ended their days in welfare institutions. The hospital doctors carried out 43 autopsies, but of the other 148 bodies only 26 were sent to the anatomical laboratory. The remaining 122 were either buried without autopsy or else were taken to the anatomical theatre on the pretence that they came from elsewhere, thus qualifying for the higher price.[15]

Soon after a similar situation emerged in Naples in regard to the management of the city's main hospital, the Incurabili.[16] This great sanatorium had several anatomical theatres for public or private lessons, the use of which was regulated by the statutes of 1839. Later, the increase in demand for such teaching prompted some private teachers, members of the hospital staff, to move their dissections to their own homes or other places, in competition with professors of the university. Consequently, a real commerce of cadavers was created and, as the number of bodies supplied to the hospital proved insufficient, some already sent to the cemetery were redirected there. The undertakers, who hitherto had been recompensed for transporting the bodies to the anatomical theatres and then returning to collect and deliver them to the cemetery, were able to acquire a sort of clandestine monopoly over the trade, with a consequent impact on teaching costs. An investigation led to proposals for a reform of the hospital's rules and a discussion about the legitimate ownership of the corpses and culminated in a ruling that only the deceased who had not expressed an objection or whose relatives had not asked for them to be honoured with obsequies could be used in anatomical lessons. It was essentially a compromise, the actual outcome of which is not known.

Nationwide Legislation: "The Rightful Needs of Science"

It was only after unification, in the unusual climate created by a succession of important scientific discoveries, by the full unfolding of the positivist culture and by the conflict between the state and the church, that the problem of the supply of corpses for research and teaching was defined in legislation. The increase in students enrolled in the medical-surgical departments—which almost doubled in the case of Turin, where between 1877 and 1885 medical and surgical undergraduates rose from 391 to 691[17]—and the process of specialisation and innovation in the discipline, which led to an upsurge in the number of classes and a concomitant number of corpses needed, induced the government to address the question.

At that time, corpses and body parts were used in lessons of simple anatomy, pathological anatomy, forensic medicine and operative medicine: the basic syllabus of the 16 medical-surgical faculties in Italy and of the Institute of Higher Studies in Florence.[18] During the academic year, lessons and exercises on human remains involved thousands of students and a growing number of courses, both institutional and public, with the University of Turin alone calculated to require 800 corpses a year, equal to around 12 percent of the city's average annual deaths.[19] And even then pockets of urban poverty were looked upon as a fundamental resource for study and research. In 1881, a hospital doctor wrote: "In Naples the hospital is sought only when one reaches an extreme seriousness, and it is sought more by families than by the infirm in order to avoid the costs of interment."[20] Not paying the cost of burial meant, quite simply, allowing the undertaker or the hospital administration to consign the body of the family member to the scalpel.

Testimony of the repercussions of the practice of anatomy at the level of public opinion, in the cultural climate of full positivism, is given by letters that mayors of university cities exchanged about the problem of supplying bodies to medical schools. Writing about the general population's resistance, the mayor of Padua asked his counterpart in Turin how the city's administration managed to make provision for "the rightful needs of Science" without undermining "the sentiment of affection and pity, worthy of full respect, whose continuation, in the human heart, is certain proof of continuing lofty thoughts and actions." His request for details related in particular to "those deceased in the hospital whose families, despite not having been able to pay the hospital's fees for treatment, nevertheless, either with the kindly help of friends or by a final sacrifice to the memory of their dead, request the bodies to give them their funeral rites and insist they be exempted from autopsy."[21]

To the need of not weakening family ties that always needed reinforcing, were added problems linked to the lack of control over the internal procedures of hospitals and anatomical institutes. The mayor of Genoa stated that sometimes the coffins returned by the Ligurian university for burial, "instead of containing what corresponds to the entirety of a corpse, are filled with parts of different limbs, so that it lacks the wholeness that determines the consistency of a body."[22] In practice, they proceeded to inhumation without attributing a specific personal identity to the body, in contravention of the rules of the Office of Civil State.[23] Similar concerns were raised by the mayor of Turin, who complained that "some hospitals carry out autopsies without informing the mayor" and criticised the behaviour of medical students: sometimes, "having finished studying the pieces removed, these were either thrown in the water or on public ground, bringing about suspicions and investigations by the judicial authority and creating alarm and fear in the population."[24] However, no explicit link seems to have emerged to the question of apparent deaths, which at least in the eighteenth century had been a subject of scientific debate and anguished concern throughout Europe.[25]

To appease the scientific community the government eventually took the initiative and passed two provisions that guaranteed a sufficient availability of corpses and reduced procurement costs. The first to take action was the Ministry of the Interior, whose director-general of prisons, Martino Beltrani-Scalia, sent a circular letter to the provincial prefects in September 1883 to give instructions that, in support of the requests of certain medical-surgical faculties, the corpses of prisoners who died in the infirmaries of penal establishments were "put to the benefit of teaching and science."[26] The ministry, he wrote, had gladly adhered to the request, both because this practice had long been in existence in some provinces, under earlier regulations, and because autopsies would give the prison administration indirect control over the quality of health services in the prisons. Therefore, following an agreement with the Ministry of Public

Education, the governors of prisons in the provinces were obliged to promptly inform the rectors of universities each time a prisoner in their charge died. If the rector accepted the prisoner's corpse for autopsies, the university would bear the cost of transportation and burial.

One should remember that Beltrani-Scalia was in correspondence with Cesare Lombroso and had published some of his writings in the *Rivista di discipline carcerarie* (*Review of Prison Disciplines*), since he shared some of his ideas on the study of delinquent men. According to criminal anthropology, the new "science" created by Lombroso, lawbreakers needed to undergo psychiatric and medical evaluations while living and, in due course, post-mortem examinations. The data gathered should be compared to those of the general population. In his later years Lombroso confessed to the "scientific crimes" that he had committed at the start of his career, when he and his pupils and friends violated old, abandoned graves.[27] Not by chance, the mayor of Turin wrote some time later of "autopsies carried out in prisons and of the transfer of limbs and especially skulls," which went well beyond what was legally allowed.[28] In short, the measure taken by Beltrani-Scalia is evidence of the diffusion of Lombroso's ideas in the prison administration.[29]

The effectiveness of Beltrani-Scalia's regulation, however, is somewhat in question in terms of its effect on what was actually happening in prisons: at the second international congress on criminal anthropology, which took place in Paris in August 1889, Ezio Sciamanna, author of the form intended to serve as a guide to doctors carrying out autopsies on convicts,[30] declared that the system had not taken root. On the one hand, the doctors found Sciamma's instructions too detailed and refused to fill out the form, while on the other the lack of psychological data on potential subjects nullified the value of such work from the criminological point of view. Because of this, he hoped that the authorities would allow criminal anthropologists to gain access to prisons so that they could study detainees while they were still alive and perform their autopsies when they died.[31]

This possibility, however, met with objections from Louis Herbette, the state councillor and director of the French prison administration, who argued that prisons were not hospitals, where in exchange for medical care patients had to accept the idea that their bodies were also of use for study and education both in life and death. Rather, prisons were places of punishment that nevertheless guaranteed inmates certain rights, including the right to retain control of matters relating to their corpses. Depriving them of this right would compromise their self-respect still further, putting at risk what remained of their consciences. For the same reason, access to prisoners' cells was granted only to charitable people committed to their repentance, that is to say, to prudent and experienced people dedicated to the public interest, qualities which Herbette evidently did not ascribe to scientists. With their hazardous theories, the latter might compromise difficult pathways to recovery, and moreover, in their thirst for discovery, they might easily fall for lies told by the prisoners.[32] Herbette then pointed out that the decision to subject the corpses of prisoners to autopsy violated the principle, enshrined in the Napoleonic code, that prisoners' sentences ended at the moment of death.[33] Finally, he declared that in his experience the display of executed prisoners caused serious disturbance in other inmates. Like in France, in England autopsies on prisoners were only carried out in cases of suspicious death,[34] meaning that the decision taken by the Italian prison administration probably remained unique in Europe: in 1891 the new regulations for prisons reiterated the provisions of the 1883 circular and Beltrani-Scalia invited doctors working in prisons to carry out anatomical research on those corpses that were not sent to the universities.[35]

As far as the rest of the population was concerned, the *Regolamento per la consegna dei cadaveri alle Scuole anatomiche* (Regulation on the consignment of corpses to the anatomical schools), created by the Minister of Public Education Michele Coppino in 1885, established the rule that all corpses of people who died in hospitals in cities with medical faculties, and all those who were to be buried at the expense of the municipality, should be handed over to the anatomical schools, if requested through the offices of civil state.[36] In the *ancien régime* the seventh work of mercy, in other words the burial of the poor, had become established through the creation of the Confraternities of the Good Death and the work of the mendicant orders, but after the revolutionary and Napoleonic age the part played by religious bodies as providers of funeral services had contracted greatly.[37] On the other hand, hospital assistance, which constituted the last haven for part of the vast number of poor affected by need and illness, was experienced as a veritable *deminutio* for the working classes integrated in economic life, while there emerged paid hospitals for the petty bourgeoisie and private nursing homes for the well-heeled.[38] The government provision reconfirmed the principles of the British *Anatomy Act* and in effect nationalised for scientific-economic purposes the bodies of the dead belonging to the most wretched groups of the big city populations. In other words, they were the marginalised and homeless, not workers inserted in the network of protection of mutual aid societies that guaranteed subsidies for the burial of their members or helped widows and children.[39]

The Beltrani-Scalia circular and the Coppino regulation had a notable impact, especially in the major cities of the centre-north, where the proportions of deaths taking place in hospital was by then reaching about 30 to 40 percent of the total.[40] In this way, the government ensured a constant replenishing of cadavers for the anatomical schools and brought about a reduction in the universities' operating costs. Previously, the Turin anatomical institute had used corpses almost exclusively from the Cottolengo Hospital, one of the city's main charities, paying 5.50 *lire* to the city gravediggers for each one they brought and took back to the general cemetery after the autopsies.[41] This was not a minor expense, considering that at the time a worker in a mechanical or chemical plant in Turin earned about 3.25–3.50 *lire* a day.[42] With the new system in operation, the university could be sure of a supply of the 800 corpses a year necessary for its teaching activities, paying to the city, as a contribution to transport and burial expenses, 750 *lire* a year which, despite being increased to 1,000 *lire* in 1889, nevertheless was a net saving compared to the past.[43]

The regulation by minister Coppino, who with the 1877 reform had established compulsory, free and non-confessional elementary schooling, substituting religious teaching with lessons on the duties of man and of the citizen, reinforced the policy of containing the interference of religious orders, of challenging local particularism and of fighting the huge intertwining of parasitic interests, in an attempt, destined to be completed only after the First World War, to transform hospitals and sanatoria erected by baroque piety for the benefit of the poor into a modern health machine. The year 1887 saw the publication of the report produced by the committee of inquiry on pious works, followed a year later by the health reform law and in 1890 by the law on care institutions. Hospitals were placed within an institutional framework distinctly marked by the prevalence of public goals. The Crispi law consolidated the contents of the Coppino regulation, establishing that in university cities hospitals were obliged to provide the rooms and to leave the sick and corpses at the disposal of the clinics, according to the needs of the teaching programmes.[44] Therefore, if the history of the nineteenth-century hospital can be understood as a battle between opposing interests and mentalities, the Coppino regulation must be seen as a victory of the lay and utilitarian outlook that belonged to the positivist ruling class, and as a step towards the transformation of the poor into clients with established rights and duties.

There was also a shift in the relationship between hospital doctors, teachers in medical faculties and institution administrators. At the city conference held in Turin for the implementation of the Coppino regulation, representatives of the private institutions expressed a desire to remove themselves from its jurisdiction, while doctor Giacinto Boetti, representative of the children's hospices, declared: "the position one would like to bring to the doctors of the hospitals with the Royal Decree is quite intolerable [. . .] the doctors of the Hospitals are low paid and if despite this they are able to render service in the Hospitals, it is precisely for the advantage of being able to do autopsies."[45] In essence, the situation in Turin was similar to that of Naples: alongside official teaching, doctors provided private lessons in anatomy to supplement their income. By ensuring the complete fulfilment of the needs of the university teachers, the new legislation treated corpses as a resource to be regulated in the public interest. The effects were immediate: as early as the start of 1887 the rector of Turin University rejoiced because the decree had made it possible to obtain "a wealth of material for our Schools of Anatomy, which previously they greatly lacked."[46] A final provision, of which, however, no trace has yet been found, also made available the corpses of soldiers who died in military hospitals: at the moment this is a hypothesis supported by the fact that a substantial part of the craniological collection of the university's Institute of Anatomy is composed of items of that origin.

"The Sentiment of Affection and Pity"

"What are you afraid of? Maybe what I just told you, about them cutting us into pieces, has scared you? But don't you understand that they do this after, when we don't feel anything anymore? What do you care?"[47] With this imaginary dialogue between two women in a waiting room, Emilia Ferretti Viola, who wrote under the pen name Emma, referred to the dark fears that the lower classes held towards autopsies, which were not the least of the many insecurities behind the persistent hostility towards hospitals.[48] In the period in which the practice came to be regulated by national legislation, the safeguarding of the feelings of families was a matter in which the municipalities intervened, by stiffening the checks on the work of anatomical institutions and hospital doctors in the area of autopsies and by formalising procedures to minimise disagreeable episodes. A provision relating to this was implemented in Turin in 1886, when the Coppino regulation was in force. The councillor for the civil state and cemeteries, Severino Casana reported to the municipal council that the need to establish better controls over the transport of corpses and greater clarity in the rules regarding autopsies carried out for scientific purposes had long been felt.

At the same time, however, the new *Regolamento dei cimiteri e del servizio funebre* (Regulation of cemeteries and the funeral service) of the city of Turin introduced a detailed list of tariffs for the burial of corpses, which took into account the requirements imposed by hygiene and propriety. While the cost of a first class funeral was 450 *lire* for the hearse alone, even those forced to choose a less expensive service had to spend a significant sum: the cost of the coffin (including the visit of a pathologist to carry out the post-mortem, the transporting of the coffin to the funeral parlour, the preparation of the body and its instalment in the coffin) cost ten *lire* for adults, and not much less for children and foetuses. And there were other amounts to be added: around 15 *lire* for the gravediggers, five for the interment, 21 for the hearse, 20 for the fee for a single burial and at least ten for the stone-laying fee. In all, over 80 *lire*, at a time when the wages of male adult workers were on average little more than three *lire* a day, and considerably lower in the case of women and children.[49] It is therefore not difficult to imagine that the cost of burial was beyond the means of those people who did not receive assistance from a religious charity or a lay association. Therefore, given the city's need to make funeral services more freely available to those who could demonstrate that they were unable to meet these costs, many citizens had to accept that their or their loved one's body would be used for scientific or educational purposes. In short, the people's disquiet about the increase in anatomical studies was answered by greater bureaucratic control over procedures for accessing and managing corpses, as envisaged by the legislator, attentive to hygiene problems and protecting the feelings of the bereaved.[50] But this raised the costs, increasing the number of people who had to resort to free municipal services.

These procedures became nationwide with the 1892 *Regolamento speciale di polizia mortuaria* (*Special regulations on mortuary affairs*). On one side, article 41 established that the bodies of those who died in hospital or at home, and whose transportation had to be paid for by the council, had to be consigned within 24 hours of their death to the medical schools for investigative or didactic purposes if they were to be regulated, unless the judicial authorities had made other arrangements. If the university did not request them, the corpses could be handed over to doctors with an appropriate autopsy room. In this way the system met the needs of private academics. Article 44 prohibited the removal of corpses or body parts from the university anatomy halls or other autopsy rooms without written authorisation from the institute's director or the mayor, which could be denied in the event of explicit family opposition.[51]

The transformation of autopsies into an ever more formalised and regulated procedure was completed by the *Regolamento per le sezioni cadaveriche relative alle cliniche* (*Regulations for cadaverous sections relating to clinics*), promulgated by the Ministry of Public Education. The corpses of those who died in university clinics had to be dissected in public, at the time set for the lesson by the school from which the body came, an operation that could be performed only by a professor of anatomical pathology or one of his assistants and not by teachers of the clinics. The teachers did, however, have to be present and might then receive the dissected body, or parts of it, to use in their own studies, before returning it to the professor who was allowed to take samples from it for the museum.[52]

Museums and Human Remains: The Case of Turin

The abundance of cadavers made available for university teaching and research by this set of provisions had an immediate impact on the activity of Turin's anatomical institute, whose history makes an interesting case study. Up to the moment of the issuing of regulations on corpses, the anatomical museum consisted mainly of the valuable collection of waxworks commissioned by the University of Turin and created by Piedmontese and Florentine artisans in the late 1830s and later expanded, as well as dry specimens or specimens preserved in alcohol. There was also an anatomo-pathological museum founded by Alessandro Riberi, a doctor in the court of Savoy, within the hospital of San Giovanni. In the second half of the nineteenth century, with the improvement of preservation techniques, wax models were gradually abandoned.

But in the 1880s the collection of anatomical samples was made systematic, the reorganising being carried out by Carlo Giacomini, director of the anatomical council from 1876 and the architect of the major expansion of the university museum. In 1898 this was moved to the new building of the anatomical institutes, a few months before the scientist passed away.[53] In an undated report from his later years, Giacomini provided an account of the notable enhancement of the collections that had come about thanks to the government provisions of the early 1880s.[54] His research had concentrated on the central nervous system, and used individual variations as a possible means of deciphering the mysteries of difficult to study organs. His areas of interest included the anatomy of the brain, to which end he sometimes studied criminals, in particular those held in Turin's female prison, and non-white peoples. Giacomini's writings have recently led to his name being cited as an example of scientific racism,[55] but in reality, while he shared the assumptions of evolutionism, his work reveals significant interpretative prudence and his general conclusions are not in the least aimed at proving the inexorable superiority of white people.[56] Indeed, his research led him to refute the theories of his colleague Lombroso: nothing, on a macroscopic level, made the brain of a condemned prisoner different from that of an ordinary person.[57]

In a way that demonstrates the ideological coherence that had led to the enactment of the law on autopsies, Giacomini arranged for his own corpse to be taken to the anatomical institute and dissected by his pupils. This was a long-standing tradition, already seen in seventeenth-century Bologna,[58] but the process of secularisation had changed its meaning. In 1876 scientists and other French positivists launched an association, the *Société d'Autopsie Mutuelle*, to demonstrate that the soul did not exist. Thus, they carried out autopsies on deceased associates, to show the relationship between the structure of the brain and the character, qualities, and intelligence of a person.[59] This strange association developed against the background of events involving the Third Republic, in the years of the struggle between traditionalist Catholicism and materialist and anti-clerical radicalism. In that context it was fairly usual for scientists to arrange, by testamentary will, that parts of their body should be preserved to help with the teaching of the pupils of the anatomical schools where they had worked or to be exhibited in the museum established by the *Société*.[60] Hence even in positivist Turin, not a cemetery nor a cinerary urn, but the anatomical museum was the place chosen by Giacomini for the preservation of his remains. After the autopsy, his skeleton, brain and other parts of his body were prepared and exhibited in a purpose-made glass case, the cost of which he had personally covered with a legacy.[61]

Figure 13.1 The skeleton of Carlo Giacomini (1840–98) preserved in the Museo di Anatomia Umana Luigi Rolando, Turin.

It was after Giacomini's death that, under the direction of his successor, Romeo Fusari, the anatomical collection of the University of Turin was set up according to the criteria of racial anthropology and biological criminology. A first section of the museum exhibited the skulls of criminals, thereby contradicting the conclusions of the collection's main architect. The second documented the ethnic stratification of the various Italian regions, for the most part using the skulls of conscripts. The third was dedicated to the display of what was openly described as "skulls of negroes and other inferior races"; the fourth and final section was made up of a collection of "skulls of microcephalics, cretins and madmen."[62] Not by chance, the construction was part of the exhibition opened to the public for the sixth international congress of criminal anthropology, held in Turin in 1906 to celebrate the 30th anniversary of Lombroso's tenure in Turin.

Lombroso had made use of the abundant provision of corpses made available by the government to expand his criminal anthropology collection, but in contrast to Giacomini he has not left us—or, more precisely, we have not received, except in a minimal percentage—information on the findings that would allow a secure identification of their provenance. He too, however, wanted to leave his body to science, an extremely contentious gesture hostile towards traditional religions and evidence of a faith in a socialist neo-Christian future, a civil religion with a scientific background that Lombroso proposed as a solution to the emergence of virulent anti-Semitism.[63] Embittered by the discrediting of criminal anthropology, Lombroso intended to transform his museum into a mausoleum, preparing it for the moment when unkind Italy would finally recognise the greatness of her son. Not only did he follow in great detail the dispositions of Giacomini's will with regard to his corpse, except for his decision to leave a cash donation, but he added the desire that a portion of his cerebral matter be examined under the microscope, as indicated by the new research perspective that was opening up for brain studies, perhaps in the hope that the small tissue sample would provide irrefutable evidence of his genius.

Notes

1. Michel Vovelle, *La mort et l'Occident de 1300 à nos jours* (Paris: Gallimard, 1983), 530; Anne Carol, "Prêtre et médicins face à la mort et aux mourants en France, XIXe–1e moitié du XXe siècle," *Rives mediterranéennes* 22 (2005): 1–5; Marzio Barbagli, *Alla fine della vita. Morire in Italia e in altri paesi occidentali* (Bologna: Il Mulino, 2018), 51–61 and 130–37.
2. Diego Carnevale, *L'affare dei morti. Mercato funerario, politica e gestione della sepoltura a Napoli (secoli XVII–XIX)* (Rome: École française de Rome, 2014), 473–74.
3. Carnevale, *L'affare dei morti*, 418–63; Angela Capellaro Siletti, "I cimiteri," in *Milleottocentoquarantotto. Torino, l'Italia, l'Europa*, ed. Umberto Levra and Rosanna Roccia (Turin: Archivio storico della Città di Torino,

1998), 217–22; Maria Giuffré, Fabio Mangone, Sergio Pace and Ornella Selvafolta, eds., *L'architettura della memoria in Italia. Cimiteri, monumenti e città 1750–1939* (Milan: Skira, 2007); Cristina Ciancio, "Requiescant in pace. Alcune osservazioni sulla protezione del cadavere nel Regno d'Italia," *Historia et ius* 10 (2016): 3–15.

4. Silvia De Renzi, Marco Bresadola and Maria Conforti, "Pathological Dissections in Earl Modern Europe: Practice and Knowledge," in *Pathology in Practice. Disease and Dissections in Early Modern Europe*, ed. Silvia De Renzi, Marco Bresadola and Maria Conforti (London: Routledge, 2018), 3–19.

5. Silvio Solero, *Storia dell'Ospedale maggiore di San Giovanni Battista e della Città di Torino* (Turin: O. Falciola, 1959), 116 and 130–31; David Gentilcore, "Poor Relief, Enlightenment and the Protomedicato of Parma, 1748–1820," in *Health Care and Poor Relief in 18th and 19th Century Southern Europe*, ed. Ole Peter Grell, Andrew Cunningham and Bernd Roeck (Aldershot: Ashgate, 2005), 201; Andrew Cunningham, *The Anatomist Anatomis'd. An Experimental Discipline in Enlightenment Europe* (Farnham: Ashgate, 2010), 111.

6. Cunningham, *The Anatomist Anatomis'd*, 99–100 and 380–83; Marco Bresadola, "The Problems of Anatomia Practica and How to Solve Them: Pathological Dissection Around 1700," in *Pathology in Practice*, De Renzi, Bresadola and Conforti, 56–74.

7. Cunningham, *The Anatomist Anatomis'd*, 225–27 and 231–32.

8. Elizabeth Hurren and Steve King, "'Begging for a Burial': Form, Function and Conflict in Nineteenth-Century Pauper Burial," *Social History* 30 (2005): 321–41.

9. Elizabeth Hurren, "Whose Body Is It Anyway? Trading the Dead Poor, Coroner's Disputes, and the Business of Anatomy at Oxford University, 1885–1929," *Bulletin of the History of Medicine* 82 (2008): 775–818.

10. Giacomo Sangalli, *La metodica sezione del corpo umano preceduta dalla storia dell'anatomia patologica* (Milan: Tip. Bernardoni, 1875), 23–26 (1st ed. 1865).

11. Luigi De Crecchio, "Sopra un nuovo indirizzo da darsi all'insegnamento ed alla pratica della medicina legale," *Il Morgagni* 9 (1867): 621–41; Sandra Menenteau, "'Un des moyens le plus puissants d'établir la verité': l'autopsie médico-légale selon Fodéré," in *Faire parler les corps. François-Emmanuel Fodéré à la genèse de la médecine legale moderne*, ed. Loraine Chappuis, Frédéric Chauvaud, Marc Ortolani and Michel Porret (forthcoming).

12. Silvano Montaldo, "Università, professioni, pubblico impiego (1814–1859)," *Annali di Storia delle Università italiane* 5 (2001): 119.

13. Archivio storico dell'Università di Torino (henceforth ASUT), Corrispondenza, Carteggio 1857–60, Istituto anatomico, c. 460, letter from the rector to Minister Lanza, 30 July 1858.

14. Barbagli, *Alla fine della vita*, 43.

15. ASUT, Corrispondenza, Carteggio 1857–60, Istituto anatomico, c. 368, lettera from Professor Tomati to the rector, 15 April 1858.

16. Marcella Marmo, "Il prezzo del cadavere. Medici, impiegati, inservienti nell'ospedale degli Incurabili a cavallo dell'Unità," *Quaderni del Dipartimento di Scienze Sociali dell'Istituto Universitario Orientale* 7–8 (1991): 121–57; Carnevale, *L'affare dei morti*, 437, 442 and 455–56.

17. R. *Università degli studi di Torino. Discorso inaugurale e Annuario Accademico 1877–78* (Turin: Stamperia Reale di Torino, 1878), 124–25; R. *Università degli studi di Torino. Annuario Accademico per l'anno 1886–87* (Turin: Stamperia Reale di Torino, 1887), 196–97.

18. Ariane Dröscher, *Le facoltà medico-chirurgiche italiane (1860–1915). Repertorio delle cattedre e degli stabilimenti annessi, dei docenti, dei liberi docenti e del personale scientifico* (Bologna: Clueb, 2002), 25–28.

19. Giovanni Battista Arnaudo, "Torino nella vita pubblica," in *Torino 1880* (Turin: Roux e Favale, 1880), 622 and 626; *Conferenza del 18 dicembre per l'applicazione del regolamento per la consegna dei cadaveri alle Scuole Chirurgiche ed Anatomiche secondo il Regio Decreto 28 ottobre 1885* (Turin: 1886), 5–7.

20. L. Romanelli, *Rendiconto statistico etiologico, climatico e terapeutico degli infermi spediti e curati nell'ospedale della Conocchia* (Naples: n.p, 1881), 24.

21. Archivio storico della Città di Torino (henceforth ASCT), Affari stato civile, 1885, c. 55, letter from the mayor of Padua to the mayor of Turin, 7 January 1885.

22. ASCT, Affari stato civile, 1886, c. 56, letter from the mayor of Genoa to the mayor of Turin, 30 January 1886.

23. Cristina Ciancio, *Il momento della morte come evento giuridico. Definire, tutelare, gestire fra Ottocento e primo Novecento* (Bologna: Bononia University Press, 2017), 74–84 and 134–38.

24. *Conferenza*, 2.

25. Ciancio, *Il momento della morte*, 13–72.

26. Archivio storico dell'Istituto di Anatomia normale, Turin (henceforth ASIAT), Corrispondenza istituto, Circular from the General Directorate for Prisons to the provincial prefects, 14 September 1883.

27. Cesare Lombroso, "Il mio museo criminale," *L'Illustrazione italiana* 33 (1 April 1906), 302.

28. *Conferenza*, 2.

29. Augusto Tamburini, "Lettera aperta all'on. Comm. Beltrani-Scalia," in *L'antropologia nelle carceri*, ed. Augusto Tamburini and Giulio C. Benelli (Rome: Tipografia delle Mantellate, 1885), 3–5.

30. Ezio Sciamanna, *Guida nelle ricerche anatomiche e antropologiche sui cadaveri dei condannati* (Rome: Tipografia delle Mantellate, 1884), 3–4.

31. Ezio Sciamanna, *Sur l'opportunité d'établir des regles pour les recherches d'anthropométrie et de psychologie criminelles dans les hopitaux d'aliénés et dans les prisons*, Actes du deuxième congrès internationale d'Anthropologie criminelle. *Biologie et sociologie (Paris, août 1889)* (Lyon: A. Storck – G. Masson, 1890), 36–41.

32. "*Discussion*," ibid., 265–68.

33. Ciancio, "Requiescant in pace," 6.

34. Archivio del Museo di Antropologia criminale "Cesare Lombroso," Turin, letter from Edwin Goodall to Lombroso, 20 June 1896.

35. Martino Beltrani-Scalia, *Relazione al Regolamento Generale per gli Stabilimenti Carcerari e per i Riformatori Governativi del Regno del 1891* (Rome: Tipografia delle Mantellate, 1957), 86–87.

36. "Regolamento per la consegna dei cadaveri alle Scuole anatomiche," *Gazzetta ufficiale del Regno d'Italia* 294 (3 December 1885): 5579–80.

37. Carnevale, *L'affare dei morti*, 167–76 and 451.

38. Paolo Frascani, *Ospedale e società in età liberale* (Bologna: Il Mulino, 1986), 97 and 184–90; Barbagli, *Alla fine della vita*, 62–65.

39. See Renata Allio, *Società di mutuo soccorso in Piemonte, 1850–1880. Attività economica. Gestione amministrativa. Ambiente sociale* (Turin: Deputazione subalpina di storia patria, 1980), 76–77 and the essays in Grell, Cunningham and Roeck, *Health Care and Poor Relief* by: Martin Papenheim, "The Pope, the Beggar, the Sick, and the Brotherhoods: Health Care and Poor Relief in 18th and 19th Century Rome," 175–80; Brigitte Marin,

"Poverty, Relief and Hospitals in Naples in the 18th and 19th Centuries," 216; Gianna Pomata, *Medicine for the Poor in 18th and 19th Century Bologna*, 235–36.

40. Barbagli, *Alla fine della vita*, 43.
41. ASUT, Corrispondenza, Carteggio, Istituto anatomico, 1883–84, c. 4.11, letter from the sector head to the principal of the faculty of medicine, 18 December 1883.
42. Stefano Merli, *Proletariato di fabbrica e capitalismo industriale. Il caso italiano 1880–1900* (Florence: La nuova Italia, 1972), 390.
43. Minutes of the meeting of 21 June 1897, in *Atti del Consiglio comunale di Torino* (Turin: 1897).
44. Frascani, *Ospedale e società*, 130.
45. *Conferenza*, 4.
46. Giorgio Anselmi, "Relazione delle cose più notevoli accadute durante l'anno scolastico 1885–86 nella R. Università di Torino," in *R. Università degli studi di Torino*, 8.
47. Emma, *Una fra tante* (Milan: G. Brigola, 1878), 35.
48. Barbagli, *Alla fine della vita*, 50–51.
49. *Deliberazioni della Giunta Municipale di Torino. Regolamento dei cimiteri e del servizio funebre* (2 June 1886).
50. Ciancio, "Requiescant in pace," 10–15.
51. *Regolamento speciale di polizia mortuaria* (Rome: Tipografia delle Mantellate, 1891), 13–14.
52. ASIAT, Corrispondenza istituto, *Regolamento per le sezioni cadaveriche relative alle cliniche* (7 February 1892).
53. Giacomo Giacobini, Cristina Cilli and Giancarla Malerba, "Il Museo di Anatomia umana," in *La memoria della scienza. Musei e collezioni dell'Università di Torino*, ed. Giacomo Giacobini (Turin: Fondazione CRT, 2003), 143–54.
54. ASIAT, [C. Giacomini], *Cenni sullo stato attuale dell'Istituto di Anatomia normale della Regia Università di Torino* (Turin: n.d. but after 1898).
55. Guido Abbattista, *Umanità in mostra. Esposizioni etniche e invenzioni esotiche in Italia (1880–1940)* (Trieste: Università di Trieste, 2013), 235.
56. Silvano Montaldo, "The Relics of Two 19th- Century Scientists. Carlo Giacomini and Cesare Lombroso," in *Savant Relics. Brains and Remains of Scientists*, ed. Marco Beretta, Maria Conforti and Paolo Mazzarello (Sagamore Beach: Watson Publishing International, 2016), 190–92.
57. Giacomo Giacobini, Cristina Cilli and Giancarla Malerba, "Carlo Giacomini, His 'New Process for Preserving the Brain' and the Dispute with Lombroso Over 'Criminal Brains'," in *Lorenzo Tenchini and His Masks: An Anatomical Clinical Collection of the Late 19th Century at the Universities of Parma and Turin*, ed. Roberto Toni, Elena Bassi, Silvano Montaldo and Alessandro Porro (Milan: Skira, 2016), 33–37.
58. Bresadola, "The Problems of Anatomia Practica," 56–58.
59. Jennifer Michael Hecht, *The End of the Soul. Scientific Modernity, Atheism, and Anthropology in France, 1876–1936* (New York: Columbia University press, 2003), 7–20.
60. Ibid., 29–39.
61. Montaldo, "The Relics of Two 19th-Century Scientists," 186–89.
62. ASIAT, Museo di Anatomia umana, registri dei reperti conservati in museo, c. 9.74, Skulls Held by the Turin Anatomical Museum (July 1902).
63. Montaldo, "The Relics of Two 19th- Century Scientists," 194–99.

14 Simulacra of Eternal Life
Ostensions, Exhibitions and the Concealment of Human Remains

Maria Teresa Milicia

Introduction

> *. . . neither doth corruption inherit incorruption . . . the trumpet shall*
> *sound, and the dead shall be raised incorruptible, and we shall be changed*
> (1 Corinthians 15, 50–53)

This chapter presents reflections on ongoing changes in the social practice of publicly displaying human remains in Italy, both in the ceremonial
form of the ostension of relics of the bodies of saints and in the museum
context of exhibiting scientific collections of human remains. This juxtaposition of cases involving religious and scientific practices is aimed at
exploring certain emerging trends in attitudes towards death and, specifically, in the relationship with the dead mediated by the material presence of the corpse or remains. The ostension of the body of Saint Pio of
Pietrelcina in the sanctuary of San Giovanni Rotondo in Puglia on 23
April 2008, 40 years after his death and almost ten after his canonisation
(2 May 1999), is at the centre of the first part of this reflection.[1]

The focal point of the spectacularity of the event was aimed at the
incorruptible nature of Saint Pio's body—one of the miraculous signs
codified in the Catholic tradition of the cult of saints[2]—despite the fact
that the apparently extraordinary state of preservation of the corpse was
the product of the aesthetic performativity of a silicone mask. The placing of masks on the face of relics of saints was nothing new: the use of
wax masks, obtained from plaster casts of the deceased's face with a significant degree of likeness, emerged gradually, starting at least in the late
nineteenth century.[3] The artifice of waxwork, derived from the Baroque
period, reveals the dissimulation in the act of transfiguring the earthly
image of a venerable body. But in the case of Saint Pio, which for the
moment is unique, the aesthetic force of the perfect imitation obtained
through the use of silicone annihilates the presence of the mask and the
signs of death that it covers.

Was this a radical break with the Catholic tradition of the cult of relics, famous for the veneration of skeletal and mummified saints that

"shockingly transport you to what feels like a dark and primitive living past"?[4] Is it a confirmation that exemplifies the "denial of death" supposedly widespread in Western societies? The idea that this attitude is pervasive has been a mainstay of the social critique of modernity since the 1950s,[5] but it is undoubtedly controversial and debated due to its excessive reductionism, which has conveyed and perpetuated the widespread idea of a "taboo of death" in Western societies and has been used to explain a disparate number of social phenomena.[6] The by now obsolete picture of the linear logic and temporality of the interdiction of death has given way to a tangle of contrasting tendencies, some of which appear to be radically opposed to the underlying premise. The spectacular centrality of the proliferation of images of corpses in popular entertainment (including even documentaries depicting the various stages of the decomposition of bodies) and in artistic productions forms a picture of cultural production involving subtler *dispositifs* of negating the experience of death.[7]

My intention, within the limits of this chapter, is to interpret the instances of this denial as forces operating within a wider complex of strategies of immortality that "incorporate" the corpse in performative actions (especially but not always visual) that counter the destructive violence of death. In this perspective, I examine the use of masks and their sensorial impact of "incorruptibility" in the ostension ceremonies of Saint Pio and of Saint Leopold Mandić in Rome in 2016, in contrast to the skeletal "nakedness" of the relic of Saint Anthony of Padua, which was exposed to the devotion of the faithful in 2010. I will go on to examine the technological surrogates of incorruptible corpses, from the "real" face of Saint Anthony created from anthropometric measurements of his skull to the digital resurrection of Egyptian mummies and extinct human species through the miraculous art of silicone. At the conclusion of the article, I will pause briefly to consider the controversial question of the exhibition of human remains in museums, which serves as an example of how the places and practices of their ostension or concealment can become a battleground for opposing conceptions of immortality.

Vi Divinitatis Adversus Naturae Decreta Pugnante

Corpses that have been miraculously saved from decomposition have been a recurring theme in hagiographic tradition since the spread of the cult of relics in the medieval period. The model is the glorious body of Christ, *a putrefatione servatu* (saved from corruption), which rose from the dead on the third day. However, it was during the Catholic Counter-Reformation that the notion that bodies preserved from decay were a sign of saintliness returned with new force. The Protestant condemnation of the "superstitious craving for relics," which culminated in the destruction of human remains exhibited in German churches—"the sacred bones were first mocked and then vandalised"[8]—contributed to the forming of an enduring alliance between the power of medicine and that of the Catholic Church in setting the boundaries between the natural and supranatural, beyond which miracles break into the world.

In the seventeenth century, thanks to anatomical knowledge acquired through post-mortem examinations of corpses, medical science was able to provide religious authorities with criteria for ascertaining the state of preservation of the remains of the beatified. Instances of "real" incorruptibility of bodies, declared miraculous thanks to the certification of medical examination, were held in high regard. The need to distinguish the true from the false stemmed from the practice of embalming the bodies of saints, widespread during the medieval period, especially in monasteries, which prompted a process of extending the symbols of incorruptibility from bone relics to entire bodies.[9] In particular, "the aromatic quality of the remains" became "one of the more densely metaphorical images of the perfect condition of the beatified":[10] the odour emanating from the bodies of saints, which contrasted with the fetid smell of putrefaction, was a manifestation of divine power over the laws of nature.[11] To this day signs of miraculous non-decomposition continue to exert extraordinary rhetorical strength in discourses on holiness initiated by the mass media. It is in fact the experts called to carry out the recognition of the bodies of saints—a true secret ritual of a medico-religious kind—who in numerous interviews reveal the miraculous details of the bodies' state of preservation. The popular expectations of signs of the incorruptibility of the flesh, an anticipation of the resurrection of bodies in eternal life, are given confirmation by the scientific attestation of the miracle.

The Congregation for the Causes of Saints—whose rules require the medical certification of the authenticity of miracles of healing that are essential for advancing the process of beatification and canonisation—and the well-known *Bureau de constatation medical* based in Lourdes both typify this alliance of powers conspiring against death.[12]

During the Extraordinary Jubilee of Mercy announced by Pope Francis in 2015, the new spectacular ceremony for the ostension of the Saint of Pietrelcina in Rome focused media attention on the phenomenon of the uncorrupted body. This time Padre Pio was placed alongside the ostension of the body of another Capuchin friar, Leopold Mandić, who was canonised in 1983 but did not become the object of mass veneration.[13] Of Croat origin, Saint Leopold is much loved above all in the northeast of Italy and in the city of Padua, where he spent most of his life humbly dedicated to welcoming into the confessional of his convent the crowds of penitents seeking the mercy of forgiveness and hope of eternal life.[14] He loved to repeat that "we should pass over the earth like a shadow that leaves no trace," and was the interpreter of a spirituality powerfully oriented towards an otherworldly meaning of life.

Random events have a mysterious cosmic potency and it was purely by chance that Saint Leopold shared the honour of the ostension ceremony with Saint Pio. About a month after the announcement of the Jubilee of Mercy,[15] on 22 April 2015 Father Flaviano Gusella, rector of the Sanctuary of San Leopoldo, took part in a public audience held in Saint Peter's Square. Thanks to a German priest who gave him his place on the front row behind the barriers, Father Flaviano had the privilege of finding himself face to face with the pope: "Holy Father, have you heard of Saint Leopold Mandíc?" he asked; there followed a brief exchange of words that was sealed by the pope declaring: "He will be one of the protectors of the next Holy Year of Mercy!"[16] Only a few days later, the Paduan friars received a phone call from the Vatican informing them that, as expressly desired by the pope, Saint Leopold's remains would be translated to Rome to be shown to the public in Saint Peter's Basilica along with those of Saint Pio.

The friars' surprise and joy were followed by hectic preparation for the examination of the relic, which had never been exposed to the public before the forthcoming ceremony. In 1942 Leopold's confrères had planned to bury him in the bare earth, inside a non-galvanised wooden coffin and without any preservation treatments, as is the normal practice among the Capuchins.[17] However, in deference to the friar's reputation for holiness, the Paduan clergy insisted that a galvanised coffin be used, and in that Father Leopold was laid to rest in a recess in the cemetery of Padua. In 1963 the body was translated into the convent's church and placed in a marble sarcophagus. Following the decree of beatification (2 May 1976), a second inspection of the body was carried out by the professor of anatomy of the University of Padua, Virgilio Meneghelli, who certified its state of natural mummification. The bishop decided to remove a relic from the body to be exposed to the veneration of the faithful, and thus the right hand, with which Father Leopold had bestowed blessings, was therefore placed first in a reliquary and, from 2004 onwards, in a shrine shielded by glass coloured to lessen the visual impact of mummification. The idea of a future ostension of the entire relic was at that time very remote.

The pope's impromptu decision highlighted the problem of the inevitable "aesthetic" comparison with the image of incorruptibility of the face of Saint Pio. The friars of San Giovanni Rotondo, whose advice had been sought by the rector of the Paduan sanctuary, recommended sending for the team of artists from London's Madame Tussaud waxwork museum, which had created Saint Pio's mask. But, after a careful evaluation of the significant work involved and the limited time available, the brothers of San Leopoldo decided to fall back on the experience of Lineo Tabarin, who had created the wax mask and reconstruction of the hands of Pope John XXIII.[18] To match as closely as possible the high-quality results of silicone, Tabarin chose to work with compacted elastic polyurethane, a malleable and versatile material widely used in the production of soft toys. The plaster death mask, made by the sculptor Enrico Parnigotto in 1966, served as a cast.[19] Like a shadow that left no trace even of her name, a nun of Croat origin who was devoted to the saint took care of suffusing the mask with colour and, with a loving touch, refined the details. The work was also supervised by a theatre makeup artist, Donatella Zancanaro.

Saint Leopold, Saint Pio and Saint Anthony

> *He looks like he's asleep. Untouched by death. The atheists of course will say it's a fake. Some kind of wax dummy. For those who understand, no explanation is necessary. For those who don't, none will suffice. Victory to Pio![20]*

When news of an upcoming examination of the body of a saint breaks, journalists lay siege to the experts in charge in the hope of receiving first-hand statements about the body's state of preservation. The enormous popularity of Saint Pio aroused equally enormous expectations on the part of the public, which were fuelled by the information released to the press and television in interviews. One of the articles from 2008 bore the title: "He is perfectly preserved." And the bishop present at the examination, referring to the state of the nails, said, "If Padre Pio would allow, it is as if he had had a manicure."[21] Nazzareno Gabrielli, a consultant appointed by the Congregation for the Causes of the Saints, revealed other details about the corpse's ongoing process of decomposition, saying that "the body was very wet," a disclosure he immediately toned down by mentioning the absence of a "bad smell," which recalled the codified olfactory sign of holiness.[22] The opinion of the expert, a privileged witness to the real conditions of the corpse, that Saint Pio "seemed to be sleeping" summed up the general impression formed before the ostension of the relic.[23]

The media coverage of the examination of the body of Saint Leopold in 2015 (6 October to 30 November), arranged in view of the upcoming ostension of the body in Rome, was limited to the local press in Padua but nevertheless extensive, focusing as it always did on the incorruptibility of the body. As was the case in 1976, pathologists of the University of Padua took charge of the examination, which had "exceptional results" according to Professor Raffaele De Caro, who told of the body's excellent state of preservation. The medical team "did not find before it merely a mummified skeleton": a CT scan of the body revealed "with a certain surprise" the presence of some internal organs that were still intact, including the cerebral hemispheres and part of the heart.[24] The "doctors' surprise" at the results of their examinations admitted the possibility of the phenomenology of miraculous incorruptibility, but this concession was not disclosed to the public. The scientific paper published by the team was more explicit about the exceptional details: the mummification caused by factors that prevent the "natural processes of decomposition" had occurred spontaneously and in the absence of favourable environmental conditions, "moreover, the preservation of the ossicular chains and larynx cartilages is to be highlighted since in his life Saint Leopold exercised for many hours a day the sacrament of confession and absolution through these anatomical structures."[25] In the perspective of the medico-religious tradition of ascertaining signs of "real" incorruptibility, the body of Saint Leopold matched them all, while that of Saint Pio did not.

When on 3 February 2016 the two relics found themselves side by side in the Basilica of San Lorenzo, the first stage of the jubilee ostension ceremony, the centre of the power structure that controls the order of the signs of "true" incorruptibility wavered. Accounts of the event focused on Padre Pio, and hundreds of video cameras and mobile phones were trained on his face.[26] One newspaper article, supplemented by photographs, merely put Saint Leopold in parenthesis: "in these days long queues are 'besieging' the Vatican Basilica to pray before the mortal remains of Saint Pio (and Saint Leopold),"[27] a disrespectful decision in very poor taste to be considered a lapse symptomatic of the visual seduction exercised by the perfection of Pio's simulacrum of eternal life. The technology of incorruptibility had produced the miracle of eternal life through the immanence of the simulation that brings "back from the dead [. . .] his deceased body, incorrupt for nearly half a century now."[28]

In the case of Saint Anthony of Padua, a cult of ancient devotional tradition managed by the Order of Friars Minor Conventual, the ostension was an exceptional event that gave pilgrims the rare opportunity to see the entire relic. The basilica ordinarily displays the saint's mandible and the reliquary containing his uncorrupted tongue, while the other remains lie in a monumental marble sarcophagus on which the devoted place their hands, hoping that the tactile contact will communicate with the power of the sacred.

In February 2010, I was among the pilgrims queuing for the ostension of the relic of Saint Anthony.[29] When we came within sight of the transparent case, I heard a soft murmur around me, not one of prayer, but of discomposure. The sight of the saint's skeleton—an authentic relic of different times—could not fail to arouse perturbation in those familiar with the imagery of the simulacra of the incorrupt body, developed within the newer "aesthetic formations"[30] of the cult of relics.

Yet a few years later, Saint Anthony had also been involved in experimental forms of devotional imagery, thanks to a digital reconstruction of his face "based on the cast of his skull, using the most modern techniques of forensic reconstruction."[31] The project, coordinated by Nicola Carrara of the Institute of Anthropology of the University of Padua in collaboration with the Saint Anthony Centre of Studies, was carried out by experts of the Arc-Team (3D imaging and forensic art) and by the Renato Archer Information Technology Centre (with its multicolour 3D printers).[32] To prevent any iconographic imagery of the Saint prejudicing the objectivity of the result, the forensic artist Cicero Moraes was asked to work on the basis of "essential" anthropometric data—"male, 36 years old and Caucasian"—without knowing the identity of the subject.[33] The operation of bringing back to life the real image of the saint did not, however, receive the unanimous approval of the devoted since the objectivity of the forensic technology was called into question when its results were compared to the iconographic tradition of the saint.[34] Their misgivings might appear to have been a reflection of the usual resistance of believers who are wary of science, but the matter was actually more subtle. The reductionist view of the objectivity of representation based on anthropometric data—the "blindness" to previous images imposed on Moraes is paradigmatic of this—produced a somewhat commonplace object devoid of the expressive force of the "true face" of a saint. After a temporary exhibition at the Museum of Popular Devotion (12–22 June 2014) and in the exhibition "Faces: the thousand faces of humanity," alongside reconstructions of the "real faces" of other famous people,[35] the "living" simulacrum of Saint Anthony discreetly left the scene.

Sacred Material

Silicone is a resistant and malleable compound that is extremely versatile and suited to the most disparate of uses. In addition to it being used to make the prostheses used in reconstructive and aesthetic surgery, the recent advance of 3D printers that can reproduce objects from digital models has made possible other sophisticated, innovative applications, such as the creation of anatomical models for use in neurovascular surgical simulation.[36] A material used in the "malleable anatomies" of the digital era, silicone restores the dream that waxwork could create perfect and lasting anatomical reproductions, which became obsolete when techniques of preserving corpses enabled the emergence of new ways to represent the human body.[37]

The potential of the use of silicone is evidenced by the success of renewed collaboration between artistic disciplines and scientific technologies that bring back to life the likenesses of mummified bodies and even remains of fossil "samples" from millions of years ago. In the Altamura Man Museum we are welcomed by the good-natured model of Ciccillo, a Neanderthal who lived in Puglia (as did Saint Pio) 30,000 years ago, while in the archaeological museum of South Tyrol we meet Ötzi, fixed in concentration on his everyday concerns of 3,000 years ago, unaware that his "real" mummified body rests nearby, barely visible behind the thick porthole of a refrigerated chamber. By visiting the online gallery of paleosculptures by the artists Adrie and Alfons Kennis and Elisabeth Daynès,[38] we step into the "miraculous" dimension of hyperreality. "Artistic imitation is, as it happens, a paradoxical notion: it disappears at the very moment that it achieves perfection,"[39] for by achieving perfection, the principle of imitation gives way to that of simulation, which in turn removes the original referent from the image and makes it "dangerously" open to new meanings.[40]

Simulation acts as a cosmic force for creating new worlds that challenge the clear-cut separation between appearance and reality, between the natural and the artificial, between the authentic and the false, and between the living body and the dead body. Only apparently questioning the principles of "Western rationality." The demiurgical power of technological rationalism is able to act directly on the code-matrix of all meanings. The creation of a synthetic DNA with an eight-letter code and the facility of genetic manipulation using the CRISPR (Clustered Regularly Interspaced Short Palindromic Repeats) technique constitute the (hyper)rational product of controlling the potential of life simulation.[41] As Foltyn has written, "as modern biotechnical societies continue to decode the secret of life and birth, it could be that one day those who have access to this death-taming technology will view the corpse as an anachronism, a relic of an era when people die."[42]

This prospect—the exploration of the new symbolic forms created by the artists of hyperrealism—has been evoked by Patricia Piccinini and Sam Jinks among others. By utilising the techniques of digital reproduction of the models and the incorruptible malleability of silicone, their sculptures reintroduce the shadow of death that the simulation of life erases.[43] In this context, the treatment of the relic of Padre Pio sets the standard. The mask-simulacrum—the immortal mask of immortality[44]—obliterates the signs of death when it absorbs the saint's dead body into the appearance of a single sacred material. The innovative choice of the silicone mask does not differ from the entrepreneurial tradition of the cult of relics that has always exploited "the omnipotence of the simulacrum"[45] to make immortality strategies effective and to successfully mediate the symbolic exchange between the living and the dead. Especially for the living who will continue to die.

Conclusions: *Detestandae Spectaculis de Mortuis?*

At the same time that the spectacular display of simulacra of eternal life continues to pervade the global imagination,[46] there has emerged with force the need for a cross-cultural ethic that opposes the public exhibition of human remains in museums, from anatomical and anthropological collections to the ancient mummies that visitors nevertheless enjoy seeing. Exhibited in the context of the "naked truth" of scientific artefacts, skulls, pieces of anatomy and mummified remains can become upsetting and disturbing signs, being of the same substance as the corpse and therefore revealing the triumph of death over life. The treatment of anatomical samples arrests the decomposition of the corpse, preserving them like relics, but in contrast to relics (except in certain rare significant exceptions),[47] which are made to celebrate the exemplary lives of the saints to whom they belonged, their treatment renders irrelevant the biographical uniqueness of the deceased. The reduction of human beings to inert substances is a reminder of the corpse, without face and without mask: only a strong symbolic order can tame the uncontrolled proliferation of its power of signification and limit its "improper" use.

In recent decades the successful activism of movements aimed at repatriating the human remains of indigenous people,[48] strengthened by the passing of Native American Grave Protection and Repatriation Act (NAGPRA) in the United States, has liberated the dead from the control of the symbolic order of the bio-anthropological and biomedical sciences established on the ethics of pursuing the wellbeing of humanity. Consequently, not only museum exhibitions, but also the very existence of scientific collections of human remains, display the genealogy of the "contemporary form of subjugation of life to the power of death," the "necropolitics" that characterises the expansion of Western civilisation and on which its global hegemony is founded.[49] In these terms, the promise of delaying death is only a mask that hides the historical connivance with the sovereign power of the biosciences, in particular racial science. The space of the museum loses the authority of representation, quickly becoming the signifier of the presentification of colonial thanatopolitics, an experiment that leads to the extermination camp.[50]

The struggle for the return of the dead to their original communities takes on the value of a reversibility of the past, the possibility of re-appropriating the symbolic exchange with the dead, guarantors of the continuity of the death-regeneration cycle of life. This is not about a change of attitudes or sensibilities in the face of the ostensive signs of the corpse,[51] but rather of the conflict for the reaffirmation of the sovereignty of symbolic control over strategies of immortality.

The use of corpses in the history of biomedical sciences, the many different preservation methods aimed at understanding the human body up to the point of dismembering it into spare parts for transplant surgery also refers back to the same symbolic death-regeneration relationship of life. On reflection, the obscenity of exhibition concerns the unsustainable awareness of the incessant work of the "sacrificial machine," the "necro-power" of the technologies governing life and death from which no living society manages to escape.

Notes

1. See Maria Teresa Milicia "Tecnologie della carne incorruttibile: maschera di santità e maschera di bellezza," in *RelativaMente. Nuovi territori scientifici e proposte antropologiche*, ed. Luigi M. Lombardi Satriani (Rome: Armando editore, 2010), 248–53.

2. Please note that in the current official provisions (2017) on the treatment of the bodies of the beatified and of saints during the process of canonisation there is no mention of the "miracle" of incorruptibility, see "Relics in the Church: Authenticity and Preservation," www.causesanti.va/content/causadeisanti/it/documenti/le-reliquie-nella-chiesa_en.html.

3. In the Christian era, the use of funeral casts is attested starting from the fourteenth century, see Philippe Ariès, *L'Homme devant la mort* (Paris: éd. du Seuil, 1977), 255–57. The use of metal or wax masks to cover the face of saints is not subject to official regulations.

4. This was the comment by the art critic Jonathan Jones in his column for the Guardian newspaper: "From St Peter's bones to severed heads: Christian relics on display," *The Guardian*, 18 November 2013, www.theguardian.com/artanddesign/jonathanjonesblog/2013/nov/18/st-peters-bones-christian-relics.

5. Starting with Geoffrey Gorer, "The Pornography of Death," *Encounter* (October 1955): 49–52, which made explicit references to the obscenity of corpses and the horror aroused by decomposition in the Anglo-Saxon context, and followed by the pamphlet by the journalist Jessica Mitford, *The American Ways of Death* (New York: Simon & Schuster, 1963) against the funeral-home sector and the use of theatre makeup on bodies, the American model became paradigmatic (and paradoxical) of the Western denial. Essential references include Ariès, *L'Homme devant la mort*, who followed across the centuries the changes of attitudes towards death, from "domesticated death" to "wild death," culminating in the new model of medicalised death and the expulsion of the dead from the domestic space; Michel Vovelle, *La mort et l'Occident de 1300 à nos jours* (Paris: Gallimard, 1983), who was more cautious, did not share the reductive idea of the taboo, and invited readers to consider discourses of death as a metaphor that revealed a general social malaise; Louis-Vincent Thomas, *Anthropologie de la mort* (Paris: Payot, 1975), contrasts the "good death" of African societies to the "beautiful death" of the West, with an implicit analogy between the civilisations of the past and "primitive" societies; Richard Huntington and Peter Metcalf, *Celebrations of Death: The Anthropology of Mortuary Ritual* (Cambridge: Cambridge University Press, 1979) relativise the *American Deathways* in a broad-ranging comparison; Luigi M. Lombardi Satriani and Mariano Meligrana, *Il ponte di San Giacomo. L'ideologia della morte nella società contadina del Sud* (Palermo: Sellerio, 1982); Alfonso M. Di Nola, *La nera signora: antropologia della morte e del lutto* (Rome: Newton Compton, 1996) also tackle the subject of the "negation of death." The most incisive critique of the use of the opposition "us-others" in the primitivist construction of "our" past comes from Johannes Fabian, "How Others Die—Reflections on the Anthropology of Death," *Social Research* 39, no. 3 (Autumn 1972): 543–67; see also Adriano Favole, *Resti di umanità. Vita sociale del corpo dopo la morte* (Rome-Bari: Laterza, 2003), 18–21.

6. Recent sociological investigations also criticise generic reductionism, see Marzio Barbagli, *Alla fine della vita. Morire in Italia e in altri paesi occidentali* (Bologna: Il Mulino, 2018).

7. Jacque Lynn Foltyn, "Dead Famous and Dead Sexy: Popular Culture, Forensics, and the Rise of the Corpse," *Mortality* 13 (2008): 153–73 and 164.

8. Paul Koudonaris, *Heavenly Bodies: Cult Treasures & Spectacular Saints form the Catacombs* (New York: Thames & Hudson, 2013), 23 and 150–77. On "Protestantism and the new iconoclasm," see Charles Freeman, *Holy Bones, Holy Dust. How Relics Shaped the History of Medieval Europe* (New Haven, CT: Yale University Press, 2011), 228–46; Alexandra Walshman,

"Skeletons in the Cupboard: Relics After the English Reformation," *Past and Present*, Supplement 5 (2010): 121–43.

9. Katharine Park, "The Criminal and the Saintly Body: Autopsy and Dissection in Renaissance Italy," *Renaissance Quarterly* 47, no. 1 (1994): 1–33; Park, "Holy Autopsies. Saintly Bodies and Medical Expertise, 1300–1600," in *The Body in Early Modern Italy*, ed. Julia Hairston and Walter Stephens (Baltimore: Johns Hopkins University Press, 2010), 61–73; Ezio Fulcheri, "Mummies of Saints: A Particular Category of Italian Mummies," in *Human Mummies: A Global Survey of Their Status and the Techniques of Conservation*, ed. Konrad Spindler et al. (Vienna: Springer-Verlag, 1996), 219–30; Giorgio Di Gangi et al., "La tanatometamorfosi in età medievale: un problema da definire," in *Morte e trasformazione dei corpi. Interventi di tanatometamòrfosi*, ed. Francesco Remotti (Milan: Bruno Mondadori, 2006), 115–36.

10. Marino Niola, *Sui palchi delle stelle. Napoli, il sacro, la scena* (Rome: Meltemi, 1995), 134.

11. Paolo Zacchia, a doctor from Rome, in *Quaestionum Medico-Legalium*, 4th ed. (Avignon: Ex Typographia Ioannis Piot, 1654), in the chapter "De Miraculis," tackles the question *De cadaverum incorruptibilitate* (235–40): "At vera cadaveris incorruptibilitas est inter miracula magnae considerationis" (239§30)—"corpora Sanctorum, cum coetera foeteant, bene olere ob id creditum est, vi Divinitatis adversus naturae decreta pugnante." (240§38). Regarding Zacchia's treatise, see Ariès, *L'Homme devant la mort*, 347 and 353. Bishop Caroli Felici De Matta Cremonensis entrusted himself to the medical criteria proposed by Zacchia for discerning the miracle of incorruptibility compared to the preservation of corpses by natural or artificial causes in his *Novissimus de sanctorum canonizatione tractatus in quinque partus diversus . . .*, "De Incorruptione," caput XIV, 187–91 (Rome: Typis & Sumptibus Nicolai Angeli Tinaffij,1678). The same was done by Prospero Lambertini, *De servorum Dei beatificazione et beatorum canonizatione*, 1840 ed., synopsis book IV (Bologna: Longhi, 1734–38), 270–76. In *Synopsim redacta ab Emm. De Azevedo S. J. Sacrorum rituum consultore* (Brussels: Typis societatis belgicae de propagandis bonis libris administratore C.J. de Mat, 1840) see Lucia Dacome, *Malleable Anatomies: Models, Makers, and Material Culture in Eighteenth-Century Italy* (Oxford: Oxford University Press, 2017), 24–55.

12. See Clara Gallini, *Il miracolo e la sua prova: un etnologo a Lourdes* (Naples: Liguori, 1998).

13. A visit to the respective websites of the two pilgrimage cults illustrates their different levels of popularity: www.leopoldomandic.it/index.php and www.conventosantuariopadrepio.it/it/home/ (showing the famous church designed by the star architect Renzo Piano).

14. "La vita del santo," www.leopoldomandic.it/index.php/san-leopoldo/la-vita-del-santo.

15. Holy See Press Office, "Information provided to the Media on the occasion of the announcement of the 'Jubilee of Mercy'," 13 March 2015, https://press.vatican.va/content/salastampa/it/bollettino/pubblico/2015/03/13/0187/00419.html.

16. For the full story, see Flaviano G. Gusella, "Sarà uno dei protettori del prossimo Anno Santo della Misericordia," *Portavoce di San Leopoldo Mandić* 7 (September–October 2015): 7–9.

17. The practices of mummification used by the Capuchins in Palermo (see chapter by Natale Spineto in this volume) are an exception. The practice of desiccating corpses in putridaria (strainer rooms) in order to turn them into skeletons was widespread in many monastic orders in the post-classical

age to the modern age in Italy and Europe: see Roberta Fusco, "Putridaria (strainer rooms) and Draining Practices of the Bodies: Anthropology of Death in the Modern Age," in *The Archaeology of Death*, ed. Edward Herring and Eóin O'Donoghue (Oxford: Archaeopress, 2018), 532–41.

18. The wax presented a problem: during the ostension of the relic of Pope John XXIII in 2018, the hands began to melt after the plexiglass display case was exposed to the sun: www.ilfattoquotidiano.it/2018/05/25/papa-giovanni-xxiii-la-salma-nella-sua-bergamo-le-mani-di-cera-deformate-dal-caldo-durante-il-viaggio/4380931/.

19. At the time of the first recognition of the body and not at the time of death, as usually occurs.

20. Comment on the video "Arrivo di San Pio alla Basilica di San Lorenzo," published 3 February 2016, www.youtube.com/watch?v=AThjqoMLpU0. Unfortunately, the video is no longer available.

21. "Esumato il corpo di Padre Pio. 'E' conservato perfettamente'," *La Repubblica*, 3 March 2008, www.repubblica.it/2008/01/sezioni/cronaca/padre-pio-riesumato/condizioni-corpo/condizioni-corpo.html. Commemorative video: "10 anni fa l'esumazione del corpo di Padre Pio," *PadrePio tv* YouTube channel, published 28 February 2018, www.youtube.com/watch?v=CUS1qo76s9E.

22. Saverio Gaeta, "Padre Pio. 'Sembrava addormentato'. Intervista a Nazzareno Gabrielli," *Famiglia Cristiana online* (27 April 2008), www.stpauls.it/fc08/0817fc/0817fc94.htm.

23. Ibid; see also the interview: "Nazzareno Gabrielli, perito biochimico Tribunale Cause dei Santi, racconta l'ispezione al corpo incorrotto di Padre Pio," *Tv2000it* YouTube channel, published 8 March 2018, www.youtube.com/watch?v=j3uS1eGcmEI.

24. Felice Paduano, "San Leopoldo Mandic, intatte parti del cuore e del cervello," *Il Mattino di Padova*, 11 December 2015, https://mattinopadova.gelocal.it/padova/cronaca/2015/12/11/news/san-leopoldo-mandic-intatti-parti-del-cuore-e-del-cervello-1.12601325#gallery-slider=undefined%20http://.

25. Veronica Macchi et al., "Friar Leopold Mandić (1866–1942): The Computed Tomography of the Body of a Saint," *Surgical and Radiologic Anatomy* 40 (2018): 967–75, www.ncbi.nlm.nih.gov/pubmed/29948041.

26. As already mentioned, and perhaps not by coincidence, the most significant videos, none of which were professional but filmed by the faithful participating in the event, have been removed. Those remaining are: "San Pio e San Leopoldo—Basilica di S. Lorenzo fuori le mura, Roma," *Stefano Mattii* YouTube channel, published 3 February 2016, www.youtube.com/watch?v=tEXUUaBcD3Q; "Spoglie di San Pio e San Leopoldo—Basilica San Lorenzo fuori le mura," *Scatenate La Gioia* YouTube channel, published 6 February 2016, www.youtube.com/watch?v=1xMIWruySIQ.

27. Particularly the photo gallery: "Corpo quasi integro Sul volto una Maschera," *Il Tempo*, 8 February 2016, www.iltempo.it/cronache/2016/02/08/gallery/corpo-quasi-integro-sul-volto-una-maschera-1001144/.

28. Ricardo Saludo, "Padre Pio, God and the devil," *The Manila Times*, 25 September 2016, www.manilatimes.net/padre-pio-god-and-the-devil/287761/.

29. "Ostensione del Corpo di Sant'Antonio 2010," *Patrick Robles* YouTube channel, published 12 May 2011, www.youtube.com/watch?v=HYGiHmbWYQY.

30. Instead of "aesthetic community," opposed to "ethic community" in the definition of Zygmunt Bauman, *Community: Seeking Safety in an Insecure World* (Cambridge: Polity Press, 2000), I welcome the proposal of Birgit Meyer, "Introduction. From Imagined Communities to Aesthetic Formations: Religious Mediations, Sensational Forms, and Styles of Binding," in

Aesthetic Formations: Media, Religion, and the Senses, ed. Birgit Meyer (New York: Palgrave Macmillan, 2009), 1–30 and 5–7. In the background is the fundamental role of new media: see for example the images shared in various Facebook groups linked to Saint Pio with millions of followers: www.facebook.com/DevotidiPadrePio/photos/a.134826989870590/246718 3186634947/?type=3&theater, *Devoti di Padre Pio* Facebook group, posted 24 May 2019.

31. "Ricostruzione del volto di Sant'Antonio," *Mostra FACCE* YouTube channel, published 12 June 2014, www.youtube.com/watch?v=xcgx9HQicMs.

32. The complete technical documentation is available on the blog: http://arc-team-open-research.blogspot.com/2016/06/.

33. The racial lexicon of the forensic identification of the corpse makes the analogy with crime fiction compelling, as highlighted by the press. "Svelato il volto del Santo: ecco Antonio in 3D," *Il Mattino di Padova*, 11 June 2014, https://mattinopadova.gelocal.it/padova/foto-e-video/2014/06/11/fotogalleria/svelato-il-volto-del-santo-ecco-antonio-in-3d-1.9402960#1.

34. The only video (in English) with comments that have not been disabled is: "What Did St. Anthony of Padua Look Like? 3D Technology Gives Us a Glimpse," *Rometv* YouTube channel, published 11 June 2014, www.you tube.com/watch?v=SaR88gApdVI.

35. From Petrarch, who welcomed visitors reciting his verses, to the face taken from a mummy of an Egyptian priest assassinated 2,300 years ago: "Facce. I molti volti della storia umana" (Padua, Botanical Garden, 15 November 2014–13 December 2015), see: Alessandro Bezzi et al., ' "FACCE. I molti volti della storia umana. Una mostra Open Source," *Archeologia e Calcolatori* 8 (2016): 271–79.

36. Justin Ryan, Kaith Almefty, Peter Nakaj and David H. Frakes, "Cerebral Aneurysm Clipping Surgery Simulation Using Patient-Specific 3D Printing and Silicone Casting," *World Neurosurgery* 88 (April 2016): 175–81.

37. Dacome, *Malleable Anatomies*, 254–59; Fabio Zampieri, Francesco Comacchio and Alberto Zanatta, "Ophthalmologic Wax Models as an Educational Tool for 18th-Century Vision Scientists," *Acta Oftalmologica* 95, no. 8 (December 2017): 852–57; Erich Brenner, "Human Body Preservation—Old and New Techniques," *Journal of Anatomy* 224, no. 3 (2014): 316–44.

38. See www.kenniskennis.com/site/sculptures/; www.daynes.com/en/hominids-reconstructions.html; an interview with Daynès is available at www.smith sonianmag.com/science-nature/bringing-human-evolution-life-180951155/?no-ist.

39. Tzvetan Todorov, *Theories of Symbol* (Ithaca, NY: Cornell University Press, 1982), 112. For Todorov the imitation of nature is always the imitation of an ideal model, simulation is the creation of a model.

40. I am inspired by the theories on simulation and logics of simulacrum discussed by Jean Baudrillard in several of his works, in particular *Simulacra and Simulation* (Ann Arbor: University of Michigan Press, 1994) and *Symbolic Exchange and Death* (London: SAGE, 2017 revised edition). For further critical analysis: Mike Gane and Nicholas Gane, "Introduction: Symbolic Exchange and Death Today," in *Symbolic Exchange and Death*, Baudrillard, 1–4; Enrico Schirò, "Simulacri e immanenza. Speculare Baudrillard," *Lo Sguardo—Rivista di Filosofia* 23 (2017): 113–25; Marina Christodoulou, " 'To Be Dead Is an Unthinkable Anomaly': Reversed Necropolitics and the Death Imaginary," *Lo Sguardo—Rivista di Filosofia* 23 (2017): 127–37; Gerry Coulter, "Baudrillard in the Future," *Lo Sguardo—Rivista di Filosofia* 23 (2017): 17–28; Zygmut Bauman, "The Sweet Scent of Decomposition," in *Forget Baudrillard?* ed. Chris Rojek and Bryan Turner (London: Routledge, 1993).

41. Matthew Warren, "Four New DNA Letters Double Life's Alphabet," *Nature* 566, no. 436 (2019), www.nature.com/articles/d41586-019-00650-8; Sara Reardon, "CRISPR Gene-Editing Creates Wave of Exotic Model Organisms," *Nature* 568 (2019): 441–42, www.nature.com/articles/d41586-019-01300-9.

42. Jacque Lynn Foltyn, "The Corpse in the Contemporary Culture: Identifying, Transacting, and Recoding the Dead Body," *Mortality* 13, no. 2 (2008): 99–104 and 103–4. See also: William Bogard, "Empire of Living Dead," ibid.: 187–200.

43. See Adam Geczy, *The Artificial Body in Fashion and Art. Marionettes, Models, and Mannequins* (London: Bloomsbury, 2017).

44. Niola, *Sui palchi delle stelle*, 134, on the subject of the incorrupt body of the saints as a "mortal mask of immortality."

45. Baudrillard, *Simulacra and Simulation*, 4. According to Baudrillard iconoclasm has always feared the inherent risk in the images "of effacing God," that is, the sole referent, and becoming "perfect simulacra, forever radiant with their own fascination."

46. I cannot develop a discussion on plastic surgery, which belongs to the same category as the simulacra of eternal life, the "cosmic surgery" of Michael Taussig, *Beauty and the Beast* (Chicago: University of Chicago Press, 2012).

47. See chapter by Montaldo in this volume.

48. Kathleen Fine-Dare, *Grave Injustice. The American Indian Repatriation Movement and NAGPRA* (Lincoln, NE: University of Nebraska Press, 2002); Paul Turnbull and Michael Pickering, eds., *The Long Way Home: The Meaning and Values of Repatriation* (Oxford-New York: Berghahn Books, 2010); Maria Teresa Milicia, ed., *The Great Laboratory of Humanity: Collection, Patrimony and the Repatriation of Human Remains* (Padua: CLEUP, 2019).

49. Achille Mbembe, "Necropolitics," *Public Culture* 15, no. 1 (2003): 11–40 and 39.

50. Roberto Beneduce, "Introduzione. Etnografie della violenza," *Antropologia* 9, no. 10 (2008): 5–47, 8 and 18–19; Adriano Favole, "Le tanatopolitiche coloniali e il dibattito sulla restituzione dei resti umani in Oceania," in *Morte e trasformazione dei corpi*, ed. Remotti, 151–63 and 161.

51. Tiffany Jenkins, "Making an Exhibition of Ourselves. Using the Dead to Fight the Battles of the Living," in *Archeologist and the Dead. Mortuary Archeology in Contemporary Society*, ed. Howard Williams and Melanie Giles (Oxford: Oxford University Press, 2016), 251–67 and 259.

Contributors

Editors

Silvia Cavicchioli is Researcher in Contemporary History at the University of Turin. In recent years her research interests have focused on the memory and celebration of the Risorgimento, the history of gender, the ruling classes in the nineteenth century, the history of the Kingdom of Sardinia and Liberal Italy, on museum collections, objects and art linked to processes of nationalism, and on the political use of human remains. Her publications include *Anita. Storia e mito di Anita Garibaldi* (Turin: Einaudi, 2017); *Famiglia, memoria, mito. I Ferrero della Marmora* (Rome: Carocci, 2004); and *L'eredità Cadorna. Una storia di famiglia dal XVIII al XX secolo* (Rome: Carocci, 2001). She has coordinated the project *Religious relics, secular relics, human remains: symbols of collective identities, instruments of power, and cultural, memorial and scientific legacy*.

Luigi Provero is Full Professor of Medieval History at the University of Turin. His research focuses mainly on peasant society and politics. His publications include: *L'Italia dei poteri locali* (Rome: Carocci, 1998); *Le parole dei sudditi. Azioni e scritture della politica contadina nel Duecento* (Spoleto: CISAM, 2012); and "Fedeltà inaffidabili: aristocrazia e vassallaggio nell'Arazzo di Bayeux," *Reti medievali*, 16, 2 (2015), www.rivista.retimedievali.it/. He is the principal investigator in the project *Beyond the Municipality: toward a new Reading of local Politics (12th–18th centuries)*.

Other Contributors

Luca Addante is Associate Professor of Modern History at the University of Turin. His books include: *Eretici e libertini nel Cinquecento italiano* (Rome-Bari: Laterza, 2010), which was awarded the 2011 "Federico Chabod" Prize by the Accademia dei Lincei for the best study in medieval, modern or contemporary history; and *Tommaso Campanella. Il filosofo immaginato, interpretato, falsato* (Rome-Bari: Laterza, 2018).

Simone Baral earned his doctorate degree in Contemporary History at the University of Turin. For the past decade he has studied the history of theories of phrenology and its impact on scientific thought and society in nineteenth-century Italy. On this subject he has recently published "Un'«armonica e magnifica fronte». La persistenza della frenologia nei discorsi medici italiani intorno al genio musicale," *Laboratoire italien* 20 (2017); and "Crani contesi. Dispute frenologiche intorno alle teste di personaggi celebri," *Il Risorgimento. Rivista di Storia del Risorgimento e di Storia Contemporanea* 2 (2017).

Diego Carnevale is Researcher in Modern History at the Federico II University of Naples. His most recent publications include: (with B. Marin) *L'affare dei morti. Mercato funerario, politica e gestione della sepoltura a Napoli (secoli XVII–XIX)* (Rome: École française de Rome, 2014); and "Naples, une réforme difficile," in *Aux origines des cimetières contemporains. Les réformes funéraires de l'Europe occidentale*, ed. Régis Bertrand and Anne Carol (Aix-Marseille: Presses de l'Université de Provence, 2016).

Maria G. Castello is Researcher in Roman History at the University of Turin. Her research focuses on late antiquity and her publications include: *Questioni Tardoantiche. Storia e mito della "svolta costantiniana"* (Rome: Aracne, 2010), which contained the essay "L'abolizione costantiniana della crocifissione: costruzione mitografica o verità storica?" dedicated to investigating the significance attributed to the symbol of the cross from Constantine to Justinian; and *Le segrete stanze del potere: i comites consistoriani e l'imperatore tardoantico* (Rome: Aracne, 2012).

Paolo Cozzo is Associate Professor in the History of Christianity and the Churches in the Department of Historical Studies of the University of Turin. His studies concern the history of religious life and ecclesiastical institutions between the modern and the contemporary age. His publications include: *La geografia celeste dei duchi di Savoia. Religione, devozioni e sacralità in uno Stato di età moderna (secolo XVI–XVII)* (Bologna: Il Mulino, 2006); *Andate in pace. Parroci e parrocchie in Italia dal Concilio di Trento a papa Francesco* (Rome: Carocci, 2014); and *Un eremita alla corte dei Savoia. Alessandro Ceva e le origini della congregazione camaldolese di Piemonte* (Milan: Franco Angeli, 2018).

Emanuele D'Antonio is a post-doctoral researcher in History at the University of Turin. He earned his doctorate degree from the University of Udine with a thesis entitled "Badia Polesine 1855. Storia di una calunnia del sangue nell'Italia dell'Ottocento." His main fields of interest are the social and intellectual history of Italian Jews and the history of European anti-Semitism in the nineteenth century. His academic publications include *La società udinese e gli ebrei fra la Restaurazione e l'età* *unitaria* (Udine: Istituto Pio Paschini, 2012); "Graziadio Isaia Ascoli e l'"Antisemitismo' di Cesare Lombroso. Una critica epistolare," in *Non solo verso Oriente*, ed. Maddalena Del Bianco, Riccardo Di Segni and Marcello Massenzio (Florence: Olschki, 2014); and "Aspetti della rigenerazione ebraica e del sionismo in Cesare Lombroso," *Società e storia* 92 (2001). He participates in a research project aimed at digitalising the papers of Cesare Lombroso.

Francesco Paolo de Ceglia teaches History of Science at the University of Bari. He is a specialist in the history of corporeality and relics. His publications include: *Il segreto di san Gennaro. Storia naturale di un miracolo napoletano* (Turin: Einaudi, 2016), which was nominated for several prizes; and the collection *Storia della definizione di morte* (Milan: Franco Angeli, 2014), which contains over 40 essays by Italian and foreign scholars investigating the evolution of the conceptualisation of death and the reification of the cadaver in the history of humanity.

Mauro Forno is Associate Professor of Contemporary History at the University of Turin. His research is mainly focused on the history of the church and the history of press and journalism. His recent publications include: *Cardinal Massaja and the Catholic Mission in Ethiopia: Features of an Experience between Religion and Politics* (Nairobi City: Paulines Publications Africa, 2013); *Informazione e potere: Storia del giornalismo italiano* (Rome-Bari: Laterza, 2012); and *La cultura degli altri: Il mondo delle missioni e la decolonizzazione* (Rome: Carocci, 2017).

Maria Teresa Milicia is Researcher in Cultural Anthropology at the University of Padua's Department of Historical and Geographic Sciences and the Ancient World. She is the author of *Lombroso e il brigante. Storia di un cranio conteso* (Rome: Salerno Editrice, 2014); and "Il grande laboratorio dell'umanità. Il dibattito sulla repatriation dei resti umani tra storia e antropologia," *Contemporanea* 1 (2017), based on the conference of the same name, which she organised in Padua in 2016.

Silvano Montaldo is Full Professor of Contemporary History at the University of Turin, Italy, and director of the Cesare Lombroso Museum of Criminal Anthropology. He has published a number of papers on nineteenth-century Italian history, including "The Relics of Two 19th-Century Scientists: Carlo Giacomini and Cesare Lombroso," in *Savant Relics: Brains and Remains of Scientists*, ed. Marco Beretta, Maria Conforti and Paolo Mazzarello (Sagamore Beach, MA: Science History, 2016); and (with E. Chiari) "Human Skulls and Photographs of Dead Bandits: the Problems of Presenting a Nineteenth-Century Museum to Twenty-First-Century Audiences," in *Museums and*

Photography: Displaying Death, ed. Elena Stylianou and Theopisti Stylianou-Lambert (London: Routledge, 2017).

Andrea Nicolotti is Associate Professor in the History of Christianity at the University of Turin. His publications include: *Esorcismo cristiano e possessione diabolica* (Turnhout: Brepols, 2011); *From the Mandylion of Edessa to the Shroud of Turin* (Leiden: Brill, 2014); *Sindone: Storia e leggende di una reliquia controversa* (Turin: Einaudi, 2015); and *Il Vangelo di Marcione* (Turin: Einaudi, 2019).

Natale Spineto is Full Professor in the History of Religions at the University of Turin. He is the editor of the journal *Historia Religionum*, the co-editor of the book series Biblioteca di studi storico-religiosi (Edizioni dell'Orso), and Scienze e storia delle religioni (Morcelliana), and a member of the scientific board of ten editorial series, among which Homo Religious Série II, from Brepols Publishers. His most recent publications include: *Storia e storici delle religioni in Italia* (Alessandria: Edizioni dell'Orso, 2012); *Raffaele Pettazzoni, Luigi Salvatorelli e la nascita degli studi di storia delle religioni in Italia* (Rome: Accademia Nazionale dei Lincei, 2012); and *La festa* (Rome-Bari: Laterza, 2015).

Index